The Provincial

The Provincial

Calvin Coolidge
and His World, 1885–1895

Hendrik Booraem V

Lewisburg
Bucknell University Press
London and Toronto: Associated University Presses

© 1994 by Associated University Presses

Associated University Presses
400 Forsgate Drive
Cranbury, NJ 08512

Associated University Presses
25 Sicilian Avenue
London WC1A 2QH, England

Associated University Presses
P.O. Box 338, Port Credit
Mississauga, Ontario
Canada L5G 4L8

Library of Congress Cataloging-in-Publication Data

Booraem, Hendrik, 1939–
    The provincial : Calvin Coolidge and his world, 1885–1895 /
Hendrik Booraem V.
        p.   cm.
    Includes bibliographical references and index.
    ISBN 0-8387-5264-0 (alk. paper)
    1. Coolidge, Calvin, 1872–1933—Knowledge and learning.
2. Coolidge, Calvin, 1872–1933—Childhood and youth.   3. Presidents—
United States—Biography.   I. Title.
E792.B66   1994
973.91′5′092—dc20
[B]   94-20106
                                                                                  CIP

The paper used in this publication meets the requirements
of the American National Standard for Permanence of Paper
for Printed Library Materials Z39.48–1984.

PRINTED IN THE UNITED STATES OF AMERICA

For David Herbert Donald

I see them in their beauty once again—
The dear Green Mountains greet my eyes today,
Not black and bare as when they met my view
But one month since; but rich with foliage green,
As if they donned a festal robe to greet
My coming feet. How still the valley lies
Beneath their shade!
                    —Achsah W. Sprague, "Thank God for Mountains."
                                    Plymouth, Vermont, 1864

   I do not think you have any comprehension of what people do to me. Even small
things bother me.
                    —Calvin Coolidge to Frank W. Stearns, 16 March 1922

Contents

Preface

People who became acquainted with Calvin Coolidge for the first time during his early manhood in Northampton, Massachusetts, were apt to think him the strangest person they had ever met. "[His] personality was apparently so arid that it at once challenged human interest," wrote a young Smith professor who lived down the street and used to walk to work with him. He was given to long, impenetrable silences; his speech, when he did speak, was dry, factual, emotionless. He never laughed. "In appearance," again according to his neighbor, "he was splendidly null, apparently deficient in red corpuscles, with a peaked, wire-drawn expression. You felt that he was always about to turn up his coat collar against a chilling east wind."

A friend of Coolidge's fiancée was more direct. The engaged couple paid her a courtesy visit before their wedding; Coolidge sat totally mute in the living room and let his bride-to-be do all the talking. Afterward, her friend exclaimed, "My land, Grace, I'd be afraid of him!" But perhaps the strangest thing about him, even then, was that he was not merely an odd, quirky person: his peculiarities were accompanied by a string of quiet successes in law, in public speaking, and particularly in local politics.

Twenty-five years later, when Coolidge burst into national prominence, the initial reaction was much the same—appreciation for his talents, fascination and astonishment at the strangeness of his personality. With his frugality, his terseness, his tenaciously rural lifestyle—going to bed early, eating pickles at breakfast—he seemed one of the most peculiar individuals the nation had known in high office, a "Grand Enigma." The article that first presented him to the country was entitled "The Silent Man on Beacon Hill."

Commentators on the national level found an easy explanation for his peculiarities—he was simply an embodiment of traditional Yankee values, a Puritan come to life in the twentieth century. In Vermont, the state where he had been born and reared, he had absorbed the simplicity and directness, the homely values that were his hallmark. He was, as the title of one popular biography put it, "Concentrated New England." "Calvin Coolidge is considered no enigma in Plymouth, Vermont," asserted Professor Dennis, his one-time Northampton neighbor. "In his early surroundings he was a perfect and exact type of what everybody was familiar with." Sometimes these explanations amounted to synecdoche; Coolidge *was* New England—or, as his Secretary of Commerce Herbert Hoover put it, "the incarnation of Yankee horse sense."

Generalizations can enlighten, but they can also mislead. The actual fact, evident at the time to observers who cared to look, was that Coolidge was as strange a figure on his native ground as in Northampton or Washington—"an odd stick," one Plymouth neighbor called him. Certainly he shared many—not all—of the cultural norms of his boyhood environment; but there was more to him than these values. He was also an individual, with intense personal needs and desires. Part of the intent of this work is to explore the line between these two Coolidges—Coolidge the Vermonter and Coolidge the human being—through a look at his early life.

In general outline, this book shares the approach of my previous study of James A. Garfield, *The Road to Respectability*. It focuses on the adolescence of a president without any explicit reference to his later career or performance in the White House; rather, it tries to tell his story simply as that of a young American male growing up in a particular place and time. The assumption is that his life can be used as a lens to focus on the culture he grew up in, that of late nineteenth-century rural New England. As with the Garfield book, there are extended descriptions of areas in which Coolidge's world differed from that of the late twentieth century—holidays, football, food, technology, theatrical performances, attitudes toward disease and death. But there are differences in focus, because the two men had very different styles as teenagers. Garfield was an avid participant in a variety of activities: house building, farm labor, canaling, debating, spiritualism, and schoolteaching, to name only a few. Coolidge was an observer, or at best took a reluctant part in the world around him, for reasons that will become clear in the narrative. Inevitably, therefore, this study contains less material on the world around Coolidge, and a greater emphasis on his own complicated, and in some ways heroic, personality.

It may seem foolhardy for a nonspecialist to undertake an account of personality development, but a cursory study of the psychological literature shows that there are competing theories on the subject, with no central body of material that could be called an orthodoxy. When doctors disagree, as Coolidge once said in a letter to his father, the disciple is free to choose; and I have felt free to explore the literature, preferring the work of clinicians to that of theorists, in search of clues to understanding Coolidge's shyness and withdrawal. A summary of my explorations is in the notes to chapter 3.

The source material available for this study is less ample than it was for Garfield, who kept a day-to-day journal through the last half of his adolescence and saved a great deal of his correspondence and schoolwork; but it is more than adequate. There are fragmentary diaries for the first months of 1886, 1887, and 1890, when Coolidge was in his middle teens, a complete series of letters from Coolidge to his parents while he was at St. Johnsbury Academy and Amherst College (1891–95), and a small amount of other correspondence and papers. The diaries are still in possession of the president's family, which has generously made them available for use; the letters are in the excellent Coolidge Family Papers collection in the Vermont Historical Society or at the Forbes Library in Northampton. (The small collection of Coolidge papers in the Library of Congress is negligible, at least for this period.) In addition, there is a huge quantity of anecdotal material; so unusual was Coolidge as a young man that he left a striking impression on everyone who knew him at all well, and many of these acquaintances later retailed these impressions to newspaper reporters, writers, or friends. And of course there is his own autobiography, a remarkable piece of rhetoric by a skilled rhetorician, much less simple than it seems. It deserves careful reading, which I have tried to give.

Coolidge came of age during the flowering of local journalism in America; small-town papers everywhere covered the public aspects of day-to-day American lives—visits, business deals, entertainments, family events—with a thoroughness unequaled before or since. There is, consequently, a wealth of material on Coolidge's social environment from the two newspapers that served western Windsor Country, the *Vermont Tribune* of Ludlow and the *Vermont Standard* of Woodstock. Reminiscences and diaries of local people supply some of the more intimate details missing from newspapers. Regarding Plymouth, Ernest C. Carpenter's *Boyhood Days of Calvin Coolidge* is a mine of information from a local resident. The published diaries of Hyde Leslie and Elmer Twombly are full of interesting detail, and there are other manuscript diaries in the Vermont Historical Society. The collections of the Black River Academy Museum in Ludlow, a model local historical organization, shed much light on nineteenth-century Ludlow, as do the valuable photographs and commentary in the *Plymouth Album* put together by Eliza Ward, Barbara Mahon, and Barbara Chiolino. Given the thrifty nature of Vermonters, it seems probable that much interesting source material, which will eventually enrich the picture of Plymouth and Ludlow during the 1880s, is still in private and family hands; but there is certainly enough currently available to construct a vivid picture of these communities during Coolidge's adolescence.

With regard to the other important setting for his early life, Amherst College, the situation is a bit different. Probably for political reasons, Amherst has always found Coolidge something of an embarrassment and has not amassed much source material on his college days, beyond a short series of letters to his grandmother. Nor has it done much to illuminate the pivotal decade of the 1890s in its own history, with the important exception of publishing Alfred Stearns's *An Amherst Boyhood*. Student publications, scrapbooks, yearbooks, and a few contemporary manuscripts at Amherst help to form a picture of college life in the 1890s; but it says something that the two most enlightening primary sources I have found on student life at Amherst in that era are housed elsewhere: the Elizabeth Cutter Morrow papers at Smith College and the Frederick A. Blossom Papers at the Wisconsin Historical Society. On the other hand, the Amherst Historical Society and the Jones Library, in the village, have considerable useful background material.

Like all biographies, this one is provisional in some ways. There are some important points in Coolidge's early life on which evidence is lacking, or almost lacking; in these cases I have gone ahead, made deductions or inferences based on whatever evidence exists, and explained them in the notes. At some points in the narrative, to make the story more vivid to readers, I have not merely said that Coolidge did something but have tried to portray him doing it. Examples are the beginnings of chapters 4 and 14 and almost all of chapter 9. In these passages, I have tried to be strictly consistent with the evidence and to explain the reasoning again in the notes. I will be grateful to any reader who can supply additional data, or point out errors of fact or reasoning in this account.

It would be impossible to thank by name all of the individuals who helped me in the search for material on Coolidge's early life; there were many, particularly in Plymouth and Ludlow. But some of them provided such effective assistance as to demand mention. Kathleen Donald, director of the Calvin Coolidge Memorial Foundation at the time I began my research, was indefatigable in rounding up sources of information, interviews, addresses, photographs, and tape recordings, and in supplying continual encouragement. Whatever its faults, this book is much better than it could have been without her help. Her successor, Cynthia Bittinger, also provided invaluable help in the last stages of writing and editing. Mary McCallum, formerly of the Black River Academy Museum in Ludlow, gave me full access to the museum's rich collections about Coolidge's school days. Earle Brown, Bertha Moore Gilman, Milton Moore, Erminie Pollard, Eliza Ward, and Allen S. Wilder, all from old Plymouth families, supplied valuable information in personal interviews or by letter. Each of them helped to enlarge and correct my understanding of Plymouth in the 1880s and 1890s. Donna Jerry, formerly executive secretary of the Coolidge Foundation, generously allowed me to use her taped interviews with older Plymouth residents.

In the Northampton–Amherst area, I am grateful to Lawrence Wikander, curator of the Coolidge Memorial Room at the Forbes Library in Northampton, who has been not only a source of information but also an acute critic, and to Elise Bernier-Feeley of the same library. Daria D'Arienzo, Archivist of Amherst College, and the staff of the Archives and Special Collections were consistently helpful. Among the libraries where I searched for material, I would particularly like to thank the following: the Fletcher Library of Ludlow; the Widener Library at Harvard University; the Bostonian Society Library; the Conant Library in Winchester, New Hampshire; the Vermont Historical Society; the Wisconsin Historical Society; the Rutland, Vermont, Public Library; the libraries of Hartford Seminary, Phillips Academy, and Smith College; the Brimfield, Massachusetts, Public Library; and the Jones Library of Amherst. I wish to thank the Baker

Library at Harvard University for permission to use information from the R. G. Dun & Co. Papers, which are housed there.

For other important contributions, I am indebted to Ada Merchant, Bob Sharp, and Daisy Welch.

In a class by themselves are: John Twombly, of Aiken, South Carolina, who shared with me his family history and knowledge of Vermont folkways; Jim Cooke of Boston, an actor who has made Coolidge's writings and personality his special study, and whose intimate knowledge makes him a keen reader and valued critic; Donald McCoy, for friendly criticism and encouragement; and Richard Bullock of Newtown, Pennsylvania, for constant encouragement and financial support.

The Provincial

1

The Fourth of July

It was 11:59 P.M., 3 July 1885, and the cool tranquility of a summer night hung over Windsor County, Vermont. A lopsided yellow moon had just risen behind the mountains across the Connecticut River in New Hampshire. On the western edge of the county, the crest of the Green Mountains outlined a black bulk against the starry sky. The clouds that had brought showers earlier in the afternoon had dissipated; now Lyra, Boötes, the Northern Crown, and all the summer constellations twinkled overhead, while fireflies mimicked them in the dim meadows.[1]

Along the main line of the Central Vermont, a trail of white smoke marked the track of the night express from Boston, chugging upgrade from Bellows Falls, bound over the mountain to Rutland and ultimately to Montreal. From the stuffy, smelly interior of its coaches, city passengers, drowsing uneasily in their coats and derbies and voluminous dresses, could watch as the train's lights raked over the white frame towns they passed through, little places with a few feeble kerosene street lamps burning; or between towns, they could peer out grimy windows into the vast, dark countryside. In the small depots up the line, stations like Chester and Proctorsville and Ludlow, lamps still burned as the railroad employees, and perhaps a few passengers, awaited the train. But beyond the railroad, the villages and farm hamlets that dotted the county seemed dark and still.[2]

The quiet was misleading. In dozens of places in Windsor County, boys and young men were eagerly readying firecrackers or firearms in their hands, grasping bellropes in church towers, or loading cannon, awaiting the stroke of twelve. This was their holiday, Independence Day, when for a few hours they could disturb the community as much as they liked, without penalty. Their noise was tolerated, even expected. They would start promptly at midnight.[3]

In many places, the first sound to break the stillness would be the clang of the church bell. Then small boys would chime in with horns and firecrackers. The young men would form a "calathumpian parade," as some called it, and march all around town to ensure that no neighborhood was overlooked, "burning powder, ringing bells, blowing horns and making things hideous" for as long as four hours. Some places had local variations. In the little factory village of Taftsville in the Ottauquechee valley, the noisemakers cus-

17

tomarily banged with sticks on circular saw blades and old boilers. When everyone was awakened, the two handmade cannon in the village would be fired until the powder ran out. Everywhere, high spirits were apt to overflow into pranks and minor vandalism of the kind later associated with Halloween—ringing doorbells, stealing signs, damaging wagons. Not everyone approved of this part. "Very few object to the boys giving vent to patriotic feelings," sniffed a Proctorsville resident in 1892, "but when they forget where fun ceases and injury to property begins, it is time to call a halt."[4]

The uproar would resume next morning. In many small villages, the celebration of the Fourth would start with a parade of "horribles"—men and boys dressed in "various and indescribable" old clothes, carrying crudely lettered signs and performing antics often intended to caricature local people. Fireworks and cannon would be detonated throughout the day, often at extreme risk to those in charge. In 1896 in Bridgewater two people were killed and sixteen injured when the six-inch cannon borrowed from a neighboring town exploded. "We boys burst a gun barrel," a Royalton teenager noted matter-of-factly in his 1879 diary. At Pittsfield, over in Rutland County, in 1891 a bursting cannon took a man's arm off; a Chester citizen lost an eye and a hand to a "cannon cracker" in 1889.[5]

Of course there were also family-oriented, more sedate activities—church picnics, fireworks displays, ball games. Once in a while a community would get up a formal celebration with patriotic speeches and toasts, bunting and brass bands, attracting farm families in their wagons from fifteen or twenty miles away. Ludlow had such an affair in 1887, complete with "gaims," as a visiting farm hand put it: "A foot race Wheel barrel race Potato race Sack race and a tug of war." In 1893 the hamlet of Felchville in the town of Reading put together a Fourth of July parade with forty-four young ladies in white representing the states, a rousing speech by an ex-state legislator, recitations, and music. But such occasions were exceptions: normally the celebrating was free-lance, and was the province of boys and young men.[6]

As such things went, the eve of 4 July 1885 was quiet in Windsor County. Noisemaking in Windsor village was confined to the small boys. In Chester, there was only a parade of horribles with music and banners; the boys even failed to ring the church bell. The citizens of West Bridgewater, busy with plans for a big festivity with music the next day, slept. At Ludlow there was next to nothing.[7]

In the small township of Plymouth at the foot of the Green Mountains, a stealthy group of men and boys eased a small cannon out of John Wilder's barn onto the stage road and rolled it up the hill past the schoolhouse. While one or two glanced down the road into the darkness, others loaded the gun with a teacup of powder, tamped it down, inserted a fuse, and touched fire to it. The resulting boom might have wakened a whole neighborhood if it had sounded in a village; as it was, it wakened very few. This part of Plymouth, a tiny settlement called Plymouth Notch, or simply "the Notch,"

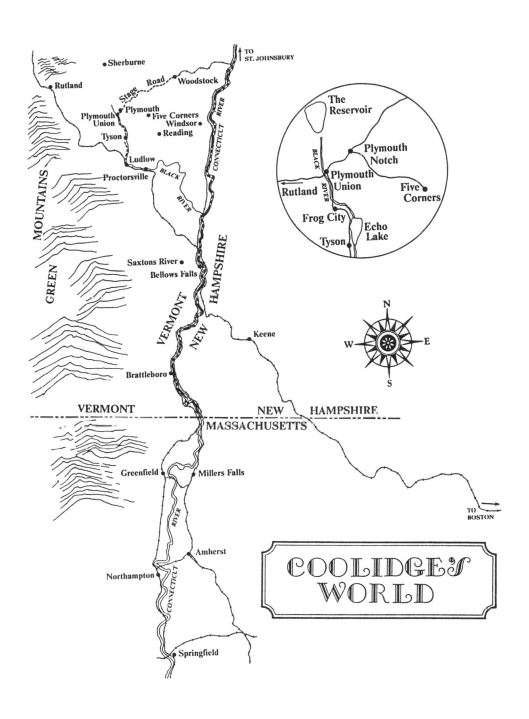

TO
ST. JOHNSBURY

Sherburne

Rutland

Woodstock

Stage Road

Plymouth

Five Corners

Plymouth
Union

Windsor

Tyson

Reading

Ludlow

CONNECTICUT RIVER

Proctorsville

BLACK RIVER

GREEN MOUNTAINS

Saxtons River

Bellows Falls

VERMONT

NEW HAMPSHIRE

Keene

Brattleboro

VERMONT

NEW HAMPSHIRE

MASSACHUSETTS

Greenfield

Millers Falls

CONNECTICUT RIVER

Amherst

Northampton

CONNECTICUT

Springfield

TO
BOSTON

The Reservoir

BLACK RIVER

Plymouth
Notch

Rutland

Plymouth
Union

Five
Corners

Frog City

Echo
Lake

Tyson

N

W   E

S

COOLIDGE'S
WORLD

had almost no one to arouse. George Moore's general store, shaded by a great elm tree, was securely closed and its owner at home asleep, if he was not among the group around the cannon. The big white church was locked; the stone schoolhouse was deserted. There were three houses adjoining the store, and perhaps a dozen houses within hearing distance on the dim slopes of the adjacent hills—and that was all. Nevertheless, the group had reason to be wary. The cannon they were firing was not theirs: it had been stolen some days before from the neighboring hamlet of Plymouth Union.[8]

The stage road west out of the Notch ran about a mile through rolling pastures and suddenly plunged down the steep, wooded sides of Notch Mountain in a breathtaking, mile-long series of bends down a rutted road that regularly gave the stagecoach's passengers the fright of their lives. At the bottom of the descent was Plymouth Union, a settlement of some size, with two dozen houses, two or three small mills on the banks of Black River, and a couple of bulky hotel buildings overlooking the crossroads where a neat wooden sign gave the mileage to nearby communities. Only two miles from the Notch, the "Union" was nonetheless a distinctly different sort of place. Its people lived by lumbering and wood products, the crash of ox-teams hauling logs through the snow in winter, the whine of steam-driven saws in the factory. The Notch was, by comparison, pastoral, a place where farmers still raised sheep, harvested wheat and barley, made butter and cheese to sell. The Union, at a crossroads, was relatively cosmopolitan; the Notch was merely a wide spot in the stage road.[9]

The young men of the Notch and the Union had been feuding over possession of this cannon for almost a generation. The origins of the struggle are obscure; probably they go back to the beginnings of the Union itself, in the years before the Civil War when the stage road was rerouted. Up to that time, Plymouth Notch, with its church and store and tiny village green, had been the focal point of the township, and the March town meetings were held there. But at some time during the 1850s its supremacy was challenged and then usurped by the Union, which was more centrally located with respect to the new road. In 1867, finally, the annual town meeting voted "to hold the town meetings for the year ensuing at Levi J. Green's Hall" in Plymouth Union. The following year, they decided "that the Town meetings shall be held at Union ville as long as the people there shall furnish a suitable place free of charge." At this time, probably, the town cannon, which had been bought for the Log Cabin campaign of 1840, was removed from the Notch to the Union. The young men of the Notch, aggrieved on behalf of their locality, began trying to steal it back to celebrate every Fourth of July. Over the years the cannon alternated between the two places. Around 1870 a band from the Notch had stolen it and kept possession of it for several years until the Union boys, in some unspecified fashion, got it back. Now, in 1885, the Notch raiders struck again—this time, actually, a few days before the Fourth. "The Notch boys came and stole [our cannon]," the Union correspondent of a local newspaper wrote wearily, "but we were used to that same caper, because they had done it before." The writer went on to gibe at the attempt of the "corn-stalk militia" from the country around the Notch to guard against an anticipated Union attempt at recapture, and suggested that the cannon blasts had not been heard at the Union because the Notch crew had been either too stingy or too cowardly to use sufficient powder.[10]

But that was several days later. In the early morning of the Fourth, up on the plateau, the thirteen blasts—one for each of the original colonies—were satisfactorily loud, loud enough to rattle every window in the place before reverberating off the surrounding mountains. The squad in charge of the cannon—young farmers, most of them, in colored long-sleeved shirts, work pants with suspenders, and heavy boots—exchanged glances of pleasure and accomplishment. Not all of them were young. John Wilder himself, wiry and dashingly side-whiskered, was nearing forty, but he had been deeply in-volved in the feud since he was in his teens and was not about to drop out of it now that he was a family man and a town official. In fact, report had it that another selectman besides Wilder—Milton Moore, who was in his for-ties—was present too. At the other end of the age scale there were the boys in their early teens and younger, sporting around among the older men, en-joying the loud noise and the late hour and the dewy air fragrant with the scent of the hayfields around the Notch.[11]

An observer might have been struck by one of them in particular—a small, skinny, sharp-featured boy who was practically beside himself with excitement. In the light of the rising moon he seemed unnaturally pale. It was possible to see that he had fair hair, although the faint moonlight could not bring out its fiery red. This was John Wilder's nephew. His name was Calvin Coolidge, and it was the morning of his thirteenth birthday.[12]

2
Pastorale

In the morning light of the Fourth of July, it was apparent just how small the Notch really was. Steep, broad-shouldered mountains rose around it on all sides: Messer Hill on the north, East Mountain on the east, South Hill or Notch Mountain on the south. Nothing was visible beyond them but the deep blue of a Winslow Homer sky. The mountains were forested at their summits, the deep green of pine and spruce foliage mingling with the lighter green of maple and birch, with occasional flashes of slim white birch trunks; lower down the slopes, pastures and hayfields lapped at their edges. At the bottom, as if at the bottom of a huge amphitheater, were the few buildings of the Notch.[1]

There were really only three dwellings in the place—four, if one counted the ell on the back of the general store. Two of them faced the triangular village green with the enormous elm tree: Cephas Moore's old house across from the store, now occupied by his son-in-law George Brown, with his wife and daughter; and Hiram Moor's house, which he shared with the family of his son-in-law John Wilder. Hiram Moor's house, large and close to the green, had been a tavern back in the days when the Notch was a place of importance, when people came there to transact town business. Now it was simply a residence, its bar dismantled, its ballroom remodeled. Adjoining it, on the side road that led up Messer Hill, was the home of Moor's other son-in-law John Coolidge, a long white house, rambling like most Vermont rural dwellings, with its kitchen connected to the shed, the shed connected to the barn, to obviate the need of going outside in snowy winter weather. Tall maples shaded it; a colorful but somewhat neglected flower garden was attached to it. At the front of the Coolidge lot, incongruously, was a small blacksmith shop.[2]

There were three public buildings at the Notch, as well—the church, the schoolhouse, the general store. The church, facing the Coolidge house, was easily the most impressive, with its Greek revival facade and two-tiered tower, but for all its impressiveness it was almost unused. It had no regular minister; there were not enough people in the community to support a pastor. John Coolidge saw that it was properly maintained for the occasions when it was open, and his mother superintended a Sunday school that met there fairly regularly. Perhaps the small, ill-kept stone schoolhouse up the

Photograph of the Notch in winter, from the middle 1880s, taken from Schoolhouse Hill. John Coolidge's home is the white house in the center. At the far right is the stone schoolhouse; at the far left are the outbuildings of Almeda Coolidge's farm. The general store is beyond the church, and John Wilder's house beyond John Coolidge's. Other buildings visible in the photo are barns or sheds. (Courtesy, Vermont Division for Historic Preservation)

hill from the Coolidge house was a better index of the village's current state. The general store stood on the other side of the church, facing the green. And that was all there was to Plymouth Notch.[3]

At least, that was all if one was counting buildings. But the farming families on the surrounding hills—other Browns, Wilders, and Moores—considered themselves, and justly so, to be part of the Notch community. They traded at the general store and sent their children to the Notch school. Just north of the village, John Coolidge's mother Almeda, "Aunt Mede" to the community, lived alone in a large, weatherbeaten, two-story house surrounded by lilacs in spring, in autumn by goldenrod. She was the Notch's midwife and nurse; people came to her even late at night when someone was taken ill or a woman went into labor. Half a mile south of the green, near the small, stone-walled cemetery that served the town, was the rambling farmhouse of James Brown, George's brother, with its adjoining rose garden that was a delight to the nose as well as the eye in the summertime. And there were others.[4]

Indeed, there were several ways to define the Notch community: the tiny village itself; the village and surrounding farms; the district served by the Notch schoolhouse. Most expansive was the definition of the United States Post Office Department, according to which "Plymouth" (not Plymouth

Notch) was one of only three post offices in Plymouth township, and served a considerable area to the north and east—all the way up Messer Hill, up the stage road to a small neighborhood called Pinney Hollow, and away beyond East Mountain to an isolated locality known as Five Corners, whose inhabitants had to travel six miles of steep, rutted hill road to pick up their mail at George Moore's store. That was the price of isolation; the stage, which carried the mail, ran only on the Bridgewater–Ludlow road, twice a day.[5]

The stage would not run today, a holiday with no mail to be carried. For one summer weekday at least, dwellers by the road would miss the usual thudding of horse hoofs kicking up dust on the blackberry leaves at the roadside, the rattle of the chains, the creaking of the leather springs, and most of all, the loud bells on the horses' harness as the coach passed. It was an old-fashioned Concord coach of the kind seen in Western movies, trim and brightly painted. It ran on wheels from April to December, on runners during the snows of winter. Today, however, it would not run at all, and its driver, whoever he was in the summer of 1885 (the job changed hands frequently), would be off attending Independence Day festivities somewhere.[6]

Whether Moore's store would be open was more problematical. Without the incoming letters to sort and distribute from behind the grate (one Plymouth resident compared the storekeeper to a caged monkey), the store lost one of its major attractions—many local people came in to hang about and chat and make small purchases while the mail was sorted. Still, there would be many families on the road Independence Day, going to and from the celebrations. Some stores definitely opened on the holiday.[7]

Moore's store was fairly typical of its kind in Vermont: a big, boxy building, painted white, with the standard columned piazza at a height convenient for wagoners to back up and unload their merchandise—barrels of kerosene and molasses, boxes of cloth and hardware—directly into the store. Local farmers also used it to bring in their tubs of butter and other items for trade. Inside, the standard wood-burning stove stood in the center of the store, ringed by comfortable old chairs where the worthies of the Notch gathered, swapped gossip, spat, played checkers, and discussed state and national affairs, as in most country places. There was the usual amazing variety of things for sale: Vermont country stores stocked overshoes, patent medicines, hoop skirts, dry goods (i.e., clothing), hardware, buggy whips, lamp chimneys, and pitchforks, to name only a few items, in addition to groceries. They stocked smaller goods as well, little drawers of corks, saltpeter, buckshot, peppercorns, and alum. (Among the things Moore advertised in 1886 were "pure gum Woonsocket rubber boots," calico, coarse and fine salt, Vermont rakes, and "Milwaukee oil grain shoes [standard screw] for women $1.50.") With this variety came a distinctive aroma from the barrels of kerosene, vinegar, and lemons, the sacks of tobacco, the bolts of cloth, the drawers of spices and glass cases of penny candy, and from the mud and barnyard dirt tracked in by customers. It was heavy and evocative; a Vermont writer of the period, in one of her stories, referred to the interior of a general store as a "great rank room."[8]

In a couple of ways, the store had not yet taken on the appearance it would have later, when Plymouth became famous. It still had only one story. John Coolidge, who owned the building, would add a second-story room the following year, and four years later would put in new cases and counters, as he felt he could afford to. A canny businessman, Coolidge believed in keeping up his property. He had owned it for a good fifteen years; for some years in the seventies he had run the store himself, but had finally sold it to his brother-in-law Frank Moor, who after a few years had moved down to Proctorsville on the railroad. Edwin Earle of the Union had purchased it from Moor and operated it only briefly before he failed; now George Moore, back from college with his education incomplete, was keeping it, renting the building with backing from his father. Clearly, it was not easy to make a living operating the Notch store. Storekeeping was a tricky job, what with the constant need to extend credit to the poorer farmers and at the same time have cash on hand to cover one's bills, and the hours were taxing enough to make a farmer's schedule seem light: open early in the morning to check in orders, and often, in fall or winter, open well after dark to accommodate the local men gathered around the stove. One had to deal with roving gypsies and their reputation for thievery, prankish local boys, and the occasional big-city traveling salesman who penetrated as far as the Notch — all this with the help of one clerk at most. Small wonder, indeed, if Moore had decided to take the holiday off.[9]

But even if the young storekeeper was not behind his counter, it did not follow that the rest of Plymouth was idle. The Fourth fell in the beginning of the hay season in this part of Vermont, and there were usually farmers who felt that it was more urgent to get in a few more loads of hay than to celebrate national independence. Hay was basic to Vermont life: from August to May it kept the horses going and the milk flowing. Farmers needed to cut prodigious quantities to carry them through the long winter. A hand on the James Brown farm in 1887 noted that Brown had put 179 wagonloads in the barn that season, huge loads piled high on the hay wagons with their bulging sides, often with a boy in his early teens riding on top to pitch the hay into the mow at the very top of the barn. Brown, to be sure, farmed 300 acres, more than many other farmers around the Notch, but his total gives some idea of how hard most farmers had to work during the critical six or seven weeks in summer.[10]

Most likely, then, the fields around the Notch that Independence Day were filled with the smells and sounds of haying season: the incomparable scent of fresh-cut grass, the halloos of the men from one field to another, the clatter of the horse-drawn mowing machine and the clang of the scythes

Jim Ayer's place, a few miles west of the Notch, was a fairly typical Plymouth farm. The man standing in the wagon, Dell Ward, was a contemporary of Coolidge's and a friend during his college years. This picture was probably taken around 1900. (Mrs. Eliza Ward, Plymouth, VT)

(the mowing machine was gradually replacing the scythe in Vermont, but in Plymouth, at least, the change was incomplete), the rattle of the horse-rake, usually driven by a boy, which followed the mowing machine and "tumbled" the hay into masses big enough for a man to pitch into the wagon. It was grueling, sweaty work, punctuated with the inevitable accidents, running over a hornet's nest and getting stung, or being punched in the hand by a pitchfork. Most serious was the threat of heat prostration. Men did die in the hayfield. The air was like molten brass, and in the barn, particularly up near the eaves where the big gray barn spiders had their webs, it was stifling. Twentieth-century workers would undoubtedly have shed their shirts, but the young and middle-aged men who worked the fields of the Notch wore the same long-sleeved shirts and work pants they had worn during the cannon escapade the night before. Some even put on an extra layer to keep hayseeds and straw out of their clothing, a long, shapeless, homemade garment of dyed wool, called a smock. Their only hope of relief from the heat was from one of the torrential afternoon thundershowers that pounded Vermont during hay season. When rain began to pour down and the hayrack was safely in the barn, it was all right for workers to stand in the door, drink in the fresh wet scent, and lave away perspiration in the cool runoff from the roof. Sometimes the smaller boys stripped and played in the cascading water as a substitute for the week's bath.[11]

The showers would come in the afternoon, if they came at all. In the meantime, part of the Notch was in the field haying, and most of those who were not were out jouncing along the dusty, ill-maintained country roads in some sort of wheeled vehicle, bound toward West Bridgewater or Mechanicsville, whichever held the nearest or most appealing holiday celebration—dressed, if not in their best clothes, at least in clean, festive attire. Few celebrants were walking. People did walk in Vermont, sometimes long distances, on errands, but not on excursions. No one rode horseback anymore: the variety of horse-drawn conveyances available had made riding practically obsolete. Farm families with lots of children used the plain farm wagon, or spring wagon as it was called; the parents rode up front on the seat, the children set behind them where the produce was usually stowed. Those with several adults were more apt to ride in a democrat wagon, a high, sturdy vehicle with two seats and a canopy. But the carriage of choice was the one that has given its name to this era, the buggy.[12]

The buggy, a small, narrow, one-seated vehicle, basically a seat mounted on a box, with a folding canopy, was a distinctively American and relatively new conveyance. Americans, because of the long hauls between their towns, had long been accustomed to horse-powered transportation, but until about the 1860s horseback was the preferred mode. The roads were too rough for wheeled vehicles, and for most families a coach or carriage was too expensive. The change, when it came in the 1860s, was not in the roads but in the carriages; manufacturers began adding elliptical steel springs to both axles, making the ride so much smoother that families began looking for a horse-drawn vehicle they could afford. The buggy was the answer: it was compact, cheap, and light, thanks to the hickory wood used for its major parts. The body was incredibly small, usually about two by five feet. Even farm boys could afford it; in fact, it was usually a young man's first big purchase. For its size, it had a certain elegance: it shone with as many as seventeen coats of varnish, striped patterns on the body, and quilted upholstery on the seat. The canopy was useful, and there was extra space under the seat for side curtains. But it could not carry much luggage, or merchandise of any kind; it was basically a business vehicle for professionals like doctors and a recreational vehicle for the rest of the middle class. On holidays the roads were full of buggies, sedately bound for the celebrations. Bigger or more affluent families could use the two-seated version of the buggy, called a surrey.[13]

Out on the road somewhere that morning, doubtless, were John Coolidge, his two children, and probably also his mother, bouncing along in a surrey to the festivities. When there was a public occasion going on, it was not in Coolidge to miss it: he took his civic responsibility seriously. He was a town leader in Plymouth. Like his father before him, he had represented

John Coolidge. (Forbes Library)

Almeda Brewer Coolidge. (Forbes Library)

Abbie Coolidge was about eleven when this picture was taken, around 1886. (Courtesy, Vermont Division for Historic Preservation)

Coolidge in his mid-teens, as a student at Black River Academy. (Forbes Library)

the town in the state legislature and had held half a dozen local offices of various sorts. He came from one of the very oldest families in town. Nonetheless, to people in Plymouth he was plain John Coolidge, or "John," never "Mr. Coolidge." New England country people frowned on the idea of using courtesy titles like "Mr." and "Mrs." with people they knew personally; bestowing honors of that sort offended their relentless sense of democratic equality ("Put us in a bag, an' we'll all come aout [sic] the same time," one Yankee countryman put it).[14]

John, nevertheless, commanded a good deal of respect in Plymouth. To most of the town, he represented the Law. Tall, dark-haired, with the blunt, rugged, solemn features of an Indian from a Wild West show, he had been town constable and a deputy sheriff of Windsor County for years. He wore no badge, but he was instantly recognizable in the town: he was one of the very few men who routinely wore "store clothes" (coat, collar, white shirt, and cuffs), and carried a watch, riding around town in a buggy behind his white horse Rarus. He was physically strong and not afraid to grapple with lawbreakers if he had to. Witness his arrest, the next winter, of a local swindler in Proctorsville:

> It seems [ran the account in a county paper] the prisoner changed his mind about going along peaceably, after having entered Coolidge's sleigh, and sprang out when the latter's attention was directed elsewhere. Coolidge whirled round, however, just in time to fasten one hand in the prisoner's coat collar, who thereupon ran round the rear of the sleigh in such a manner as to tumble his captor over backward into the box, where for a few minutes he held him down. Coolidge, however, finally got on to his feet, and ordered Fitton into the sleigh again, which Bob obeyed with very poor grace, throwing out the robes, etc., as fast as the officer could pick them up and replace them. It took threats of hand cuffing to end this play.[15]

Not only did John have to pick up wrongdoers and take them to the county jail, but in many years he was also Plymouth's town agent, that is, the collector of town taxes. Finally, he was the only insurance agent in town: the fire insurance policies he wrote protected almost every farm in Plymouth. When he appeared in a neighborhood, stony-faced and laconic, it usually meant serious business of some kind.[16]

John's strength also came in handy on the farm. Like every other man in the Notch, he was a farmer to some degree; less so, perhaps, than most of his neighbors, because he had realized early that farming in the Green Mountains in the late 1800s was a losing proposition, and carefully supplemented his farm income with a host of other activities, politics, insurance, blacksmithing, renting properties, and doing credit ratings for R. G. Dun & Company. But he had been raised on a farm and was thoroughly familiar with farm work. "If there was any physical requirement of country life which he could not perform," his admiring son recalled, "I do not know what it was."

He built stone fences and laid foundations; he was a skilled mason. He was adept in the theory and practice of maple sugaring. He could repair harness and do delicate operations on farm animals. The best buggy he had for twenty years was one he made himself. He was also a capable blacksmith, although usually he hired a smith to do the time-consuming shop work— most recently Hen Willis, a burly, bearded man who had now left the Notch and worked down in the Union.[17]

John Coolidge was, in short, a hard worker and a sharp trader. He had the defects of his qualities. Tight concentration on the tasks to be done and the profit to be earned had made him an unsympathetic man, demanding of others and of himself. He did not like to see things wasted; he observed strict economy and expected those around him to do so. His humor merited the adjective H. L. Mencken later applied to his son's, necrotic: real New England country wit, tight-lipped, quiet, and always at someone else's expense. Finally, his silence and his massive, unsmiling face made him, at an elemental level, a rather scary figure.[18]

John was a recent widower. His wife had died earlier that year (hence the untended flower garden next to his house), leaving him with two red-haired children: pale, silent Calvin (really John Calvin Coolidge, the same as his father, but no one ever used his first name), who turned thirteen that day; and plump, outgoing, ten-year-old Abbie. John's mother, Almeda, pious, active, and black-haired despite her sixty-one years, was helping to raise them. There was no reason why the arrangement should not work. John was prosperous as Plymouth people went, with good business and political connections, well able to provide. Probably he would marry again in time; most widowers did. In the meantime, John, Almeda, Calvin, and Abbie made up a tight little family, close, hardworking, respectable.[19]

They sat in the surrey, probably not smiling a great deal, probably sitting straight up as they rolled on toward the celebration, down roadsides lined with midsummer flowers: black-eyed Susan, orange and yellow hawkweed, yarrow, ferns, Queen Anne's lace. A few red clover and daisies lingered. The mountains, far less forested than they are now, shimmered in the midsummer heat. Cattle and sheep grazed in the pastures that extended far up their sides. In the valleys were fields of ripening wheat, oats, and barley, as well as hayfields where men were out working. The Coolidges' surrey disappeared down the road. Every now and then the distant report of a cannon cracker, the boom of a firearm, proclaimed that it was still Independence Day.[20]

3

The Invalid's Son

That July of 1885, a number of people around the Notch were talking about the Coolidge boy.

People in the Notch had few diversions. As in most parts of rural New England, they spent a lot of time observing and discussing one another. They were constantly on the watch for something novel and interesting to talk about; when someone passed the Browns' farm on the stage road, recalled their granddaughter Blanche Bryant, eyes and ears were always at the window to see who it was. Any happening could be a subject for discussion—analyzing, for instance, why a neighbor went to town by a road different from the one he normally used, or calculating how much money he might have made from selling his produce, or speculating why his wife had a new shawl and where she bought it. Conversation on topics like this was as much a staple of farm households as salt pork and milk gravy.[1]

Often these observations coalesced into stories about the neighbors, usually dwelling on their peculiarities. These were stories to be told in the family circle or to one's cronies at the store, to be heard with a chuckle, sympathetic or malicious as the case might be. Best liked were the ones that ended with a pithy phrase or sharp retort at another person, like the old lady in Gaysville who let fly at her mild-mannered husband's fondness for swapping jackknives: "Jackknives, jackknives, jackknives. Stand on the corner and trade jackknives, you damned old fool; you don't know as much as a chickadee-dee-dee." There was a whole cycle of stories going round Plymouth in the 1880's about the Reverend Mason Moore, a college-trained pastor over in Plymouth Kingdom who was trying to cobble together a living by farming and preaching to a sparse congregation. The pastor was a good-hearted man and a learned preacher, but he knew nothing about farming, and the stories mostly dwelt on his ignorance: how he tried to tap maple sugar out of elm trees; how he raised a pair of steers to draw his carriage; how he tried to tailor his own breeches and ended up with a pair that came almost to his shoulders. Parson Moore, the educated eccentric, had become for his neighbors the protagonist in a continuing story, a live situation comedy as it were; and doubtless some of the same people were considering young Calvin Coolidge to see what sort of story, tragic, comic, or moral, his life might constitute.[2]

Physically, there was nothing remarkable about him. He was small for his age, short and rather delicate, with a sharply chiseled face. His most striking feature was his flaming red hair, which he kept cut short as farm boys generally did. He had a redhead's skin, pale and freckled. His hands and feet were small. He was not particularly agile or graceful—he didn't run or play much—but he had no disabilities. He could work. His personality, however, offered a wider field for comment.[3]

Since his mother's death that March, he had seemed especially subdued and depressed. Victoria Moor Coolidge had been only thirty-nine, but her death was not unexpected; she had been an invalid for years. About an hour before she died, she had called Calvin and Abbie to her side and spoken to them for a last time. Nonetheless, her death had hit her son hard. (Years later he was to call it "the greatest grief that can come to a boy.") He carried her picture everywhere, a picture of the fair-skinned, brown-haired comforter who had knitted mittens for him and Abbie, who had read them poetry and had sat in the doorway and commented on the beautiful sunsets behind Notch Mountain. Months after the blustery, snowy day of her burial, the Browns would still see him around dusk, walking slowly down the stage road to the town cemetery to visit her grave. He seemed lost, devastated by grief.[4]

But even before her death there had been something peculiar about him. He was a strangely quiet child for a thirteen-year-old. He seemed to have no rough-and-tumble in him. Neighbors later described him in unusual terms: "kind of stately," "distant." He almost never played with boys his own age partly, no doubt, because he was physically small and not strong, partly because, as one teacher of his put it, "what appealed to them didn't appeal to him"—but also because something in him seemed to shrink from contact with them. He was uneasy with strangers, even though his father, who often had legal business at the county seat, generally took Calvin with him to meet people and observe things. He was not always comfortable even in the company of friends and neighbors. A picture of a church picnic around this time shows him staring warily, blankly at the camera. When he had the chance, he enjoyed solitary amusements; he spent more time reading than most boys his age.[5]

His gravity was not, as silence often is, a cover for a limited intelligence. Calvin was as smart as any boy in the Notch, perhaps smarter. He did his chores competently, milked the cows, sawed wood in the woodshed, kept the kitchen box supplied. He worked in the field to the satisfaction of his father, who was a stiff taskmaster: in summer he drove the horse rake, in spring he plowed. Despite his small size, he had been able to plow by himself from the time he was twelve. In earliest spring he helped rebuild the rock fences pushed over by the frost and worked in the sugar grove collecting and boiling sap. In the district school he was an above average student.[6]

No, there was nothing wrong with Calvin mentally. The people of the

Notch were familiar enough with mental disturbance to recognize pathol-
ogy when they saw it. There was old Ben Sawyer, a town charge who lived
with the family of farmer James Brown, who could often be found out in the
stage road reading his Bible upside down; or the Wheeler family, said by
one cantankerous descendant to be tinctured with "fool in the head."
There were the usual number of lonely, depressed people, principally
women, who attempted suicide (sometimes successfully) every year. Calvin
fit none of these patterns. He was simply a very quiet, rather withdrawn
boy. For him to be wildly excited as he had been the night of the Fourth
was exceptional.[7]

Another clue to his behavior was both more convincing and more disturbing. He was his mother's son; despite his name, he was no Coolidge. The
Coolidges tended to be tall, corpulent, stolid people with strong personalities, good New England farm folk, like his sister Abbie. Perhaps he was
more like his mother. Victoria Coolidge had been pale, delicate, sharp-featured, and bookish. Her small, compressed mouth had turned down at the
corners, like his. Though not red like Calvin's, her hair had had a "golden
gleam." Hiram Moor, her father, who lived next door, was a busy, intense,
verbal little man, a constant reader, open to new ideas and prone to lecture
people earnestly about them. But if Calvin was indeed like his mother's
family, the fact cast a shadow over his future, for two reasons: Victoria
Coolidge had died young, and she had died of consumption.[8]

Consumption, to the twentieth century, is tuberculosis, and to many late–
twentieth-century people tuberculosis is merely a name. But to the nineteenth century consumption was a horrifying reality, a "dreaded and dreadful disease," as one newspaper advertisement called it. In 1880 it was the
leading cause of death in the United States, responsible for twelve percent
of all fatalities. (In Vermont the percentage was higher, almost sixteen percent.) It was dreaded less because of its high incidence than because of the
prolonged suffering and weakness associated with it. Like AIDS and cancer
in the 1990s, it was a wasting disease for which there was no known cure. It
came on subtly; the first sign might be persistent coughing or hoarseness,
fatigue, night sweats, or loss of appetite. Only after it had taken root was it
fully identifiable, when the coughing up blood and the intense fatigue began.
After that it could go on, steadily downhill, for years; a magazine article in
the 1890s estimated an average two years of illness for every death from
consumption. Many cases lasted a good deal longer. Victoria Coolidge, for
example, had been an invalid for twelve years. In every neighborhood in the
United States there were known consumptives, living people doomed to
death within a few years. As a group they had a clear-cut image—they
were pale, frail, languid (though a few might display a kind of fevered viva-
city), and often intellectually inclined. And young: over half of all deaths
from consumption in Vermont occurred in people under forty.[9]

Though the disease and its victims had a definite image in the public mind, there was less clarity about how it spread, why some people caught it and others did not. Actually, Robert Koch in Germany had solved the problem in 1882 with his positive identification of the tuberculosis bacillus. His achievement was easily missed in the America of the 1880s, amid the confusion of traditional beliefs, faddish claims by self-styled medical experts, and real scientific discoveries. Most Americans seemed to feel that consumption was largely or entirely hereditary. Some sort of weakness, a predisposition to the ailment, was passed down the generations of a family. Experience seemed to support this view. Almost everyone knew of a family with more than one consumptive; in Plymouth, for instance, a few miles from the Notch in a rural neighborhood known as Frog City, there was a family of Coolidges, distant kin to the Coolidges of the Notch, in which the father, his brother, and three children had all died or were dying of consumption. If the disease struck one family member, the most natural thing in the world was for it to strike another. Thus, in the case of the Coolidge boy, a number of factors combined to explain his behavior, to most people's satisfaction: his resemblance to his mother; his mother's invalidism and death; and the fact, known to many in the Notch, that Victoria's brother Frank Moor, who had once run the Notch store, had recently been diagnosed with a suspicious lung disease. Calvin seemed a little boy traveling slowly down a deadend road: the end, sooner or later, was death by consumption.[10]

Calvin would go on living in the Notch, attending school, doing chores for his father. If he lived to manhood, he might take up doctoring or teaching in a small way; both professions suited with his quiet seriousness. Some day, perhaps a year away, perhaps longer, he would develop a cough that would not quit or would begin losing weight from his already spare frame. In time John would send for a doctor. (There was no doctor at the Notch, but Dr. Boyden of Bridgewater was well thought of, as was Dr. Lane of Ludlow.) The doctor would pronounce the official verdict. After that, Calvin would weaken steadily. He might remain at home, particularly if John had remarried by that time. More likely, however, he would go to stay at his grandmother Coolidge's place. There he could read and think as his body gave way. Little treatment was possible. He would probably wear woolen clothing year round to combat chills. One doctor might prescribe fresh air; another might advise him to avoid it. It would make no difference. One day his sufferings would be over. Neighbors would prepare the body for burial and comment on the appearance of the corpse; someone, probably Levi Green at the Union, would make a coffin; a minister would be sent for, probably Dr. Kidder, the Universalist pastor from Woodstock, who was popular in Plymouth because he avoided uncomfortable talk of Hell. A small procession of carriages would accompany the family to the graveyard, where Calvin would be laid to rest beside his mother, and John and Abbie would mourn another loved one.[11]

Only, of course, it did not work out this way at all. Abbie, fat, jolly Abbie, was the Coolidge who died young. Calvin not only survived but achieved a distinction few people in the Notch would have dreamed of for him.

But if he was not in the early stages of consumption, what in fact was the matter with the Coolidge boy? And why had he been so excited the night of the Fourth?

Part of the answer was that Calvin and his family believed, like everyone else, that he was dangerously prone to consumption. They very likely reasoned that he could improve his chances of not catching it if he was careful not to overtax himself in childhood sports or in excessive work. And they probably worried about his general health.

John Coolidge later asserted that his son was always in good health as a child, but the facts suggest otherwise. From his early teens, when evidence first becomes available, it is evident that Calvin was very susceptible to colds, severe ones that might send him to bed for a day or two. Frighteningly, they often interfered with his breathing and left him weak. They were not serious enough to warrant sending six miles for a doctor, however, and the family had learned to treat them on their own. By adolescence, Calvin had decided, probably at his grandmother's urging, that oranges were good for his colds. (This was twenty years before the identification of vitamin C, and probably without any knowledge that would be considered scientific today.) He was fond of them anyway, as he was of most sweet-tasting things. Thus oranges, though still a little exotic by Vermont standards, and more expensive than, say, apples, were what the family bought when Calvin was sick.[12]

Another alarming health problem was loss of appetite. Sometimes for a day, sometimes for a week or more, Calvin would just sit at table, pale, pinched, and silent, and pick at his food. Here again, the symptoms were disturbingly close to those of consumption.[13]

His family indulged him to some extent. John never spanked his son as many Vermont farmers did. Calvin was punished, to be sure, mostly by his stern grandmother, who devised measures like locking him in the attic. But at the same time, Almeda was forever warning him to be careful of his health. He did have his share of chores, some of them physically demanding, which he did without complaint, if without enthusiasm. But there was little pressure on him where farm work was concerned, because farming was not John's major source of income, merely one of those activities he carried on out of a sense of the fitness of things, like keeping the unused church clean. Calvin's labor, unlike that of most Notch boys, was not needed for family survival. As he commented in maturity, "Perhaps my lot was as easy as any boy's who grew up here." When there was heavy work to be done, his father's or his grandmother's hired man did it; he got mostly the lighter chores, and on rainy days simply went over to his grandmother's house and read.[14]

But there was another reason, more potent than health, why Calvin shunned activities and held back from playing with boys his own age. He was painfully shy with other people, and had been since early childhood. Even to encounter a neighbor in his mother's kitchen was "little short of torture" to him. He disliked these feelings and for a couple of years had been struggling to control them, with mixed success. By age thirteen he had at least learned to hide his anxiety behind a mask of composure. As a disguise, it was effective; few people who knew the boy could imagine him as anything other than calm and reticent. His cousins from Proctorsville who came up in the summer found him, not timid or nervous, but odd and rather uninteresting. Neither they nor anyone else, apparently, sensed the ordeal he was going through.[15]

There is still not much of a theoretical framework for understanding shyness. Students of the problem have usefully delimited different varieties: "audience anxiety," or shyness associated with a particular situation, like public speaking; the classical adolescent shyness, triggered by sudden changes in physique or social role; and finally, the basic, long-term shyness, which one writer calls "reticence," the behavior pattern of people who "avoid communication because they believe they will lose more by talking than by remaining silent." But there is no general agreement on how or why shyness originates. It is probably unnecessary, and certainly impossible, to isolate the factors in Calvin's background that made him the kind of person he was. What one can do is examine how it feels to be shy, to explore some typical responses of shy people, and to see how they applied in Calvin's case.[16]

Shy people tend to have low self-esteem. They typically accept high standards of performance, but then perceive themselves as unable to measure up to their own standards. They are anxious because they believe that by communicating with others they will somehow look like fools; this anxiety, as one student of shyness has put it, "is a subjective and entirely horrifying experience." There is a good deal of evidence to suggest that this was Calvin's situation. Though he was, in fact, bright in school and competent with his hands, he dreaded opening his mouth for fear of making a gaffe, or taking any action because it might prove to be a misstep. Particularly threatening to him were situations of rapid personal interchange, of give and take, where the environment changed rapidly from one instant to the next and multiplied the possibility of a mistake; so he avoided contact sports and conversation, at least conversation with strangers.[17] (It is probably worth noting that physical fear, which often accompanies shyness, apparently was absent in Calvin's case. Both his favorite pastimes in adolescence, horseback riding and sledding, had an element of physical danger. An incident from his days at Black River Academy, to be narrated more fully later, in which he broke his arm, shows both his physical daring and his comparative indifference to pain. Disapproval, not pain, was apparently what he feared.)[18]

For people in doubt of their own worth, reticence is only one way of coping. Almost all attempt to carve out of the alien terrain of human relationships a small area in which they feel at home. According to one therapist, virtually none of the thousands of shy people he has counseled "failed to identify a situation in which they felt confident." Certainly this was true in the case of the Coolidge boy. There were areas in which he was not shy at all. With immediate family and close friends, he talked without constraint and with considerable wit, in the long, unhurried drawl of rural New England. This was true, however, only with very close friends, and he had few of those, perhaps only two: a boy his own age up the road, and his grandmother's hired man. In recitations at school, where he had the aid of a prepared text, he could memorize a piece and deliver it with poise, although there was always the lurking fear that he might "break down," forget his lines, and be exposed to neighborhood gibes.[19]

Like many shy people, he found comfort in animals, with whom it was possible to have a relationship without the strain of verbal communication. There were numerous cats around the Notch, as in most dairy farming areas, to keep down the mice in the barns. Many farm children, and farm families for that matter, were fond of them; many a farmhouse in Vermont had a "cat door" in its kitchen. To Calvin they were real friends. His letters home from college in later years contained comments or questions about the family cats almost as often as any reference to humans at the Notch. One of the stories of his childhood involves his going to some trouble to save a litter of kittens from being drowned. He liked teasing cats, not like other boys, for the amusement of his comrades, but for his own and, one could almost say, for that of the cats. His attitude toward horses was quite similar. His grandfather Coolidge, who had died when he was six, had been a horseman and stock breeder, and had taught him to ride. He rode horseback by himself a lot, because, as he put it, "a horse is good company."[20]

Another technique for decreasing his discomfort in the presence of others—a classic technique of the shy—was to devote himself to the performance of routine tasks. In Calvin's case, this meant mainly the chores John imposed on him around the house and farm. Immersed in his chores, he had a perfect excuse for not socializing with other people. Moreover, successful performance helped to placate his stern, frightening father, who was much more given to criticism than to praise. Every boy in the Notch, of course, was supposed to take orders from his father, but to Calvin obedience was almost a pleasure. As he put it in his recollections, "the contemplation of a task performed, the consciousness that the farm work was all being done on time, became in themselves a form of recreation." So he strove hard to do all his tasks right. If by some chance he forgot to fill the woodbox during the day, he would get out of bed at night and do it, as he did one night to the amusement of an aunt who was visiting. For a thirteen-year-old, he was remarkably reliable. In later years John Coolidge always praised his son, significantly, for his willingness to work: "He was a trusty kind of a boy. Whatever I left for him to do, I never had to ask later if he had done it." But his devotion to routine carried over to tasks outside his home, and made him stand out even in the Yankee culture of Plymouth, with its emphasis on duty. "He was methodical, faithful to the tasks he was set to do, honest, and punctual," remembered one of his teachers. "Worked hard, Cal did," agreed a classmate. Apparently no one realized that this solitary hard work mainly helped him to keep the demons of personal dread at bay.[21]

In other ways, too, he strove to please his father. John's interests were his interests. The general store, for instance, which John had operated for some years, was one of his favorite places. The quiet, the routine, the repetitiveness of the work and the desultory conversation with familiar people were all congenial to Calvin; often he imagined himself as a country storekeeper. Or there was politics. Every year at the March town meeting John, though by no means a glad-hander, was one of the half dozen dominant men. He won repeated election to town office because of his extensive business interests, his family connections, his money, and, of course, his ability. Since the town meeting was important to John, it was important to Calvin too. Every March (and every other September, when Freemen's Meeting was held) he solemnly accompanied his father down to the Union, to the big, drafty upstairs hall behind Levi Green's store where dances and theatricals were held during the winter, and sat and watched the men thresh out the town business and spit tobacco on the sawdust-strewn floor while their wives socialized outside and prepared hot dinners for the whole crew. Most people in town were there, and the atmosphere was that of a civic holiday. Other boys his age diverted the crowd with wrestling matches and other antics, not Calvin. As a small boy, he recalled later, he carried "apples and popcorn balls to the town meetings to sell, mainly because my grandmother said my father had done so when he was a boy, and I was exceedingly anxious to grow up to be like him." Now, as he grew bigger, he sat and observed; he was equally anxious to learn the ways of town politics.[22]

Legal advice was another example. John was not a trained lawyer, but because of his long service as deputy sheriff and town agent he was more familiar with law than anyone else in the Notch, and local people came to his house to discuss legal problems, just as they went to his mother's house with medical problems. He advised them in his taciturn, gruff way; he frequently drew up papers; when necessary he referred people to a practicing lawyer like his friend J. W. Stickney in the hamlet of Tyson on the Ludlow road, or Stickney's son William, an attorney in Ludlow. At most of these meetings Calvin would be present, a silent, thin, redheaded presence observing everything through keen blue eyes.[23]

In fact, that was what Calvin was doing most of the time—observing. He was one of a rather small group of people: shy persons who are good observers. Many reticent people, according to those who study shyness, care deeply about their fellow humans, and many believe themselves good listeners, but most in fact are not because of their own inner turmoil. By adolescence, Calvin Coolidge had managed to suppress his anxieties to the point where they did not usually interfere with his observations. He still refused to take part in most activities. In games, according to a teacher, he took no part, or took part in some irregular, outside-the-rules way that posed no threat of exposing his (supposed) ineptitude. At dances he stood and watched. But wherever he was, he was storing away information about other people. "I am as much interested in human beings as one could possibly be," he said of himself in adulthood, "but it is desperately hard for me to show it."[24]

To an observant eye, there was an abundance of human interest in Plymouth. The town had been settled for almost a century, and had been remarkably stable for two generations: very few new people moved in, though there was a steady trickle of outward migration. Community experience had been distilled into a rich oral folklore of aphorisms about life and farm work ("Load of hay in June's worth a silver spoon; load of hay in July isn't worth a fly"; "When the days begin to lengthen the cold begins to strengthen"), stories about pioneer days, Indians, the War of 1812, and the Civil War from the men who had gone off to fight, and picturesque stories and turns of phrase that one could hear any day from the crowd at the general store. Like any isolated, settled community, Plymouth harbored a number of odd residents, who were perfectly accepted: whether physically odd like Orson Butler, the son of the miller at the Union, who weighed over three hundred pounds at age thirteen, was very handsome "with long curly hair down to his shoulders," and had been approached by Barnum's circus; or temperamentally odd like James "Strawberry" Brown of Five Corners, a farmer as well known for his luscious strawberries as for his radical agnosticism and his habit of letting his farm buildings fall to ruin through lack of maintenance; or the stubborn, independent Lynds family, who lived crowded into a tiny house meant for a barn, and blithely ignored community comment about their doings. Plymouth was not quite the collection of grotesques, physical and social, that Rollin Hartt was to depict a few years later in his classic article, "A New England Hill Town"; but it was demonstrably in the same category.[25]

Probably the Plymouth neighbors who observed and commented on Cal (as they called him in the Notch) missed seeing how peculiar he really was. His most prominent characteristics, silence and hard work, fitted in so completely with those of the Plymouth culture as to be almost invisible. Silence and diligence, in New England, were not peculiarities; they were highly admired virtues that went with the image of the shrewd, prudent Yankee trader, whether they were the terrified silence and obsessive hard work of the shy or the disciplined silence and industry of the Puritan. Many adults had them, not only his father. A Vermonter from another part of the state, recalling maple sugaring with her grandfather, remembered "no conversation ... but only silent companionship." A visitor to St. Johnsbury from a Western state found it hard to talk even to a well-read man: "Until he knew one, it was difficult to draw him out of a habitual reserve." A Stowe farmer who represented his town in the state legislature in the 1890's was known for his laconic speech. Economy of speech in general was prized. Unnecessary speech might lead to unnecessary emotion, to "breaking down," as a Connecticut woman described it.

Cal's shyness, too, did not seem entirely strange. Probably most youngsters in Vermont, growing up in placid, self-contained communities, feared strangers to some degree. The people seen as peculiar in Plymouth were those who socialized too readily and talked too much, like James Kavanagh, a Civil War veteran who lived between the Union and the Notch, a glib, lazy, Irish-born ne'er-do-well with a house full of children.[26]

But some traits of Cal's stood out as peculiar even in the Notch. His lack of high spirits, his deliberateness, his preference for solitude probably explained what his neighbor was trying to convey by the description "stately." To other boys his age, he was "a bit of an odd stick." "Kind of kept to himself," one schoolmate put it. His cousin Dallas Pollard was once asked if Cal might have become a more outgoing person if his sister Abbie had lived to influence him longer. "Well I don't know I'm sure," Pollard responded. "I never knew anybody that would have much influence on him, did you?" At the core of his personality, people sensed, there was a basic detachment, a refusal to engage with others.[27]

Strangely, however, there was one way in which he had learned to relate effectively to other people—through practical joking. A trick was an ideal vehicle of communication for someone as withdrawn as Calvin: it required keen observation of, and interest in, another person, a good deal of care and forethought, and no emotional investment at all. Probably for the same set of reasons, practical joking was a favored activity in New England culture. One cannot read far in the personal documents of late nineteenth-century Vermont without coming across a host of practical jokes, most of them simple, often cruel. Boys at sugaring parties fed their dogs balls of warm maple sugar so that their jaws stuck together and they rolled about in the snow as though dying. A young man fashioned a blowpipe through which he shot balls of soft putty great distances at unwary passers-by. Adults fooled each other by sending out notices of nonexistent meetings. Young men tied strings across a neighbor's walk at ankle level and watched to see who would trip. The crowd in the general store would drill a small hole in some man's favorite seat and plant a small, sharp object in it. These were the ways in which many rural Yankees amused themselves. Ingenuity was valued. Calvin praised his grandfather Coolidge for his ability to "entice a man into a nest of bees and make him think he went there of his own accord."[28]

Coolidge loved practical jokes all his life and played them most often on the people he was closest to. The prospect of having, and sharing, fun by observing someone else's embarrassment was one of the few things that could break through his reserve. An anecdote from his school days supports this point. Some of the older boys in the one-room school surreptitiously cut the teacher's birch switch almost through, so that it would break on the first stroke. Little Cal was not the joker, but when he learned of the trick he was so eager to see the payoff that he deliberately defied the teacher and became the one on whom the rod was used and broken.[29]

For a boy from the Notch, stealing the town cannon from the Union and firing it was the summit of practical joking. It was bound to annoy the Union boys and might cause all sorts of unexpected and delightful consequences. Moreover, the feat had a wonderful legendary aura. The contest reached back almost a generation in time, and its episodes were rare enough so that each one took on the special quality of a myth. Friends and neighbors were involved. More than just a prank, it was the culmination of a community saga of practical jokes. It is no surprise, than, that the early morning hours of the Fourth when the cannon was stolen were the only time in a long acquaintance when a boyhood friend could recall Calvin's showing excitement about anything.[30]

4

Six Miles from Anywhere

Long before dawn on the morning of 22 July 1885 there was light in the Coolidge house. Upstairs in his cramped bedroom (they called it a "chamber" in Vermont), Calvin got up and lit his candle with a safety match. It was cool, but not cold, and crickets trilled outside the window. The darkness was like a midwinter morning, but getting up was not the ordeal that it was in wintertime: no icy floor, no rush to grab his clothes and run downstairs to the freezing kitchen and dress, shivering, while the fire got going in the stove. As he got out of his nightshirt and into his underwear, he could hear that others were up too, Abbie moving around upstairs, John downstairs. He probably dressed a little more carefully than usual and slicked down his red hair with water from the basin. This was a big day, an annual event for the Coolidges. He, John, and Abbie were going to Rutland for the circus.[1]

He descended the steps candle in hand and came out opposite the double doors to the parlor. They were shut as usual; the family rarely used the best room, chilly even in summer with its shiny store-bought horsehair furniture, except for funerals and visiting ministers. On his right was the small bedroom where his mother had died. He turned left, then left again, and crossed the dark sitting room, where she had lain during her illness, to the kerosene-lit, whitewashed kitchen. Mattie McWain, the hired girl, a second cousin of John Coolidge, was up. There was a fire in the big cookstove. The scrubbed wooden floor, the scrubbed iron sink, the shelves with their collection of kitchen things, gleamed in the yellow light. Between the windows, the mirror where John shaved every morning reflected the glow. On the table were glasses and china for the light breakfast they would eat before setting out. (Or, rather, John and Abbie would eat; Calvin was too excited to have an appetite.) Breakfast itself was almost ready—there were pickles (as always at breakfast), rolls, doughnuts, coffee, maybe bacon.[2]

The door on the opposite side of the kitchen, the one Calvin had been afraid to pass through as a boy, led out to the horse barn. John, perhaps, was already there, hitching up the buggy in the darkness. The barn was under the same roof as the house; the enclosed space between them was the woodshed, the scene of Calvin's labors during the winter. Off to the left, if he needed to use it, was the privy. As in many Vermont houses, it

45

too was connected with the house, although in winter it was still fiendishly cold. Its furnishings were spartan: two holes, with lids, and a pail of corncobs. Next to it was the shed bedroom where John sometimes put up men he had arrested but not had time to take to the Woodstock Jail before nightfall; usually he had them give him all their clothes before he locked them in.[3]

Calvin would not have to go out to the cow barn; this morning probably Warren Spaulding, the tough, independent young farmer who worked as his grandmother's hired man, would take over for him. For many Vermont boys, though, milking was not nearly as irksome a chore as chopping and bringing in wood. You sat drowsily on the stool in the morning, your head buried in the cow's warm flank as the milk sizzled into the pail. Now and then you directed a jet of milk at one of the expectant cats. Your lantern hung on the wall, and the barn seemed warm and friendly. But Calvin would not milk this morning; some time later he would fill in for Warren.[4]

It was still dark when they left the Notch and descended the mountain into the sleeping Union. A tiresome two-hour ride lay before them, up the long, climbing road from the Union to North Shrewsbury, at the top of the Green Mountains, then down into the valley on the other side, then a few miles farther to Rutland. Across the narrow Shrewsbury road there were frequent "water bars"—places where a channel of rainwater had washed out the dirt roadway and created a bump. These provided places to stop, brace the buggy wheel, and give the tired horse a rest. The three Coolidges probably did not talk much: the children were sleepy, and in any case the family was not much given to idle conversation. As they went, the day brightened behind them, first the false dawn, then the real one. The forest air was fragrant with smells of evergreen and humus.[5]

Several other Plymouth families, doubtless, were going to the circus that day, but not many started that early. The parade, after all, was not scheduled to begin until nine o'clock, and the main show was at two in the afternoon. But John, stiff and solemn as he appeared, was partial to circuses and wanted to see the show from the very beginning. Calvin, of course, was all eyes; the pageantry particularly appealed to him. Besides, the circus this year happened to be one of the best: Barnum and Bailey's traveling two-ring circus with its giant elephant, Jumbo. So superbly managed was Barnum and Bailey that the circus's arrival in a town was almost as great a spectacle as the show itself—the bustle of unloading the forty-eight railroad cars, deploying the animals, setting up the tents, and serving breakfast to 420 employees. So it was not for the main street of Rutland that the Coolidges were headed, but for the railroad yards and the baseball field beside East Creek, where the tent was to go up. Calvin, on the seat beside his father, was uneasy. "It seemed to me," he recalled years later, "that so many things might happen to prevent us from being on the scene before a stake was driven or a car unloaded."[6]

This year, as it turned out, they were early. When they arrived in Rutland, there was no circus there at all. No doubt they had a couple of anxious moments before learning that the circus trains had left Brattleboro late and were on their way. The three trains were several hours behind schedule when they pulled in later that morning, and the circus people had to scramble to make up the lost time. The street parade did not get off until after ten. But when it did, it was as exciting as ever: there were Jumbo and JoJo, the famed elephants (Jumbo was to die later that year, in a railroad accident in Canada); the "menagenary," as some people called it jocularly, of wild beasts in cages; the glass cart full of snakes; men on stilts and women on horseback, both in rich, dazzling costumes; wisecracking clowns; perhaps a "golden chariot," a multitiered, awe-inspiring wooden float painted gold, ornamented with moldings and carved reliefs, inlaid with mirrors, riding on brilliant sixteen-spoked wheels and carrying a seated band; and at the end, in its traditional place, a raucous steam calliope.[7]

What the Coolidges were seeing was the American circus at the very beginning of its golden age. For the next generation, up to the end of the First World War, the great circus companies would tour the nation annually with their big top and ringmaster, their brass bands and wild animals, and leave a permanent mark on American culture. But in the 1880s that was just beginning. Only in the previous decade had a wider railroad net and improved technology made it possible to move a circus by rail. Now the splendor and sophistication of the city could be brought to the countryside by the trainload. The scale increased every year. The first three-ring circus dated only from 1881; Barnum and Bailey's two-ring circus still evoked complaints in Rutland that "so many performances going on at one time and all meritorious made it difficult to 'take anything in.'"[8]

By afternoon the troupers had made up their lost time, and the main show started at two as advertised. As usual, a majority of the acts were equestrian: bareback riding and acrobatic feats on horseback, graceful leaping and somersaulting that fascinated Calvin, whose Grandfather Coolidge had taught him to ride standing up as a child. But there were high-wire acts as well, and music, and clowns. The clowns illustrated how the circus was changing. Previous clowns had been stand-up comics, masters of one-liners and repartee, and often singers as well, popularizing songs that lingered for years in public currency. Now, with the expanded scale of the circus, that kind of close dialogue with the public was harder. The new generation of clowns spoke and sang less; instead they "knocked about in pantomime" and went for visual effects, though Barnum and Bailey still had at least one clown of the old school, dressed up as "Whitfield, the Vermont farmer," who got off a "few solemn jokes" to which his audience could relate.[9]

They left the show in late afternoon, satisfied, passing the sideshow tents of freaks and wild animals ("big, little, and sacred elephants ... the Patagonians, and the wild Quiche midget") and its ballyhooing barker on his high

box, loudly dressed in checked material, broad-brimmed hat, and big dia-
mond ("Everything on the inside *ex-act-ly* as represented on the outside.
Come *o-n*, good peepul, the small sum of a dime ..."). In the glow of late
afternoon their buggy rode by barns with big red-lettered circus posters
affixed, reminding them of what they had just seen. They exchanged comments about it in short, factual, pointed sentences.[10]

For Calvin and Abbie, at least, part of the thrill of this annual trip lay in
the visit to Rutland itself and the urban world it represented. (John was
more familiar with city life. When he had operated the Notch store he had
visited Boston regularly on business.) Rutland was no metropolis: it had
only twelve thousand people, though that population was enough to make
it the second largest city in Vermont. But its position at a main railroad junction put it in touch with the larger world of the major cities. It had the appurtenances of a city: five-story brick buildings and gaslight, soda fountains
and horse cars, barber shops and band concerts, livery stables, ice houses,
telephones, all the things that signified comfort and pleasure to Americans
in the later Victorian era. Rutlanders kept up with the times, too. That summer they were gathering subscriptions for an electric light system, an invention only three years old, to be tried out that fall. ("Most everyone seems
satisfied with the new light," the *Herald* reported after the trial; "[it] is un-
wavering, mild and pure and the absence of all flickering is apt to give it an
impression of weakness at first sight.") In Rutland indoor plumbing was
real; in Plymouth it was only something one read about in newspapers or
magazines.[11]

All these wonders were only a tantalizing two hours away, but they were
hours of toilsome, relatively primitive travel. It was no wonder that young
people, aware of all the pleasures and opportunities as near as the nearest
depot, found it a "positive hardship," as one contemporary student of New
England said, to live back in the hills. A Felchville woman summed it up in a
letter to her grandson: "Things remain just about the same here in Felchville, only duller if possible." One could sympathize with "Strawberry"
Brown's wife, the Five Corners correspondent for a local paper, when she
wrote, "It is a trifle inconvenient to 'write for the paper' when one lives six
miles from anywhere."[12]

Summer twilight lasts long in the Green Mountains, and doubtless it was
still light as the Coolidges' buggy rolled down the slope from North Shrewsbury toward the Union. The thick woodland around them bore testimony to
the attractiveness of cities like Rutland. Few farmers had ever tried to settle
these steep mountainsides; most of those who tried had given up and left.
Now and then they passed an old cellar hole half reclaimed by forest, a tot-
tering chimney, a collapsed shed, what was left of an abandoned farm. The
abandoned farm had become virtually a signature of rural New England, not
only in Vermont, but also in New Hampshire and the hillier parts of Massachusetts and Connecticut. Since before the Civil War, the younger people

had been yielding to the lure of the urban-railroad complex, leaving the boredom and privation of the hills, and moving to the railroad towns and cities of Vermont or sometimes to the bigger cities farther south. Their parents tried to keep farming, but eventually grew old and gave up, or died, and another deserted farmstead was added to the Vermont landscape. The immediate consequence had been a spectacular drop in the population of the hill country. From 1870 to 1880, three-fifths of all the towns in Vermont, mainly those along the spine of the Green Mountains, had lost residents. From 1880 to 1890, four-fifths would do so. (At the same time, the larger towns in the state were growing, so that Vermont as a whole remained stationary in population.) Towns like Plymouth were particularly affected. Between 1870 and 1880 one-sixth of its people had left: the town's population dropped from 1,285 to 1,075. By 1890 it would be down to 755; in other words, one-third of those remaining would emigrate.[13]

Signs of emigration were apparent all over Plymouth, but perhaps most so in the southern part of the town. In the southeast corner, near the Reading line, was an old neighborhood known as Plymouth Kingdom, the first part of the town settled after the Revolution. Now it was almost unsettled again, full of abandoned farms, its imposing church falling into disrepair and disuse. Several miles west, in the southwestern part of town on the slopes of the Green Mountains, the community of Ninevah was literally disappearing from the map as its farmers moved away. Its schools were closed for lack of pupils, its pastures and grain fields were reverting to forest, and the area was becoming, as to some extent it had always been, a haunt for several kinds of illicit behavior—liquor stills, sexual escapades, violent family feuds. To a degree, the whole town was acquiring the image later ascribed to it by a poet from a nearby town, that of a remote mountain fastness

> ... where snow hangs on till May,
> Where hunters range the hollow woods;
> Where smugglers go to buy up pelts
> And pedlars go to peddle goods.[14]

To the town as a whole, the declining population meant pretty much the same thing: less ability to support public institutions like schools, churches, and roads. During the eighties, the number of school districts in the town of Plymouth dropped from eighteen to fourteen. The number of schools actually taught per term (for some districts, lacking enough pupils to justify a school, sent theirs to a neighboring district) declined still further, from sixteen to twelve. As to churches, in 1885 there was only one full-time clergyman in town, the Methodist pastor at the Union, who left that year and was not replaced. Plymouth roads in 1885 may already have been decaying to the state they were in a few years later, when, according to one native, travelers knew they had crossed the town line by immediately plunging into a mudhole. (The man who told this story blamed the poor roads on John Coolidge's unwillingness, as a town official, to spend public funds. John's own explanation was different. He could afford the necessary taxes to maintain the roads, he told Calvin, but he didn't want to place an additional burden on the poorer farmers who were just squeezing by.)[15]

For the shy residents of Plymouth like young Calvin Coolidge (and surely there must have been others), the sparse population was a positive blessing. Having to see only a few people each day, and those probably the same ones every day, made life bearable—in fact, made it interesting. Less sensitive residents simply accepted the loss of population as a fact of life, except occasionally during the summer, when farmers might complain about the lack of available hands and lament that all the young men had gone off to other towns to work in the mills. Indeed, if provoked, Plymouth people were capable of defending their town because it was depopulated, as John Coolidge's cohort J. W. Stickney did in 1887 in a spirited letter to a local paper:

> In Plymouth there are no large villages; the population is widely scattered among its hills; the churches are too small to make trouble with one another and too weak to have trouble among themselves—which gives the town a quietude unknown to places of strong churches with large membership. The absence of railroads, and of a foreign population consequent upon railroad towns, is escaped, and no real cause exists here for trouble.[16]

Others were much less tolerant of outside criticism, as witness the reaction of a Plymouth correspondent in 1885: "If we are 'isolated, gloomy, and peculiar,' and abounding in illicit distilleries, our people have it yet to learn. If strangers so judge, why we do not feel very bad about it here."[17]

Even for those who resisted the flight to the cities and chose to stay, the gradual abandonment of the town was enough to shake their confidence in farming as a way of life. There were good farmers in Plymouth, but none of them did much more than break even—not "Strawberry" Brown with his luscious fruit, nor Henman Sargent with his thousands of maple sugar trees, nor John Wilder with his flocks of prizewinning Merino sheep. In a less isolated town, with better access to the railroad and a little more available labor, some of these men might have shifted to dairying as alert farmers were doing elsewhere in Vermont, to tap into the profitable business of supplying the cities with fresh milk. But in Plymouth such a shift seemed pointless. Most of the land in Plymouth farms was not really suited to farming at all, at least not for profit. According to one classification, not a single acre of land in town was capable of being farmed productively.[18]

There were alternative ways to make a good living without leaving Plymouth, lumbering, for instance. The Black River ran through the whole western part of town, under the foot of the Green Mountains, widening at two points into broad ponds, providing a way of moving timber cut during the winter logging season and a source of power for sawmills to cut the logs into lumber. Plymouth men were not slow to take advantage of their town's resources. In 1883 Plymouth had ten sawmills, more than any other town in Windsor county. Some, like Parker and Piper's steam mill at the Union, turned out over a million and a half feet of lumber a year. Moreover, the business created other mills manufacturing wood products, like Sanderson and Knight's chair stretcher factory, which the Coolidges passed as they crossed Black River in the deepening dusk and rolled into the Union. Logging was very much a seasonal trade, beginning with the first really good snow in November or December and running through the spring thaw; because of this fact, it coexisted well with farming. Young men who wanted to earn good money year round could cut and haul timber during the winter, and then hire on as farm laborers in time for spring plowing. It was also lucrative. An artist who lived a bit farther north in the Green Mountains was told by his neighbors "in this part of Vermont that the lumber business pays better than any other."[19]

Lumbering had its unattractive features. Lumber camps were commonly (and correctly) associated with profanity, drinking, and foreigners, and so were the mills and factories dependent on them. All three enterprises attracted numbers of young single men from all over; in Plymouth, about half were likely to be French-Canadian. Where one had dozens of men boarding together for months, as at the steam-mill boarding house at the Union, there were bound to be "frolics," with occasional injuries, incidents of public drunkenness, and even labor disputes. It was no wonder that the young people of the Notch tended to think of the Union boys as "toughs." Then there was the purely aesthetic aspect. A large sawmill, say Alonzo Hubbard's big mill at Tyson Furnace, was apt to be a really ugly place, its buildings crazily pieced together, wreathed in smoke and steam, and surrounded on all sides by a chaos of sawdust piles, logs, wood scraps, and rubbish. Finally, lumbering was not a way to permanent prosperity. It was, after all, an extractive industry. When the supply of trees in Plymouth, vast as it seemed, began to be used up, the loggers and their mills would go elsewhere.[20]

Much the same could be said of another moneymaking method, mining, which had recently enjoyed a brief flurry at Five Corners. There was no doubt that Plymouth was rich in minerals and geological curiosities. Iron had been mined and smelted at Tyson Furnace since the 1830s, and indeed had given the Furnace its name. For years there had been a steady, though small, production of crushed lime from the limestone ledges above the Union. Colored marble was known to occur in several parts of town, and north of the Union were two deep caves that Calvin, like most Plymouth boys, had entered and partially explored. But the mineral that captivated people's imaginations was gold. Flakes of it were fairly common in the brooks in the eastern part of town, and from the 1850s on a constant trickle of outsiders had poured into Five Corners and the Kingdom, men interested in panning and casually exploring, men who hoped for a strike to rival those in the western states. Around 1880 two groups of these outsiders, believing they had found the gold-bearing quartz vein, between them acquired nearly three hundred acres near Five Corners and began full-scale mining operations. Their activities had prospered for several years. Miners had come to the Corners to work; the community had sported two hotels, and had even developed a rudimentary social life. But now, in 1885, the mines had abruptly shut down, and several of the leading men in the outfits had left. To Calvin, whose knowledge of the mining boom had been filtered through his father's chilly skepticism, the collapse was probably no surprise, but it did underscore again the difficulties of making a living in shrinking, isolated Plymouth.[21]

The real economic future of Plymouth, though no one realized it at the time, lay not in the Five Corners mines or in the Plymouth Union sawmills, but in the little community of Tyson, at the south end of Lower Plymouth Pond, where a sleepy little hotel, the Tyson House, had been packed with summer boarders every year for fifteen years. The boarders were a quiet lot. They mostly rocked on the veranda or took quiet walks and drives to enjoy the gorgeous scenery around the pond, which sometime in the 1860s or 1870s had been renamed Echo Lake to appeal to the visitors. (There seems to have been a vogue in these years for renaming pieces of Plymouth scenery to suit tourist sensibilities. In 1886, a party of gentleman visitors from Bethel, Vermont, rechristened the upper pond "Lake Adsulule" after their wives and wrote a letter to the Ludlow newspaper about it; local people, offended by the "outlandish" name, came up with a better one of their own devising, which has endured, Lake Amherst.) Tyson was not a noisy community either. The iron furnace had been closed some ten years, and Hubbard's sawmill operated only in winter and spring. Some summer days on the veranda of the Tyson House the loudest sound was a bumblebee droning or a fish jumping in Echo Lake. The fresh air and tranquility were why the city people came back, year after year, some for as many as fifteen summers. And there were more who wanted to visit. "The Tyson House has twenty-five summer guests," the Woodstock newspaper noted in August of 1885, "and might have a hundred more if it could accommodate as many." In 1888 Alonzo Hubbard took the logical next step; he bought the Tyson House, tore it down, and erected the much more modern and spacious Echo Lake Inn.[22]

The Tyson House boarders, middle-class families from Boston or New York, or occasionally as far away as Chicago, were not a showy group, and they made little impact on Plymouth. Yet they, apart from some of the laborers in the mills at the Union, were the only considerable group of outsiders in the town. Occasionally tramps or gypsies, scary vagrants, might pass through en route from Ludlow to Woodstock. Prudent storekeepers closed their doors until the gypsies were gone, and children avoided the tramps. But for the most part, the outside world was simply not a compelling factor in Plymouth people's lives.[23]

To say this is not to assert that Plymouth was cut off from outside. On the contrary, the Coolidges' trip to Rutland, from which the drowsy trio were now returning, illustrated that communication with the world beyond Plymouth was perfectly possible. The stage regularly brought Rutland and even Boston papers to Plymouth. Grandmother Coolidge ordered Sunday school materials from Chicago. And the dress patterns, patent medicines, and the fruits that appeared in the stores around Christmas all came from far away. At the store, the men often discussed national politics in the evenings as they chewed and filled the spittoon, though mainly as a diversion and ordinarily ending with a comforting symbolic reaffirmation of their own values: the Civil War had been right, the big-city Democratic politicians were wrong, Vermont Republicanism was right. There was no urgency in these discussions; they were merely a pastime. People in Plymouth were free to ignore the rest of the world, and most of the time they did. They were, with respect to the great world, like members of a large audience seated in the back rows of a vast arena, immeasurably bigger than Barnum's tent. They were in the same room as the action, and with careful attention they could make out what was going on; but most of the time it was easier and more rewarding to pay attention to their immediate neighbors.[24]

For this remoteness there was, inevitably, a price. The people of Plymouth and similar townships missed out on a good deal that was interesting and fine in Victorian culture. The few city dwellers who spent much time observing rural Vermonters were apt to feel sorry for this deprivation. But as one perceptive observer noted, in connection with a village much less isolated than Plymouth, the local inhabitants "would be full of wonder and wrath if told that their lives are narrow, since they have never seen the limit of the breadth of the current of their daily life. A singing school is as much to them as a symphony concert and grand opera to their city brethren, and a sewing church sociable as an afternoon tea."[25]

Calvin Coolidge, in his maturity, felt that the lack of contact with the outside was a positive gain. "Experience," he wrote,

> was sufficiently meager so that it could be carefully considered and digested. Contemplation was possible.... There was nothing to suggest to a boy that conditions would change violently. I never mistrusted that history was not all made, public questions about all decided, and the world—at least our part of it—was not destined to go on indefinitely as it was then going.
> Each year brought the same seasonal routine.[26]

5

Winter in the Notch

Plymouth school District 9 (which comprised the Notch school district) operated with the wheezy regularity of most other town institutions, so it was quite natural to see the stone schoolhouse, one early morning at the end of August, surrounded by a crowd of some twenty students, farm children roughly between the ages of five and fifteen, awaiting the arrival of the teacher, Miss Ina Davis of Reading. Miss Davis was coming to teach the eight-week school term that ended in late October, the second term of the school year as it was understood in Plymouth and other rural towns. The first, the summer term, had begun in May and lasted ten weeks. Also taught by Miss Davis, it had ended just after the Fourth of July. The final, or winter, term would start the week after Thanksgiving and run through late February. According to this schedule, the school year ran from May to February: the long vacation for schoolchildren came not in summer but in spring, at the time of maple sugaring, spring plowing, and mud-clogged roads.[1]

Calvin was waiting with the other boys outside the school, probably talking with his best friend Thomas Moore, who lived just north of the village on the stage road. He and Thomas were constant companions after the fashion of country boys; they hunted and fished together whenever they could get away from their chores. At thirteen, they were nearly the oldest students in the school. Only George Chamberlin and Calvin's cousin Allen Wilder, both fourteen, were older. Boys and girls older than thirteen were also supposed to attend school, but most did so only in the winter term, since Vermont state law required only three months' attendance. (Those whose parents were really serious about education did not attend the district school at all, but went to an academy in one of the towns nearby.)[2]

The fields were alive with bird calls and the roadsides aglow with goldenrod, the harbinger of autumn, as Miss Davis arrived, attired in the long, high-collared dress proper for a woman teacher. She had been driven over from Reading, the next township to the east, and she would stay in the Notch for the eight weeks of the term, boarding with the families of the students she taught. Twenty-seven and an experienced teacher, she was old enough to have acquired the name of an old-maid schoolmarm (or "unclaimed blessing," as some young wags in Plymouth called unmarried lady teachers). In fact, she was old by the standards of some districts. Vermont set no minimum age for teaching. A person who could pass the teachers' examination, given once or twice a year in most towns, was qualified to teach; many districts hired teenage girls as teachers, particularly during the summer term, when most of the students were small children. Miss Davis alighted, greeted her students, and went into the schoolhouse. Calvin and the others followed her.[3]

District 9 was, in most respects, a typical Vermont country schoolhouse. That is, it had a bare floor, a big, smoky box stove in the center, high-backed spruce benches around the walls, polished with wear and whittled with years of disrespectful carvings, a blackboard of some sort, a pail and dipper for water for the pupils, a chair for visitors, and two privies, more or less filthy, behind the building. But the school was made of stone rather than wood, and it was in awful condition. The three teachers who had taught there the previous year, in response to Question 16 on the School Register, "Is the school house in good condition?", had each put down "no"—the third, Ernest C. Carpenter, in emphatic block capitals. Even the district school board was convinced it was inadequate; the following year they would order it torn down and replaced by a frame structure. The exact nature of the problem with it was not specified. Probably it was drafts. It must have been brutally cold in winter, and even now, in August, there was quite possibly a fire, built by Calvin or one of the other boys, to ward off the morning chill. Winter was not far away; there had already been frost in Plymouth on the twenty-eighth. To signal the beginning of classes, Miss Davis rang the handbell on her desk at nine o'clock—more or less, since no one in the school possessed a watch. For Calvin and his companions, another seasonal routine had started.[4]

School work was largely memorizing and reciting memorized material. Calvin and the rest sat in the desks and benches—younger children at the desks in front, older ones on the benches in the rear—with their slim, well-worn textbooks covered in heavy brown paper or odd pieces of gingham, works like Greenleaf's *Algebra*, Hall's *Geography and History of Vermont*, or the *New American Reader and Speller*, and studied their assignments. One age group after another trooped to the front of the class and stood in a row, toeing a crack in the floor in front of the teacher's desk, to recite. If reading was the first subject of the morning, as it was in many districts, the smaller children would be saying their *a*, *b*, *abs*, as the alphabet drill was called in New England, or stumbling through sentences from an easy reader, while Calvin and his contemporaries worked at memorizing "pieces," famous orations or classic poems, to recite when their turn came. A new method of learning grammar, which consisted of diagramming sentences, was being taught over in one of the Reading districts, and Miss Davis may have imported it to Plymouth too. A little later, during the arithmetic period, the room would be full of the screech of chalk on slates and the drone of the small fry saying their multiplication tables, while the older ones stood up front and went through the complications of "mental arithmetic":

> How many miles is it from Boston to Providence? It is six miles from Boston to Mt. Hope and two miles from Mt. Hope to Readville, nine miles from Readville to Sharon, and so on. The pupil must say: if it is six miles from Boston to Mt. Hope and two miles from Mt. Hope to Readville, then it is eight miles from Boston to Readville.[5]

During the lunch hour, students from nearby, like Calvin, went home to eat. The others, in the schoolyard, ate doughnuts, johnnycake, apples or whatever was in their lunch pails. Afterwards the teacher went on to other subjects—government, geography, science, U.S. and Vermont history—all conducted in pretty much the same way, with a lot of didactic verse to memorize, especially for the smaller children. In some Vermont districts, there were written examinations in subjects like history; but probably not in the Notch district, where writing materials were scarce and costly, and where the teacher simply put oral questions from the textbook. In the hands of an uninspired teacher, this rote repetition, textbook-question-and-textbook-answer exchange was a dull, almost meaningless routine—and few teachers in the Notch school were inspired. As the afternoon crept on, doubtless, Calvin and his classmates watched the sunlit rectangles from the windows inch across the dusty floor and tried to calculate how long it was until four o'clock.[6]

The monotony of the teaching made trivial events—student pranks, teacher discipline, fights between pupils—stand out by comparison. Generally, in the summer and fall terms, little "government," as one Vermonter called it, was needed; most of the pupils had been brought up to be obedient and orderly. But not the best parental training could keep children from dozing off occasionally, or boys and girls from whispering while Miss Davis heard someone else's lesson. The offender was switched, or grasped and thoroughly shaken, or had to stand in the corner, or, if he was a boy, had to sit with the girls. At recess, all these punishments were rehashed with delight by the other students.[7]

Recess was the time for games and pranks of all sorts, or children's games inside the schoolhouse if the weather was stormy. In one nearby district, a favorite trick of the boys was overturning the privy while a schoolmate was inside and forcing him to crawl out through the hole in the bottom. They then claimed that he had been "through college." Fights also took place at recess. Boys usually were involved, though at times girls were too. Calvin, when he was smaller, had been thrashed by one of the Kavanagh girls one winter day for pestering her by putting snow down her neck.[8]

Calvin behaved himself in school this term. Even though he was at the age (the "between age," one teacher called it) that ordinarily gave teachers most trouble, he received an above average mark for conduct. Not all pupils did. His little cousin Johnnie Wilder and an irrepressible nine-year-old named Harry Rowe both got low grades. Meanwhile, as the term progressed, the mountains around the Notch turned from green to spectacular gold, red, and orange, a little earlier than usual, reaching their peak around the first of October. Probably most Plymouth boys took this splendor for granted; but Cal, with his eye for natural beauty, may have stood still at times, his hair as fiery red as the mountainside, admiring it silently.[9]

By term's end the splendor was gone and winter was approaching in earnest. It had snowed twice already, though the snow had not stuck. The Windsor County Fair at Woodstock, which Calvin loved, with its horses, races, and rides, had come and gone. Farmers had about finished their fall tasks: the potatoes had been dug and stored, the corn cut and put up in stooks, the apples gathered. The mown fields had turned brown, and the cattle had been turned loose in them to graze on the last hay in the corners. It was pitch dark in the mornings now when Calvin went to milk. John was very likely mending the walls around his place, a favorite task of his in October, and had his son busy after school and on Saturdays splitting stones and hauling them on the wooden sledge. The cold, raw smell of winter was in the air.[10]

Although report cards were apparently not in use in the Notch, as they were in some nearby districts, it was evident that Calvin had not wasted his time this term. On the last Saturday in November, the common school teachers' examination was given at the schoolhouse. John was serving as town superintendent of schools again this year, and it was probably at his suggestion, certainly with his permission, that Calvin, though only thirteen, took the test. He passed. As far as the state of Vermont was concerned, he no longer needed to attend district school; he was ready to teach.[11]

Calvin had no idea of teaching. He was too young; besides, he lacked the forceful personality that the job required. But his score did raise the question of why he should continue to attend district school. The proper place for him was an academy, one of the private educational institutions with a larger faculty where the ambitious boys and girls of the New England countryside—the "intellectual aristocrats," one New Hampshire boy of modest family called them—went to prepare themselves for professional careers or local responsibilities. There were quite a few academies in Vermont. Like modern high schools, they offered a mix of courses: practical studies like English and bookkeeping for students who would finish their education there; Latin and Greek for the few who aimed to go on to college; science, history, and literature for everybody. Calvin could benefit from an academy education. It would help in his career, assuming he survived to adulthood. Moreover, from what he had heard of academies, he thought he would enjoy one. But of course the final decision was not his, but John's.[12]

John had had a busy fall and was having a busy winter. He had been chosen town superintendent in September to replace a man who had moved West, and the post entailed visiting all thirteen schools functioning in the town. This was no great burden. His duties as constable took him all over, anyway: in October he was in the Five Corners area investigating a burglary at John Lynds's; the first week in December he was in Woodstock serving on the grand jury. Perhaps he was just too busy to come to a decision about Calvin's schooling. In any event, young Coolidge attended district school for one more term.[13]

Winter school was somewhat different from the other terms. It smelled different, to begin with. Boys and girls bathed less in winter, and the schoolroom was shut as tightly as possible against the cold outside, so there were lots of pungent human odors, which the heat of the wood stove brought out. One got used to these, but there were also the boys who came to school in the same boots they used for tending to the barn animals, with manure still on them; and invariably a boy or two who trapped skunks for extra money in winter and had the distinctive scent clinging to him (and was usually nicknamed "Skunk" by the other students).[14]

The students were different, too. The "mean jobs" of late fall were now done: the chickens and turkeys killed (and a couple served for Thanksgiving dinner); the first hog of winter butchered, and the soap and sausage made; the winter's firewood gotten in. Now the older adolescents were free from farm chores for a while, and since the New England ethos forbade idleness, most of them employed their time in going back to school, even if it meant simply studying the same old lessons again. Besides, school was socially the place to be in winter—all the other young people were there. No longer were Calvin and his contemporaries the oldest students: now they were outranked by the boys and girls in their middle teens, physically bigger (the boys in particular; Plymouth males tended to be tall) and socially almost adults, with less awe of the teacher. At the same time, some of the youngest children were absent, their mothers keeping them at home during the cold weather. Winter term, thus, found the class more crowded and the students less respectful than in the other terms. It was the real challenge for a teacher. There were apt to be more pranks than in summer or fall, and not just the usual spitballs, or tripping other students up, but pranks designed to harry the teacher—making animal noises like a cat trapped in the loft, for instance, or setting a piece of rubber on the hot stove until it melted and scorched and the stench drove everyone from the schoolhouse.[15]

Miss Davis was again the teacher this winter, and the scraps of evidence that survive suggest that the students gave her a bad time. At the New Year Calvin began keeping a diary (someone in the family, evidently, had given him the little blank book for Christmas) and among the first of his terse entries, on 6 January, he noted, "The boys broke the desk all to the devil." ("The desk," presumably, meant the teacher's desk.) The next day, having made their point, the boys "fixed the old desk.... They put in a pound of nails and done a good job," he added with dry rural humor. A couple of weeks later, "the boys," again, took the swivel out of the teacher's chair during the noon hour. A look through the teacher's register makes it clear who "the boys" were. Not Calvin or Thomas: they maintained their above average marks in conduct, though Calvin did get a "talking to" when he hit two younger boys who were bothering an older girl student. But most of the older boys got low marks in deportment: Herbert Moore, George Moore's lanky, humorous younger brother, a great hunter and fisherman; Matt Hall, the hardworking, boisterous son of the farmer and lime-burner Chris Hall, who lived toward the Union ("They [the Halls] was devils," one neighbor recalled); Allen Wilder, Calvin's cousin; Dell Ward, Perry Kavanagh, in short all the older boys but Calvin, Thomas, and Henry Brown, who at seventeen was perhaps a little above it all. Whatever the exact nature of Miss Davis's problems, one can note that this was her last term teaching at the Notch, and that she failed to end the term with the customary student exhibition.[16]

She was, however, involved in another, more pleasant exhibition early in the term. This was the annual community Christmas tree, at which many of her students had pieces to recite. The celebration of Christmas was not a tradition of long standing in Vermont, or indeed in New England. Only since the Civil War had Christmas been accepted at all, thanks to the steady, imperceptible pressure from the outside urban culture, exerted mainly through commercial publications and magazines, and through natives returned from living in the cities. Now, however, it was gaining in importance every year, surpassing even Thanksgiving. In most rural Vermont households there was a family dinner, Thanksgiving-style—turkey, potatoes, soda biscuits, gravy, and several kinds of pie. Children sometimes hung up their stockings; whether they did or not, they usually received a small present or two, often of a practical nature, like stationery or a blank book. In some families adults exchanged gifts too. In the previous generation, most of the gifts would have been homemade; now they were more apt to be "boughten" from the local store. As for decoration, Vermonters in many rural areas, including Plymouth and neighboring towns, harvested boxcar loads of Christmas greens every year for shipment to the cities; but they were sparing when it came to decorating their own homes. An occasional household would have its own tree, hung with oranges and popcorn strands. Typically, however, the only Christmas tree in town was the one at the church or schoolhouse, and on some night near Christmas—it might be Christmas Eve or Christmas Night—this tree was the focus of the community celebration.[17]

At Plymouth Notch, the tree was erected in the church. It was large and impressive, hung not only with decorations but also with gifts for the children and others in the community, to be given away by some member of the organizing committee dressed up as Santa Claus. Individuals also exchanged gifts, sometimes real presents and sometimes gag gifts directed at the foibles of a neighbor, which left the victim with a smart that might last a whole year as he figured how to get back at the perpetrator. There was music, too. At the 1885 tree Clara Moore, Thomas's seventeen-year-old cousin, played the portable pump organ, while her mother, Rhoda, sang in the choir. The rest of the choir that year consisted of Coolidge kin and employees: John Wilder; Warren Spaulding, Almeda's hired man; and Mat McWain, John's hired girl. (What they sang is conjectural; most of today's Christmas carols were not yet current. "Jingle Bells" was perhaps the only exception.) And, finally, there were recitations, pieces spoken by the best students at the school, which in 1885 meant Calvin, Thomas, two Kavanagh boys, and a host of girls, large and small. They had an ample audience. In addition to the local folks, some people from other neighborhoods had driven over the rainy, slushy roads to the Notch celebration, as they did every year. The spectators applauded, and sometimes cheered lustily, after each recitation. All the performers, no doubt, had prepared with Miss Davis's help; probably she had also helped them choose their selections. Abbie recited a selection called "The Three Wishes." Thomas's piece was called "The Sale of the Bachelors." The piece that Calvin declaimed, intentionally or by chance, had a title that suited well with his quiet, withdrawn nature: "The Grey Cold Christmas."[18]

The Christmas tree was only one of the amusements Plymouth people got up for themselves during the winter. In Plymouth, as in the rest of rural New England, winter was the most social of seasons. The load of farm work was comparatively light; though wood had to be chopped and the animals fed, most of the cows were dry, and the weather did not permit undertaking major projects. Farm families, thus, had more time to spare. Travel, moreover, once a good blanket of snow had covered the roads, was easier than at any other time of year. Snow, wrote an English visitor to New England, "is the best—I had almost written the only—road-maker in the States." One needed only to harness the horse to a sleigh, bundle the family up warmly, and take off down the glistening double ribbon of track in the center of the road with a smooth, silent glide. To be sure, there were stinging winds, numbed noses, and reddened cheeks as the sleigh flew along, with minute bits of ice, kicked up from the road, flying over the dasher, and occasional spills, particularly after a fresh fall of snow; but these were more than compensated for by the joy and speed of the ride. "This was the chosen time," as one Plymouth resident put it, "for parties, visiting, dancing, courting, and merry-making."[19]

The winter of 1885–86 had its full share of social activities, even though the weather was less than cooperative; by 8 January there had been lots of rain and very little snow, and the ground was almost bare. Nevertheless there were spelling bees for adults and children, perhaps the kind at which a prize was offered. Calvin went to one on 15 January and "had a splendid time." There was a singing school at the church on Saturday nights, too, as there was most years. This one, to practice part singing of traditional hymns, was conducted by Albert Bennett of Woodstock and attracted a lot of participants, including the musical Moores, Alfred and his family, and Warren Spaulding. Calvin attended occasionally, but he was basically not a musical person, nor were any of his family. At the final concert on 30 January, he was in the audience.[20]

Most of all, there were the parties and dances. At the latter, dancers joined in traditional figures, quadrilles and contra dances with complicated evolutions (the popular Portland Fancy began "eight hands around—right and left—ladies change—half promenade—half right and left—forward and back—pass by one couple"). These were tremendously popular. At the Union, where the bigger dances were held in the hotel parlors (there was no room at the Notch big enough for them), sometimes as many as forty couples attended, to dance well into the early morning to the music of bands from Woodstock or Chester and vex the stable hands with the task of handling all forty teams. But just as much fun were the kitchen dances—"kitchen junkets," or "kitchen tunks," some called them—at private homes in the Notch. Some family would clear the chairs, tables, and other furniture from their kitchen, John Wilder would come over with his fiddle, and Stella McWain, Martha's younger sister, would play the pump organ if there was one. Then the dancers would form in two lines opposite each other and begin the Virginia Reel or Fisher's Hornpipe while a caller sang out the steps. Often there would be a card game going on elsewhere in the house. Most young people seem to have enjoyed these affairs and joined in energetically, but not Calvin. As often as not, he found a health reason for not going to dances. When he went, he avoided dancing.[21]

Calvin's idea of winter fun was more typical of a thirteen-year-old boy. He and Thomas Moore skated a lot, on the shallow meadow ponds. When the hoped-for snowfall finally arrived, in mid-January, both boys started bringing their sleds to school and sliding down Schoolhouse Hill during recess. "Sliding" (this or "coasting," rather than "sledding," was the commonly used term for the sport) was young Coolidge's favorite diversion, something he consistently enjoyed despite what the Woodstock paper called the "bruised limbs, mangled noses, and such incidents as are necessary as seasoning to the sport." On Saturdays, the two friends shouldered their shotguns and went out, warmly bundled up in short overcoats, leggings, rubbers, and sealskin caps, with perhaps a handkerchief or woolen muffler around their faces, into the bare woods that enveloped the Notch. Their quarry was generally birds; larger game was not abundant in the area. There were almost no deer in Plymouth, or indeed in Vermont; they had been all but exterminated in the early 1800s and were just beginning to return. (In fact, the head of the last buck shot in Plymouth was on the wall of grandmother Coolidge's kitchen.) Probably there were more bear than deer in the area, but Cal and Thomas saw none of either. Herbert Moore did get a fox one day in January, but the younger boys usually came home empty-handed. "Went shootin [sic] with Thomas. Scat up 6 partridges. Didn't get one," was a fairly typical entry.[22]

In any event, it was good being out among the sights and sounds of winter: the roaring of the treetops in a rising wind; the surprising variance in the color of the snow under different lights, yellow in direct sunlight, lilac or rose in the distance; the flash of bright blue as a jay swooped down from a tree; the almost unbearable glittering of the woods the morning after an ice storm, like the one that hit at the end of January. "We have a good time sliding," Calvin wrote on 1 February. "John went out collecting tax as it is loaded with ice (the trees)."[23]

Calvin's diary reveals some surprising features of life in the Coolidge household. Since John was away on town or private business so often, Cal and Abbie spent as much time at their grandmother's house as they did at their own. In fact, it appears from the diary that Cal thought of both houses equally as his home. That is, an entry like "I stayed over with Grandma tonight" (6 January), which seems to be written from the perspective of his own house, is balanced by one like "Warren drawed wood to John's house" (22 January), where he seems not to be claiming a share in his father's house. Sometimes both houses appear in a single entry, like that of 10 January: "I am to home now. Am going to go to the house." His Grandmother Coolidge was not quite a surrogate mother to him. She was partly the stern grandparent, lecturing him on his behavior (as she had disciplined him when he was smaller by locking him in the attic) and monitoring his faith by her strict Baptist code; but she was also the indulgent grandparent, genuinely fond of him and willing to let him have time by himself to lie on the couch in the big old kitchen and read, or just daydream and watch the firelight on the enormous colonial hearth. Later on, in college, he was to remember the gaunt Coolidge manse, with its old books and Revolutionary heirlooms, as a second home.[24]

When he was at his father's house, moreover, he was often there alone: John was off on business, Abbie was staying at their grandmother's, and the hired girl was also off for some reason. Cal's solitude was, in a way, John's tribute to his son: it represented a judgment that Cal was capable of handling all the small daily chores of farm life, keeping the stock fed and the fires going, by himself. But it was also lonely. Much of the time Calvin saw more of Warren Spaulding than he did of his father; some diary entries suggest, too, that he got along better with Warren than with John. Certainly he lent a sympathetic ear to Warren's recurrent frustrations (John, stern and demanding, was a very difficult boss). On 21 January, with regard to some unspecified problem, he recorded, "Warren is mad as hell scat-oxen. Don't know what J. will do." He also seems to have enjoyed sharing vicariously in the hired man's life. Warren was a singer, a dancer, and a bit of a ladies' man. Cal was none of these things, but he enjoyed following Warren's activities.[25]

At some point during January or February—the diary gives no hint when—he brought up the question of his education with John again. That he did so shows how strongly he felt on the subject. It was rare for Cal to express strong feelings about anything, and there is no indication of how he conveyed to his father his desire for a different kind of schooling, his belief that he could do well and (in a favorite phrase of his) "have a good time" at an academy, his timid longing for new people and new experiences of the kind he had seen on his trips to the circus. Maybe it was over supper in the kitchen, by the light of the kerosene lamp; maybe out in the horse barn or the woodshed, during a pause between chores. In any case, to John the question also involved using resources efficiently. Tight-fisted and painstaking, John did not like to waste money, and there was a real question whether it was a waste to send Calvin to an academy when his future career, if any, was completely uncertain. But there were also strong arguments to the contrary. There was nothing for Cal to study profitably in Plymouth; his labor was not really needed on the farm; and perhaps most telling of all, it was difficult for a widower who was often away from home to look after two children. Even though Cal was young to be going off to school, maybe it was the most economical course in the long run.[26]

On Monday, 8 February, two weeks from the end of the term, father and son went to Woodstock, the "shire town" (county seat), some twelve miles from the Notch, to look at a school. The tranquil little village, with its stately houses and oval common, had a good high school that was attended by some youngsters from the Five Corners area. For some reason, however, the Woodstock school failed to work out, if it was ever a real possibility. In the end, John decided to send Calvin in the other direction, not east to Woodstock but south to Ludlow, to Black River Academy, which John himself had attended years before. There was much to be said for Ludlow. Many Plymouth people sent their children to school there: Henry Brown of the Notch, James Brown's son, had been attending recently and had probably been telling Cal all about it. Moreover, lawyer William Stickney, the son of John's friend and collaborator, had an office there and would be a useful local contact. The schedule of Black River Academy ("B.R.A." to local people) was set up to dovetail with that of most rural schools; its spring term began 22 February, the Monday after the winter term in the Notch school ended. And the fees were reasonable: fifty cents a week for the basic English course, sixty cents for the college preparatory, which included Latin. (Calvin would sign up for the English course; whether this decision stemmed from John's parsimony or from his own hesitancy is unclear.)[27]

On Saturday, 13 February, while Cal went out hunting with Thomas, John went to Ludlow to see about the boy's getting into B.R.A. After his return the next day, the whole family had supper at Almeda's and John announced that Calvin's admission was "a cast-iron arrangement." It was a big step, not only to the shy thirteen-year-old but to the rest of his family, Abbie, his grandmother, even Mat, the hired girl, and Warren. Almeda worried that he might be too sensitive to be happy at Ludlow; he might get homesick and have to come back.[28]

The week before his departure was full of excitement and activity. There was careful packing to be done, selection of his best clothes, fit for wearing in town—not his farm-work, hunting, or district-school wear. (In the end it all fitted easily into two small handbags.) There was a party at John's house Thursday night, in part no doubt to wish Cal well in his new undertaking. Perhaps there was dancing, although maybe not. John did not dance, but he had no objection to others' doing so. If there was no dancing, probably the young people played one of the popular kissing games, like "Copenhagen," in which they all formed a ring around the kitchen holding onto a long rope, and two or three people inside the ring tried to slap the hands of the others, with a kiss as a reward if they succeeded. Calvin, with his pronounced sweet tooth, made molasses candy for the guests and himself. In addition, those invited brought their own refreshments. Calvin said he had a good time, but his mind was probably less on the party than on his upcoming departure. John had already secured longings for him; he would be rooming with one of Stickney's law clerks, Alva Peck.[29]

The great morning finally arrived. It had snowed all weekend but had stopped the night before, so that when he woke the room was full of the eerie glowing light of daybreak reflected from new-fallen snow. The snow meant that it would be a cold ride into Ludlow, but a quick and easy one. He put on his newly-bought best clothes. There was time for a quick breakfast, and then he told Abbie goodbye. Perhaps he kissed her, although New England culture frowned on displays of emotion. He and John climbed into the sleigh, with his bags and a calf his father was taking to market. It was bitter cold, but Calvin was so excited by the new direction his life was taking that he barely noticed it. What was for John just another trip to Ludlow was for his son a journey of cosmic significance. The sun had just risen as they passed the Brown farm and turned the horse's head toward the Union. "As we rounded the brow of the hill the first rays of the morning sun streamed over our backs and lighted up the glistening snow ahead," Coolidge remembered years later. "I was perfectly certain that I was traveling out of the darkness into the light."[30]

6

A Railroad Town

The layout of Ludlow differed from that of most Vermont railroad towns. Ordinarily a Vermont town adjoined the river that furnished power for its mills; the railroad tracks, following the smoothest gradient, paralleled the riverbank, so that the railroad depot was beside the river, at or near the center of town. But at Ludlow the Central Vermont main line was already well up the grade that was to carry it over the summit of the Green Mountains, only three or four miles away. The depot, consequently, with its ramshackle wooden buildings, was high on a hillside, overlooking the red-brick mill and the big frame stores and houses that made up the village, huddled into the crooked valley of the swift, shallow Black River.[1]

In the brilliant, cold sunlight father and son drove down the snowy main street in their sleigh. John had at least two destinations in mind: Calvin was to be dropped off at Miss Eliza Boynton's, where he was to room; the calf was to be taken to the depot, to be shipped to Boston. In fact, John's parting words to Calvin alluded to both, in a characteristically dry comment on his son's ambitions: "Well, Cal, here you are in school in Ludlow.... Study hard and maybe you'll get to Boston some day, but remember that the calf will go there first." And he went on to the depot.[2]

Calvin's room was on what was called lower Main Street. Just east of the business district, Main Street crossed the river on an iron bridge and opened into a narrow, triangular green, shaded in summer by elms, fronted by the Baptist church. Behind the church, High Street, where the academy was located, went steeply uphill, so steeply that on icy days in winter B.R.A. students who were coming from Main Street had difficulty negotiating it. At least once a neighbor had to come out and toss a rope to some academy girls who found the slippery climb impossible. Today, however, with fresh snow underfoot, the hill was no problem. Calvin left his belongings at Miss Boynton's and went on through the icy chill of early morning to register, wearing shoes with rubbers instead of the countrified boots he normally wore in Plymouth.[3]

The vaguely Georgian two-story brick building toward which he was heading, with its squat white tower in the center, looked like an old church. In fact, it had begun existence as a church, but for over forty years it had sheltered B.R.A. The town owned it, and used the hall on the second floor

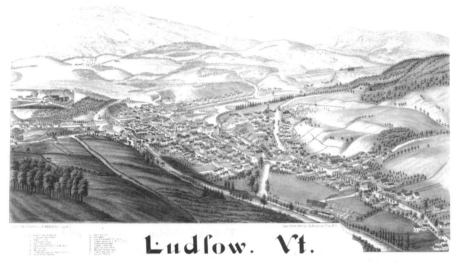

Lud1ow. Vt.

This 1885 lithograph of Ludlow, too small to convey much detail, does show the principal features of the village—the railroad curving from upper right to left center, and
then back to lower right; the Black River following a similar course through the center of the picture; and the main street of the village squeezed between them. Black
River Academy was located just above the iron bridge in the center of the picture.
(Courtesy of Special Collections, University of Vermont Library)

for town meetings and other public business. The academy occupied only
three rooms on the first floor. Small as it was, however, it was the pinnacle
of the Ludlow school system: in practice, it was Ludlow High School. About
half the students who attended it were from Ludlow; the rest were mostly
from the surrounding country towns. In an arrangement fairly common in
Vermont, the town school district paid tuition fees for local students; those
from outside the district had to pay their own fees.[4]

There were a few outstanding academies in Vermont (Vermont Academy
in Saxtons River, for instance, or St. Johnsbury) from which most of the students went on to one of the New England colleges. They belonged to a
rather small group of academies that were beginning to be called "feeder
schools," or "preparatory schools." B.R.A. was not among them. The overwhelming majority of its students, around eighty percent in most years, were
enrolled in the same English course young Coolidge was taking, designed
for "those who may not have time or means for the more extended
courses, but who desire a solid English, business education." The subjects
they studied were the same ones that in the twentieth century would form
the core of the American high school curriculum: English and American
literature; grammar; arithmetic, algebra, and geometry; Vermont, American, and "general" (i.e., world) history; "civil government"; and a few prac-

tical courses like bookkeeping. A small contingent of students pursued a Classical course organized along the traditional academic pattern: less American history and literature, heavy emphasis on Latin, Greek, and the classical authors. This was the course for those who were going on to college. There was also a middle course, the Latin Scientific, for students whose parents wanted some classical learning for their children, but wanted to avoid overdoing it.[5]

Similar in many respects to a modern regional high school its multiple-track curriculum, its coeducation, the fact that it served both Ludlow and the surrounding townships—B.R.A. was radically different in one respect. Attendance was wholly voluntary. In any of the three terms, fall, winter, or spring, students were there because they were not needed on the farm or had chosen not to look for employment in town. Thus, in many cases a student's stay at B.R.A. was brief: illness, financial need, a desirable job, or any of a number of factors could cause him or her not to enroll for the next term. Particularly for young people from the outlying towns, attendance was apt to follow a choppy pattern, one term one year, another term the next, perhaps two terms a year later. In 1888–89, for instance, less than half of the 123 students attended all three terms at B.R.A., and two-thirds of those who did were from Ludlow.[6]

With regard to attendance, then, B.R.A. was less like a twentieth-century high school than a twentieth-century community college, at which many students take courses sporadically and for "enrichment." Students and their parents evidently believed that there was absolute value to be derived from a course in geology, English literature, or ancient history, whether or not such courses added up to a coherent program. At B.R.A. as at other high schools and academies, the administration periodically urged upon parents "the great advantages of finishing the course and graduating from the School." Indeed, in 1873, like many similar schools, B.R.A. had begun holding commencement ceremonies with all the trappings of higher education: class speakers, class colors, class mottoes, the awarding of diplomas, and the like. The intent, evidently, was to promote the notion that an academy education was, in its way, as coherent and complete as a college course. But just as evidently, the families who patronized B.R.A. had not yet accepted this novel idea. Less than two-fifths of the students who enrolled graduated; the others either went on to other academies, or, more likely, dropped out after a brief taste of academic learning and began their careers.[7]

Calvin slipped into the main entrance hall, hung up his coat and hat (if he could find room for them among the mass of outerwear hanging from pegs on both sides), and went on into the crowded assembly room, where the wood stove was going full blast. This was not a day of classes; students showed up on the first day merely to register and sign up for the classes they wanted to take, leaving the faculty to devise a class schedule and have it printed up for distribution at next day's morning assembly. Some students he already knew. Henry Brown was there, with his niece Florence Blanchard; she was two years older than Calvin and a good friend and neighbor. One of them, doubtless, helped him through the process and pointed out the faculty, all five of them, busy enrolling students. Actually, there were only three full-time faculty; two women taught only a few specialized subjects, like music. As was customary in New England schools, the principal was a man—Henry Kendall, a Ludlow boy just graduated from Harvard who had returned to take over the academy. He was all of twenty-four years old. As the only college graduate on the staff, he would be handling all the classical courses, Latin and Greek. His two assistants, Rowena ("Miss Rena") Pollard and Clara Prior, both more experienced, would take care of the heavy teaching in English, mathematics, and history.[8]

Slender, red-haired, and anemic, Calvin looked even younger than his real age. Nonetheless, the faculty agreed to enroll him in some fairly advanced courses: algebra, grammar, and civil government, the first in the morning with Miss Prior, the others later in the day with Miss Pollard. The two ladies, both of them thoroughgoing teachers in the style of the 1880s, prim, earnest, and authoritarian, occupied the two recitation rooms at the rear of the assembly room. (Kendall taught his classes in the assembly room itself.) Calvin had until the next day to purchase his books and prepare for the first lesson.[9]

The easiest way to summarize young Coolidge's progress in this first term is to say that it was a shock. He made some of the lowest marks he had ever made in school or was to make again: his overall average for the term was 83.8 percent. Individual subject grades were not given on that year's report card, but it seems evident that Miss Prior's algebra class was his Waterloo. Civil government he liked, though he may not have done too well in it; the class was taking up the study of the Constitution, which he found new and mildly interesting. Grammar was not a hard subject for him. But algebra was a different matter.[10]

Calvin was to study algebra, off and on, for the next eight years, and it is fair to say that he loathed almost every step of the way. He was good enough with figures, but he saw neither use nor enjoyment in algebraic formulas. Eventually he arrived at a point where, with plenty of hard study, he could make respectable grades in algebra, but this first encounter must have been an ordeal. To begin with, he was somewhat afraid of Miss Prior, with her sharp-featured face and her hair pinned up in a bun. "Don't know what Miss Prior will say and don't care either," he wrote bravely in his diary one Monday morning when he got into Ludlow a little late from a weekend at home, and decided to skip algebra class. But the following day he was careful to record, "Miss Prior did not say anything about my being tardy or absent and I was very glad she did not."[11]

Absences and tardies like this, plus a few days out with a bad cold later in the term, gradually added up. As the term went on, the "good lessons" he had bragged about in the first couple of weeks vanished, and he found himself behind. At least once, probably more than once, he sought help from other students, notably Henry Brown. Henry was rooming with his sister Nellie and Florence Blanchard, the three cooking their own board in an arrangement not uncommon with children of economy-minded rural families. Cal came down to their tenement, algebra book in hand, and deadpanned in front of the landlord, "I thought I would come down, Henry, and help you on your algebra." (This sort of solemn kidding was not just Calvin's brand of humor; it was rural Plymouth style, as shown by a letter to Calvin in March from his friend Thomas Moore. Commenting on an excursion of Calvin's, he wrote, "You must not eat so many fish that will make you sick." Then he added, "I wish I was there to help you eat them.") One way and another, Cal managed to get by; but it was not, all in all, a good term for him. When the academy honor roll came out in April, Henry was on it; Calvin was not.[12]

The obvious explanation for Calvin's performance was that he was getting used to the ways of an academy; this was his own explanation, in retrospect. There were certainly differences that took some getting used to. Learning in his classes was generally by rote, as it was in district school; but the recitations were longer and more concentrated, the homework correspondingly heavier. "The Arithmetic is about 4 times as hard and you have to get 7 or 8 pages of it besides," a Felchville boy wrote his father from Vermont Academy. The grades, reckoned on a basis of one hundred, were more stringent than in district school, and there was more emphasis on them. In addition, there was the bother of wearing formal clothing—coat and trousers, wing collar and tie—day in and day out, with the obligation it entailed of dignified, solemn behavior, plus the anxiety about looking one's best. "I have got to have a new suit of clothes for best," the same student wrote home, "... for these are getting thin on the elbows and knees and seat."[13]

Probably, too, the new environment distracted Calvin from his work. He was not too difficult to distract; he was a steady worker but not a particularly concentrated one. It was not an abundance of B.R.A. student activities that held his attention, however; the academy offered its students very little in that way. At one time there had been a student literary society, but it had lapsed. The beginnings of organized student athletics were about a decade in the future, and in any case they probably would not have appealed much to young Coolidge. Occasionally a student social would be held at some Ludlow student's home, but these affairs were not school-sponsored and were not for all students. The only time that the whole student body was together was at the morning assembly, where every morning at nine o'clock some student played the organ, Mr. Kendall offered a prayer, and Miss Pollard wrote some inspirational sentence on the blackboard in her neat copperplate (something like "In the bright lexicon of youth there is no such word as *fail*"), while the more mischievous boys and girls sat behind the big wood box with its open cover, where they could whisper and chew spruce gum unobserved. Even then, it was not really the entire student body that assembled. The old sanctuary was too small to hold them all, and those who had classes later in the day were encouraged to go home after roll call until time for their class. In these circumstances, there was really no such thing as school spirit.[14]

No, the real distraction for Calvin came from the mere fact of living in a town. For a shy, impressionable thirteen-year-old from the country, Ludlow offered a host of things to observe. The sounds were different: not only the academy bell, but the incessant hum of the woolen mill on Main Street and the shrill whistles that announced a change of shifts, the periodic wails and rattles of the Central Vermont trains up on the embankment, and, on Sundays, the bells of five different churches—Baptist, Methodist, Congregationalist, Unitarian, even Catholic.[15]

In some ways, Ludlow was not quite a full-fledged town. It had no gas light, only kerosene. It had no water or sewage system; residents used privies and cesspools as they did in the country. It had no concrete sidewalks, no curbs; there were only rudimentary boardwalks and, as the warmer weather of spring wore on, a horribly muddy main street filled with melting slush or what Rudyard Kipling, in writing about his years in Vermont, referred to as "horsepondine." But it did have many other appurtenances of a town—telephones, for instance. In April the local newspaper counted eleven. They were fairly primitive contraptions. Vermonters, at this stage, regarded them as high-powered speaking tubes, so that most were in stores and offices; few citizens wanted them in their homes, especially after a thunderstorm the preceding July in which lightning had hit the telephone line attached to Deacon John Hall's house. The deacon, according to the Ludlow *Tribune*, had been "standing beside an iron sink in his kitchen, to which the electric fluid was conducted by some unexplained means, giving the old gentleman a shock that threw him over backward, and heating a knife in his pocket so hot that it burned him."[16]

The boy from Plymouth probably had no occasion to use the Ludlow telephones in any event. They communicated only with each other; long distance was still some years in the future. But he recognized the wooden boxes with their jutting mouthpieces in the stores he visited. The stores themselves were perhaps the most visible index of the difference between town and country—they were so numerous and so varied. At the Notch, or the Union, or Five Corners, there was only the general store, which handled all the retail trade there was. Here in Ludlow, there were also general stores downtown, but there were specialty stores as well: like Charles Raymond's store at the corner of Main and Depot Streets, which sold only clothing, mainly "gents' furnishings"; or Bixby's jewelry store; or the bakery, with its tempting aroma of baked beans and warm brown bread on Sunday mornings; or that great American institution, the drugstore, which was just begin-

ning to assume its classic form in the 1880s and was bound to appeal to
Calvin, with his love for quiet, propriety, and sweets. There were two drugstores in Ludlow, one run by Daniel F. Cooledge, who was a doctor and a
distant relation of the Plymouth Coolidges, the other by Alvah F. Sherman.
The doctor carried schoolbooks as well as medicine; Sherman also sold
pianos, organs, sheet music, and the Boston and New York dailies, in a
two-story frame building across the muddy street from the mill. At least one
of them, probably both, had a soda fountain, a wondrous counter topped
by jars of colored syrups that could be mixed with soda water or poured
over shaved ice to create exotic drinks for consumption there in the store.[17]

Walking downtown through the slush to buy school supplies or to pass the
time of day with his roommate Peck at lawyer Stickney's office, Calvin saw
more signs of town culture: John Keating's billiard parlor; Hammond Hall,
the large frame building where traveling musical and dramatic groups occasionally performed and where young people roller skated during the winter;
the hitching posts in front of the stores where clerks liked to lounge and chat
idly with acquaintances when the weather was fine; the town lampposts,
newly painted red that spring; the Ludlow House, with its broad first- and
second-floor piazzas, where drummers (traveling salesmen) from Boston
and New York put up. (Calvin probably did not go into the Ludlow House
often; it was a slightly raffish place, perennially in trouble with the law for
selling alcoholic beverages, which were supposedly prohibited in Vermont.)
Horse-drawn vehicles one would not see in the country passed by down the
muddy streets: the cart of the fresh meat vendor; or a grocer's delivery wagon, square, trim, and conspicuously painted with the store's name. Finally,
there were the people's clothes, many of them much spiffier than anything in
Plymouth, with a distinct city cut. Most men wore coats, derbies or top hats,
stand-up collars, and neckties. Women dressed up with elaborate flowered
hats and few women, perhaps, displayed the latest and most absurd style of
city couture, the bustle, a skirt with heavy padding in the rear to show off
the drape of the material. All of them wore long skirts whose hems grazed
the filth and slush of the thoroughfare.[18]

The crowning token of Ludlow's status as a town, however, was the railroad that connected it with the greater wealth and sophistication of the bigger cities. It brought entertainment to Ludlow: next year, for example, Cal
would go up to the depot to see a boxcar filled with products of the Canadian Northwest ("saw a fir tree 24 ft in circumference it was a monster"). It
also brought excitement, in the form of weather-related delays and minor,
occasionally major, accidents.[19]

Young Coolidge used the railroad occasionally. On weekends, he often
climbed the stone steps from Pleasant Street to the depot and took the 5:15
train to Proctorsville, the next station, where his aunt Sarah Pollard lived. If
the weather was good and has wanted to save the sixteen-cent fare, he
would walk the four miles to Proctorsville on the railroad track; its gravel

bed made for more pleasant walking than the muddy road, and there was always the possibility of encountering a handcar—one of those three-wheeled, hand-powered, bright-colored affairs that railway workers used—and maybe getting a ride part of the way.[20]

Calvin went to Proctorsville about as often as he went home to Plymouth, perhaps more often; it was not always convenient for John to come down to Ludlow to bring him home. Proctorsville was fine with him, anyway; he enjoyed his aunt's family. She was his mother's oldest sister, and her kindness to him conjured up poignant memories. His uncle, Don C. Pollard, was a prosperous local businessman and storekeeper much like his father, who invariably greeted him, when he came in the door, with a loud "Hello, Mr. Calvin Frog City Coolidge," in reference to the Plymouth neighborhood. There were three boys in the family, two of them, Park and Dallas, near Calvin's age. Fred, the oldest, helped his father run the big general store in the center of Proctorsville, and often Calvin spent virtually his whole weekend with the Pollard boys in the store's back room, under his uncle's severe direction, shelving, inventorying, sometimes helping deliver groceries, inhaling the mingled smells, and dreaming of being a storekeeper himself someday. Occasionally he walked down to Cavendish Gorge, a spectacular waterfall on the Black River a couple of miles below Proctorsville. Aunt Sarah was sweet-tempered, fond of him, and almost indulgent; more than once she let him and Park have the use of the kitchen to make molasses candy, a favorite snack with Vermont country boys.[21]

There is no mention, on his visits, of going to church. Apparently the Pollards did not attend regularly, which suited Calvin, to whom Sunday morning churchgoing was not natural either. Even when he spent a weekend in Ludlow, more often than not he skipped church, though once in a while he attended Congregational services. It was not that he was irreligious; years of reading the Bible to his grandmother and listening to her homilies in Sunday school had convinced him of the essentials of Christianity. Worship service was simply unimportant to him, as it was to many Plymouth people.[22]

Aunt Sarah's household was probably the closest Calvin ever came to the model nineteenth-century Vermont household with a mother (not a grandmother or hired girl) constantly busy in the kitchen, washing, mending, and turning out meals for the family. His weekend visits put him in Proctorsville for Sunday dinner (doubtless the big meal of the week in the Pollard home, as it was almost universally in Vermont) and undoubtedly he made the most of the opportunity. Sunday dinner was, as a later Vermont writer put it, "halfway between a normal day and Thanksgiving when it came to eating." It lacked the incredible variety of dishes that characterized Thanksgiving and Christmas dinners: pork, roast beef, turkey, and chicken; baked beans and brown bread; plethoras of pies, mince, pumpkin, apple, custard, and berry; potatoes; vegetables of all kinds; six or seven flavors of cake; and every kind of relish known to humanity. It also lacked their almost avowed purpose of stuffing the members of the family until they could barely waddle away from the table. Sunday dinner was not that grand, but it was a big meal, with a first-class main dish like roast beef, turkey, chicken pie, or tongue. There were potatoes, as a matter of course, and several kinds of vegetables. As at all meals, the beverage was coffee. (One gets the impression from the sources that there were only two nonalcoholic beverages in rural Vermont of the 1880s: coffee and sweet cider. Tea was rarely mentioned. Milk was drunk occasionally as an evening or bedtime snack with crackers or johnnycake. Cider was for festive occasions and hot weather. Otherwise, people drank coffee.)[23]

Sunday dinner, in most homes, stood in sharp contrast to the meals eaten the rest of the week. Vermont cooking was based on thrift, so that meals tended to be simple preparations of whatever happened to be on hand, boiled or fried, without any trimmings. Often meals were meatless, or virtually meatless. Boiled turnips, for instance, might be the main dish at a winter meal (turnips kept well in the cellar during the winter), or it might be beans, or macaroni, or oatmeal. During the summer "boiled victuals" were a staple. This dish consisted, basically, of all the vegetables on hand—beet greens, dandelion greens, onions, squash, and beets, for instance—put together in a pot and boiled. Its wintertime version, based on the vegetables that kept well in cold weather (turnips, beets, carrots, potatoes, and cabbage) with the addition of some salt pork, was known as a "New England boiled dinner" and was a frequent main dish.[24]

When meat was served during the week, it was often codfish, which kept well. Many families kept a salt cod hanging in the cellar during cold weather and broke off pieces as required for meals, serving it creamed, fried, or hashed. Most families, too, had no objection to serving whatever the menfolk brought home from hunting or fishing—rabbit, squirrel stew, trout, or even woodchuck (young woodchuck, according to a Grafton boy of this era, was "truly excellent"). Chicken was popular year round, although it seems to have been reserved for special occasions to some extent. But the basic meat, day in, day out, was salt pork from the barrel in the cellar. With these meats generally there would be biscuits or potatoes or both.[25]

The consensus seems to be that Vermont cooking in this era was generally poor. To say this is not to condemn Aunt Sarah's cooking, which was well above the norm; Calvin, at any rate, loved her steamed brown bread. But as a rule, the boiled dishes were cooked too long, the fried foods tended to be greasy, the dough was on the heavy side, and foods were used long after their prime. Nevertheless, people who grew up in Vermont during these years often remembered certain dishes with fondness: the doughnuts served at breakfast, fresh from the frying pan, often with maple syrup; the Indian pudding (cornmeal, milk, cinnamon, and raisins boiled together); the dishes peculiar to a working farm, like buckwheat cakes or fried tripe; even the salt pork. Calvin was partial to pickles, and to the whole grain cereal and sugar frequently served at breakfast.[26]

This diet had been standard in New England for a couple of generations, but Vermonters who lived near a railroad had the opportunity to add some new items to what they ate, oysters, for instance. Like all New Englanders, Vermonters were partial to oysters and tended to serve them—fried, steamed, stewed or raw—on festive occasions. Obviously, they were easier to get when one had ready access to the coast. Then there were the tropical fruits made available by rapid ocean shipping: oranges and lemons, which had become an accepted part of Christmas and were carried at that time of year even by country stores like Moore's; and bananas, which had first appeared in Vermont in the 1870s and were still regarded more as curiosities than as fruits. (They impressed one Rutland boy as tasting "smooth and slippery, and rather horrid.") More or less in this category, too, were the flavored chicle-based chewing gums, sold mainly in drugstores, which would eventually supplant the sticky, tasteless natural spruce gums enjoyed by Calvin and his contemporaries.[27]

No matter what Aunt Sarah's cooking was like, chances are that it was better than what Calvin got in Plymouth; John economized on food as he did on everything else. In rural Vermont there were continual tales, often brought back by schoolteachers who boarded around the community, of stingy farmers who fed their families little or nothing. John was probably not in that league, and his home had such standard farm fare as home-baked bread and a big barrel of apples (sometimes mushy or questionable in winter) in the cellar, but meals at his house were certainly not feasts. Whether Calvin's meals at the Pollards' were better than what he had to eat in Ludlow is more problematical. There were a lot of boardinghouses in nineteenth-century America, and boardinghouse food was the subject of many jokes ("What American production outranks all others?" ran a riddle a Newbury farmer copied into his diary. The answer was "Boarding house butter"), but some boardinghouse fare equaled home cooking. Elmer Twombly, boarding at Saxtons River, enjoyed meat, bread, tomatoes, and pie for supper at one meal in early fall. Calvin, a few years later, felt that the board he had gotten in Ludlow had been rather good, on the average. Little specific information survives about what he liked to eat. At a later boarding house, he ate only oatmeal for breakfast. He enjoyed oysters on occasion. On a visit to Proctorsville, the one he wrote Thomas Moore about, he ate a lot of fish. When he went to a local entertainment, he was apt to buy a ten-cent bag of peanuts.[28]

Much of young Coolidge's experience at Miss Boynton's was typical of boardinghouse life in Vermont, and not much different from that of other B.R.A. students. He and his roommate, for instance, had to supply their own wood for the stoves that heated their rooms, kindling, logs, and wood in big thick pieces called "chunks," which burned slowly and kept putting out heat all night. Calvin had his sent down from Plymouth. He also had to deal with his dirty clothes. Many landladies were willing to wash their boarders' clothes for an extra charge, but Calvin or John preferred to send his home.[29]

In other ways, however, his experience was quite dissimilar. He was, very likely, one of the youngest boarding students at B.R.A. Moreover, where he boarded there were few or no B.R.A. students, and he was thrown almost entirely into the company of the young clerks and professionals who boarded there. Possibly one other boarder at Miss Boynton's was a student, Fred Colburn, and he was a most unusual student, dark-haired, rugged, and mature for his nineteen years, who had knocked around the West two or three years before returning to Vermont. Alva Peck, Calvin's roommate, was twenty-seven and, as Stickney's clerk, was evidently supposed to be a sort of mentor to him. "Do what you can to help Miss Boynton," John wrote his son the second week of school, "and keep things in your room to suit Peck."[30]

As it happened, Calvin and Peck got along famously. "I like Peck very, very well," wrote Calvin in his diary three weeks after his arrival in Ludlow. "I hope him well for life. He said he would help me anytime." Peck somehow got through Calvin's shyness and established a rapport with him very much like his relationship with Warren Spaulding, back in Plymouth. He bought oranges when Calvin was sick ("[He] said he would not take the pay, but he did," Calvin noted with amusement) and kept him posted on the town gossip, the doings of the storekeepers and lawyers. The two shared secrets: "Get round to everything with my *usual* regularity, especially nights," Peck wrote him cryptically in June after school was out.[31]

Perhaps through Peck, Calvin became acquainted with other young men in their twenties (rather than the students who were his contemporaries) like Win Bixby, the young jeweler just out of college, George Raymond, Raymond the haberdasher's twenty-year-old son, Frank Day, twenty, who clerked in a Main Street grocery, and Dick Lane, the son of a local doctor. To some degree, allowing for his age, they acquainted him with the faster, flashier life of a young man in town. In Ludlow, to be sure, there was not a great deal of organized immorality, beyond drinking on the sly. Vermont was a prohibition state, so that anything to do with alcohol was illegal, other than its use for "medicinal" purposes. Occasionally the authorities uncovered a whorehouse or dive, but circumstances suggest that these were lower-class establishments. Among Peck's associates there was a lot of smoking, ribaldry, and talk, usually about going out of town and doing something forbidden. For instance, in June Peck met Calvin's cousin Park Pollard on the Bellows Falls train. "He said he was going on a bust," Peck reported. "Didn't know just where himself—to the Falls, and probably to Saxton's River."[32]

Calvin seems not to have picked up any bad habits. He was still young and dependent on his father, whereas it was understood that smoking, drinking and so forth were appropriate marks of an independent young man. It seems likely that he did not drink until his college years. (John apparently did not drink regularly, nor did many other men in the Notch.) Calvin may have had his sexual curiosity stimulated; a scribbled address in the back of the diary he kept in the winter of 1887 was that of the Murray Hill Publishing Company, a New York City concern run by the birth-control advocate E. B. Foote and best known for its relatively frank publications on sex, which included "Sexual Physiology for the Young," "Illustrated Treatise on Gynaecology," "Spermatorrhea," and "Controlling Conception." As a farm-bred boy, Calvin surely had a good basic knowledge of reproduction, but he may have been curious about some more specialized subjects. If he did look at any Murray Hill books, however, it was only to satisfy curiosity. In this as in many other areas of his life, he absorbed information, kept his own counsel, and did nothing.[33]

As spring term stretched out into the mud and occasional warm sun of April, Calvin realized that, for the first time in his life, he was away from home at perhaps his favorite time of year—maple sugaring. Sugar making was big business in Vermont. Tin pails of the delectable stuff sold by the thousands every year, all over the country; almost every farmer, large or small, had a sugar grove of some size where he headed every year as the days got warm and dark moist patches of earth appeared in the woods and the sap began to rise. Maple sugar season began at different times in different places, according to the weather and lie of the land. In Plymouth, at least on the Coolidges' land, it might start at the end of March and run as late as the end of April. Calvin loved the season and everything connected with it: tapping the trees with spouts ("spiles," they were called), hanging the sap buckets ("a cow being milked into a thimble gives some idea of the disproportion," wrote a visiting Englishman), collecting the watery sap from the full pails and conveying it to the sugar house in pails hung from a wooden yoke over a boy's shoulders—he and Thomas Moore had made a sap yoke of their own, which Thomas now had. Then there were the red firelight and flying sparks of the fire that burned day and night in the sugar house, the "mild yet heavy sweetness" of the place, the warm sugar that candied on the sides of the big pans, and (later) packing the light brown sugar into ten- or twenty-pound tin pails for export. He loved the process, and he was also very good at it; even John, who was not given to idle praise, admitted that Calvin could get every last drop of sap from a tree. He was a real epicure when it came to taste. On warm April days at the academy he sat and dreamed of the sap rising and calculated how much syrup could be made. He could not know, luckily, that his apprenticeship had ended when he began his academy education; from now on he would be only briefly in the Plymouth woods during maple sugar season.[34]

The academy's term ended the first week in May, in time for its students to go out into the rural districts and teach the summer term of district school. Final examinations, both written and oral, were 4 May through 6 May. Once he had finished these—including the hated algebra, which came last—Calvin gathered his few belongings, waited for John's arrival, and was off to Plymouth like a shot, surprising even Peck with his sudden departure. Not that he had a teaching job in front of him; on the contrary, he had only months of rural idleness, as much idleness as John would let him achieve, doing chores in the field and around the house. It was a beautiful time of year, when the signs of full spring, bobolinks and bumblebees, first appeared in the fields, when the grass was tall enough to wave, and maples leafed out, and hillsides were covered with white violets or forget-me-not, when the mountains were "soft and cloudy in spring foliage, and open places, pastures, and meadow of a bright emerald green." It was the time when the stock, let out after a winter in the barn, romped around with a joy described by one recorder of rural Yankee life: "the cows wanted to career all through the neighborhood, and they kicked and capered and galloped and hoisted their tails in the air." There would be milking and fence mending, but there would also be time for reading over at Almeda's and for fishing with Thomas, subtly proud of having been off at school. ("Rich feels as big as pusley now that he has been to Barre to school," wrote a boy in Calais in 1891.) For a summer, Cal—well aware that most of the time for the next few years he was slated to be an academy pupil—could go back to being a Plymouth farm boy.[35]

7

The Academy Dude

Young Coolidge spent most of the next four years of his life at B.R.A., and established a distinct image for himself, quite different from the one he had had in Plymouth. Serious, bespectacled Clara Pollard, one of many B.R.A. students who helped Cal with his algebra assignments at one time or another, remembered him clearly: "He was known as the 'dude' of the Black River Academy, because he always carried a cane, wore a derby hat and a carefully starched dickey [shirt front]." Roy Bryant, a Ludlow doctor's son who was several classes behind him, had much the same impression. Coolidge, he recalled, would play ball with the other boys occasionally, always with his derby hat on. Other students' memories touched on other characteristics—his quiet aloofness, his violently red hair ("You are a red woodpecker," one fellow student wrote in his autograph book), his extreme slenderness—but the most surprising and vivid trait about Coolidge at B.R.A. was the way he dressed. In a school where boys were required to wear coat, tie, and stiff collar, he overdid it. In a remarkably short time, the nondescript country lad in overalls and copper-tipped boots turned into a sort of slick town dude.[1]

This transformation, so improbable at first sight, is supported by other kinds of evidence from the boy's own diaries. In 1887 as in 1886, Cal began keeping a diary on New Year's Day, during the winter term at Ludlow. (As in 1886, he kept it only a few months; this year, until mid-April.) He referred to his father in it with fair frequency, almost always using the sophisticated, slightly urban term "Papa"; in 1886 he had used the plain Plymouth "John." Clearly, somewhere in the intervening year he had picked up a signal: the proper term to use was the one favored in his middle-class Ludlow environment, not in his family. Similarly, in the 1886 diary he had sometimes used mild profanity of a rural sort—"Warren is mad as hell," "The boys broke the desk all to the devil." In the 1887 diary, and indeed for most of the rest of his life, that sort of profanity was notably absent; less, one suspects, because it was profane than because it was coarse, the mark of a hayseed. By 1887 he had become conscious not only of clothes but of accessories; he had an active business selling his schoolmates mail-order jewelry of a small sort, cufflinks, pins, and the like, and he wrote home to have his ring sent down to school.[2]

Usually a change in behavior of this sort signals a change in audience; that is, one changes his style to meet the expectations of his elders, or the opposite sex, or a new group of peers, or God, or some other individual or group that has suddenly become relevant. But in Coolidge's case the audience is hard to identify. It was not girls. "[H]e wasn't a great hand with the girls," a classmate recalled. According to his cousin Dallas Pollard, he "wasn't interested in girls at all" at this age. In the four years he spent at B.R.A., he seems to have gone to only one dance, and that was a leap year dance in 1888 to which he was invited by witty, fun-loving Ada Barney, a Ludlow girl who was secretary of the class above his and had almost as much trouble with algebra as he did. (He didn't dance, of course, having never learned how.) Not until the last half of his senior year, when he felt safely ensconced at B.R.A., did he begin showing serious interest in girls.[3]

But if he was not trying to impress the opposite sex, he seems not to have been trying to adapt to the ways of his male schoolmates either. Then as now, a lot of schoolboy socializing involved informal sports, especially baseball. Cal was not terribly interested. "I had some skill with a bat," he recalled vaguely in his autobiography, and others' recollections suggest that he played baseball once in a while. But as a rule, it seems that the memory of Albert Sargent, the president of Coolidge's class, was accurate: "He didn't play ball with the rest of the boys." Nor did he talk like the rest of the boys. The sort of mild profanity he was trying to excise from his vocabulary was, in a slightly different idiom, a way many town boys expressed rebellion against their parents' strict respectability. "Oh, hell" was a kind of universal expression of mild disgust or mock resignation, and probably one of the "shocking oaths" the editor of the *Vermont Tribune* claimed to have heard on the streets from Ludlow boys, "even children of God-fearing parents." In a scribbled note on a B.R.A. program, Arthur Spaulding, a Ludlow boy in the class behind Coolidge, asked a classmate "who in h____" had said something. On the same program, Spaulding and Albert Sargent had an exchange in another vocabulary of no interest to Coolidge, that of cards. "You'll pass," Spaulding assured Sargent. ("Pass" was a new and somewhat slangy term for making a satisfactory mark in school.) "I won't," Sargent responded. "I will order and play it as I sit." There was also the matter of clothes. Coolidge did not dress like his peers; he outdressed them, like an adult.[4]

Most likely, the audience that Calvin was trying to please was himself, or something inside himself. From boyhood he had been a little finicky about dress. Jennie Chamberlin recalled how annoyed he had been when his first pair of long pants developed holes; a classmate at Ludlow remembered that the only time he ever saw Calvin really angry was when he tore a hole in his pants climbing a fence. In brief, he had an image of propriety that he wanted to present, and he was fussy about getting it right. "I am a trifle hard to fit and suit," he would later write John from college when discussing clothes, and he seems to have begun to be that way in his academy days.[5]

The same quality carried over to other areas of personal care. Calvin really enjoyed the luxury of bathing; his baths were long and elaborate ("took a 2 horse bath today," he wrote in his 1887 diary). Apparently he felt real pleasure in being clean. Suggestively, one paragraph in his autobiography is a virtual hymn in praise of cleanliness. He must have been one of a very few boys in Plymouth or Ludlow who felt this way. He loved neatness; his clothes, even the ones he had had for some time, were always immaculately kept. His hair was another example. Once away from the Notch, he began letting it grow, and by the time he was ready for graduation it was long, silky, and striking. On the farm he had had few opportunities to satisfy these tastes; in Ludlow, perhaps, he made the most of the chance to dress up to his new role, be the sort of proper young man he had always wanted to be, and in a muted masculine way express the same sense of beauty his mother had had so strongly. Also, by wearing adult clothing every day, he was moving up to the kind of attire his father habitually wore.[6]

Calvin's room at E. C. Pinney's on Pleasant Street doubtless contained a mirror, and as he glanced at himself in the morning prior to leaving for school, he saw an image that was correct but did little for his sense of beauty. Men's formal wear in the 1880s made little pretense to either elegance or comfort. "At present we [men] have lost all nobility of dress," lamented a dandy of that era. A modern authority on clothes has described men's wear of the period as "practical, dull, and uniform." The basics were a morning coat, about the same length as a modern suit coat, trousers, and a waistcoat or vest, all of heavy, scratchy woolen cloth in dark, drab colors, occasionally checked or striped. The modern idea of a suit, of having all three articles made from the same material, was beginning to take hold, but as often as not men wore a vest and coat of one pattern and trousers of another, or vest and trousers of one pattern and coat of another. Under the vest were a shirt, invariably white, with a high starched collar (another source of discomfort), and a narrow necktie, barely visible behind the high cut of the waistcoat. All the garments, shirt, trousers, vest, and coat, were tightly buttoned, so much so that they often looked too small. Long, narrow, pointed black shoes (instead of the copper-tipped boots of the country) and a derby hat finished off the outfit. Under everything was a two-piece set of long underwear, worn year round—flannel from fall to spring, cotton in summer. So heavy was the ensemble that it must have felt a little like armor. Indeed, in Calvin's case, the too-formal clothing may have been a psychological shield as well.[7]

In his letters home, he found frequent occasion to mention clothes, whether it was to ask for his clothes brush and shoe brush or to ask for new purchases, which he always did carefully and delicately. Suits were the most expensive item. He seems to have asked for and gotten at least one a year, although he always got full value out of them, wearing the same suit day in and day out until it became worn or faded.[8]

Calvin was not quite as remote from his fellow students as this formal attire might suggest. When he returned to Ludlow in the fall of 1886, he began rooming with fellow students his own age, rather than with Peck, and continued doing so until he graduated in 1890. He had no close, inseparable friend in these years; on the contrary, he seems to have roomed with almost every other boy in his class at one time or another. A partial list of his roommates (who usually shared rooms in fours, two beds to a room and two boys to a bed) would include S. R. Kendall of Pittsford, Henry Lawton of North Springfield, Fred Colburn of Ludlow, Newton Turgeon of Mechanicsville, Loren Pinney of Rutland, George Harris, Henry Hicks of Perkinsville, and probably Albert Sargent of Ludlow. In the fall of 1888 he roomed with fellow Plymouthite Herbert Moore at Mrs. Parker's on Main Street. He seems always to have gotten on well with his roommates, in a casual, kidding way. They argued over swapping possessions and over who was hogging the bedclothes. Like any schoolboys, they were forever playing tricks on each other: switching George Harris's bay rum for a similar bottle full of water; yanking Loren Pinney, who rarely bathed, out of bed and dousing him with cold water; inserting bogus sentences into a letter to Abbie that Calvin had left on his desk ("I have the dearest little darling for a best girl that you ever saw").[9]

Probably the most vivid surviving example of schoolboy high spirits comes from the fall of 1886, when Calvin was rooming with Kendall and Lawton at Pinney's. He and John and Abbie had attended John B. Doris's circus ("New England's Favorite") when it was in Rutland in August with its bareback riders, strong men, contortionists, and a young woman on the flying trapeze. Calvin, fourteen, was demonstrating the trapeze act for his roommates in their room when something slipped. He fell to the floor and broke his arm. It was a serious break; Dr. Lane set it for him, and fortunately, since it was a Friday, he managed to find transportation home. But on Monday, though the arm was still hurting and he could easily have stayed home, he insisted on John's taking him back to Ludlow so that he would not miss classes. The broken bones healed in the course of the term.[10]

Against these instances of horseplay and friendship, however, one must set the times when Calvin avoided social events, when he was alone and acutely conscious of his solitude. To judge by the number of entries on the subject in his brief 1887 diary, there were many such times. 2 February: "There was a play here tonight but I did not go." 3 February: "Did not go to church tonight. Most all the other boys went though. I had to stay at home and study." 2 March: "Colburn and Turgeon are out to a sociable at the Baptist C. I did not go but staid at home and studied." 13 March: "It is a beautiful day and all the boys are out but me." 30 March: "There was a nice crust and every body was out sliding but me." Very often, one notes, he used study as a pretext for not associating with others. It was more than just a pretext, no doubt; he was genuinely worried about not doing well in his studies. But as he himself admitted, a good deal of the time he was at his desk he was daydreaming not studying. As at home, his devotion to duty helped him to limit contact with other people.[11]

In many ways, then, he functioned at B.R.A. as a near-adult—formally dressed, diligent at his studies, holding a little aloof from schoolboy sports and making no close friendships. He kept up his acquaintance with Alva Peck, and spent odd hours hanging around Stickney's law office, enjoying the casual, dry companionship of the clerks. Perhaps he frequented other law offices too; by the time he left Ludlow, he claimed, he was well acquainted with all the lawyers in town.[12]

For a brief time he even had a job. Out at the east end of town, on the Black River, there was a factory, usually called the "cab shop," complete with a mill wheel and pond where local men and boys were in the habit of swimming on Sundays. Its name, actually, was the Ludlow Toy Manufacturing Company. It was owned by substantial local men and in good times employed about thirty hands, making products like doll perambulators, with frames of bent or jigsawed wood covered with enameled cloth in "bright, tasty colors" and running on "neatly striped" or "bright vermilion" wheels, or boys' "real Toy Express wagons," complete with seat and springs. It was one of several similar enterprises in Vermont; its compact scale and the simple operations involved—working a forge and a bench saw, gluing upholstery on and painting neat stripes on the wheels—just suited a small town on the railroad with a good local supply of wood.[13]

John got his son a Saturday job here, probably in the fall of 1886, when the factory had a big backlog of orders and was running evenings. It was not that the Coolidges needed the money, of course; the idea was an object lesson in thrift, with Calvin depositing his small wages (he was paid by the piece) in the Ludlow Savings Bank at a decent interest. So for most of the fall, until he broke his arm, Calvin probably did not go home weekends, but worked at the cab shop. The typical work day was ten hours, from seven o'clock to five or six, with a break at one for a smoke and "baiting" (i.e., lunch). His fellow workers were rural Yankees like his Plymouth neighbors. Dressed in work clothes from the farm, he did his work conscientiously, but apparently made no friends. He did come to know, as he said, "how toys and baby wagons were made." His broken arm ended the job temporarily, or perhaps permanently. He did not work there in the spring 1887 term, and in fall 1887 the place was sold.[14]

One reason why the experiment with an outside job was not repeated was that young Coolidge's studies were becoming more and more demanding, by his own choice. He had entered B.R.A. as a student in the English course in the spring of 1886. By fall, having gotten his feet wet, he decided to move up to the Latin Scientific curriculum, which meant that he would be taking Latin from the principal, Mr. Kendall, as well as a good deal more science. Latin, he found, was easy for him. ("We went only 50 pages," he commented on his work in the winter term. "I think it is a shame we did not go more than that.") Botany was not; it was harder than he had expected. And algebra ("this thing," he called it) continued to cause him endless frustration. He gave vent to his feelings in his diary: "I have 30 ex. to do and cannot do one," or "do not understand my algebra," or "algebra is so hard that I do not half get my lessons I did not do a single example today." To Abbie he wrote in February: "I do not expect to pass in Algebra but still have a faint hope that I may squeak through with about 71%." Somehow, amazingly, he did, thanks perhaps to Clara Pollard's last-minute help. In fact, he was under the impression he had made a grade of ninety-five on the written exam, a feat that seems incredible. But, for whatever reason, his grades were good that term, and he decided to take the next step, enrolling the next year in the Classical course.[15]

It seems a momentous decision, since it put him definitely in the tiny group of B.R.A. students who were committed to preparing for college, but almost no clues survive as to how or why it was made. It does seem clear from the recollections of both Coolidge and his father that the decision was mainly Calvin's. This fact, however, confuses more than it clarifies, for there is no evidence to suggest that Calvin was enthusiastic, then or later, about the idea of going to college. He liked Latin, liked town life, found study more and more congenial; perhaps those were reasons enough. Calvin's future horizon was short, to all appearances. He made few long range plans, perhaps because he did not expect to live long. "I don't think he had any burning ambition," a cousin observed. As his father said of him, reminiscing years later, "He wanted to conclude his education. If he did have plans for the future, he never made them known to me." More than likely, he signed up for the Classical course because it interested him, without any clear idea of attending college; he was content to let the future take care of itself.[16]

The next school year, 1887–88, turned out to be full of dramatic changes at B.R.A. The most dramatic had been several years in the making. There had been general agreement in Ludlow for some time that the old B.R.A. building was too small and too antiquated. At an 1885 town meeting the voters had agreed to turn title to the property over to B.R.A. if it could raise money to put up a new building, and in 1887, after several alumni reunions, the trustees managed to do so. On Friday, 7 October, a local Baptist minister delivered a farewell prayer in the main hall before classes began ("probably the last one that will be made in the old building," Calvin wrote his father cautiously). That evening there was a "farewell sociable" in the building, which Calvin did not attend, although he was in town. The following week workers began demolishing the old academy. Construction of a new one, with all modern conveniences, would get underway as soon as possible.[17]

In the interim, the hundred-odd students of the academy had to attend classes in what was called Whitcomb and Atherton's Hall, the second story of a commercial building on upper Main Street, at the opposite end of the village. In terms of classroom size, it was not much more cramped than the old building; the boys and girls in their wraps filed up the wooden outside staircase into an assembly room with a platform and a stove, about the same size as the old one. The difference was that there was nowhere to put their coats, and many of the students kept them on through the class. During recitations, luscious odors would come wafting up to the rooms from the first-floor bakery—fresh bread, or crackers straight from the oven, cooling before being put into barrels—making it harder than normal to concentrate on algebraic formulas or the French Revolution. In addition, there were all the shouts and noises of teams and wagons usual for a business area. So for the spring term, the academy classes were moved out of "bakery hall" to the town grammar school on High Street adjacent to where the new academy was being built. One term there seems to have convinced the administrators that the noises of a grammar school next to a construction site were as hard to cope with as those of downtown. At any rate, when the next school year began in August, classes were back in "bakery hall" and stayed there until the new building was ready in December 1888.[18]

At the same time, there was almost a complete change in administration. Young Mr. Kendall, who had been ill a good deal of the 1886–87 school year, did not come back; his place was taken by George Sherman, a bewhiskered, serious man in his early thirties, a Massachusetts man and Amherst graduate who had recently been a principal in New Hampshire. Like Kendall, he handled the Latin. Calvin took to him at once; "I like the new Prof. very much & think he is a good teacher," he wrote John. At the same time, Miss Pollard and Miss Prior both left. The new teacher who moved up to replace Miss Pollard, Belle Chellis, a round-faced, cheerful young woman from New Hampshire who taught Greek, French, and history, had already been there a year, and her history class had made a profound impression on young Coolidge, whose romantic imagination loved to weave daydreams about exciting eras like the Middle Ages or the French Revolution.[19]

Sherman, it seems clear, came to B.R.A. with all sorts of ideas for upgrading the school. He had not been there a month before he had the boys wearing neat dark-blue military-style caps lettered "B.R.A." He got them to revive the defunct debating society. After the model of the schools he had attended, particularly Amherst, he strove to develop class identity among the students, setting up elaborate class day exercises. He planned to introduce a new department of music. But his main goal, not stated as such but clearly inferable from the evidence, was to make Black River Academy something more than a local institution, to make it mainly, as he was to

Coolidge was not in this photo of a class at B.R.A., taken probably in 1887. Mr. Sherman is third from the left in the back row, Miss Chellis is seated first from left in the second row. The costumes give some idea of what B.R.A. students ordinarily wore. The building is the old B.R.A. (Black River Academy Museum)

write in an 1889 advertisement, "a Fitting school for TEACHERS and College Students." He seems consistently to have encouraged students to transfer from the English into the Latin Scientific or Classical track.[20]

Calvin adapted well to the new regime. His grades stayed satisfactory, mostly in the eighties. (He was never an outstanding student; at no time during his stay at B.R.A. did he make the honor roll.) He enjoyed Miss Chellis's Greek classes and felt he learned a lot. Moreover, for the first time he seemed actually happy to be there. During the first two years he had often been miserably homesick, despite his denials to his grandmother. The longing to get back to Plymouth had come out strongly in his 1887 diary, in entries like "I wish I could go home but I cannot I suppose," or "I am in hopes to go home this week but am much afraid I shan't," or "I should like to go home tomorrow but I do not expect I can for I was home this week." Now he was not only reconciled to being in Ludlow but eager for Abbie to join him. The year before, in contrast, he had been lukewarm to the idea. Now he urged that she should enter in the spring term: "It takes one term ... to get used to the ways and know what you are about."[21]

Abbie did enter the academy in February of 1888, just in time for the famed blizzard of that year, which struck on 10 March and dumped two to three feet of snow on the Black River valley, covering Ludlow streets up to the fence tops. The storm paralyzed the entire Northeast, halted rail travel for four days, and made travel in the hills virtually impossible. Within Ludlow, however, it was no more than a major inconvenience. "Snow in any quantities," the editor of the *Tribune* observed, "has no terror for the Vermonter." Classes at the academy were interrupted for two or three days. Abbie and Calvin, at any rate, did not room together that term and led largely separate lives at B.R.A. She had her own circle of friends, her own interests, and her own goals. Her main goal that spring was to teach school in the summer, even though she was barely thirteen. "I hope you can get me a school," she wrote John, "and I think you can if you try I don't care where it is." (He did get her one, in North Shrewsbury, and she taught it successfully.) Calvin, however, was not the type who required a great deal of contact to enjoy another person's presence. He enjoyed merely knowing Abbie was there.[22]

Calvin was a bit more sociable as he became more comfortable at the academy. Smartly dressed, he went out that winter to a set of four magic-lantern lectures on the wonders of the world (his favorite type of entertainment, sitting and observing), also to a drama at Proctorsville, and also, more surprisingly, to a couple of social events at Perkinsville with his roommate Henry Hicks. When there was something to watch in town, he generally went to see it. Back in March, for instance, when the Kickapoo Indian Medicine Show came to Hammond Hall, heralded by vivid posters in the windows of the post office, he had gone and seen the comic Irishman and Ethiopian, plus Texas Fred the sharpshooter and an Indian contortionist. A crowd of farm families from the country were there to hear the barbs at conventional physicians and the plugs for Indian Sagwa, Indian Oil, Indian Worm Killer, Indian Salve, and Kickapoo Cough Cure. Calvin apparently bought none of these, but like most Vermonters he did believe in patent medicines. When he felt rundown, which was not uncommon, he took Hood's Sarsaparilla, a preparation of sarsaparilla and herbs made in Massachusetts and advertised as good for scrofula, salt rheum, boils, pimples, catarrh, dyspepsia, biliousness, headache, and "that extreme tired feeling."[23]

His favorite amusement, however, as in Plymouth, was still solitary: walking. He walked to the surrounding hills for a view of the town, or along the sinuous, willow-fringed banks of the Black River, which despite its industrial uses was an attractive stream, "darkly gleaming in the night-time, showered with sun-gold in the day," to quote a local poet. He enjoyed getting home for the weekend, too, though he did not manage to do it as often as he liked. But periodically throughout the year, neighbors on the stage road would peer through their lace curtains to check passing traffic and see John's buckboard, with Calvin sitting up grave and straight beside his father.[24]

The year 1888 held especially memorable spectacles, in Ludlow and all over Vermont. It was the year of a presidential election, that great civic festival of nineteenth-century America, with its banners and torchlight parades, buttons, puns, bets on candidates, and mass meetings. There was no doubt that Vermont would vote Republican—it always had—but the national elections for over a decade had been exceedingly close, and Vermonters both Republican and Democratic followed them with passionate interest, cheering on their respective sides in a contest whose outcome they could not influence. From the moment in June when the Republican convention named Benjamin Harrison of Indiana to oppose incumbent president Grover Cleveland, the main street of Ludlow blossomed forth in bunting and party banners. "The republicans have two campaign flags fluttering in the breeze, and the democrats one, and all within the space of ten rods," a local observer reported in August. More were added during the fall. The B.R.A. students, most of whom were soundly Republican (seventy for Harrison to nineteen for Cleveland, according to a straw poll), were still attending classes in bakery hall that fall, and were outraged when the new barber from Rutland who occupied the first-floor storefront hung out a large Cleveland–Thurman flag. Some of them made a conspicuous detour into the street to avoid the shame of walking under it. One student, Jane Spafford, recalled that on election day the barber moved the flag to hang over the walk they had to traverse to get to the second-floor stairs, saying, she was told, "Now that God damn Spafford girl will have to walk under my flag." But the Republican boys managed to hoist her and the other Republican girls up the steps without using the walk.[25]

The election was uncommonly close. On election night several leading citizens stayed up till twelve o'clock with a special telephone hookup to Bellows Falls, but could learn nothing conclusive. Not until Wednesday night were there enough returns, by telegraph and from the Boston and New York newspapers, to claim a Republican victory. That night "the boys of Republican proclivities" built a large bonfire in front of the mill and paraded around town with bass drum, dinner bells, tin pans, and fish horns from nine until midnight. Some leading Democrats still refused to concede. Not until the following Monday was it certain: Harrison had won. The academy bell pealed; the windows of the woolen mill and all Republican homes were illuminated. Just as on the Fourth of July, the other great secular feast in the democratic calendar, the "calathumpian orchestra came out again in force ... and went the round of the principal streets; while the cannon at intervals woke the mountain echoes."[26]

Young Coolidge was certainly an avid spectator of all this, and probably a participant in the victory bonfire and parade. Politics remained a consuming interest to him, and he followed the national campaign closely and in detail. On 28 October, nine days before the election, he awoke from a vivid dream that he recorded, just in case it turned out to be a valid, perhaps supernatural, prophecy: "dreamed C carried Ind by some over 4000 and N.Y. by 30." His numbers were wrong, as it turned out; Harrison carried both states.

The new B.R.A. building, completed in 1888. (Black River Academy Museum)

But the dream was the dream of a political adept, complete with numbers in crucial borderline states, remarkable for a sixteen-year-old; consciously or unconsciously he had learned a lot from John.[27]

That fall, the second most absorbing pastime in Ludlow, after the presidential campaign, was watching the new academy building rise on the site of the old one and speculating when it would be done. The deep snows of the preceding winter had slowed construction, but by September it was approaching completion and it was becoming apparent that, according to one correspondent, "it [was] to be the ornament of the village." It was taller than the old building, with a square, pointed, assertive brick tower, generous arched windows on the upper stories (there were three stories in all), and a monumental Romanesque entrance whose imposing brick arch, supported on squat slate columns, sat atop a flight of eight granite steps. Stained glass squares in all the stock Victorian colors—amber, green, deep blue, wine, and turkey red—surrounded the big green wooden doors with their horizontal panes. The floor of the porch was checkerboard marble and slate; the windowsills were slate, and an ornamental slate band ran around the first story.[28]

It was finally ready just in time for winter; it was the second week of December, in fact, when the new seats arrived and were installed. When students and townspeople were able to go inside, it was apparent that the new building was a vast improvement on the old in practical terms as well. The stairs, the corridors, the classrooms, all wainscoted in black ash, were wide, roomy, and well-lit. Gone were the old wood stoves; now there was central heating from a coal furnace in the basement. Boys and girls had separate cloakrooms and even separate entrances. A broad double stairway led to a large assembly room on the second floor, where the principal's office was. There were separate rest rooms in the basement, as modern as they could be for a town that had no water or sewer system. (One wonders just how modern that was.)[29]

It was in this new building that Coolidge had the supreme experience that sooner or later comes to most adolescents, that of finding an area of subject matter that had strong, compelling personal meaning to him, quite apart from grades. In his case, the subject was Cicero's orations, for generations the staple of third-year Latin students. His teacher was Professor Sherman, in Room 1, the second-floor assembly room. The class, which met just after the noon break, must have been small; only six juniors and three seniors were enrolled in the Classical or Latin Scientific Courses. ("Junior" and "senior" were the current words, then as now, for the two upper classes; "sophomore" and "freshman," however, were not used. The class behind the juniors was the Third Class.) As in most classics courses, a class session consisted basically of students taking turns in translating the text, the four orations against Catiline plus a few others. Calvin had a basic competence in Latin by now, but the supercharged, highly rhetorical Ciceronian style presented new problems.[30]

Later in life, Coolidge more than once mentioned these orations and the way they held his attention, particularly the speech on behalf of the poet Archias with its ringing affirmation of the value of literature ("alunt adolescentiam, oblectant senectutem, ornant secundas res, adversis praebent perfugium et solatium, delectant domi, non impediunt foris": it fosters youth, it delights old age; it adorns prosperity and offers refuge and comfort in adversity; it delights us at home and does not hinder us abroad). At the end of the year he went home and systematically began trying to read all the great oratory he could find in his grandfather's library. But even during the year their influence was apparent. Encouraged no doubt by Mr. Sherman, who was also in charge of the "rhetoricals" (preparing student speeches and vetting the texts before delivery), he began composing and delivering orations of his own. By the time of Sherman's Class Day exercises in May, he gave a graceful speech of farewell to the seniors as secretary of the junior class.[31]

Although Coolidge never explained in so many words what it was that attracted him to Cicero, the conclusion is evident: Cicero opened his eyes to the possibility of using oratory in his own life, of becoming an orator himself. That a teenager so withdrawn and hesitant with others should be attracted to public speaking is only superficially surprising. Public speaking actually offered him another way, and a powerful one, of communicating with others without too much investment of self-esteem. In the past, to be sure, he had felt fear before speaking. An 1887 diary entry is a good example of his mixed feelings: "I rehearsed my piece again. I have it learned well.

I do not dread it much if any. I would not any if I knew I would not fail."
But from Cicero he learned that a skilled orator could string words together
to produce strong effects on his hearers, making them feel laughter, sympathy, determination, outrage, or whatever he wanted them to feel. He could
speak without interruption and express his own thoughts without equivoca-
tion. (Young Calvin, always fearful of being proved wrong, was apt to hedge
his statements till they were like caricatures of Yankee caution, for instance:
"I do not think she [a cow] is gaining much, so I guess she will die but hope
she will not," or "I shall not be glad when I go back to school again but
should be much more sorry if I could not go back," or "It does seem a relief
not to have to study Algebra although I like it very well.") If he did his work
well, an orator could count on making his point without the stresses and
shocks of face-to-face conversation.[32]

During his junior year, then, Calvin began working at reaching his classmates and—who knows—perhaps a wider public, through rhetoric. An indication of his success is the grudging recollection of his classmate Albert
Sargent: "I recall no great thing he ever did or anything he ever did that
would be of interest to the public.... He was a good speaker; could write a
good speech and deliver it well."[33]

The thing most people in Ludlow remembered about Coolidge in the long
run, however, was not a speech or anything like it, but an event that took
place in the first part of his senior year, in November 1889, when he was
seventeen. It was mysterious and controversial at the time, and Coolidge's
part in it remains cloudy to this day. It seems a fitting way to close this chapter on his years at B.R.A.

The new building was almost a year old on Wednesday morning, 13 November, when the janitor opened the academy and heard peculiar noises
upstairs. They came from Room 3, the classroom of Miss Cora Butler, who
had been teaching English at B.R.A. since the preceding year. Investigation
showed that some unknown persons had managed to smuggle a jackass from
a farm outside town into the building and shut it up in Room 3 overnight.
The room was a wreck. The animal had kicked the wainscoting and the
seats to splinters, to begin with, and, as the local paper, the *Tribune*, delicately put it, "the defilement that followed can easily be conjectured."
Once the jackass had been removed and the mess cleaned up, questions began. The prank was offensive but not unheard-of, locking a stock animal inside a building was a fairly common trick in Vermont, and though it had a
slightly rural flavor, well, so did Ludlow. The motives, too, were not hard to
come by; Miss Butler was strict, and not popular with her students. The real
questions were who had done it, and how they had gotten in.[34]

Egged on by the *Tribune*, which called the act one "of the most out-
rageous pieces of mischief that has been perpetrated in this place in many
years," the Executive Committee of the B.R.A. Board met in special session
the following Saturday to grill students about their knowledge of the prank.

They got nowhere; all the students questioned, Calvin included, denied knowledge except tall, somber Henry Hicks, Calvin's friend and ex-room-mate, who admitted he knew who had done it but refused to say who it was. Some of the students' parents, who were present (John Coolidge was in Ludlow that day, probably because he was on the Board), expressed the opinion that "boys will be boys" and that the affair should be treated as a harmless joke. In any event, no one was found responsible, and editor E. G. Allis of the *Tribune*, in his next issue, denounced the investigation as a whitewash and suggested that the members of a local political "gang" with whom he was at odds were shielding their sons from the consequences of their misdeeds.[35]

Perhaps they were. No one was formally disciplined by the academy or legally charged; or if anyone was, the record of it has vanished. One student, years later, recalled that there had been one expulsion. A new janitor—Henry Hicks, in fact—was installed in January; if the old janitor was likewise a student and was dismissed in December, it could well have been in connection with the jackass incident. In fact, if this conjecture is valid, it would explain how the pranksters were able to get into the building. But the *Tribune* recorded no further action in the case. That omission was not accidental. Three weeks after the affair, Allis abruptly sold out his paper and moved to Alabama. The new editor dropped the incident entirely.[36]

From the time of Coolidge's rise to national political prominence in 1920, there were persistent rumors that he had been involved in the prank or had some special knowledge of it. (The animal in the case was often referred to as a "donkey," "mule," or "four-footed animal" by those who found the term "jackass" intolerably crude.) Coolidge did not try to squelch the rumors; indeed, he gave them some credibility by a coy passage in his 1929 autobiography which ends: "About as far as I deem it prudent to discuss my own connection with these escapades is to record that I was never convicted of any of them and so must be presumed innocent." Other people in a position to know, however—his father, for instance, and his Pollard cousins in Proctorsville—denied that he had any connection. Reporters never found any witness who claimed to have the true story of what happened, and in the absence of firsthand testimony it has been possible to believe anything at all. One recent fictional account portrays Calvin as the ringleader of the prank-sters. Vermont mores being what they are, it is quite possible that a full account of the affair by one of the participants is reposing in someone's attic and will not become public for another century. In the interim, however, it may be of some use to assess the evidence as it now stands.

It is beyond doubt that Calvin was one of the students questioned about the prank. But he had never studied under Miss Butler and had no reason to hold a grudge against her. Moreover, he liked and admired the other two teachers, Mr. Sherman and Miss Chellis. He had no reason at all to embarrass the academy. He does not seem the right sort of person to have instigated or taken part in the joke. On the other hand, he might well have known about it beforehand, especially if he was acquainted with those who committed it. There is good reason for supposing that this was actually the case.[37]

George Sherman was an active administrator and nobody's pawn; yet he disciplined no students, or almost none, for the action. The fact may not mean that he knuckled under to parental pressure. What it probably means is that the perpetrators were beyond his disciplinary reach—they were not students at all, but young men of the village. The one name mentioned, years later, as having been among those responsible is that of George Raymond, twenty-two, the son of the Main Street haberdasher. He had just graduated from Tufts; his younger brother, Charles, was a B.R.A. student. Another likely participant, Frank Agan, twenty-one, worked in the dyeing department at the woolen mill. Coolidge's cousin Dallas Pollard, who mentioned Raymond and had secondhand knowledge of the episode, said two or three others were involved. More than likely they, too, were young village bachelors, the same sort of group as the Plymouth men who had executed the cannon caper, always ready to do something to shake up their staid little community.

As it happened, Calvin had been friends with this very group of young men since his first year in Ludlow, when he roomed with Peck. Peck had moved to Boston, but Calvin still hung around with George Raymond, Agan, Dick Lane the doctor's son, and their contemporaries. He could easily have heard of the prank in advance. His love of a good joke might well have led him to watch the preparations and maybe even collaborate in some small way.[38]

Probably the best way to imagine Coolidge, then, that chilly November night when the jackass was put into B.R.A., is not leading the animal or opening the door, but standing at a distance with his hands primly in his overcoat pocket, watching, as always, intently.

8

Graduation and a Change in Plans

Once again, as often during the winter, the respectable men of Ludlow, their wives and children in tow, were thronging into Hammond Hall after dark. The gentle light of candles or kerosene lamps diffused from the imposing frame building onto the icy main street. The attraction, this cold January evening, was not an operetta or a traveling play from Boston or a lecture series; it was homegrown entertainment, the Ludlow Trades Carnival.[1]

For a few years past some Ludlow community leaders had been concerned about the village's future. In comparison with nearby towns, theirs seemed to be stagnating. The cab shop had closed a year ago, in 1889, and a number of workers had left. Moreover, there was a still a steady, small trickle of emigration out to the West and to the cities of southern New England. In the trading of barbs between local newspapers that was so much a part of nineteenth-century small-town life in America, Ludlow often had to absorb some rather hard blows; a Springfield newspaper, for instance, had recently called it, not entirely implausibly, a "backwoods village." The Trades Carnival, a new event in Ludlow, a sort of showcase where local businessmen and professionals could display their wares and services, was probably an outgrowth of this concern, an attempt by village leaders to instill a little civic pride.[2]

At any rate, a great many people in the village were involved, either as participants or as spectators. The format was that of a variety show: the acts succeeded one another on stage, each exhibitor trying, with original wit and props, to amuse the audience and boost his business. B.R.A., for instance, had an entry, with bantam Albert Sargent, square-jawed and confident, imitating the spiel of a patent-medicine salesman and demonstrating, with charts and models, how study at the academy could enlarge a student's brain. Abbie Coolidge, self-possessed as always, wearing a smart frock coat and derby, carrying a cane and doctor's bag, represented Dr. W. N. Bryant.[3]

Calvin was not on stage, but he was in the audience, which in itself was something. In his senior year he had become a lot more active socially. He was still studying as hard as ever—recently he had decided to take on French in addition to Latin and Greek, and was getting up at four o'clock most mornings to catch up on it before going to class—but he was also getting out. During the very cold weather at the beginning of January he had been out skating on the river or one of the ponds almost every night, probably with Sargent, Amos Pollard, and tall, burly Rufus Hemenway, the other boys in his class. These were not only classmates but almost neighbors; for four years now Calvin had roomed pretty consistently in the same block on Pleasant Street, below the railroad embankment about two blocks from the academy, and most of these boys lived on that block. (Abbie roomed there too—at the Hemenways', in fact. Sometimes neighbors saw the two of them walking home from school together, Abbie in long overcoat and fashionable tam o'shanter talking animatedly while Calvin listened. Usually, however, they went their separate ways. After the Trades Carnival, to give one example, she went home to Plymouth with John while Calvin went over to Proctorsville for the weekend.)[4]

With Sargent, Pollard, Hemenway, and some younger boys like Roy Bryant, Dr. Bryant's blond, handsome son, he also attended sociables at the academy or Hammond Hall, or in the cozy, cluttered homes of his classmates on Pleasant Street, ate ice cream and cake, drank coffee or cider, and played party games. He was not conspicuous, but he was there, and like most of his male classmates, very much interested in the opposite sex. In fact, association between the sexes was the point of most of the parties. The games—bobbing for apples, blowing soap bubbles, forfeits with kisses for prizes—were designed to bring boys and girls together in a relaxed but respectable setting. For many a boy, walking a girl home from a sociable provided the earliest occasion for close contact. Jane Spafford, the girl who had refused to walk under the Democrat's flag, described her experience after a Hammond Hall sociable: "When time came to go home a schoolboy asked to 'see me home.' To my surprise and shock, he kissed me 'goodnight.' I was terribly 'green' and embarrassed, also I decided that 'Now I am a tough girl,' and never would I tell my father. O no!"[5]

There is no record that Calvin ever escorted a girl home from a sociable, or that he used any of the other time-honored approaches, like reading poetry together (his schoolmate Romeo Quimby read Tennyson's "The Princess" with a female B.R.A. student) or turning a casual encounter into a long, intimate conversation ("B.R.A. students are reminded that the post office is not a public trysting place," warned the *Tribune* in 1891). But he did go to sociables, and he was quite relaxed around girls. Alice Lockwood, who lived in his block on Pleasant Street, remembered seeing him "skirmishing with Lena" on the lawn next to her house. In March, when the whole senior class bundled up and went for a long sleigh ride through the hills northeast of Ludlow, he noted in his diary, "Took Lena."[6]

Who this girl was is not clear. Improbably, there seem to have been three Lenas, all attractive and eligible, connected with B.R.A. in 1890. Lena Sargent, Albert's older sister, is perhaps the least likely, even though she was the beauty of the class of 1889 and lived on Pleasant Street; she was a year or two older than Calvin and, then as now, it was uncommon for boys to go with girls older than themselves. Lena Levey, on the other hand, two years younger than Calvin, was the daughter of the man who owned the woolen mill and probably the most popular girl in the school, petite, curly-haired, and charming; Calvin would have faced stiff competition for her. Even Arthur Spaulding, who critically scribbled "P.I.G." by the names of all the girls in his class in the catalog, had a special and different category for Lena Levey. Then there was "vivacious" Lena Clark, a black-haired New Hampshire girl five years his junior who was in Ludlow that year staying with relatives, and friendly with the B.R.A. crowd; young Coolidge was definitely friendly with her sister Nell, who was his own age. If one must guess, Lena Clark was the one he had his arm around on the sleigh ride.[7]

For boys of Calvin's age and social class, these contacts with girls were not serious in any sense. On the physical level, a relationship between a male and a female student rarely progressed to more than a kiss and an occasional squeeze. As for social consequences, there were none. A boy could not even consider engagement or marriage until he was graduated and had a steady job—and he did not need to do so then. In terms of emotion, finally, there was almost no mention, in this age group, of romantic love or crushes. Doubtless they existed for some young people, but New England culture, unhospitable to emotions on principle, did nothing to encourage them. For Calvin and his friends, the parties and sleighrides were simply a pleasant diversion—"aimless play," one New England writer called it— copying the activities of older people.[8]

Apart from socializing, Calvin became active in many academy functions this winter. He was elected secretary of the senior class; Sargent was president. Both boys were in the debating society, and one can perhaps detect a muted rivalry between them. When the academy boys got up a minstrel troupe in February, Coolidge was probably on it; he had been in such shows at the Notch, and made a good end man. His wit was good, and his sense of timing for jokes was remarkable. After five years, he had at last come to feel as much at home in Ludlow as he was at the Notch, and could discard his shyness and do the things a typical Academy boy would do.[9]

Like almost every other academy student, too, he was sick a couple of times in the winter term. That winter, although relatively warm, was a bad one for illness; a new variety of flu, nicknamed "la grippe" in the newspapers, was going round, and B.R.A. had as many as ten students out with it one week in January. Calvin, with his generally parlous health, was a natural victim.[10]

An illness later that winter had a more tragic outcome. The winter term ended on 21 February, and Calvin and Abbie went home to Plymouth for a week of vacation. The first day of the spring term was 4 March. But this Friday before they were to go back, Abbie began running a fever and having abdominal pains. Dr. Boyden of Bridgewater, the nearest physician, was sent for. Whatever his treatment, it produced no immediate results. The next day, Sunday, 2 March, was the day the young Coolidges had planned to return to Ludlow, and the need to go back seemed obvious; a severe snowstorm, the first of the season, appeared to be on the horizon. Though Abbie was no better, John either sent or took Calvin back to Ludlow. The snowstorm did indeed set in, and Calvin heard nothing from home for a day or two, as he went to the academy and registered for the final courses of his senior year: French, Virgil, and American Literature. Then on Wednesday, the first day of classes, he heard that Abbie was worse and that Dr. Bryant had been sent for from Ludlow. He rode home with Bryant in his sleigh, and of course talked of the situation. "Inflammation of the bowels" was the doctors' name for what Abbie had. Like much nineteenth-century medical terminology, it was totally descriptive: none of the three medical men involved, Bryant, Boyden, or another doctor who had been called in, had any idea what was making the abdomen sore and causing the fever, nor any notion of what to do for it. All they could do was wait while Abbie suffered terrible pains. (What she had was appendicitis, as Bryant was to recognize years later; but this, as Coolidge put it in his *Autobiography*, "was a disease not well understood in 1890.") She died around noon on the next day, 6 March.[11]

The death of a person Abbie's age was not unusual in 1890, in Vermont, or for that matter in the United States. Abbie's case suggests why: physicians lacked the facilities, the medicine, and most of all the understanding to treat most illnesses. There was not even a single accepted standard of medical practice; doctors had different theories about the kind of medicine to administer in a given case, none of them based on any knowledge of the causes of disease. It was still the age in which country doctors carried medicine in their saddlebags, white powders that they dispensed with a penknife and wrapped in tiny paper squares of various colors. As often as not they were useless, or gave only symptomatic relief: one of the most popular, Dover's powder, was simply a mixture of ipecac and opium. The popularity in rural Vermont of laudanum, an addictive painkiller made with opium, was staggering: four Woodstock druggists reported that they annually sold enough opium to make one hundred gallons of it. Again, Abbie's case, with the agonies involved, illustrates why. It was an age, finally, in which most families still relied largely and desperately on patent medicines and home remedies for illness: eating lemons to cure diphtheria, carrying a horse chestnut to avoid rheumatism, applying skunk oil and onion poultices for spring ailments.[12]

Schoolchildren, thus, were accustomed to the idea that any one of their classmates might die during the year. Calvin had often seen death strike among his own age group. Three years before, Meda Kavanagh, one of the numerous girls in that family, had died of consumption at fifteen. Orson Butler, the Plymouth Fat Boy, had died the year before, age fourteen, of complications caused by obesity. His first year at Ludlow, eighteen-year-old Willey Winn of Mount Holly had been run over by a train in the railroad cut. Martha Lynds, Levi Lynds's niece, had died in 1889 at the age of nineteen, and Lula Hall, Matt Hall's sister, had died at the same age just a month before Abbie. All of these deaths, and others, occurred in the tiny world of Plymouth and Ludlow. Abbie's death was mourned—fifty people came up from Ludlow for the funeral, which was held amid a deep blanket of new snow—because she had been a cheerful, assertive person; but it did not evoke the shock that such a death would in the later twentieth century. B.R.A. printed a memorial program for her, with her favorite quotation: "Count the day lost / Whose low descending sun / Sees from thy hand / No worthy action done."[13]

To Calvin, Abbie's death was a painful loss. She had been the jolly one in the dour Coolidge family; a couple of years later he was to compare her life to a "happy day" in a letter to John. He had no easy way of consoling himself for her departure. The promise of heavenly bliss for the deceased, which bulked so large in nineteenth-century Christianity, seemingly did not attract him; at any rate, he made no mention of it. Abbie, to him, was just a memory, a beautiful, joyful memory to be sure, but only a memory, like his mother's portrait that he still silently carried around everywhere. Calvin's understanding of death was perhaps more Roman than Christian.[14]

One wonders, in passing, how much Calvin's ideas of the afterlife were influenced by the rather peculiar views on the subject in Plymouth. In the 1850s, the town had been a center of spiritualist activities in Vermont, and as late as 1890 one of its leading men, the lumber merchant Alonzo Hubbard, was a leader of the movement in the state. Large meetings took place fairly regularly at Tyson for conversation with departed spirits. The Coolidges were not spiritualists themselves, nor were most people in the Notch; but there was a general feeling in the community that conventional Christian ideas on the subject were inadequate. Visiting preachers who spoke of Hell, for instance, were coldly received.[15]

Formal religion could offer little consolation, for he had little to do with it. Abbie, however, had joined the Congregational Church of Ludlow the year before her death. Calvin had never joined. After five years in Ludlow, he was still not used to attending church. Unlike proper language and proper attire, proper behavior on Sunday mornings was not central to him, though he knew it should be. "Am ashamed to say I did not go to church," he recorded in his diary one Sunday that January. But in fact he went to church only one of the five Sundays recorded in that diary. In the widest sense, religion was important to him. He knew the Bible well, and was sure that the world was an orderly system guided by moral and spiritual as well as physical laws. Unquestionably Abbie's death fitted into this system somehow, but Coolidge's surviving writings give no clue how he fitted it in. In the meantime, life had to go on. He returned to Ludlow, gave John's writeup of the death and funeral to the new editor of the Tribune, and got back to the studies that he needed for graduation.[16]

One likely reason why he did not agonize more than he did over his sister's death is that it was overshadowed by a more immediate question, that of his own future. He was about to leave B.R.A., having absorbed about all the knowledge it was capable of giving him. The question was what he was going to do next, and the answer, by the spring of 1890, had been worked out between him and John: he was going to college.

Much about the decision to attend college is unclear—when it was made, or why it was made. Coolidge's surviving letters and writings give no clue when the decision was taken. The earliest possible date could be the fall of 1887, when fifteen-year-old Calvin first enrolled in B.R.A.'s Classical course, but it seems likely to have been much later. His sudden move in the winter of 1890 to begin studying French in addition to his regular classes may be the tip-off. Many colleges had recently begun to stress modern languages like French and German in addition to the classics. This fact may have prompted him, once he had definite plans to attend, to make the extra effort and get prepared. Certainly the sketchy planning evident in his first attempts to go to college suggests a last-minute decision.[17]

The really interesting question, however, is why he planned to go at all. He was not a particularly good student at B.R.A.; for instance, he had never made the honor roll. He had no ambition to become a doctor or lawyer or anything of the sort; his hope, rather, was to be a storekeeper. No one in his family had attended college before. Finally, as the events of the next year were to show, he did not want to leave Plymouth. In fact, his reluctance to go away to college was to become so obvious in the next twelve months that one has to question his statement in the *Autobiography* that it was in any sense his idea. Almost certainly, it was John's; though John, in later years, disclaimed responsibility for it and sought to portray it as his son's decision.[18]

Three factors seem to have led the older Coolidge to this unusual step. The first and governing one was simply that he had enough money to do it. Calvin, writing him about a similar matter five years later, was to say, "The only question you will consider in the end is whether you have the means ... so that may as well be settled first." College was an expensive proposition for ordinary people. At the University of Vermont, for instance, tuition was sixty dollars a year, board about the same, room rent up to thirty dollars annually, fuel, lights, and washing twenty-five dollars, and library privileges nine dollars: one hundred and eighty-four dollars total at a time when the average American family income was three hundred and sixty dollars a year. Thanks to his labor and thrift, John Coolidge was capable of taking on that expense. Moreover, he had a son whom he wanted to see successful, and not much else to spend the money on. College, then, was a real possibility for Calvin.[19]

Another consideration may have made it seem virtually a necessity. If Calvin was to be a success financially (which was doubtless the way John defined success), he would have to find a line of work he could do well, and it was not obvious what that would be. Farming was out; in the hill towns of Vermont, no one made money in agriculture. Business was a more likely possibility—keeping store, in fact, was what the boy wanted to do—but he was so alarmingly absent-minded at times that his father must have shuddered at the thought of his managing a business. It was odd: Calvin was an acute observer most of the time, and there were few individual foibles or pertinent details that escaped him; but at times he could fall into fits of abstraction that were almost incredible. At least twice during his years at B.R.A., and probably more often, he had visited Uncle Don and Aunt Sarah in Proctorsville for the weekend, had left some important possession there, and had had to return to Proctorsville, skipping school, to pick it up. Once it was his schoolbooks, once his clothes. He would begin studying and then lose himself in a fog, staring up the street. His father had stopped scolding him about the trait and accepted it with resignation and even dry humor. Jennie Chamberlin, who was working for the Coolidges around 1890, recalled a time when Calvin

brushed himself up carefully, pressed his pants and got the old calico horse and harnessed the same and backed him into the thrills, but things did not seem to go together right. Colonel Coolidge came out and said, "What is the matter, Cal?" Calvin replied, "I dunno, something is wrong." The Colonel went back and brought out the harness breast-plate and tugs and said, "Well, if you will put these on the horse I guess it will go better."

In the view of a hardheaded insurance agent like John Coolidge, such a capacity to get lost in thought may have made the boy unfit for anything else but college.[20]

Calvin's propensity for reading was another trait that pointed toward a college education. It was a taste neither John nor anyone else in the Notch shared, a product, of course, of his fear of social interaction. By graduation he had read a remarkable amount—not just schoolbooks, but histories, orations, poems, novels, almost anything he could find—looking for "insight," as he put it twice in his diary, into remote historical eras. His Grandmother Coolidge had given him a complete set of Shakespeare, which he had read. He had also read, among many other works, *Ivanhoe*, a life of the Empress Josephine, various historical novels of early Vermont, and quantities of Tennyson's poetry. For a seventeen-year-old from a rural hamlet, he had a rich fund of knowledge. To be sure, his conversation and writing often did not reflect it; Calvin was, in the parlance of communications specialists, an "information sink," good at absorbing information, poor at passing it on. But if all this reading was ever to be of use to him, it would be in a college setting, and nowhere else.[21]

Besides these two reasons for sending Calvin to college, there was one more immediate factor—the influence of Professor Sherman. Sherman had become more and more impressed by the boy's ability the longer he stayed at B.R.A. He liked Calvin's seriousness and what he perceived as his maturity, and since he was trying to promote B.R.A.'s reputation by sending his best students on to colleges where they would do well (and reflect luster on their alma mater), he naturally felt that young Coolidge should go. From the fall of 1888, when the senior Coolidge was chosen to the B.R.A. board of trustees, Sherman had had ample opportunity to present his viewpoint.[22]

Which of these factors influenced John the most is impossible to say, but by the winter of 1890 the plan had been made: Calvin was to go to college. The prospective collegian, however, was so uncertain of his own ability to do well in a new environment, no matter what Professor Sherman said, that he had managed to talk his father into a compromise: he would not enroll immediately. He was only seventeen, a little young to be off on his own. Instead, he would register in one "of the larger preparatory schools"—most likely Vermont Academy in Saxtons River, where Park Pollard had studied—and spend a year getting ready. Moreover, he would go not to Middlebury College, where most college-bound B.R.A. graduates went, including his classmate and rival Albert Sargent, but to a university, probably the University of Vermont. This was the arrangement as the snows melted, the lilacs budded, and the graduating class of 1890 headed into final preparations for commencement.[23]

Commencement season at B.R.A. was full of little social ceremonials borrowed from the colleges. The junior class gave a reception for the seniors; the seniors wore "generous" bows of pink and goblin blue, the class colors. Calvin used the occasion to wangle some new clothes out of his father. He had already purchased a new suit, gloves, and shoes for graduation, but now he persuaded John he needed another suit of clothes for classes and parties. "These that I have I have worn every day for almost two terms and do not look hardly fit to wear for best." He not only managed to get a new suit at Raymond's, but also two ties, hose, another pair of shoes, and an overcoat.[24]

He also had a speech to write and memorize, as did all the other seniors. The class was so small, only nine members, that every member had a chance to speak at least once during the program; Jessie Armington and Albert Sargent, the valedictorian and salutatorian, spoke twice. (It was actually a rather large class for B.R.A.; the year before there had been only seven graduates, all girls.) The five boys would deliver orations, the four girls essays; the difference between these genres is not clear, but perhaps the boys' offerings were more rhetorical and delivered with more flourish. Certainly Calvin's ten-minute oration on "Oratory in History" was full of embellishments and rhetorical devices. Although the commencement ceremony was not until 23 May, he had it ready by mid-April. It dealt with two of his favorite topics, history and oratory, and gave him a chance to invoke Demosthenes, Cicero, Peter the Hermit, Savonarola, William Lloyd Garrison, all the great orators of whom he had studied; writing it was a labor of love for him. Professor Sherman was highly complimentary of the speech, and told him it was the best one he had seen.[25]

The reporters who covered the commencement ceremony (it was common to review such occasions critically, as with theatrical performances) substantially agreed; Calvin's speech, along with those of Sargent and Hemenway, was the best of the afternoon. It was a beautiful afternoon, cool and spring-like, May in Vermont at its finest. Hammond Hall was packed; a multi-colored flower arrangement dominated the center of the stage as the graduates filed in, wearing brand-new suits or long pastel dresses. Calvin was pale; his red hair shone like fire. When Ellen Adams had completed her essay, he stood up and, in a deliberate high baritone, with the slightly artificial enunciation favored by speakers of that era, began: "To fully estimate the degree in which oratory has influenced the history of the world, would be a difficult task; the history of every country and of every age teems with miracles wrought by this necromantic power."[26]

There were four more speeches after he sat down, including Sargent's on "The Power of Truth," and Rufus Hemenway's on "National Pride." (Henry Hicks, who spoke on "The Boy of To-day," had grown a mustache for the occasion.) Then the piano played again and the crowd dispersed, some going across the street to sup at the Ludlow House. In the evening there was a concert at Hammond Hall by the Temple Quartette of Boston, with Miss Ella Chamberlain, whistling soloist. Perhaps Calvin and John stayed for it. Next day, at any rate, Calvin was back in Plymouth, looking forward to a summer of rest and moderate labor before he had to leave in the fall for Vermont Academy.[27]

It was a busier summer than usual at the Notch, at least in some ways. The Fourth of July was not busy at all; since 1885 there had not been a really exciting Fourth. Somehow the Union had managed to regain possession of the town cannon in the intervening years, and there was little for the Notch boys to do. Most who wanted to celebrate independence went to the ceremonies at Ludlow. But on the positive side, the second story that John had had put on the store building a couple of years earlier, with its large room (forty-seven by twenty-four feet) directly over the store, provided a focus for dances, theatricals, and social events. Periodically throughout 1890 there were sociables in "Coolidge Hall," as it was called by some local correspondents. The real focus of attention, however, was the new cheese factory.[28]

The idea behind a cheese factory was simple and appealing to hard-pressed farmers. Wool, for generations the main farm crop in Vermont, was no longer viable because of competition from the West; grains were not profitable and never had been; but dairying was a possible option. The big cities of southern New England offered a market for dairy products, and most Vermont farms had a few cows anyway. The problem with dairying was that it required more labor and more machinery than sheep raising, and, on a large scale, was much smellier. If, however, a lot of small farmers all agreed to sell their milk to the same place and have it processed there, then they saved by consolidating the labor and machinery needed, and could still keep their operations small if they chose. This central plant, called a "creamery" if it produced butter and a "cheese factory" if cheese was the product, could then sell its product at a profit, which it shared among the participating farmers. The idea had been current in Vermont since the 1870s, but there was a major flurry of interest in it around 1890 as the depression in the mountain towns deepened and dairying seemed more and more like the only way out. West Bridgewater farmers organized a cheese factory in January; in February the farmers around the Notch met and agreed to build one up the hill from John Coolidge's house, near the new schoolhouse. John was, of course, a leading incorporator; nothing of substance could be done in the Notch without him.[29]

Framing began in mid-April. By the time Calvin got home in May, the large barnlike building was up, but the machinery was still arriving and being installed. Eugene Aldrich, a master cheesemaker from Shrewsbury, had been hired, and on 6 June the factory opened and began buying milk. The sour smell of cheesemaking permeated the Notch that summer. More visibly, the road at John's front door was full of farm wagons bringing milk, three thousand pounds a day more or less. Day in, day out, it was more activity than the Notch had known for years, and endlessly entertaining to residents.[30]

The most entertaining show in Plymouth, however, was a local controversy: the Taylor case. In 1890 it had been going for six or seven years without letup. Though no spectacular episodes took place that summer, the case bears relating, first because it was constantly on everyone's lips, secondly because it closely involved John Coolidge, and last, because it serves to illuminate how complex and embittered life could become in a small place like Plymouth.

Warren Taylor, a second cousin of John Coolidge and about John's age (he was in his early forties), farmed with his father on the stage road south of the Union, not terribly successfully. He also dabbled in sawmilling, and he had married a woman from the neighboring town of Sherburne. Beginning in the early 1880s, he had been feuding with the Plymouth town government over the size of his tax assessment. He finally hit upon a stratagem to avoid taxes: every March, when the assessment was made, he moved most of his taxable property to a place he and his wife owned in Sherburne. It was impossible to conceal this trick in a community the size of Plymouth, and the selectmen were enraged. In 1884, they ordered the tax assessor to go to Sherburne as well as Plymouth and assess all of Taylor's possessions he could find.[31]

This was where John Coolidge came in. In May of 1885, he had to arrest his cousin and carry him to Woodstock jail unless he paid his newly-augmented tax bill. Under the threat of going to jail, Taylor paid; but he promptly turned around, sued the town for seizing his property, and contested the justice of the assessment. For a couple of years the case wended its way through the courts, to the great interest of Plymouth people, who went over to Woodstock in droves to hear it tried. Finally, in 1887, the county court decided against Taylor; the following year the town assessed him the then hefty sum of two hundred and sixty-nine dollars sixty-three cents, including back taxes and penalties. John was again the person responsible for seeing that the tax was collected.[32]

On 9 January 1889, at Coolidge's invitation, he and Taylor met at the general store at nine o'clock in the morning. It was more a confrontation than a discussion; the relation between the cousins had degenerated into animosity. Taylor, according to Coolidge, "neglected and refused" to pay his taxes, and instead offered all he had, "which consisted of a five dollar bill, a little change, one button, one key, and one pocket knife." If Coolidge would not take this in full payment, he said, he was ready to go to jail. The day was cold and stormy, and John did not feel like taking him to Woodstock then. He said "he would attend to the matter some other day," and so he did. Three days later, he caught up with Taylor walking down the road from West Bridgewater to the Union, demanded his taxes, and when Taylor again refused to pay, grabbed him, put him in the buckboard, and carried him to Woodstock, where Taylor, in his words, spent the night in the "stone house with an iron bedstead for a couch," among "thieves and ruffians." On his release, predictably, he sued Coolidge in state court for illegal arrest, and the town for an unjust assessment. That was where the matter stood in the summer of 1890. John was busy gathering all the testimony he could in his favor, for instance on the question of whether Taylor was, as he claimed, a bona fide resident of Sherburne. William Stickney, his friend and lawyer, was preparing to argue the case when it came up, which would be soon.[33]

The pleasant rhythm of Calvin's summer in Plymouth—working in the field, reading, visiting with neighbors—was interrupted in August by a disturbing piece of news. It came from Professor Sherman, of all people. Sherman was a graduate of Amherst College, "down below" in Massachusetts, and proud of it. He had just learned that an old acquaintance of his, from the same part of Massachusetts where he had grown up, had a son attending Amherst College that year and was planning to move to Amherst and open a boarding house there so that he could keep an eye on his son's progress. Quite possibly he had asked Sherman if he knew of any young men who might be attending from Vermont and needed a place to room. Sherman thought of Calvin at once. Here was a way for his shy, talented pupil to attend a good college and still have the benefit of a familiar, supportive environment as he adjusted to the college atmosphere. There were obvious problems with the idea. Most seriously, the basic costs of an Amherst education were about twice those at the University of Vermont, approximately 370 dollars a year. Also, freshmen had to pass an entrance examination in the classics, history, and mathematics. But he proposed the idea to John Coolidge, and John, surprisingly, accepted.[34]

One can only guess why. Amherst was certainly a prestigious school. It had one of the highest reputations in New England for traditional Yankee piety and simplicity combined with thoroughly up-to-date learning. It was actually no more distant by train than the University. Albert Weaver, Sherman's friend, could be a needed help for Calvin in a strange environment. And John shared Sherman's confidence in Calvin: he could pass the entrance examination; he could do well in a challenging institution. These must have been among the reasons that persuaded him that the costs, though high, were not excessive. Now he had only to tell Calvin the good news.

This last-minute change left Calvin aghast. He was not naturally an adaptable person, and this particular idea brought out all his worries about studies and feelings of inadequacy in general. If he had known earlier that he was going to be faced with the Amherst entrance examination, he could have spent the whole summer in study. Now there were barely three weeks to prepare. Moreover, he was being sent far away from home—it seemed far to him—just after suffering a great loss in his family. He must have made his feelings known to John, but there cannot have been a confrontation on the order of John's with, say, Warren Taylor or Warren Spaulding, no trading of charges and threats. It was not in Calvin to confront his father.

Whatever method he used to convey his fears, it failed. Plans for his departure were made rapidly and without his input. He was to leave for Amherst on 15 September.[35]

9

Nerves

This chapter, unlike the others in this book, is an imaginative recreation of an event that is almost totally undocumented: Calvin's first journey to Amherst. The specific actions it narrates are based not on direct evidence but on deduction; they are, in my view, the best approximation of the actual journey. To underscore this difference for the reader, and also to present the information in this chapter with more immediacy, I have used the historical present.

The station yard is filthy, knee deep in mud as always in a wet spell. For the past couple of days it has been raining or threatening rain most of the time. The mountaintops are invisible in the morning mist. Telegraph wires fade away into the grayness.[1]

The horses that pull the Ludlow House carriage stamp and snort as they wait for the mail train from Rutland. Also on the platform, despite the early hour (it is just after seven-thirty in the morning), is the usual depot cast of characters: railroad workers in bib overalls, checked shirts, and shapeless hats; idlers lounging, wearing caps and pulling at their pipes; one or two women, clearly passengers, in dark dresses and flowered hats. Calvin shivers inside his overcoat, as much from nervousness as from the chill. He has his ticket. His trunk is ready to be checked on board.[2]

The low blur of noise in the distance to the left becomes the rush of the train; the hoarse, surprising whistle is unmistakable. Gradually the locomotive draws nearer, with its overpowering noise, its squeals and hisses. Clouds of steam hover around; choking torrents of coal smoke flood out of the tall, flaring stack. (The smell of coal smoke is new. Back when he had first gone to B.R.A., the Central Vermont had burned only wood, and meeting the train had been like entering a steam bath fragrant with burning pine and cedar. Coal smoke almost makes him stop breathing.) The engine, the mail car and the passenger coach, its wooden sides painted a dark olive drab, grind to a halt. Calvin's grip on the handle of his bag tightens as the passengers dismount. He has brought no lunch; the trip is not that long. According to the schedule, by eleven-thirty he should be in Amherst.[3]

Amherst—an unknown and terrifying place. Professor Sherman is sure he will do well there. The entrance examinations start tomorrow, 16 September, in Walker Hall, wherever that is.[4]

He barely perceives the thump of the mailbags being tossed on board, and the "All aboard" of the conductor. The interior of the car is warm and smoky. He looks for an empty red plush seat near the big stove in the center, and hopes the floor is not too cold. The train jerks to a start, and Ludlow begins disappearing backward—the brick tower of B.R.A., the white iron bridge on Main Street—just as it did when he used to take the train to Proctorsville for the weekend. The conductor comes through and punches his ticket with one of those strange miniature shapes—moons, trees, geometrical figures—that you see only on the railway. His fellow passengers are dozing or reading the *Rutland Herald*. The train hurtles across the flats toward Proctorsville. He will pass right by Uncle Don's big frame store, Uncle Don's house and yard, but will not be able to get out and visit. The train stops in Proctorsville; Calvin, with a slight effort of will, stays in his seat.[5]

Misty fields, streaks of rain on the windows, an occasional glimpse of a fiery pink rock maple next to a farmhouse. The train rattles and lurches around bends, never very fast. With all the stops, it takes an hour to cover the twenty-seven miles to Bellows Falls, the junction, where it meets the main line down the Connecticut Valley. The stations are familiar: Cavendish, Gassetts, Chester, little collections of houses and stores like Proctorsville. The atmosphere in the car is smoke-laden and stuffy. The floor is cold, as he feared. So many rail travelers complain of coughs and sick headaches; one can see why.[6]

Latin prose composition and pronunciation will be the first examination, at nine-thirty. It will not be easy; Calvin has never really mastered the rules of composition, word order, when to use "atque," when to use "et." The next is easier: Caesar and Cicero. Then, after lunch, comes Greek: Xenophon, Homer, and sight translation. At best it will be challenging. At worst it may be too much for him. Of course, even if he fails a portion they will admit him, but with a "condition"; he have to make up the work, with the help of a private tutor, while carrying the full freshman load. It sounds almost impossible.[7]

The conductor's shout rouses him. They are entering the largest railroad yard he has ever seen, an expanse of wet gleaming steel rails crisscrossing in the mist. Other engines snort and puff on side tracks. There are sounds of hammering. A two-story red brick station stands on a sort of peninsula that projects into the yard. This is Bellows Falls, and already the Boston passengers, who have to change here to a Boston and Maine train, are gathering their packages and preparing to get off. Calvin's route is simpler; he just has to stay in his seat while his train switches to a new engine and prepares to go on to Brattleboro. As the train stops, he pulls out his pocket watch to check the time: according to the schedule, it should be 8:55 A·M·[8]

Bellows Falls is a town of some size, but smaller than Rutland, with a lot of big paper mills next to the river. Presently the train begins moving again, southward; on their left appears the Connecticut River, a wide gray sheet of water under a gray sky, with the rocky hills of New Hampshire on the other side. There appears to be a railway over there too, paralleling the river. The scattered red and orange of early fall foliage punctuate the scene. Now they are moving faster; the track is straight and level, and there are no stops before Brattleboro unless the train is flagged at a local station. There is time to walk around the car if he likes, take a drink from the common water cup at one end, use the toilet in its tiny cubicle, dry his hands on the common towel, prospects his fastidiousness rejects. Besides, the ends of the car are cold, and he already feels miserable enough without tempting illness, which would worsen the terrible two days ahead.[9]

The second day of the examinations is a torture he is ill equipped to suffer. It begins with French, and although he studied French at B.R.A., his one and a half terms of the language were not much. Then come ancient history and English, both easy, and then, in the afternoon, of all things, geometry and algebra, the subjects that had always bedeviled him in the academy, the awful problems he thought he had seen the last of. Calvin's heart sinks when he thinks of this part, the perplexity, the embarrassment ahead. Could he possibly do badly enough to be sent straight home?

The stations fly past, some of them just gilt-lettered signboards and a small cabin by the tracks: Westminster, Putney, East Putney, Dummerston. Cows graze in the broad meadows. The hills are a constant presence in the background. Shortly they are approaching Brattleboro, a large brick town by the river, its skyline dominated by two tall church steeples. Again there are paper mills and other factories, as at Ludlow and Bellows Falls—again the Vermont pattern, small industry encircled by mountains and farms. The depot, a quaint sort of brick cottage, perches on a ledge between the town and the river; the graceful curve of its platform roof recalls some marine creature. A covered bridge spans the Connecticut River. Many of the organs Calvin has seen in Plymouth came from a factory in Brattleboro, the Estey Company. He also knows the place as the home of the Brattleboro Retreat, the place where insane people, or neurasthenic people, in the language of the time, are sent for treatment.[10]

He has to change trains here, but the connection is quick and easy. The New London & Northern Train that will carry him to Amherst is on an adjacent track and leaves in only a few minutes, the conductor tells him. He doesn't need to wait in the depot. On the platform he can buy a New York or Boston paper or a magazine to read, and look around unobtrusively to see if anyone else his age seems to be taking the Amherst train. It is strange and novel being out in the world by himself like this. Annoyingly, his nose feels stuffy, his chest tight. He seems to be catching a cold after all.[11]

The first thing to do in Amherst will be to find Weaver's house. He has the address; it is near the college. He will introduce himself, get his trunk, go to his room, and begin studying.

Off again. It is raining now. There is not much poetry to this New England September. They enter Massachusetts—probably the first time he has ever been outside Vermont—and cross the Connecticut on a long bridge. Now the track veers away from the valley, and the train slows as it follows the winding rails through forested hills. The names of the stations are unfamiliar—Millers Falls, Montague, Leverett—but the landscape still looks a lot like home. After about an hour's ride, as the side yards and backyards of large, well-kept houses are beginning to appear by the track, the conductor bellows "Amherst!" and there he is. The cars clank to a stop opposite two straw-hat factories.[12]

With a deceptive composure on his pale, narrow face, ready to deal with the mundane problems of finding the college and finding Weaver's house but not nearly so ready to confront being away from his community and proving his worth to strangers, Calvin takes his bag, buttons his overcoat, dons his derby, and descends from the train. It is pouring rain. He sniffles. This is Amherst, prospectively his home for the next four years. As the hack rolls through dripping trees and falling yellow leaves, carrying him to South Pleasant Street, he peers through the curtain of rain to make out the outlines of the town. There are surprises, things he never saw in Ludlow. On the same street as the depot, large, dignified houses of brick or stucco, in an unfamiliar style, stand far back from the street surrounded by gardens or clipped, iron-fenced lawns. Up the hill from the station they come to the main street and the large Common, rolling, rectangular, tree-covered. The business district at one end is composed of brick store blocks like Rutland rather than frame ones like Ludlow, snug, prosperous-looking stores with trim awnings. There is, to his surprise, a Renaissance Revival stone church half-covered in ivy, facing the Common; a big brick-and-sandstone building, not wholly unlike B.R.A. but much more massive, seems to be the new town hall. There at the Common's end, visible as they turn down Pleasant Street in that direction, is the college.[13]

As he has been told, it is on a hill, a rather steep hill, dominating its end of the town. The oldest part of it is on the crest, a pair of antique brick buildings, with a square-towered chapel between them, facing west. Below them on the slope are an odd octagonal structure and a classroom hall with a tower; behind them, still on the crest of the ridge, hints of other big buildings in the trees. The whole ensemble, college and town, conveys a feeling of authority and complexity unlike anything he has encountered in Vermont. Far to his left, as he nears the end of the Common, stands a massive Second Empire pile, rather new-looking, with a strange jutting central tower and gables, and a long flight of granite steps in front. This, he learns, is Walker Hall, where the examination will begin tomorrow, where he will

College Hill in Amherst, viewed from the business district in the 1880s. The towers in the photograph, from left, are the College Church; Walker Hall; Grace Episcopal Church on the common; Williston Hall; and Johnson Chapel. (The Jones Library)

trot out the scraps of learning he has acquired at B.R.A. and lay them in front of the examiners, where he will be judged. The sick oppression on his chest, partly a product of the well-timed cold that is overtaking him, is also partly raw fear. The hack rolls on, down South Pleasant's crushed gravel, down to the very foot of College Hill.[14]

All that Coolidge ever said about this first attempt to enter Amherst in 1890—all, in fact, that anyone in a position to know ever said—was a single sentence in his *Autobiography*: "On my way there I contracted a heavy cold, which grew worse, interfering with my examinations, and finally sent me home where I was ill for a considerable time." A little more about the episode can be inferred from other sources. For instance, he stayed at Weaver's boarding house; he completed one day of the examinations, but probably not the second; and John had to come for him and take him back to Vermont. From contemporary weather reports it appears that on Wednesday, 17 September, the second day of the examinations, the central Connecticut Valley experienced a deluge of rain unmatched in recent memory. Probably the foul weather, coupled with his cold symptoms and the prospect of failing the examination, was enough to make him telegraph his father that morning that he was sick and unable to complete the examination, or ask his landlord to do so. Yet, for a dutiful son, it was an act of desperation. To justify sending for John in this way, he would have to have been very ill, almost on the brink of death. The *Autobiography* hints, without actually saying so, that he was. On Thursday John returned with him to Plymouth.[15]

The illness was so opportune that it was probably stress-related. Faced with the unwelcome prospect of entering Amherst, Calvin, whose health was not good at the best of times, simply let himself go and became very sick, so sick that probably he and his father both mistook his illness for the first stage of the terminal consumption that threatened him. The real question is why he found the thought of college so threatening. Certainly it was not study in itself; he had always enjoyed books and languages. Probably the basis of his fear was twofold: first, dread of the unknown, fear of living isolated among strangers; and second, fear of failure, dread of doing badly at a task his father had set him and thus revealing his basic inadequacy. During his adolescence, Calvin had overcome the demons of anxiety many times with sheer dogged quietness and self-control; but his stoicism had limits. Confronted with these two terrors, he decided, unconsciously of course, that it was after all easier to surrender to the familiar terror that had haunted most of his boyhood, death by consumption.

Lying alone in the unfamiliar bed at Weaver's, sweaty and feverish, scared to cough for fear of bringing up blood, he hears a familiar voice, opens his eyes, sees his father's heavy, stiff face in the lamplight. The face utters words of comfort in a gruff voice. Sick as he is, dark as his future may be, at least John has come to take him home.

10

Performances

"J. Calvin Coolidge is gaining slowly," ran a cryptic one-line notice 10 October in the *Vermont Tribune*, among the Plymouth news. The item was totally lacking in context; it contained no identification of Calvin, no mention of what ailed him or how he had contracted it. An outsider would have passed it over without a thought. But to readers in Plymouth, Ludlow, Proctorsville, and Bridgewater it was pregnant with meaning, one of the "paragraphs of genial and friendly interest" Rudyard Kipling referred to as indices of the way New England country folk lived "on terms of terrifying intimacy." Like other October items—the news that Fred Colburn, back from Massachusetts, had bought a half interest in a Ludlow clothing store, or that Perry Kavanagh had gone to Springfield looking for work—it was matter for analysis and discussion among interested readers: why Cal had come back, whether he was likely to recover, and what would happen next.[1]

No evidence at all survives of the community's reaction to Calvin's return. There was doubtless a range of opinions. Warren Taylor and other local people who did not care for John Coolidge probably had to suppress a sardonic snicker when they heard the news. John's sickly, hesitant son, his one extravagance, on whom he had lavished an academy education, had never been real college material. It had been a waste to send him. Perhaps he actually had gotten ill; perhaps he had found the courses too challenging. Either way, it was a failure for Coolidge.[2]

Another more charitable and probably more general view would have seen Cal's illness as the beginning of the long-expected last act in his life. Like his Uncle Frank, who had died of consumption one year earlier, he had "great capabilities" but was not fated to live long. He had performed well enough at B.R.A., but apparently would not be spared to show what he could do in college. He might as well stay at home and prepare for the end. John may have felt this way himself.[3]

Calvin's recovery was slow; "I was ill for a considerable time," he wrote in his autobiography. It was, in other words, a severe illness, its severity validated by the length of time needed for recovery. Doctors no doubt were called in and prescribed treatment, but there is no record of what they recommended. In fact, there are no records at all of what the Coolidges, father and son, did that fall. The weather continued wet and chilly, not a

111

bad time to spend six weeks confined to the house. About the beginning of November, it seems, Calvin began to get out, but there was apparently no thought of sending him back to college or providing him tutoring. On the contrary, the next thing John did, in mid-November, was to begin renovating the general store building—putting in new counters and display cases, repainting the walls—at considerable expense. Les Walker, who had bought the store from George Moore back in 1888, had to move all his stock upstairs into the Hall during the two or three months while the craftsmen worked. Cal was well enough to help, but the main work was done by Chapman, the carpenter from Ludlow, and M. M. Dimick, the local painter. Perhaps it is not too far-fetched to suggest that John was fixing up the store for Cal to take over when Walker's lease ran out. Calvin would be able to fulfil his long-held dream of keeping store; he would do a good job; and he would be able to stay in the Notch, where he was among friends and could be looked after.[4]

Secure in the feeling of returning strength, Calvin began to enjoy being at home during a school session for the first time in five years. He hung around the cheese factory and observed its operation in his leisurely way. More quickly than was usual for him, he made the acquaintance of the master cheesemaker, Eugene Aldrich, and his family. He was sorry when the factory closed for the winter and the Aldriches returned to Shrewsbury. But with the ample leisure of the dying, he could devote more time than ever to solitary pursuits. That winter he spent hours reading the poetry of Sir Walter Scott, immersing himself in the romance of the Middle Ages and the Renaissance. Once before, when he had been at B.R.A., he had come home for the summer and tried to work at his desk, following a suggestion of Benjamin Franklin's about the value of turning poetry into prose; but his father had shooed him out to work in the field. This winter, there was no objection from John.[5]

It began as a classic New England winter, without the alternations of thaw and blizzard that had been so annoying the preceding few years—just honest, severe, snowy weather straight through. By early December, the temperature had already gone down to four below zero at the Union, plenty of snow was on the ground, and sleighing was excellent. Good sleighing, of course, meant socializing, and 1890–91 in the Black River valley was a winter full of festivity: a grand opening ball at the Echo Lake House, with forty couples dancing to the music of Proctorsville's Amphionic Orchestra; Fred Pollard's gala wedding at New Year's in Ludlow, to Dr. Bryant's daughter, in a house decked with greenery and mistletoe; evening parties where the new "Tiddle-de-wink" game was all the rage. Even Calvin, who was supposed to be doomed, got drawn in.[6]

It happened more or less like this. A small group of young people at the Notch realized in December that they were all together with time on their hands. They were mostly Moores and Wilders, mostly young women in their late teens and early twenties. The notion struck them that it might be fun to get together and work on an amateur theatrical performance, as young people of the Notch had done in the past. Shows of this kind were a fairly common entertainment in rural Vermont in the winter, usually as benefits to raise money for some worthy cause like the local free library. Scripts were readily available; one simply sent a couple of dollars to some publishing house in Boston or New York. It is not recorded who the leader was in getting this project going. Certainly it was not Calvin. All indications point to Clara Moore, Thomas's cousin, one of the musical Moore girls. The oldest of the group at twenty-two, she had taught school and probably had some experience in directing programs.[7]

The script they chose was called *Under the Laurels*, a standard romantic melodrama set in the exotic southern Appalachians, complete with a contested will, a conniving villain, a beautiful orphan heroine, and a humorous darky. There were ten parts in all, four women and six men. There was no difficulty in casting the female parts (Clara, for instance, took the role of the romantic lead, Rose Milford), but the male parts required more ingenuity. Len Willis, who had worked as John Wilder's hired man for several years now and who was probably sweet on Clara then, as he was a few months later, took the male lead, but that exhausted the Wilder household; Allen was clerking in Proctorsville, and the other boys were too young. Almost all the other young men of the Notch were pressed into service. Clarence Blanchard, Florence's brother, took a comic part. Elwin Bailey, John's hired man, was the sheriff. Thomas Moore was the hero's sidekick. Dell Ward, one of Jim Ayer's nephews, took the blackface role. And Calvin was lured away from his reading with the long and juicy part of the villain, Kyle Brantford.[8]

Probably it did not take much coaxing to get Calvin involved. He may have acted before in theatricals at the Notch. In any case, acting was very similar to what he had been doing in real life for six or seven years: projecting an image, in his case the image of the quiet, correct, detached young man. The Brantford part was right for him, too; there was little emotional involvement with the other characters (though at one point he did have to steal a kiss from Clara), but a great deal of smooth deception and menacing asides. He seems to have thrown himself into the part. At any rate, his rendition of the line "Jealousy is a bitter passion to nourish" tickled the rest of the cast so that they were forever repeating it to one another. Recalling the production a few years later, he remembered "I had all the work to do."[9]

Probably they practiced at the Wilders' house, maybe in the old ballroom upstairs. At length they decided that they were good enough to merit an audience. Since the hall over the store was filled with Les Walker's stock, they would have to take their production somewhere else. They decided on the Union, specifically the old Institute building next to Daniel Wilder's hotel. (The Vermont Liberal Institute had been the Union's short-lived attempt at an academy, back in the 1870s.) Scenically, the play presented no problems; it required only a sofa, a few benches, and some chairs. The script gave helpful hints for special effects—"Lightning may be produced by blowing finely powdered rosin into a candle flame. Thunder by rattling a large piece of sheet iron," and the like—so that they could give a workmanlike performance, good enough to warrant charging admission.[10]

Some time after the New Year, accordingly (a plausible guess would be late January or early February, though there is no notice in the newspapers) the troupe from the Notch gave two performances at the Union. No record exists to tell whether the performances were any good, but in one crucial department at least they were successful: the players ended up with eight dollars in receipts. "That was the only money any of us ever had that we didn't know what to do with," Dell Ward recalled. "It belonged to all of us and not any of us.... Fact is, we were all pleased that we'd got eight dollars out of the Union." Finally one of the girls came up with a solution: "Let's eat it up. Let's have a party in the hall." "That suited us boys," Ward reminisced. "We felt gingery—havin' money to spend in a frolic that we'd earned actin' in a play. I don't remember what kind of refreshments we had—likely oysters. Anyhow we had plenty of music and we didn't care whether school kept or not." Maybe there was a piano in the hall and Clara played it; if so—and it is hard to imagine what other kind of music they could have had—Calvin probably sat and tapped his feet while the others danced. But he enjoyed the party.[11]

It may have been this frolic that convinced John he did not have a dying son on his hands. In early March, at any rate, Calvin's period of idleness came to an end. He enrolled for the spring term at B.R.A., as a postgraduate student. The step was not unusual in itself; in almost any term at B.R.A. there were a handful of students who had already graduated but, for one reason or other, had leisure to take another course or two. So Calvin signed up for Greek prose and algebra. He would board with his old classmate Rufus Hemenway, who was living at home while clerking at Ball's hardware store. What was noteworthy about this action was not simply that he was well enough to go to Ludlow to study; what it meant was that he was going to try again to get into Amherst. Nothing else could have induced him to confront algebra again.[12]

In all likelihood the decision to try going back to Amherst was John's. The basic idea behind it is clear: if Calvin was not dying, he needed to get busy securing an education. Moreover, John had other fish to fry. For some time he had been thinking of remarriage, to Carrie Brown, George Brown's daughter, a smart, well-liked spinster who had taught school and clerked in the Notch store. It was a little difficult to propose marriage while his son's future was so uncertain; with Calvin established in college, remarriage would be simple.[13]

The snows of early March, then, found Calvin back in Ludlow, reconciled to if not happy with the thought of trying the Amherst examination again. As he wrote his father in a characteristically ambivalent sentence, "I have not the training of a man from a school like St. Jonsbury [*sic*], Saxtons River, or Phillips Exeter, but I hope I have the ability yet to secure it, though not having it would cause me some embarrassment." In any case, it was pleasant to be back at B.R.A., where he now felt entirely at home. He saw many of his old Ludlow friends. Dick Lane, for instance, was now working in the front office of the woolen mill; he had shaved his mustache, and was trying to project the air of the suave young businessman. (Dick had shaved his mustache, and Rufus was growing one; young men their age frequently experimented with whiskers. Calvin, however, seems never to have tried, although by this time he was probably shaving.) Dick was interested in Calvin's plans; he had been a Delta Kappa Epsilon at Middlebury and had heard that fraternities were of major importance at Amherst, so he was trying to persuade his friend that they should make an advance visit to the college and start "scheming" to get Cal into DKE.[14]

B.R.A. itself had not changed much. Sherman was still principal, and still eager to help young Coolidge enter Amherst. Miss Chellis had left. A new marking system was in effect, with letter grades instead of numbers. There were some new students there; Calvin became particularly friendly with a local girl, Ada Wilder, two years his junior and no relation to the Plymouth Wilders. Later that spring, in fact, he sent her his photograph, a gesture that often signaled serious interest. Nothing came of it in this case, however; three years later she married one of the Ludlow Warners.[15]

Rufus, during the month and a half Calvin stayed at his house, was deeply involved in the current American craze that was sweeping Vermont in 1891: bicycling. Besides his work at Ball's, he sold Columbia bicycles on the side—the new "safety" bicycles with the chain drive and without the high front wheel that had made the earlier models so precarious—and during the spring of 1891 he could barely keep up with the demand. Every young person in Ludlow, it seemed, wanted a Columbia, including Lena Levey, the Raymond boys, and Henry Brown. Editor Crane of the *Tribune*, an ardent cyclist, plugged them in his paper at every opportunity, and his son Ephraim, who was studying at B.R.A., lost no chance to whiz around town on his. They were sporty, cheap, easy to repair, and safe. (Relatively safe; three years later, the elder Crane was to die of a fractured skull suffered in a bike accident about a mile from the Notch.) Calvin and Rufus, one can be sure, talked bicycles a lot, and Calvin rode Ephraim Crane's at least a few times, but in the mud of March and early April he had no chance to become a real devotee.[16]

Besides, his return to B.R.A. proved to be unexpectedly brief. He had finished Greek prose by the end of March and was sweating over algebra when Mr. Sherman, who knew about his collapse at the Amherst examinations, came to him with a suggestion. Graduates from the better academies, the preparatory schools as they were beginning to be known, could enter Amherst directly without the necessity of passing the examinations. If Calvin could manage to enroll for the final spring term of such a place and graduate with its senior class, then he could enter Amherst "on certificate," as the phrase went, and not have to undergo the September ordeal. It was a little late in the year for him to enroll at such an academy, but as it happened, an Amherst classmate of Sherman's was the assistant headmaster at St. Johnsbury, one of the favored schools, and Mr. Sherman thought it might be possible to get Calvin in on his recommendation, providing John was agreeable. John, it turned out, was wonderfully agreeable, despite the extra expense of getting Calvin to St. Johnsbury, finding rooms for him there, and paying his way through mid-June, when the spring term ended. It was a chance to achieve his and Calvin's goals without the pressure of the September examinations. By 12 April everything was set. Coolidge moved out of the Hemenways', returned to Plymouth in John's buckboard to pack his bags for a two-month stay, and the next day went over the hills the other direction, to Woodstock, where he could catch a train for St. Johnsbury, fifty miles to the north.[17]

The train ride to St. Johnsbury was slightly shorter and less complicated than the journey to Amherst. Calvin left Woodstock on the short-line Woodstock Railroad, an elegant little line that ran seventeen miles to White River Junction and en route offered travelers one of the more spectacular sights in Vermont: its bridge over dizzying Quechee Gorge, where an occasional nervous traveler had been known to leave the train rather than take the risk of riding so much iron and steel over so high a drop. At White River Junction, he caught the northbound Boston and Maine train along the Connecticut Valley, where the maples and birches were just beginning to bud out, to his destination.[18]

Larger than Ludlow or Woodstock but smaller than Rutland, with a population of around seven thousand, St. Johnsbury was an impressive town. Young Coolidge, at any rate, was very much impressed by it. Granted, he saw it at a beautiful time of year, when May flowers were beginning to bloom and foliage was leafing out on the awesome elms that shaded the broad streets; but he also found it full of imposing houses, with a "beautiful" Congregational church and "the nicest [store] I ever saw." "The town is situated a great deal like Amherst," he explained to John a couple of days after his arrival, "the depot is down low and you come up the street to the hotel just the same." He did not mention the numerous fountains that dotted the town, or the brand-new system of electric street lights, though he did refer in a later letter to the brick sidewalks, and a park with a herd of tame deer that ate out of visitors' hands. All these amenities were due to the money of the Fairbanks family, who owned the scale factory on the river just outside town and lived in gleaming colonial houses on St. Johnsbury Plain, a sort of plateau above the river, where the academy also was located. Fairbanks money accounted for the uncanny serenity and quiet splendor that pervaded the town and often startled visitors from large cities. As one European observed, "Here are a dozen churches, public library, reading room, schools, and a lecture hall that will seat over a thousand people. Who, after this, would consider himself an exile if he had to live in St. Johnsbury?"[19]

Most important to Calvin, of course, were the arrangements for his schooling, and as soon as he got in to the train station he climbed the hill for an interview with the headmaster, Mr. Putney, who recommended that he take rooms on Main Street across from the academy. Calvin was delighted with the rooms; they had not only hot-air heating but a modern bathroom like the ones he had read of in magazines, with hot and cold running water. This may have been the first chance in his life to get acquainted with a flush toilet (itself a very recent invention), not to mention the chance to enjoy a hot bath without all the effort required at home. John had cautioned him about spending too much, so he took pains to ask around and make sure that the rent was not out of line.[20]

Putney promised him nothing with regard to graduation or a certificate. He would register as a senior and take the regular courses—Homer, Cicero, and a review of algebra—with the senior class. If his work was found satisfactory, he would graduate; the certificate would automatically follow. So on 15 April he began the regular routine of morning prayers at nine o'clock, classes until noon, and a Greek class after lunch, much the same as at B.R.A. The work was hard, but he went at it conscientiously. "I am full an average with the class here in Latin I think," he reported nervously to John in May, "in Greek I am an average in translation but insufficient in verb formation and grammatical construction somewhat." Putney himself, an exact grammarian, taught the classics; the algebra class, fortunately, was under Mr. Sherman's friend Audubon Hardy, who was inclined to be lenient.[21]

In many respects—its curriculum, its small faculty, its piety—St. Johnsbury was cut from the same educational pattern as B.R.A., but the resemblance was deceptive. St. Johnsbury was altogether larger, higher-powered, and more cosmopolitan. Its faculty was three times as large as that of B.R.A. The senior class contained seventy members to B.R.A.'s nine. No one there was from Ludlow or even from Windsor County. Most of the young men, and several of the young women, were planning to go on to college, the boys principally to Dartmouth. A few had Amherst in mind. Of the casual acquaintances Calvin struck up during his two-month stay there, several were with young men he would see again at college. In a way, though he was unaware of it, he had crossed an important divide by coming to St. Johnsbury. He was no longer in a good local institution, but rather in a good regional institution, among a very different group of contemporaries.[22]

Calvin had been at St. Johnsbury seven weeks when Mr. Putney called him into his office on the first floor of the academy building, a monumental brick structure with a tower, like B.R.A. but larger, with two grand brick-and-granite entrances, and told him he would receive a certificate. This good news was not totally unexpected: he had already told Calvin the week before, as Calvin reported it to John, that "he had never had any one come into the class so late that did as well as I have." It was a real achievement, his making good in this strict, competitive institution, and he was quietly proud of it; avoiding the appearance of boasting, he merely wrote his father, "I have not accomplished this without any effort." Not only that, but he would not have to attend graduation; at St. Johnsbury, unlike B.R.A., the ceremony was underplayed, and only a small part of the graduating class spoke. He would be able to come home as early as 19 June.[23]

His homecoming, nevertheless, was not a joyful or even a particularly pleasant occasion. It was raining as he arrived in Woodstock—good weather for the farmers, who had been complaining of drouth all spring, but not for the long ride home up the Ottauquechee Valley and Pinney Hollow. He had spoiled his return by letting his pocketbook, containing fifteen dollars cash, be stolen just three days before, while he was bathing. He had put the matter in the hands of the police (St. Johnsbury, modern in law enforcement as in everything else, had a police force), but without much hope. "I am very sorry and know I deserve much blame," he had written John stoically. John, moreover, had just lost the latest round in the unending Taylor lawsuit. A state circuit court judge had just ruled that the justice who had issued the warrant in 1885 had done so without statutory authority, that everything done subsequently by the town in the case had been illegal, and that therefore John owed Warren Taylor eighty dollars and costs. John cannot have been in a happy mood, nor can Calvin; probably the buggy ride from Woodstock to the Notch was even more silent than usual.[24]

All the same, it was pleasant to be home, knocking around John's house (oddly empty now without Abbie) and his grandmother's big, bare mansion. Grandmother Coolidge was happy; there would be regular preaching at the Notch Church this summer, and two Congregational missionaries were coming in September. Every other Sunday Calvin in his academy best sat beside John and Almeda in the pine-paneled sanctuary, faintly redolent of varnish and peppermint, listening to the sonorous Scriptures and the long Congregational prayers. (It is not clear who the preacher was or where he came from.) Weekdays, as it was hay season, he shucked his coat and tie and worked in the fields if John needed him; if not, he might go for one of his long, solitary rambles on horseback, or hunt up Dell Ward to go fish for bullpouts in the reservoir off the West Bridgewater road near where Dell lived, fighting off the mosquitoes that infested the woods. Later in the summer, Dell's cousins, the Gilson girls, would be coming up from Brooklyn to stay in a cottage by the reservoir. There were three of them, and each played a musical instrument; together and separately they gave entertainments throughout the summer. Calvin enjoyed their visits.[25]

Since it was summer, the new Echo Lake Inn was full of city visitors; wagonloads of excursionists from Woodstock might come through the Notch in the dusk laughing or singing, and there were parties of cyclists on weekends, including local boys like Herbert Moore, gliding down the road on their shining new Columbias. People got in their buggies and drove to the Fourth of July celebration at Ludlow despite the cloudy weather. There were lawn parties at the Notch church and baseball matches with West Bridgewater. Thousands of pounds of milk flowed into the cheese factory daily. More and more, John squired Carrie Brown everywhere. Calvin liked her; she was precise and kind, like a good teacher. She and John were to be married in September, just before he left for college. But amid the pleasant rituals of summer it was hard to imagine going to Amherst College again, much less becoming a student there this time.[26]

One special event late that summer of 1891 made it stand out in his mind. That year was the centennial of Vermont's statehood, and a proud time for many Vermonters, who ever since the Civil War had been feeling quietly smug about their state. The downfall of the Confederacy had proved the rightness of the Green Mountain way of life, thrift, industry, simplicity, and idealism, as against the extravagance, dissipation, and immorality of Southern culture. To celebrate, the state had commissioned a granite obelisk over three hundred feet high, comparable with the Washington Monument, to be erected on the site of the Revolutionary victory at Bennington. It was to be dedicated 19 August by a host of national and state officials, and thousands of patriotic Vermonters felt a duty to attend. The Central Vermont was running special trains to the dedication from all over the state. Even from tiny Plymouth almost a score of people were going, not only the professional war veterans like Levi Lynds, Chris Hall, and James Kavanagh who regularly marched at old soldiers' rallies, but town notables like Levi Moore of the Union and his wife Mary Ann, the town clerk, or Jim Ayer, Dell Ward's uncle and guardian, or farmer James Brown. The general stores at both the Notch and the Union would be closed for the occasion; both Levi Green and Les Walker were going. It is hardly surprising that John Coolidge and his son joined the party.[27]

Probably most or all of the Plymouth people went as a group. Some time early that morning, one can assume, they caught sight of the monument towering over the countryside as they approached by train. The day was clear and beautiful, an ideal Vermont summer morning, and perhaps they had time to puff up the iron steps inside the shaft and look out from the top over the thousands of visitors—thirty or forty thousand, estimates said—massed in the village for the occasion. Downtown Bennington was so jammed with visitors in their proper Sunday coats and collars that it looked like some New York City block on a festive occasion; and the arrangements for the long military parade at noon, which featured President Benjamin Harrison and Governor Page of Vermont, were as elaborate as those for a major city. There was a canvas-covered arch made to resemble hewn stone, so cunningly that it looked like the real thing, with carved patriotic mottoes and a live "Goddess of Liberty" in a golden throne on top, not to mention hundreds of electric lights outlining it. Here and there men were hawking "Ethan Allen Souvenir Spoons" as mementos of the day.[28]

What really interested Calvin was the oratory. There had been some speaking before the parade; there was more after the dinner in midafternoon, at which he, John, and over three thousand others sat under a tent and feasted on "consomme glace, salad of lobster, potatoes, sardines, dressed tomatoes, cold chicken, turkey, ham, lamb, tongue, veal, rolls, crackers, etc.," plus tea, coffee, and "a great variety of fancy ices." Three hundred young Bennington girls waited on the diners; the presidential party had its own black waiters. It was surely the most elaborate dinner he had ever been to. After dinner he could see President Harrison rise for his remarks, a physically unimpressive man, stout and short, with a full white beard. The president's high, melodious voice was a little scratchy: he had already spoken at length that morning. He repeated his praises for New England's institutions, Yankee schools, churches, town meetings, and God-fearing homes. "The love of social order and respect for laws which has characterized your communities," he declared, "has made them safe and comfortable abodes for your people." John, Calvin, and most of the audience no doubt caught the implied contrast: in the great cities, where there was no love of social order, people organized strikes, threw bombs, sold liquor, exploited the weak. Greed and ignorance reigned. But here in Vermont the flame of liberty still burned pure. People should be thankful that they lived in Vermont. Calvin was stirred, especially at hearing these praises from a man who, as he wrote years later, represented "the glory and dignity of the United States."[29]

After the speeches, when it grew dark, there were fireworks, spectacular ones: "sun-fire showers, electric flames, Japanese wheels, willow trees, exploding and contorting serpents, floating star-signals, changeable and magnesium lights in great variety," and then "Roman candles, massed in groups and sections about the grounds," and "golden fountains of the largest size, fired in unison, and producing the effect of living geysers of fire."[30]

Calvin's mind was running on fireworks and oratory as he boarded the train home. The cars were packed with drowsy celebrants and perhaps a few drunk ones; though Vermont was officially a prohibition state and this gathering generally respectable, there was always a tendency to overdo on these occasions. He settled into his seat to the accompaniment of snores from heavy bodies. He went back to thinking over the virtues of Vermont and the splendors of the day; it was certainly easier than thinking that a month from now he would be descending into the maelstrom of college, close to those scenes of social disorder. If he thought of this at all, he could hardly be blamed for fidgeting uneasily in his seat as the crowded train rattled toward Rutland.[31]

11

Into the Vortex

They stood, nervously alert, in front of the massive stone facade of Walker Hall—forty-five freshmen in coats and ties, the tight-fitting, drab men's clothing of 1891, many of them looking very young. Some had on derbies, but many wore the small beanie-type caps of newly pledged fraternity men. They stayed as still as they could while the photographer fiddled with his tripod and camera. Seven, mostly up front, held up pasteboard signs with the legend "'95", the year of their class's graduation. Most were looking directly into the camera as the shutter snapped, but on a higher step toward the rear of the group, one of the very few derby wearers, a slender figure in a dark suit, a book under his arm, stared seriously into the distance. The derby concealed his red hair, but the nose and jutting chin were prominent as ever. Coolidge was now on record as an Amherst man.[1]

There was good reason for the freshmen to be uneasy. What they dreaded was hearing a yell of "ninety-four!" and seeing a crowd of rampaging sophomores coming down the walk at them. Fierce conflict between the two lower classes was an accepted part of Amherst student life. Sophomores no longer "hazed" individual freshmen, so it was claimed (not quite accurately). But for the freshman class to try to do anything as a group, like having its picture taken in the middle of the campus on a fine October morning, was to invite a collision with the sophomores.[2]

There had already been at least one mass collision between the two classes, the traditional "cane rush" on the first Saturday night of the fall term. Much about the Amherst cane rush in the 1890s is a little hazy; originally, it seems, the sophomores had had the custom of carrying canes and not permitting any freshman to do so. The rivalry expressed itself in a series of small group encounters in which sophomores went after any freshman bold enough to sport a cane in public. (Two of the freshmen in the class picture, in defiance, displayed canes.) By the 1890s, however, these small encounters had been consolidated into one big, formal bout at the beginning of the term, held at night, by the light of flickering torches, between the college church and the chapel. The "cane" was now a long broom handle, and the object of the contest was to see which class had more hands on it after an eight-minute, no-holds-barred brawl. The classes waited, separated by a distance of several yards, while six men, three sophomores and three fresh-

The freshman picture of the Class of 1895. (Amherst College Archives)

men, laid their hands on the cane. Some impartial third party, probably an upperclassman, fired a pistol, and everyone plunged in. Instantly a "mass of fighting and yelling human beings," as one participant described it, formed around the cane, jammed to the point of suffocation, while combatants from outside the mass tried to make their way over the packed bodies and dive into the center. Fights broke out on the perimeter; one freshman recalled "los[ing] all native timidity and exchang[ing] blows with complete indifference to personal consequences." It was not unheard of for students to be carried away injured or unconscious. Most tried to come prepared for the scrap, in old clothes or football clothes. The more athletic students stripped down for the event, like boxers.[3]

Coolidge, with his distaste for physical contact and lacking any old clothes to sacrifice, was doubtless on the outskirts of the 1891 battle, watching as his classmates of 1895 struggled, grunted, cursed, and fought for the cane, particularly Theodore Penney, the strongest man in the class, "his shirt torn from him, his body bleeding and a finger broken." As usual, the sophomores, with their extra year of experience, won, but for the class of 1895 it was a bonding experience; as Coolidge recalled four years later, "We lost the rush, but we found our class spirit."[4]

But in October of 1891, it was far from obvious that Coolidge had found his. Like his pose in the class picture, his stance at the edge of the cane rush epitomized his relationship with the rest of the freshman class: he was there, but isolated, somehow different from the rest. It was not a wilful, self-imposed isolation; on the contrary, whenever his class gathered, the fiery-haired freshman from Vermont was there. In chapel, every weekday morning at eight-thirty, he sat with the freshman class in the gallery, in his alphabetically assigned slot between Isaac Mayhew Compton, an awkward, bumptious ninny from rural New Jersey, and Frank (Jeff) Davis, a breezy, athletic fraternity man from Minneapolis, and listened to fifteen minutes' worth of stock piety while looking down on the heads of the upperclassmen. (According to Amherst tradition, 1891 was the year in which the sophomores varnished all the freshmen's seats in chapel one night in hopes of embarrassing them publicly, but were foiled when the freshman learned of the plot and brought newspapers to sit on. Coolidge, however, mentioned no such incident in his letters home, nor does any other contemporary source.)[5]

With the other freshman, he took part four afternoons a week in another traditional Amherst ritual, the compulsory gymnasium drill. Under the leadership of the humane, magnificently eccentric Edward Hitchcock ("Old Doc," he was called), a generation before, Amherst had been the first college in the United States to make physical education a major part of its program. The idea, as Hitchcock explained to the freshmen in his famous health lectures, was to promote physical fitness as an aid to learning, improving bodily health so that the mind could learn more readily. Over the years the drill, organized by classes, had become a central part of Amherst college life, and the Pratt Gymnasium, built in 1884 at the south end of the campus, was an imposing brick-and-brownstone shrine of physical culture unlike anything Coolidge could have seen in Vermont. It had steam heat, cold shower baths (or "sprays," as they were called), punching bags and exercise rings hanging from the rafters, parallel bars, a locker room (though the term was not yet in use in the 1890s) and a 208-foot indoor track encircling the main hall on an upper level. It was on the cutting edge of college education in 1891 and was immensely popular with Amherst students, most of whom came there to work out daily even when there was no required activity.[6]

The friendly aura the gymnasium presented was due mainly to Old Doc Hitchcock, who had invented the drill. Short, bearded, and spry despite his sixty-three years, he was a constant benign presence in the building, constantly popping out of his first-floor office to watch the proceedings even when not actively engaged, usually wearing a black skullcap and carrying a notebook. His Yankee twang, his obvious enjoyment of young men's high spirits, and his almost compulsive frankness won over most Amherst students immediately. Certainly they conquered Coolidge; two days into the term he had already written his father and stepmother all about "good Old Doc" and his fatherly manner. Hitchcock was also counselor for students with financial, disciplinary, or personal problems—in short, almost the whole student body—and, as one of his assistants said, saw a good deal of the "seamy side of human nature." He had a massive research project going in the field he called anthropometry, which would later be included in physical anthropology, charting the physical growth and development of young males. At the beginning of every year, every Amherst man was called to Pratt Gymnasium, stripped, and was measured in fifty-five different ways by the doctor and his assistants, including weight, girth of head, neck, chest, belly, and hips, height to knees, to crotch, to navel, to breastbone, and total height, length of arms, breadth of shoulders, distance between nipples, lung capacity, vision, number of pushups completed, and "general pilosity" or hairiness. The findings were used to counsel the young men about needed exercise, changes in diet, glasses and so forth; they went into Hitchcock's anthropometric tables; and they were summarized in the *Student*, the college newspaper. Thus, in December members of the class of 1895 could learn, if they did not already know, that Ernest ("Fat") Hardy was, at 191 pounds, the heaviest man in the class, or that Henry S. Lane could do the most pushups in one minute—twenty. Coolidge could see that his five-foot-nine height was about average for the class, but that in weight he was near the bottom, with only 120 pounds.[7]

Hitchcock had borrowed the movements for the drill from Upton's Infantry Tactics, adding several touches of his own. One was the piano, played (in the class of 1895) by "Bish" Bishop, a waggish freshman from Minnesota. To the sound of a lively march or galop, the freshmen, in platoons under the command of their class officers, drilled on Monday, Tuesday, Thursday and Friday afternoons. The dark blue flannel "gym" suits they wore—baggy shirts and loose pants bearing the class number, 95—anticipated the later sweat suit. From racks around the sides of the main hall each man took down a pair of one-and-one-quarter pound rock maple dumbbells, and the class as a whole began a series of complex exercises, raising, lowering, extending, touching the dumbbells in time to the music. The exercise lasted half an hour, long enough to work up a good sweat, and often when it ended some freshmen, tired of the monotony, shied their dumbbells across the hardwood floor, persuaded Bishop to strike up a waltz or two-step, popular dances of the day, and did some mock ballroom exercises on their own until Old Doc came out to order them to the showers, with his passionate "Gentlemen, gentlemen!" Old Doc had a wonderful tolerance for disorder, and even in his presence the class could seem like "a boisterous group of howling dervishes." Later in the fall, when he was out sick for a few weeks, freshman drill collapsed totally; "we don't do much but yell and get out the blanket and toss up some of the boys," Coolidge wrote his stepmother.[8]

He attended freshman drill faithfully, despite his distaste for hard exercise, because it was his duty, part of the course. For the same reason, he was at every class meeting, though he scarcely participated. The freshmen as a body met in the chapel several times during the year, to elect officers, arrange the class dinner, and select class athletic teams. Lacking the enforced silence of morning prayers or the enforced activity of gym drill, these meetings provided a better opportunity for a freshman to size up the other boys in his class, to get some idea of their characteristics as a group. Young Coolidge must have noticed, for instance, that despite his delayed entrance into college he was about the same age as the rest of his class. He was by no means the oldest; there were several men in their twenties. He stood out in another way, however, being one of only four or five redheads in the class. Probably his most striking discovery was that students like himself, unassuming eighteen- or nineteen-year-olds from small towns in New England, were a slight minority. The majority, who set the tone for the class and the college, were sons of well-to-do families in the large Northeastern cities, particularly New York and Brooklyn (still two separate cities in 1890), or occasionally from Western business centers like Chicago, St. Louis, and Minneapolis; they were sleek, well-educated, sophisticated young men from a wholly different background.[9]

To Calvin, with his experience of town-meeting democracy, it must have been obvious from the first meeting, when officers were elected, that certain freshmen were running the show and that others, himself included, had almost no voice in the proceedings. These dominant freshmen, it turned out, were all fraternity men; indeed, the election of class officers was basically a contest between rival alliances of fraternities. Coached by the upperclassmen in their houses, the fraternity pledges managed to take all the offices. Dick Lane, back in March, had been right: the societies were "a great factor" at Amherst, virtually all-important. That was the other striking statistic about the class of '95: they were fraternity men. By the end of October, of the ninety-seven freshmen all but thirteen had pledged a secret society. Coolidge was one of the thirteen.[10]

Taken together, these two measures, the social background of the students and the percentage of fraternity members in the class, signaled a far-reaching change that had begun overtaking Amherst in the 1880s and was still far from complete at the time of Coolidge's entrance. Young Coolidge may or may not have recognized it, but the fact is that the Amherst College he had entered was substantially different from the Amherst his patron and teacher, George Sherman, had attended only ten years before. In 1880, about half of the student body had belonged to one of the Greek-letter societies; by 1890, the figure had climbed to eighty percent. Most Amherst graduates of the early 1880s had become teachers or preachers, as Amherst men had traditionally done; by the early 1890s, a majority were instead going into law or business.[11]

These changes, in turn, were the product of several converging trends. For one thing, the growing industrial and commercial wealth of the Gilded Age was generating numerous good jobs in law and business; for another, among

businessmen and professionals a college education was beginning to be accepted as a desirable prelude to a business career. Even though it taught
nothing about business as such, the polish it supplied conferred a certain
status. In addition, the traditional professions were losing their prestige. In
New England, the controversies surrounding the Darwinian theory and the
rise of critical religion made the ministry less and less influential every year;
many young men had an increasingly hard time believing Christian doctrines, and even for those who did, the cloth seemed a less desirable calling
than it once had. In short, a revolution in values was sweeping Amherst College, especially among the students. Religion, solitary prayer and soul-
searching, ascetic simplicity, and the search for abstract truth were being
replaced by the genial values of respect for wealth, success in competition,
cordial friendliness and team spirit, and elegant display.[12]

The anonymous student author of the poem "Some Ideals," published in
the college newspaper during Coolidge's freshman year, had a sure grasp of
the things that mattered to the new breed of Amherst student:

> To be a College gymnast, that is grand;
> To be an athlete known throughout the land
> Is better still.
> To play at ball, both foot and base,
> And in the hare and hounds to race
> Is just my will.
>
> To be a banjo player, there's the rub;
> To be a singer traveling with the club
> Is greater fame.
> To play at chess or with the cue,
> To be at whist surpassed by few
> Is just my aim.
>
> To be an earnest student, there's a bore....[13]

The nine Greek-letter societies were already a well-established part of
campus life when this revolution began. Amherst had historically been far
more hospitable to them than some other colleges; as late as 1888 the president had endorsed them as promoters of academic excellence and manly
character, and several faculty members, Old Doc among them, were spon-
sors or members of particular societies. They were the first on campus to
reflect the new values. As more and more affluent students came from the
seaboard cities, with their eyes on worldly status rather than on eternal
Truth, they gravitated to the societies, who welcomed them and used their
money and sophistication to create a new sort of Amherst style: urbane,
mannerly, supercilious about the religious values that had been central to
the old Amherst, frankly interested in secular success. The keen competi-

tion between them for college offices and honors reflected less a love of scholarship than a desire for status, a drive to boost their organizations.[14]

A quick stroll around Amherst gave a clear idea of the wealth and influence of the fraternities. All of them occupied imposing houses near the college, built or bought during the 1880s. The Alpha Delta Phi house, on Pleasant Street facing the Common, was probably more splendid than any college building—classroom, administration, library, even the gymnasium. Built in 1890 in Georgian style, with a granite and brick facade, it had electric light, elegant oak furniture, banquet and reading rooms, and living quarters large enough so that many of the brothers could bring pianos from home for their suites. One could practically call it a little bit of Manhattan; as a later historian of the college said, it "set a new standard of costliness in Amherst."[15]

Granted, the Alpha Delts were in a class by themselves when it came to money; even the individual brothers tended to "dress up." But other societies, even though they occupied frame houses, were close behind. The Psi Upsilon house next door, with its spacious rooms, had previously housed the president of the college. The Beta Theta Pi house across the Common, big and rambling, with a wide piazza on which the brothers used to gather to smoke, play their mandolins, and sing, displayed, according to one writer, "several independent styles of architecture, among which predominated, but without much conviction, what might be called the Franco-American style of 1880." Both the Chi Phis and the Chi Psis, the latter the smallest and rowdiest of the nine societies, had built new houses during the 1880s. The Delta Upsilon house on Pleasant Street, and probably most of the others, had a billiard table. The Dekes' house was big enough for them to stage a minstrel show.[16]

Every member of the class of 1895 had an opportunity to get into one of the societies. Eager to outdo one another in prestige, the societies recruited actively among each year's new freshmen. The process, which was later known as "rushing" at many colleges (it was not yet named in 1891; most often it was referred to by the military-political metaphor of the "campaign"), began even before school officially opened. Members of each society, all urbanity and polish, awaited freshmen arriving at Amherst's two train stations (the New London & Northern where Calvin had arrived and the Massachusetts Central on South Pleasant Street), accosted them, and made appointments for them to interview the brothers at the house as soon as possible. Often they even spoke to likely-looking newcomers on the train before arriving at Amherst. As an 1890 account had it, every "freshman who gave any indication of having a solitary natural ability was hurriedly siezed [sic] upon and treated with all honor and respect due a governor." At the house, a dozen or more of the members spoke with each candidate, scrutinized his clothes and his manners, and tried to decide whether he repre-

sented a potential asset. Quite often the competition for especially
desirable prospects was keen, but when the dust settled, the great majority
of freshmen had been invited to join.[17]

There were probably a handful of students who deliberately avoided the
process and became "oudens" (from the Greek word for "nothing") by
choice. In Coolidge's class, for instance, twenty-nine-year-old Fred Gray
may have considered himself a little old for late-adolescent power games.
Harlan Stone of the class of 1894 thought fraternities "a rather artificial
way of forming friendships" and ignored the bids he received. Others perhaps forewent fraternity membership because of the expense: there were
initiation fees and assessments, as well as pressure to buy all sorts of expensive society jewelry. "As the men wear them all their lives," a breathless
freshman Alpha Delt wrote his mother a few years later, "it is imperative
that they should get as nice ones as they can afford. A pin with whole pearls
and a genuine emerald costs twenty-five dollars *at the least*."[18]

In most cases, however, including Coolidge's, it was style, or rather the
lack of it, that accounted for a man's failure to be invited to join a society.
The smooth young urbanites at the core of each fraternity scanned their
fellow students' clothes, their speech, their attitudes, their eating habits
for telltale signs of anything rural or "common": in the words of one, "the
scent of the farmyard." They rejected those who seemed too countrified,
"too natural, too animal-like," as one New Yorker put it. A freshman of
modest attainments like Coolidge, with his Vermont twang and peculiar
habit of sitting silent as though tongue-tied, was to them, as one classmate
put it in retrospect, merely "a sandy-haired boy with freckles and trousers
which [did] not come down to his shoes." His seatmate "Jeff" Davis, the
fraternity man par excellence, called him "unattractive and uncouth."
Apparently most of the fraternity men who talked with him shared that impression; he did not receive a single invitation.[19]

It must have been painful for Calvin, who had spent five years at Ludlow
quietly living up to his ideal of village elegance and propriety, to come to
Amherst and discover that he was now dismissed as a hayseed. So were
most of his fellow oudens in the class of '95; with only one exception, they
shared Calvin's rural background. Most were homely or awkward or both,
and three of them, Compton, a local boy named Fairbanks, and another
named Booth, were to become the perennial butts of class humor for the
next four years. But not Coolidge.[20]

Not belonging to a society put severe constraints on an Amherst man's
social life. He saw very little of his classmates who belonged once classes
were over; their time was taken up with society activities. The fraternities
generated most of Amherst's formal social life. For example, on Mountain
Day, a college holiday during October, some of them hired stagecoaches
and took their members on all-day excursions, often to one of the nearby
female colleges. On Tuesday night, "Goat Night," all freshmen had to be

in their fraternity houses for various rituals, and often on other nights they had specific things to do. Even in their free time they tended to run with their fraternity brothers. Oudens, therefore, had to socialize with each other.[21]

Calvin's lodgings put him at an extra disadvantage here; he was the only freshman in the house where he roomed, Mr. Trott's, far down Pleasant Street near the Massachusetts Central bridge. In fact, he and his roommate, Alfred Turner, were the only two students. Trott's was a solitary two-story brick house with peculiar pointed windows, roughly across the street from the house Albert Weaver had kept the preceding year. (Neither of the Weavers, father nor son, had returned.) Calvin had not originally intended to room there, or to have a roommate at all, but sixty dollars for half of a double room seemed the best deal he could find— though, according to the college handbook, it was on the expensive side.[22]

Parenthetically, there was no question of his rooming in a college dormitory in 1891. The Amherst administration, unwilling to truckle to the new student taste for creature comforts, had refused to remodel the old college buildings on the crest of the ridge, North College and South College. By 1890 even the neediest students could hardly be induced to stay in their chilly, spartan cells, with their ambience of, say, 1850. Practically all Amherst students lived off campus, a great many of them in the fraternity houses, where a man and his "chum" or "wife" (college slang for roommate) could have a room in the approved late-Victorian-collegiate-clutter style, with steam heat, gas or electric lighting, a bay window and window seat for lounging, shelves of pipes and knickknacks, afghans draped across tabletops and chests, hangings in purple and white (Amherst colors), and a closet full of suits, sweaters, and tennis outfits. In 1891, under the leadership of a new college administration, remodeling finally began.[23]

Coolidge and Turner's room, by fraternity standards, was monastic: kerosene-lit, drafty in cold weather, and sparingly furnished. (It was heated by a stove that burned wood or coal, which they bought themselves; they also supplied their own kerosene and bedclothes.) The two got along well— Turner, a Massachusetts-born junior whose family now lived in Rutland, struck Calvin as "a good fellow"—but their interests were different. Turner was an athlete, college champion in the hammer throw, who spent a lot of time in the gym and the darkroom there (he was also in the Camera Club). Calvin, terrified of failing in his studies, spent most of his time at his desk. In his spare moments he was conscious of his isolation. "I am in a pleasant place and like [it] very much," he wrote his father, "but suppose I shall like [it] better as [I] become better acquainted, I don't seem to get acquainted very fast however." To his new stepmother he was more direct: "I have not seen much of the pleasant side of college life yet, I don't think I am enjoying myself as well as I do at home."[24]

It was probably because Turner was an athlete that Calvin formed the

habit of going out to all college athletic events, yet another area in which
he stood faithfully beside his classmates but not really among them. Nothing in his background had prepared him to enjoy or appreciate these
contests at Pratt Field, only a couple of blocks from his lodgings, on
Northampton Road. Two different kinds of contests were held there: intramural matches, like the October "Cider Meet" in which the three lower
classes competed in track and field events, with the prize a keg of cider,
and intercollegiate competition (football in the fall, baseball and track in
the spring). Historically, the intramurals had been the important matches,
but in the new metropolitan-oriented Amherst of the 1890s they were being
eclipsed by the intercollegiate events, especially football, which was surging
in popularity though baseball remained important too.[25]

Probably the first athletic event Calvin attended was the "Cider Meet" on
14 October. In all likelihood he had never seen a track meet before, and the
pole vault, broad jump, shot put and the like, though they had some affinity
with the contests sometimes held at Fourth of July celebrations in Vermont,
were new to him, as were the athletes in shorts. The events themselves were
easy enough to understand, however, and he enjoyed the meet. (Turner
took first place in both the hammer throw and the pole vault.) His rather
vague report of it to John reveals his lack of a vocabulary for talking about
athletics: "The sports went off very well yesterday, but they tell me it was
not much of a day, that is the sports were not carried out so well as usual."[26]

Football must have been a complete mystery to him. Baseball was popular
in Ludlow with both students and townspeople, but football was something
played only at colleges, and the game as it was played in 1891 probably
looked even stranger to him than it would to a late-twentieth-century spectator. It was a sport in the throes of rapid change: numerical scoring had
been introduced only seven years before, and there was no scoreboard on
most fields; offensive blocking had been legal for only three years; there
was no forward pass, no substitution, no time out; and most important,
there was no coaching to speak of. "We were trained mainly for endur-
ance," a Princeton player of this era recalled. "We had no great strategy."
Some things about the game were the same as in modern football: there
were eleven men to a side, who wore heavy shoes, shin guards, padded trousers and jerseys—no helmets, however; there was a quarterback, a snap
from center, a field goal (although the field goal then counted five points,
one point more than a touchdown); and there was passionate involvement
among the spectators—"students will not keep behind the lines during
foot-ball games," the college newspaper complained. To a newcomer like
Calvin, it must have seemed a gigantic brawl; and indeed, at times it was.
"I witnessed two important games between Yale and Princeton in 1890 and
1891," a contemporary recalled, "when at least twenty minutes of the ninety
were devoted to battles between linemen." Young Coolidge, totally be-
mused, tried to make sense of what he was seeing: "to and fro, hammer

and hit, kick and return ... battering-ram work in the center of the field," as a contemporary writer described it. Though he didn't understand the game, he had paid three dollars for his season ticket from the Football Association, and he attended regularly. Bert Pratt of the class of '95, one of the few freshmen on the team, a devoted athlete from the same family that had donated money for the field, had little use for nonathletes but did notice who came to the games. He remembered Coolidge's consistently following the team "in his own quiet way."[27]

The great football event of 1891, which Coolidge attended, did not involve the Amherst team at all. It was the Harvard–Yale game, played at Hampden Park in nearby Springfield. Enthusiasm for it was not limited to graduates of the two colleges involved; people came to it from all over New England, especially college students and alumni, on a sort of athletic pilgrimage. "Among the thousands of graduates and undergraduates from Yale and Harvard there were scattered hundreds from smaller colleges," the Springfield paper reported the day after the game, "and it was as much a day of reunion for graduates of the smaller institutions as of the larger." It seems to have had some of the social cachet that would belong to, say, a polo or lacrosse match in late-twentieth-century America—a sporting event for the elite.[28]

Coolidge was among the 150 Amherst students who came down to the game on three passenger cars of a special train from Northampton. The trip furnished more than one new experience for him: not only was it his first major sports event, it was also his first venture into the real industrial heart of the United States. As the train chugged south from Northampton, the little city west of Amherst on the Connecticut River that served as an urban center for Amherst students, it passed the Holyoke Range of mountains, lonely and impressive, on the east. These were, in effect, the last outriders of the New England mountains. South of them lay the large manufacturing complex of Springfield and its satellite towns, Holyoke and Chicopee, smoky and crowded, with acres of brick and frame tenements, narrow streets, Catholic churches, electric wires, and large factories with high smokestacks. It was not quite New York or Chicago. There were no tall buildings yet, just an expanse of city blocks where all the houses were three stories high. There was no single dominant industry; it was an area of many different manufactures. As the train entered Springfield, for instance, it passed the spacious railroad-car plant of the Wason Manufacturing Company. Springfield was not that big, only about forty-five thousand in population. Still, it was by far the largest place Calvin had seen.[29]

Just as the train drew level with Hampden Park, a big, rather seedy racetrack-and-grandstand complex surrounded by a board fence, quite reminiscent of the Windsor County fairgrounds at Woodstock, it stopped dead for no apparent reason (the paper next day said that a cylinder head had broken in the locomotive); the Amherst boys, jumping from their cars, charged directly across the tracks and made their way over the fence to join the enormous crowd. Calvin followed along.[30]

It was certainly the largest crowd he had seen. "[T]here were many more people there than I ever saw at a circus and seated on benches going clear around the field," he wrote John. The Harvard side seemed a solid mass of crimson flags and clothes, the Yale side an equally spectacular array of blue. The atmosphere was even noisier and more excited than that of a circus. He had arranged to meet Dick Lane and George Raymond there—Lane a Middlebury man, Raymond a Tufts graduate—and somehow managed to find them, as well as seeing several boys he had known at St. Johnsbury. Probably he paid only intermittent attention to the game, the "shrill penny whistle" of the referee, and the strange classical cheer from the Yale stands, borrowed from Aristophanes: "Bre-ke-ke-kex, co-ax, co-ax!" He did know the final score: Yale 10, Harvard 0. Some idea of the atmosphere, however, can be gained from the comments of Betty Cutter, a Smith student who attended the game the following year and probably knew little more about football than Coolidge: "There was the open field in front of us and those men tumbling over each other with reckless disregard of life and limb.... I don't know much about football, but I knew enough yesterday afternoon to be wildly excited.... It was thrilling though awful to see Harvard's best man carried off the field...and then to think that his collar-bone was broken his ankle sprained and his leg in the same condition!" (There were no injuries, miraculously, in 1891.) And after Yale won: "Every particle of dignity was gone; men jumping up and down for joy, hugging each other, and cheering like mad."[31]

This was the most exciting of his diversions. Generally they were more sedate and involved merely passive observation. He had a season ticket to the college lecture series and attended regularly. Occasionally he would take in a show at Town Hall (in November a company put on "The Gondoliers," Gilbert and Sullivan's new operetta), or even take a train to "Hamp," as Amherst students called Northampton, for a performance at the Academy of Music, returning on the late or "drunk" train to Amherst. He also enjoyed gazing at the autumn leaves. During Thanksgiving break, which he spent in Amherst, scared to miss a recitation by taking time to travel home, he walked around town and went up the old chapel tower to take in the long view across the Connecticut Valley. He could see Northampton seven miles away, he wrote his stepmother, even the buildings in Smith College.[32]

Most of the time, however, he was not out observing, but studying, studying as though his life was at stake. "I do not suppose I know anything of college life," he wrote John in September, "but can say it more than meets my expectations in the large amount of work required. I recite 16 hours a week besides chapel, lectures and gymnasium." Initially he felt able to handle it, but as the term went on he became less sure. "We have to study pretty hard here to get along," he wrote Carrie B. Coolidge in October. "I used to suppose a man in college did not have to do much to get through but I see now that he does." The farther he went, the worse it seemed to get. "Winter is the time we do hard work," he reported home in November. "I heard one of my professors tell one of my class the other day that his winter work just took the life right out of the boys."[33]

Apart from classwork, he took part in nothing. His singleminded concentration on work, his leisurely walking across the campus always with a book or notebook in hand, his seeming disinterest in casual conversation, suggested the unpopular Amherst type of the "plugger," the student who sat "from morn till late at night, / His eye upon the page," as a bit of college-yearbook verse had it, in an effort to impress others with his superior grades. Calvin did study hard. He rose usually between seven and eight o'clock, by his or Turner's alarm clock, in time to prepare for breakfast and chapel, and often stayed up late enough to hear the chapel bell at midnight. The problem was that his work was not that superior. It was always adequate, but rarely more. The classmate who called his grades "moderate" was correct; to one professor, he was the classic B student.[34]

Other students who knew him only slightly (and no one knew him well at this time) automatically classed him with the "poor boys," country students of limited financial means who typically worked part-time in college boarding houses to earn money for tuition and avoided other activities because they had no time for anything but study and work. But here again, he failed to fit the stereotype: no one ever saw him working at a job; his clothes, though not the latest cut, were appropriate and well kept; he did not seem to need financial help.[35]

In sum, to most of his classmates, Coolidge was a "puzzle," "a perfect enigma," when they thought about him at all. "He was tall, thin, somber, usually alone," one of them recalled. "A drabber, more colorless boy I never knew," said another. Most of the time his classmates simply ignored him. His obscurity was, in its way, striking. In his first two years at Amherst, he was the only man in his class not mentioned in the student newspaper, in any context, at any time.[36]

One other man in his class knew him slightly, according to one classmate's recollections: a Massachusetts country boy named Royal Booth. Booth was blond, handsome, and eager, but also very rustic and not very bright, which was doubtless why he had failed to get into any of the societies. His good looks made him conspicuous; a poem in the following year's annual would mockingly describe him as a "remarkable youth" who was "fair but uncouth." He had passed the entrance examination with a host of conditions, extra work he had to make up, and now was working doggedly, morning to night, trying to stay in school. Calvin, who was doing nearly the same thing, befriended him and gave him what help he could spare. This was the only friendship he had time for. "[I]t worries me to be behind much," he wrote John.[37]

In the midst of his studying, like any freshman, he looked forward to winter vacation and a chance to get home—in his case, with a little more longing than most, to escape a place where he felt inadequate and rejected. "In just one month I will be at home," he wrote his father on 22 November. He watched anxiously for the first snowfall, which came at the end of November, late by Vermont standards. As winter weather set in, his room at Trott's got colder and draftier, and prolonged study uncomfortable. (He also had to put up with loud snores from the Trotts, whose room was next to his and Turner's.) Finally, in December, came the end of the fall term, two-hour examinations in all his courses—he had no idea whether his work had been good enough—and a quick departure for Ludlow on the afternoon train. He carried only a small bag of clothes as he waited at the New London depot, with the other Vermont boys who were homeward bound, for the northbound train to puff laboriously up the incline as it always did, belching dense clouds of wood smoke. Maybe he would see some of his friends in Ludlow; he had written Rufus Hemenway several times but had gotten no answer. A couple of hours later he stepped down into the dark Ludlow station yard and rejoiced to see the face of Elwin Bailey, John's hired man, or Len Willis, the blacksmith's son, who had come with the buggy to pick him up. There was scarcely more snow on the ground than there had been in Massachusetts. An hour or so after that he alighted at his house, kissed John on the lips as was his custom, and carried his bag inside.[38]

There are no specific memories of this vacation, but one can imagine the warm interiors, the glittering community Christmas tree, the lamplit homes, maybe a kitchen dance, his affectionate grandmother, and the quiet of the Notch countryside. One important thing apparently did happen: some time during this vacation, Calvin got up nerve to speak to John about Amherst. He did not want to go back. He pleaded to be allowed to stay in Plymouth, farming or clerking at the store. It was a mirror image of their conversation six years earlier, when he had begged to be sent to school in Ludlow. Now he had reached the limit of his capacity, he felt; he was ready to come back to Plymouth and work. He had the necessary business sense, he thought; he was a close observer of people and knew commercial law. Sometimes he offered his father advice on his finances. He was familiar with farm economy, could keep the books on raising an animal or figure the probable yield of maple sugar (his favorite subject) from year to year. John, unreceptive, put him on the 6 January noon train back to Amherst.[39]

The ride back, through falling snow, was like the first grim journey to Amherst over a year before, only worse. That night, alone at his desk in his frigid room at Trott's, so deep in blind misery that he failed to finish his name at the close of the letter, Calvin wrote his father:

> I hate to think I must stay here 12 weeks before I can go home again. I think I must be very home-sick my hand trembles so I can't write so any one can read it.

It is just 7 o'clock I wonder if you are most home there is some snow here but it has stopped snowing now....

Each time I get home I hate to go away worse than before and I don't feel so well here now as the first day I came here last fall but suppose I will be all right in a day or two.

Let me hear from you as soon as you can

With Love, J Calvin Coolidg[40]

12

The Sophisticate

The mood passed over in a day or two: Turner came back from Rutland with projects for rearranging their rooms to keep the cold air out; recitations got under way Thursday morning, only a few at first because so many men still had some of last term's work to complete. The weather turned still colder—two below zero, Calvin heard someone say.[1]

Most important, in the first week after his return his grades for the fall term arrived, in the form of stiff-paper cards printed over the signature of the Registrar, Edward B. Marsh (or "Swampy," as he was universally known in the college). The format was brief and precise: "Your rank for last term is _____. Your average for the course thus far is _____." The marks were reckoned on a five-unit scale, in which five represented 100 percent, or perfection; in practice, it was never awarded. Four signified "excellence," three "satisfactory work," two "low passing," and one "complete failure." To Calvin's relief, he had "pulled a two"—he had passed everything. Indeed, he may have done better than that. The peculiar Amherst marking system gave no credit for fractional marks: a mark of two might represent a 50 percent performance, the lowest passing mark, or it might represent 73 percent or 74 percent; only at the level of 75 percent did the mark go up to three. But the important thing was that he had avoided failure in the eyes of his family and the few students who knew him. Now all he had to do was to explain the grade to his father ("probably not a man in the class got a 4, the marks seem pretty low don't they.")[2]

Strangely, the class that had contributed most to keeping his grade up was mathematics, the dreaded algebra. There he had been fortunate enough to run into one of the best Amherst teachers of that era, George Olds, who was also in his first year. Short, sandy-haired, and unprepossessing, with a scraggly little mustache, Olds had an unusual ability to make figures interesting, and an uncommon warmth and interest in his students. He had first put Calvin at his ease by calling on him, early in the term, as "my red-headed brother in the second row." Students who were above average in the subject thought highly of him too. Dwight Morrow, a freshman from Pittsburgh who excelled in mathematics, wrote his parents enthusiastically, "The finest professor we have is the math. man—and he is a daisy." By midterm Calvin had come to think of the big, dim classroom in Walker Hall, with its feeble

136

gas jets and the enormous blackboard covered with graphs and calculations, as a place where he could do well. On the final exam his paper was one of the three best—a real testimony to Olds's ability to overcome what modern teachers would call "math anxiety." The performance entitled him to move up to the "rank" class, the first division, which would be formed for the winter term. But Olds would not be teaching that class, and Calvin turned down the opportunity. "I do not care to be in the first division," he wrote John, "for we have the same Prof. as last term and he makes all so plain I do not want to leave him."[3]

The classes that had caused him the most worry during fall term were the ones that had been his best at B.R.A., Latin and Greek. Both met in Johnson Chapel, in the afternoon. Levi Elwell, the professor of freshman Greek, was a bearded man in his late thirties who acted like a crochety old codger twice his age, going off on tirades about nothing in particular, punctuating his sentences with a dry, hacking cough, as if he were perpetually trying to clear his throat. His way of teaching was numbingly repetitive: set translation by the students in a fixed order, without comment. The reputation he was to leave at Amherst was that of a professor who could take the *Odyssey*, his text for the fall term, and make it dull. His students, Coolidge included, cannot have been sorry when it was announced that he was leaving for a midwinter Mediterranean vacation.[4]

His replacement, however, was no better: Henry Gibbons, the new sophomore Greek instructor, who took Euripides's *Alcestis* as his text but whose real mania, on which he spent an inordinate amount of time, was Greek word derivations. His teaching was memorably disorganized, and his classes, variously described as a farce, a circus, or an adventure, were punctuated by his frequent explosions of ill temper. In his classes, where it was never quite clear what material was supposed to be learned, the more conscientious students generally suffered most. William Boardman, a classmate of Coolidge's from St. Johnsbury and a first-rate classical student, regarded getting through "Gibbie's" Greek class as one of the major accomplishments of his Amherst career.[5]

"Eph" Wood, the professor of freshman Latin, about the same age as Elwell and Gibbons, in his midthirties, was better organized than Gibbons and a good scholar in his field, but cutting and unsympathetic in class. He was a professor students loved to hate. They caricatured his staring eyes and heavy glasses, his peculiar walk, his tendency to preen just a little too much in matters of dress. His class somewhat resembled a relay race, with one man after another standing up to recite and being "flunked"—asked to sit down for inadequate performance or poor preparation—often with some sarcastic comment at his expense. Eph was finicky about details, and so critical of students' performance that his blue-penciled prose composition papers, one Amherst student remarked, could pass for maps of the new New York City rapid transit system. Students dreaded seeing his penciled

"In view of this flunk, you will please to consult me later," at the foot of a written assignment. A student like Calvin, with his fear of ridicule and exposure, must have dreaded Wood's class in particular, although the material included his favorite Latin author, Cicero. The difficulties experienced by other, better students like (again) his friend Boardman disheartened him. "Prof Wood told me I was in the first 12 of my division in my last exam.," he wrote John in November, "that don't amount to much." Eph had the knack of making even his better students feel incompetent.[6]

Professors like Elwell, Gibbons, and Wood were both a cause and a symptom of what was happening in the 1890s to the teaching of Latin and Greek. The prestige of the ancient languages was plummeting, not only in Amherst but across the nation. Fewer and fewer students perceived them as the keys to absolute Truth, revealed in the Scriptures and in the ancient authors; more awarded that role either to natural science with its experimental certainty or to the new cluster of social sciences and philosophy. Latin and Greek were coming to seem mere obstacles, "drudgery" to be surmounted one way or another before a man got on to the real business of getting an education, and their professors tiresome, irrelevant pedants who stood at the door of the academic establishment and kept students out. As the perceived importance of the classics declined, the classicists' exactitude came to seem finicky and obstructive, their passion for the subject boringly eccentric. At Amherst, moreover, this change coincided with the larger shift in student population and values from the views of Puritan New England to those of the urban Northeastern upper class. By 1900, the classics had lost their primacy at Amherst and had come to be seen as secondary, dull subjects.[7]

In the circumstances, it was not surprising that classes in Latin and Greek were charades. "Some time ago, in spring it was," began a poem about J. Sitlington Sterrett, another sophomore professor of Greek, "Pa Sterrett bored us all / To death in Greek about some quirk." Another, about Professor William S. Tyler, started, "The class in Greek was going on: Old Ty his lecture read." Students dozed, ate candy, or surreptitiously read popular magazines, paying as little attention as possible to the material; those who had penknives amused themselves carving names, fraternity emblems, and occasional epithets on the seats, or pried the cardboard pads off the writing surfaces and threw them at other students when the professor was not looking. Those who could afford to do so got through the classes by using "cribs" or "horses," prepared translations of the classic texts, although the practice was anathema to the professors and could cause serious trouble if detected. Most students cut class up to the allowed limit, one-tenth of the total number of meetings; those who overcut were assigned still more translation as punishment. A student in this situation might well hire another, better student to do the assignment for him. If Coolidge had been thinking of majoring in the classics, which he had enjoyed so at B.R.A., classes like these went far to change his mind. In the end, he took only the minimum of Latin and Greek required at Amherst, though he continued to like both languages.[8]

With regard to his other enthusiasm from B.R.A., oratory, he was luckier. The class in declamation, taught once a week by Professor Henry A. Frink in the chapel, was taken very seriously indeed by most students. The societies, in fact, competed keenly to produce champions in declamation; each customarily assigned an upperclassman to drill each of its freshman members and prepare him for the speaking contests. Just as there was a consensus among students at the end of the nineteenth century that the classics were drudgery, there was also one that public speaking was important, for a host of occasions: on the political platform, at civic banquets, in the pulpit. Frink, moreover, was as popular as Elwell and Wood were unpopular. A meticulous, immaculately dressed man (like Wood), he was known (unlike Wood), for taking a personal interest in each of his students' progress and giving extra help when necessary. Freshmen, consequently, put a lot of genuine effort into the course, going to the small, luxurious library with its wide study tables, classic busts and portraits, and hanging brass lamps (Edward Dickinson, the poet's nephew, was the assistant librarian) to read the books Frink put on reserve and take copious notes.[9]

Like the cane rush and the drill, declamation was a bonding experience. The whole class took it together, and every man had to face the same ordeal—public speaking—twice in the year. Most of the speaking was declamation of memorized texts, and several of the lines, because of the theatrics required, became clichés that the freshman laughed over together and remembered, it turned out, practically for a lifetime—"Room! Room in Hell for the soul of Maximilien Robespierre!" or "Ten degrees, twenty degrees, wet the ropes!" Calvin must have made the required speeches, but he said nothing about them in his letters and none of his classmates mentioned them in retrospect. One can safely guess that, unaided by the coaching of upperclassmen, he did not distinguish himself; but he did enjoy the course.[10]

By far the most memorable course for most freshmen, however, was not really a course at all, but the freshman health lectures that were given by Dr. Hitchcock weekly in the gymnasium and were popularly referred to as the "smut course." The student handbook described them as lectures on "anatomy, physiology, and hygiene," but in fact they covered a range of practical topics from proper diet and exercise to the much more exciting subject of the reproductive organs and what attention to give them. For freshmen who were still growing up—many of them would begin shaving regularly for the first time that year, using the dangerous long folding razors of the era—this section was a fascinating one; they followed Old Doc with rapt attention, sometimes asking deliberately naive questions to see how frank they could coax the doctor to be. Old Doc, whose discourse ran to "terse, vivid Anglo-Saxon expressions" anyway, required little coaxing; it was not his object, however—at least not his main object—to shock or titillate the boys. A devout Christian, a leader in student and faculty prayer meetings, famous for his long, earnest prayers, he had taken on the responsibility of being medical and moral counselor for the students and honestly believed that all these subjects, proper or not, needed to be addressed. His counsels, without being dogmatic, had a Christian slant: for example, "Show a Christian manliness whether it is manifested to you or not"; or "Always speak the name of God or Christ reverently"; or "At bottom each one of us is solitary, alone with God."[11]

Much of what he had to say in his lectures was simply the conventional wisdom of the 1890s on health and morality; but the students found it arresting because of the way he presented it or the fact that it was being publicly discussed at all. Young Coolidge listened intently as Old Doc commended frequent bathing: a daily cold sponge bath was a "necessity," and a weekly hot bath very desirable—with soap, if the sweat and oil glands had been "excessively stimulated" or if a man was worried about the odor of his armpits or feet. As to diet, Hitchcock's advice was in line with contemporary thinking: pork, pastry, and fried foods generally were harmful, coffee and tea admissible in moderation. Meat was good but not adequate by itself; about one third of a meal should be meat. Tobacco was an understandable temptation because of the sensation of comfort it afforded, but it was, after all, a narcotic, and as Old Doc reminded his listeners, "Narcosis is paralysis." Calvin and probably a fair number of other freshmen listened to this part of the lectures with some detachment; they were not in the fourth of the class that used tobacco, mostly in the form of cigarettes. (There was a strong movement in the New England colleges that year toward pipes and away from cigarettes, which were thought to be too effeminate; "If you must smoke, be a man and smoke a pipe," one student was portrayed in the college literary magazine as saying to another.)[12]

Where sex was concerned, Old Doc shared the preoccupation of the nineties with venereal disease, and his strongest argument against sexual intercourse was that a man could infect his system for life with the "rottenness" of syphilis by indulging in it. He recommended chastity. Wet dreams— "seminal emissions"—were the price one paid for abstinence, and were to be expected occasionally. This view was no doubt a comfort to Calvin and his companions, who as a group were experiencing the highest rate of such dreams ever documented among young American males, one every other week on the average, with much higher frequencies in some individuals. Late-nineteenth-century ideals and religious beliefs had convinced many of them that abstinence from sexual relations before marriage was desirable and attainable, and they were trying (Calvin no doubt among them) to achieve it. Most of them masturbated, and most felt guilty about it. Old Doc's advice gave them little comfort here. Masturbation was to be avoided, he said, because, like tobacco, it was "progressive" (i.e., addictive), with all sorts of mental and physical ills likely to result from overindulgence. Coolidge and his fellow students, most of them committed to the quest for sexual purity, had no doubt heard the catalog, which included loss of weight, fatigue, weak eyes, feeblemindedness, deformity, and a whole chamber of medical horrors.[13]

There was a small group of students, whom Calvin knew mainly by reputation, who ignored Old Doc's precepts in this area as in others. These "sports," as they were called, spent a good deal of their time in Northampton, seven miles away, where liquor was legal and where there was a small hotel near the depot with "none too good a reputation." "Hamp" was, of course, the home of Smith College and thus a frequent destination for young Amherst men in pursuit of courting and respectable female society; but as even a rather staid Amherst man conceded, it had attractions "other than the strictly social." One was alcohol. Quite a few students drank, not just the sports, mainly beer, which had become increasingly available in bottles in the 1890s with labels like Anheuser-Busch and Milwaukee. ("Fortynine [sic] bottles of beer on the wall" also made its debut in this era as a college song.) In Northampton, Bruno's beer garden was the popular hangout, and a number of the societies brought beer from there to Amherst and stored it in care of their black janitors, who doubled as cellarers. Many Amherst men tolerated or indeed secretly envied the sports; not Coolidge, however, who disliked their foul language and their disrespect for authority.[14]

Old Doc's lectures ended in early December. Almost two months later, Calvin walked into the gymnasium and found it radically changed: a white cloth was spread on the floor, potted palms were around the sides, and there were beautiful decorations hanging overhead. The occasion was the Junior Promenade (already abbreviated to "Prom"), by common consent "the great social event of the season," and another part of Amherst social life almost completely closed to him. "I did not go of course for I cannot dance," he explained to his stepmother, but in fact he did not go because he was not invited. Few freshmen were, only those with good fraternity connections and money enough for a white-tie-and-tails outfit and the expense of having a girl over from Smith or one of the other women's colleges. As for dancing, he was doubly disqualified, for the dances at the Prom were not the old New England country dances which he had seen all his life but could not execute, but rather the sophisticated metropolitan ballroom dances, waltzes, two-steps, and polkas. A burlesque letter published in the college yearbook, "Eddie Writes to Pa," purporting to show a rural student's first impression of the prom, probably came pretty close to Calvin's view of these dances: "The band plays, and each man puts his arm most round a girl, then they whirl round and round, and bump into everybody, and everybody bumps into them. But it's awful pretty, Pa."[15]

The anonymous student author of this letter came remarkably close to hitting off Calvin's attitudes toward a lot of things at Amherst. Time and again the simple sentences in country idiom almost echoed thoughts that young Coolidge had expressed in his letters home, for example his judgment of the Prom: "it was so nice and a dance is such a different thing here from a country ball." "Eddie"'s letter went on, "The band is better than ours, but it makes me homesick. Oh! Pa and Ma I wish you were here"—a poignant reminder of Calvin's homesickness after Christmas vacation. Its final sentences—"Has the cow got over her cough? Did you have a hen to eat Sunday? Is the wood sawed yet? I forgot it before. I like to work real well"—were meant as humor but sounded much like Calvin's in a letter home later that spring: "I shall be all ready to help hoe corn when I get home, It is easy hoeing where the corn is this year and I shall like it."[16]

The fact is that there was apparently a deep cleavage between the metropolitan students and their rural classmates in the early nineties—not surprisingly, since the city boys had just become the dominant group in college—and that language was one of the principal ways it manifested itself. Country students like Calvin expressed themselves in a plain, slightly rustic style; a few expressions in his letters home, which occur mainly in his freshman year, are probably typical: "I felt awful mean"; "it don't seem best"; "it makes no difference as I know of"; "she [the cow] was some unruly." Their urban classmates, on the other hand, spiced their conversation with the exuberant slang that was being created in American cities in the late Victorian era: words and phrases like "nifty," "Ta ta," "slicker than a meat ax," "the glad hand," "out of sight"; and longer utterances like "Hello there, gents, how do you think you feel? Have I had a good time? Well, I should snicker, a regular James-dandy."[17]

The main function of slang, of course, is to confirm one's belonging to a particular group and knowing its current catchwords. In using it, the city boys were flaunting their membership in the great metropolitan community. The lushness of their own language amused and fascinated them. Some tried to reproduce it at length in print, as in the following specimen, attributed to JoJo Sampson, a Cincinnatian who was in Coolidge's class. Probably overdone, like most such reproductions, it nonetheless conveys the ebullience of urban student talk in the early nineties:

The good Bruiser blew in and gave us the glad hand; and it was such a dead-smooth night we sailed down pleasant street to queer the queens. Met Bish ragged out to beat the carpet, headed for a skirt party at the convent—he thinks he cuts all kinds of fog with the girls. Bruiser and I smoked just a few, joked some beauts, got our legs jerked, slipped our trolleys, and meandered back to our stys.[18]

That this rendering was not wholly fanciful is apparent in a letter one New York freshman wrote to another in the nineties, which contained such sentences as "Hell of a lot of 'fruits' up here. 'Missing links' just own the town," or "She was nice and pretty to beat the band," or "I may get sick of this place and haul out inside of a week," or "Really they are out of sight things."[19]

Coolidge, on the basis of the evidence, did not acquire this slang during his Amherst years. He did purge his language of rural dialect and ended with a plain, unadorned style that he was to keep refining throughout college and, broadly speaking, throughout his life. This style, not the ornamented one of his B.R.A. orations, was to become the language of his later speeches and books.

When the freshmen had their class supper in February, Coolidge was not one of the twenty-four men, nearly a third of the class, invited to speak. He was there, of course, as he always was when the class got together. The supper was the last act in the freshman–sophomore conflict for that year. As Coolidge explained it to his parents, it was a triumph for the freshmen if they managed to hold a supper before Washington's Birthday without its being invaded and broken up by their rivals. Customarily they arranged to hold it in a nearby city or town, renting the dining room of the main hotel for a night and feasting until the small hours. In 1892 they waited almost until the last possible date, 18 February; Westfield, a moderate-sized town on the railroad southwest of Northampton, was the lucky site. To escape detection by the sophomores, they hid near the Massachusetts Central station until the 8:27 came in; then they boarded en masse and were off to a night of revelry at the Park Square Hotel in Westfield. Almost everybody went; "Bish" Bishop missed the train despite a "heroic sprint," and seven or eight others could not attend. Those who did feasted on a true Gilded Age menu in both amount and variety. (When the class had been discussing arrangements for the supper, Guido Metcalf, one of the leading sports of 1895, at a critical moment had leaped on a table and shouted "Damn the expense!"; his advice had evidently been heeded.) It began modestly enough, with celery, blue points, and consomme, proceeded through bluefish, turkey, beef, oysters, and lobster salad, and terminated in a blast of sweets: "English Plum Pudding with French Sauce; Pineapple Jelly; Orange Jelly; Frozen Pudding; Neapolitan Ice Cream; Assorted Cakes; Apples; Oranges; Grapes; Bananas; Figs; Layer Raisins; Edam Cheese; Coffee; Tea; Lemonade." Calvin complained that after the supper he did not get his appetite back for a week.[20]

Some '95 men perhaps partook of stronger beverages than those on the menu, for the student newspaper reported that a number fell into "the meshes of the law" and were "forced to give up a small quantity of plunder in the shape of porcelain and gilt letters which they had taken from the store windows." Three months later the bill for their depredations was still unsettled. This sort of casual vandalism by rich young collegians, one of the less attractive features of college life in the 1890s, was in its way another manifestation of the metropolitan–rural cleavage; Coolidge not only would not have participated but would have had nothing but scorn for those who did. He wrote his stepmother merely that after the banquet was over at two-thirty they "walked around town until train time and got home at six this morning."[21]

All in all, the winter and spring terms (Amherst, like B.R.A., was on what modern colleges call the trimester system) were far more pleasant for Calvin that fall term had been. He was reconciled to being at Amherst; when he came back from Easter break in April, he did not experience even a pang of homesickness. He subscribed to hometown papers from Ludlow and Rutland and read them thoroughly. Except for his loss of appetite, he felt well most of the time. At the end of January he even got out his skates and went out on the ice of the Fort River, east of the college, as a lot of Amherst students did in winter. Classes were still dull and unrewarding, particularly the ancient languages, but the work no longer terrified him. His grade remained the same, a two.[22]

Some time during the spring a peculiar thing happened. A senior, Charles Stebbins, wrote him to ask for a meeting, and Calvin agreed to talk with him in the living room at Trott's. Stebbins, it turned out, wanted to ask if he would like to join in founding a chapter of a new fraternity, Phi Gamma Delta, at Amherst. Another senior, Bobby Clark, had suggested his name.[23]

Calvin must have felt a rush of satisfaction. According to a fellow student who knew him later, he, like many other oudens, thought of the existing societies as closed and autocratic; this offer gave him a chance to get even with them. Moreover, it was pleasing to think that on his alien, formal campus, where speaking his pieces in class and nodding to acquaintances made up the bulk of his social life, someone had been watching him and deciding that he was a person worth cultivating.

Nevertheless, he asked Stebbins no questions and gave only a noncommittal answer. Native timidity was partly responsible, no doubt, but there was also the question of finances. John never tired of reminding him how much his education was costing, and indeed had recently tried to take out insurance on his life in case he died before his education was complete. The added expense of initiation fees, dues, jewelry and the like was too great to incur, or rather not worth the criticism he would have to take from John in order to get it. In the end, Coolidge, formal as only he could be in his suit coat, tie, and stiff collar (on a campus where many men wore tennis trousers and sweaters outside class), limited his reply to vague interest: "I don't know but I would." Stebbins left, puzzled by his silence, and nothing came of the idea.[24]

After Easter vacation the work seemed to become easier, and Amherst seemed bearable, indeed almost pleasant. There were lectures and political rallies; there was old "Unk," the maple-sugar man from the Pelham hills, crying his wares all around the town. May came with its fickle weather, its hepaticas and white violets, lilac and apple blossoms. The seniors, for the first time ever at Amherst, donned caps and gowns for the last month of their college career, a step criticized by some as a piece of pseudo-English affectation. There was the baseball season, in which Amherst's team won twenty of twenty-nine games, and the intercollegiate track meet at Springfield, won by Amherst; Old Doc led the parade to welcome the returning heroes at the Massachusetts Central station. At Amherst, unlike B.R.A., the spring term extended well into June and culminated in Commencement Week, a sort of regional celebration, like a county fair, where people from the surrounding country towns flocked into Amherst and set up lemonade stands, roast chestnut booths, and so forth; in 1891 it ended with a week of terribly hot weather that made young Coolidge doubly glad to pack his trunk, ship a box of books by freight, and set out for home and, as he had written in a letter that March, "all the associations that are dear to me."[25]

Some of the associations were inanimate: the clipped grass on his mother's grave and Abbie's; the uninterrupted sky beyond the green hills; reflections in the reservoir; the smells of the general store, of the cheese factory, of the attic at his grandmother's house. Others were animate but mute: Ned the cat, the black horse, the woodchuck that raided his grandmother's garden. Then there were his grandmother, Uncle John and Aunt Gratia, all the families up and down the road. And, of course, the chores he would do for his father, as much now out of nostalgia as out of duty.[26]

One of the first people he sought out when he got back was Levi Lynds, the bachelor Civil War veteran who lived with his brother John's family on the Five Corners road. Perhaps as early as his last year at B.R.A. he had begun seeing a good bit of Levi and going over to his house for visits; he had written him from Amherst. Levi regularly wrote back, though his handwriting was so dreadful and his spelling so eccentric his letters took time to decipher. He was one of the regulars at the general store, where Calvin had no doubt first met him; he was a critical, profane man about John Coolidge's age who was always running somebody down and may have been too opinionated even for the gang at the store, especially when he got started on Christianity, the church, and religious hypocrisy. Without accepting all his opinions, Calvin enjoyed Levi, who was more widely traveled than most Plymouth people. He had fought at Cold Harbor, The Wilderness, and Petersburg, and the pension he received for his war wound gave him funds to travel to veterans' meetings in New York and elsewhere. He dressed well and knew his way around; he was an odd blend of urban sophistication and backwoods Vermont. He was also a man of ideas, despite his limited education; he thought a lot about social questions and was a fascinating storyteller. A lot of people in Plymouth may have been a little afraid of his sharp tongue, which spared no one, including John Coolidge. Calvin, nevertheless, spent a lot of time with him, often talking local and national politics (Levi was a belligerently partisan Republican).[27]

Among the people his own age, he looked forward to seeing Midge Gilson, the youngest of the three Gilson girls who came up to Plymouth in early

July every summer. She was darkhaired, pretty, well dressed, a violinist, three years older than he—and like him and Levi, had a foot in both camps, the big city and Vermont. Her parents lived in Brooklyn, but her roots were in Plymouth; she was a cousin of Dell and Oric Ward. The high-gabled Victorian cottage the Gilsons occupied on the other side of Black Pond, surrounded by a brilliant flower garden, was a place he had become fond of, and he preferred Midge as his companion on picnics and excursions. Like other young women, she liked him but found his silences unnerving.[28]

Dell Ward had become his principal male friend in Plymouth. Calvin had written him a lot from college, and now that he was back he was eager to resume the routine of riding up to Dell's house near Black Pond and getting him to go fishing or picnicking. (Dell remembered his horse later as a spotted Arabian, but from Calvin's letters home it appears it was a black horse.) When Dell was not busy pitching hay, they would go wherever Cal suggested: he "just naturally took charge," Dell reminisced years later. It was fun to get back to simple Vermont ways, catching bullheads in the lime-kiln pond and baking them between squares of turf—even when things did not go according to plan. Once, Dell recalled, Cal decided the fish were done, took off the top layer of earth, and saw their tails still moving. It had been only ten minutes; the fish were not only uncooked, they were barely warmed through. "His expression was so comical that I lay back on the grass and laughed and rolled until I was weak," Ward remembered.[29]

Most of the time Calvin controlled the laughs. One story from these years, impossible to place exactly but probably from a summer vacation, concerns a party that Cal, Dell, and a group of young people were having in the hall over the store. Les Walker finally had as much as he could take and sent up word for them to quiet down, whereupon Cal brought out a twelve-foot board from a storeroom, got Dell to stand on one end while he lifted the other as high as it would go, and then released it to slap down on the floor like a pistol shot. They waited breathlessly for Walker's reaction from below, but none came. "Guess I put him to sleep," Calvin drawled.[30]

A year in college, Calvin discovered, could do wonders for a young man's prestige. Typically a local boy who had been to college was recognized at home by the dandified, up-to-the-minute clothes he wore, and this may have been true in Calvin's freshman summer, as it certainly was in later ones. But even apart from the clothes, many a collegian from a small hamlet returned with, as one Vermont writer put it, a "gay swagger," an aura of self-confidence along with his Latin and Greek. Calvin was the last person in the world to swagger, but he did find that his year at Amherst commanded for him a certain deference, in subtle ways, that he had never felt before.[31]

One indication of his new status was evident almost as soon as he got off the train. For the first time in years, the leaders of the Notch—that is, his father, Ephraim Moore, John Wilder, and James Brown—had decided to have a local Independence Day celebration. It would be a flag-raising and a basket picnic, and, since the Notch was virtually all Republican, a Harrison rally for the presidential campaign. They wanted him, the young scholar-orator of the Notch, to deliver the main address. It would be a wonderful way to celebrate his twentieth birthday. Calvin accepted, and probably spent most of his time for the next two weeks preparing the oration.[32]

He delivered it from a platform under the great elm in the center of the green, to a crowd mainly of neighbors (the men of the Union had gone to a celebration at Bellows Falls), as they finished their hard-boiled eggs, cold pork, sandwiches, and tomatoes, and looked forward to the custardy home-made ice cream that was packing in the churns as they listened. Levi Lynds was probably there listening, as were his genial, alert Uncle John and his father, stern and serious as always. A Harrison–Reid flag (Reid was the vice-presidential candidate) fluttered at his side, also a national flag with its forty-four stars. The elegant frock coat he wore only underscored his youth, and he began, becomingly, with an apology:

> I know not why youth has been condemned to speak to you today, while men of maturity are doomed to listen. Unless the proverb, 'old men for council and young men for war,' has been reversed. But if age will agree to bear the battle's shock, I will undertake the perils of council and consider the exchange to my advantage. I esteem it one of the first privileges of my boyhood to be permitted to address an assemblage of my own townspeople on an occasion like this.[33]

It was a ringing, elaborate oration, full of all the words and rhetorical tricks he had learned at B.R.A. and Amherst: alliteration, vivid images, pounding rhythm ("Let trembling tyrants hold their sway with arms and fleets, and ride to empire through a sea of blood"), dramatic gesture ("While that flag floats [pointing to it] our rights shall be preserved"), and a grand peroration; "Roll on, America! Roll on, bearing rich blessings with o'erflowing hand through the endless ages of all eternity, until freedom's golden course has traversed all the earth, and tyranny and oppression are no more." It was also to be the last speech he would ever write in that nineteenth-century stem-winding vein; but neither he nor his hearers could know that. They were much impressed with it and with him.[34]

Grandmother Coolidge had been unwell and unable to attend the celebration, so when Calvin came over to her house the next morning she naturally demanded a report. He recited the speech for her, in hesitant, lame fashion, until she stopped him and said, "Calvin Coolidge, didn't you do any better than that?" "Worse, I guess," he answered. "Then you ought to be ashamed of yourself," she pronounced, but then she caught sight of his grin and realized she had been the victim of another joke by her grandson. He was actually very pleased, both with his speech and with his joke, and also for another reason that his grandmother and everyone else in the Notch knew of.[35]

In the two weeks since his return, between bouts of working on his speech for the flag-raising, Calvin had been pondering whether it would be possible to wrest the town cannon back from the Union this year. He and his contemporaries were in their early twenties now, heirs to the rivalry with the Union and old enough to do something about it. Moreover, he had found out where the Union boys were hiding it: in the very center of the Union, in the grove behind the Wilder House hotel, where no one ever stayed but where Norris Wilder and his father lived. It was probably John Coolidge, who traveled all over town and noticed everything, who gave him this piece of information, including the vital fact that the cannon was alarmed—there was a string tied to it that rang a cowbell in the Wilder House. Armed with this news, Calvin tried to get up a force from the Notch to go down the mountain and spirit off the cannon. He may not have been the only leader of the effort, but he was certainly one of them. Before long, he had enlisted Dell Ward, his old friend Tom Moore, his cousin Allen Wilder, who was up from Proctorsville for a visit, Herb Moore (who was always game for anything, though he had already tangled with the law once that year), Frank Willis, the Wilders' hired man, and possibly Hen Brown, who was married and working in Ludlow but may have been home visiting. It was the first time, on the basis of surviving evidence, that Calvin had taken the lead in anything at the Notch. Maybe his college smoothness and flair, invisible in Amherst but conspicuous at home, were paying off.[36]

Anyway, one night before the Fourth, at about three in the morning, the Notch boys stole down the mountain and into the Union. As Dell Ward remembered it, there was a dance ending at the hotel. There may have been; at the Wilder House for some weeks past, they had been exhibiting the new invention called the "phonograph," which made it possible to give dances without the need of a band or piano. Dell and his crew avoided the lighted windows, found the cannon in the grove and cut the string on the alarm, and began the backbreaking work of moving the five-hundred-pound piece of iron on its big wheels up the Notch road. It was work enough for seven healthy young men, but they made it and, amid the insect trills of early morning, stowed it in John Wilder's barn. On the Fourth, after Calvin finished speaking, they hauled it out and fired a victory blast, or several.[37]

To make sure that their Union rivals could not get it back, Calvin suggested taking it apart: the carriage could stay in the barn, while the cannon itself could be carried upstairs in the Wilder home and hidden under his grandmother Moor's bed. That would clinch the Notch's victory; the Union boys would never be able to retrieve it.

And they never did.

13

The Sunny Dream

Calvin sat at his desk, a letter in front of him, gazing eastward out the window at the blue October sky over College Hill. It was Sunday. "It is a beautiful day," he wrote his father, "so clear, with just enough bracing air and cool enough so a fire is not uncomfortable." Wood crackled in the stove behind him. "The scenery too is now charming," he went on, "the woods just taking on the mellow richness of autumn and tinged here and there with purple and gold." He had been to service that morning at the College Church, on the other side of the campus, drinking in the tang and cleanness of the autumn air; some said the autumn view east from there, over the Pelham hills in the hazy distance, was one of the most beautiful in western Massachusetts.[1]

Calvin was in a mood to share his reveries, although he knew his attempts at fine writing made John impatient. He had been to the Walter Emerson concert at the town hall the night before, not terribly enjoyable, he confessed, for most of the music was over his head; but the sound of a violin solo—the fiddle music of his Plymouth boyhood, transfigured—sent him into rhapsodies, and he also enjoyed the harp, which woke echoes of the Scott poems he had loved and memorized; "I think I should [have] loved the old days of minstrelsy."[2]

As often when Calvin was daydreaming, medieval pageantry was involved. Perhaps, indeed, the stained glass and hewn stone of the campus, so different from Vermont, were one reason why he enjoyed being back at Amherst, as he unmistakably did. Two years later, in his rhetoric class, he was to write an essay that began "The days of chivalry are passed," with praise for Scott's "gorgeous imagination" in *Rokeby*. Two Sundays before, he had attended worship at the stone Renaissance-style Episcopal church on the Common, with its single, slender, off-center spire—"God's saintly toothpick," one student wag called it. To be sure, he had not gone to savor the architecture, but to listen to Bishop Huntington of New York, a famous pulpit orator. But the experience was part of the contentment he was feeling in school that fall.[3]

He had gotten in on the 14 September afternoon train, the day before registration, nursing a serious cold, as he had in 1890. But this one, although it tightened his breathing and made the morning climb up College

149

Hill painful, was not an apocalyptic event like the one two years before; it was just a cold. He would go to Deuel's drugstore at the corner of the Common, buy some quinine or patent medicine, and treat it; it would go away in a few days. He had found Turner back at Trott's, wearing glasses, to his surprise. He had been having trouble with his eyes, and his doctor had prescribed glasses for a few months. There had been registration the next day—he was taking Greek, German, rhetoric, and geometry, typical sophomore courses—and the cane rush the day after that, for which his cold had provided a good excuse for not taking much part. (The sophomores, his class, had won by a large margin; sophomores usually did.) There had also been the first sophomore class meeting.[4]

It was odd how this collection of men, a faceless mass only a year ago, a strange jumble of sack coats, sweaters, tennis trousers, Midwestern breeziness, languid New York accents, New England country drawls, tall, short, blond, brunet, had turned into a gallery of individuals. Calvin knew nearly all of them, though with most he had exchanged hardly a word in a year of college. But he had sat in class with them, sweated in the gym, laughed at Old Doc's "choice indecencies," stolen onto the train to the class supper, yelled (or at least watched) at football games. He recognized dark-haired "Kid" Morrow, Dwight Morrow from Pittsburgh, a bright, well-liked fellow who was becoming a sort of unofficial class leader; Nelson Kingsland, one of the leading sports of '95, who swore more fluently, cut more often, and drank more heroically, in Amherst and in Northampton, than his classmates; Harry "Twich" Twitchell, another sport, whose thick furry hair on his arms and legs drew a lot of jokes in gym class; Theodore Penney, the giant from Utah, who (it was said) had never seen a football before coming to Amherst but had ended up playing on the varsity; little blond Charlie Andrews. Royal Booth's blond hair and rosy cheeks were visible; he had made it through freshman year with Calvin's help, but he and Calvin were no longer close. A few men were gone; there were also a few transfers, including a studious chap from Illinois named Blair who looked like a full-blooded Indian.[5]

Calvin, of course, was not the only '95 man feeling this sudden sense of class unity. Many other sophomores perceived the same tightening web of acquaintance, which included bonds of friendship forged sometimes in fraternity associations, sometimes in class activities, and quite often in the most democratic of Amherst institutions, the boarding house.

For an Amherst student in the early 1890s, there was only one answer to the question of where to take his meals. The college, conservative in this respect as in most others that entailed expense, had no dining hall, though it would open one in 1893. The societies had at one time operated dining rooms for their members but no longer did so. The dining room of the Amherst House hotel was the only restaurant in town. And cooking for oneself, popular in some small freshwater colleges, was all but unheard of in

Amherst. That left the boarding houses, or "feed stables" as some Amherst students called them. They numbered a couple of dozen, located generally in the rooming houses that crowded the streets next to the campus—Pleasant, Prospect, College, Maple—and run by the same local men and women. They varied a good deal in quality and price: the Amherst House and Mr. Houghton's charged six dollars a week for board, while the weekly price at Merrick's, held to be the worst as well as the cheapest, was a mere three dollars.[6]

There was variation in size as well as quality. Some houses, like Morse's on South Pleasant, had as many as forty-five students at each meal, and fed them at a number of tables located in several rooms. At other houses there was only one table and six or eight students, who were served family style by the landlady. In the larger houses, waiters served the food, restaurant style; the waiters were college men who needed the extra cash. For a middle-class boy from New England, there was nothing degrading about waiting on tables; indeed, some students, like Albert Tibbitts of '95, organized tables of their friends and classmates and waited on them. A New Yorker, on the other hand, might find that donning a towel and carrying trays led to social snubs from some of his acquaintance.[7]

Food at the boarding houses was, naturally, simple and cheap. Beef was served a lot, because it was the cheapest meat available: beefsteaks for breakfast were almost universal. At other meals there were steak or roast beef. The commonest drink was milk, often rather "chilly and purplish" (as one student described it) due to watering down, or cocoa. Chicken, turkey, or goose might turn up on Thanksgiving, and also oysters on occasion. Fruit was cheap around Amherst, and pie was a popular dessert; Calvin reported that at Thanksgiving Trott's served seven kinds of pie, in true Vermont holiday fashion. "Pie you know has great attractions for growing boys," he commented blandly.[8]

As a freshman, Calvin had boarded at the same place where he roomed and found the food acceptable ("not elaborate ... but good and substantial"), but he was not typical in this respect; Amherst students seem to have liked to board elsewhere, and even Calvin, in his sophomore year, joined the majority, shifting his boarding place from Trott's, where there were twenty-six boarders, too many for the help to handle, and Mr. Trott was "on a strike," as Calvin put it ("the old man ... sat out on the piazza all day and did not do any thing"), to a house up the street run by the black janitor of the Beta Theta Pi house and his wife ("coons," Calvin called them, using standard New England vernacular), where there was a table of his own class. Since board was paid for by the week, switching houses was simple and apparently rather common; one switched until he found a table with agreeable company at a price he was willing to pay.[9]

Much socializing went on at these tables—not at breakfast, where everyone was wolfing down his breakfast to be able to take his assigned seat in chapel on time—but at lunch ("dinner"), which was served around a quarter to one. In the absence of girls, table manners were primitive. Banter was spirited, loud, and free. There was a lot of joshing; students were likely to heckle the hostess or the waiters when the food was not up to expectations. (Calvin recorded an instance where the boys at his table, after finding a hair in their pies once or twice, ostentatiously brought their razors to the meal the next time pie was served.) Calvin himself was remembered by a fellow boarder at Trott's for pushing back his plate whenever mutton was served and drawling, "I don't eat sheep."[10]

Quite possibly it was through his new boarding place that Calvin began to make friends. By the middle of sophomore year he had several, including the two who were to remain closest to him throughout college, Ernest Hardy and John Percy Deering. Deering's explanation for his acquaintance with the solitary, sober-faced Coolidge, which was to ripen into friendship, was that neither was a fraternity man, so that they were thrown together often—presumably on evenings when all the fraternities scheduled activities, and perhaps too at class meetings where men from the same society were likely to sit together. The same was true for Hardy, who was an ouden probably for financial reasons; he was the only son of a widowed mother and needed to economize. Deering was an independent sort who may have disdained fraternities on principle.[11]

The two young men were alike in many ways. Neither belonged to the metropolitan urban culture; both were, like Calvin, small-town Yankees. Deering was from Saco, Maine, Hardy from Northampton. Both were physically larger than Calvin; Deering played football, and "Fat" Hardy has already been mentioned as the heaviest man in the class. Perhaps more to the point, both were witty and articulate. Hardy, a bright student and talented orator, qualities which doubtless impressed Coolidge, was the archetypal jolly big man, with curly red hair, genial, friendly, a good mixer, but also sharp in repartee: "one of the most cheerful, fun-loving and pleasure-giving men who ever came to Amherst," a historian of the class called him. His other nickname, "Chipmunk," suggests the class's affection for him. Deering, on the other hand, was a quiet, tough, undramatic young man from a locally prominent Republican family in Maine, fond of debate and athletics. His sudden flashes of dry wit resembled Coolidge's, and he had a good deal of nerve. He was capable, for instance, of taking out his enormous pocket watch in Professor Gibbons's chaotic Greek class freshman year and imperturbably counting its rotations at the end of its chain while the annoyed professor shouted at him to put it up. Both men seem to have struck up an acquaintance with Calvin and then cultivated it after they discovered his talent for quiet, mordant wit.[12]

It seems likely, although the sources do not permit certainty, that what really cemented the friendships was common participation in the college Republican club. Both Hardy and Deering, like Coolidge, were fond of local politics and politicking, and 1892 was a presidential year, full of party activity on the Amherst campus. In the spring of Calvin's freshman year, the College Base Ball Association sponsored a mock Republican convention at College Hall, with Calvin a fascinated spectator. The student delegates paraded around the campus beforehand, singing for their respective favorites, President Harrison and his rival, former Secretary of State James G. Blaine. (Harrison won, as he was to do at the national Republican convention that summer.) Then in May, a College Republican Club was formed. Dwight Morrow was the only freshman on the board, but Coolidge was probably down in the ranks along with Deering and Hardy.[13]

When they returned to college in the fall, the presidential campaign was in full swing. It was a rematch of the 1888 Harrison–Cleveland contest. This time a number of high-principled "Mugwump" Republicans for whom Harrison's administration had been too corrupt were supporting Cleveland, but not many Amherst students shared their reservations; those who could vote supported Harrison about seven to one, and fully a third of the whole student body was active in the Republican Club. The Club at once swung into action on Harrison's behalf with large-scale torchlight parades around town. The classic mode of mass political expression in presidential campaigns, torchlight parades had lit American streets on nippy fall nights for at least fifty years, and techniques and equipment had become standardized: the torches, for instance, were not flaming pieces of wood, but conical metal reservoirs full of oil, with a thick wick on top, very often with a metal cap to keep the rain off. The marchers, all of whom were male, wore oilcloth capes, and often military-style caps, to protect themselves from dripping hot oil. (The caps were also a reminder of the Union Army that had saved the nation under a Republican government.) Usually they carried transparent banners of oiled paper mounted on a wooden frame with a torch inside, shrieking political slogans. The order of march was quasi-military, and often a torchlight parade was a rather solemn affair; probably not at Amherst, however, under student platoon leaders like "Twich" Twichell.[14]

Illumination of various kinds was central to torchlight processions. Usually Republican homes along the route of march were illuminated, and often decked out with paper Chinese lanterns glowing in different colors while Calvin and his companions marched along under the flickering light of open flames. For the 31 October parade, the Common was enlivened with "Roman candles, rockets, and red fire." At the procession of 24 October there were a lot of placards and banners, for eighteen Amherst professors had published an open letter in support of Cleveland the week before. Among them were some of Calvin's favorite professors, like Olds and Frink, as well as less popular ones like Eph Wood and "Pa" Sterrett. This fact probably did not bother him; he had learned years ago in Vermont that political opposition and personal esteem were quite compatible. The most respected man in his Republican home town of Plymouth was H. F. Pinney, a Democrat, who was always chosen moderator at town meeting. But as political enemies, the professors had to be answered, and a banner in the procession read "18 Profs can't fool us—Tammany Faculty—Christian College," tying the pro-Cleveland faculty to the notorious New York City Democratic machine.[15]

The processions were exhilarating, and student Republicans felt good about the election; "Republicans here are very confident," Calvin wrote John on 30 October. He was doubtless among the crowd that assembled at the commercial end of the Common after dark on 8 November, to watch as the election returns were projected from a stereopticon onto a sheet hung over the front of Williams's Block. But the result itself was a total surprise. Cleveland beat Harrison by a healthy margin, and the Democrats took control of both houses of Congress. Calvin doubtless analyzed the outcome with his friends in the Republican Club, but it was a puzzle to them too; "nobody seems able to account for it satisfactorily yet," he wrote John a few days later. (Levi Lynds, oddly enough, had "got it about right" that summer when they were talking.) He went on nevertheless with a fairly shrewd, though general, analysis: "The reason seems to lie in the never satisfied mind of the American and in the ever [recurring] desire to shift in hope of something better and in the vague idea of the working and farming classes that somebody is getting all the money while they get all the work." A letter from the vice president of the Republican Club, Harlan Stone, to a Democratic acquaintance shows the combative spirit in which the young Republicans conceded their loss: "Gen. Grant used to say that 'Give the Democrats enough rope and they will surely hang themselves.' There is no doubt but what they have a sufficiency of rope, and four years will tell us whether they will reduce suicide to a fine art."[16]

Besides the excitement of national politics, young Coolidge's acquaintance with Hardy and Deering, and the few other friends he had made, began to admit him to the real life of the college—discussing professors and their ideas, philosophical questions, and issues affecting Amherst. There were plenty of the latter, mostly petty controversies that stemmed naturally from the presence of affluent city boys in a conservative New England small town—complaints about the young college swells' riding their new Columbias too fast on the asphalt sidewalks and endangering innocent pedestrians, or college men's complaints that the local authorities had arbitrarily torn down signs the Base Ball Association had posted on trees around the village. There were the faculty and their peccadilloes, like the glamorous Mrs. David Todd (Mabel Loomis Todd), the wife of the astronomy professor, who was understood to be having a romantic affair with Austin Dickinson, the treasurer of the college. (Mabel Loomis Todd, parenthetically, represented a side of American metropolitan culture—elegant, wide-ranging, intellectually sophisticated—that existed marginally in Amherst but had no impact on Coolidge. City life, to him, was merely the football, polkas, beer, and slang of his urban classmates.) Two issues, however, stood out from the rest and were to become more and more divisive during Calvin's years at Amherst. They were intertwined: one was the new president of the college, Merrill E. Gates, the other the question of compulsory chapel attendance.[17]

Calvin's first contact with President Gates had been at a chapel service in the first week of his freshman year. He had been much impressed by the suave, eloquent president; "he is such an earnest man and offers such a prayer," he wrote home. This was not just the reaction of a naive fresh-man; the forty-three-year-old Gates was an impressive figure by any standard. An avid tennis player and football fan, an elegant dresser and handsome man with a flowing mustache, a superb public speaker with the perfect manners of a diplomat, he was decidedly not a typical Methodist minister. His unusual combination of clerical soundness and worldly polish seemed exactly suited to a place like Amherst. He had arrived only a little before Coolidge, having been inaugurated at the commencement ceremonies in June 1891, and had been well received.[18]

By Coolidge's sophomore year, however, Gates's superhuman aura was disappearing. It was not just the inevitable puns—"Prexy" Gates happened to have the same surname as Lanford Gates, the college janitor, and they were called "Big Front Gates" and "Big Back Gates" respectively—or all the Christian in-group wordplay on Psalm 24, with its repeated "Lift up your heads, o ye gates!" It was not just Prexy's egotism and name-dropping about famous acquaintances in Washington, or even the comments that were starting to float around faculty and town circles about his deviousness in college matters. Gates's real problem was his religious style. Despite his sophisticated veneer, he was a believer in using religion to influence others and to advance his own ends. (Calvin's first impression had been perceptive; Gates's fervent, earnest prayers were meant to sway his hearers.) The problem was that this style was wholly unacceptable to most Amherst students, and a good many faculty.[19]

The impact of Darwin and the higher criticism of the Bible in the years just after the Civil War had split American Protestantism into two camps; it had, in fact, created two different ways of being Protestant. On the one hand, many Protestants in the North, especially in cities and in New England, had had their faith badly shaken by science's new revelations about human ancestry and the text of the Bible. Their faith, they felt, had misled them in some ways, and they were in no frame of mind to be dogmatic about it or to push it on others. The proper role of religion in their society, they felt, was to harmonize, to sweeten, and to comfort—not to command. The other group of Protestants, most numerous in the West and South but not unknown in New England, felt that religion should keep the role it had had in America for most of the early 1800s: an active, transforming force, inculcating beliefs through revivals, converting souls, stimulating people to act on the basis of revealed Truth. To avoid compromising their own faith, they tended to reject or ignore the new scientific ideas. One might call them "aggressives," and their more doubtful brethren "accomodationists."[20]

Amherst, like all the traditional New England colleges, was accommodationist; the higher criticism and the theory of evolution were accepted without serious question. As one undergraduate, who went on to become a clergyman anyway, put it, "The Department of Biology ... shattered my Book of Genesis; The Department of German ... excised my conventional Northfield idea of the atonement." But many of the boys who came there in the nineties had few beliefs to be shaken. Most were church members, willing to participate in freshman prayer meeting, but few could accept the faith of their parents without reservations; doctrines like immortality, the divinity of Jesus, the atonement, or the efficacy of prayer carried little conviction for them. Though not "pious," as they called it, not many of them were outright skeptics; most were looking for something they could honestly believe in. Consequently, they respected the search for religious truth, but resented any effort to impose religion on them or anyone else. Some, at least, were apt to turn out and annoy revivalist preachers who tried to hold forth in Amherst, and most were impatient with the new "Christian Endeavor" groups that were supposed to drum up interest in Sunday school.[21]

It was only recently that the students had become so overwhelmingly accommodationist in their outlook. There had been successful revivals at Amherst in the 1880s; the last was in 1890. But that year, according to one professor, marked the transition from the "evangelical period" to the "all-round-man period," in which athletics and fraternities took over the central place religion had formerly occupied in student life. Doubtless the continuing influx of metropolitan students was connected with the change, one symptom of which was the new nickname acquired by the "Day of Prayer for Colleges," a one-day break in January traditionally consecrated to religious activities. Fraternity men now knew it as the "Day of Poker." Coolidge had arrived at Amherst just at the time of the shift in values.[22]

So had Gates, but the president seemed unaware of the change. Despite his cultivated exterior, he was very much an aggressive believer, determined to use religion to transform people and situations. In conferences with students and faculty, he was quick to resort to prayer, delivered kneeling, in which his superb command of Christian rhetoric gave him dominance over the situation. He taxed faculty members with their low attendance at prayer meetings, outprayed even Old Doc at chapel, and made life especially difficult for professors like Charles E. Garman, professor of psychology and philosophy, whom he suspected of insufficient enterprise in promoting Christian faith.[23]

The issue that arose in Calvin's sophomore year was ideally calculated to test the firmness of a Christian like Gates. Five times during the week and twice on Sundays Amherst students were required to attend religious services: on weekday mornings in Johnson Chapel, on Sunday morning and evening in the college church. The requirement had been natural enough in the days when almost all Amherst students were preparing for careers in the ministry or some paraclerical field like teaching, but now that the majority were oriented toward business or law it seemed to many irrelevant and demeaning: as one fired-up undergraduate put it, "a blot upon our civilization, the descendant of old religious persecution, a misshapen monument of folly and stupidity." Even Calvin, docile believer and conformist that he was, confessed to his parents as a freshman, "I don't like to be compelled to go to church very well but there is no other way here."[24]

There were pleasant features of Sunday morning service—the ornate Gothic interior of the college church, the stained glass, the beautiful altar, decorated with flowers in season, the soothing organ music—if one could cope with the long sermons by the college pastor, Dr. Burroughs (who was, to the students' relief, called to the presidency of a western college in the fall of 1892). But no one seems to have had a good word for morning chapel, barring the ironic praise of a student humorist, Bertrand Snell:

It teaches elocution by the improved modern practical method. By their critical study of the preachers, the students have forcible illustrations of how to speak and gesture—and how not to. It establishes good habits.... There is no better discipline than making young people do what they don't want to.[25]

The bell of Johnson Chapel began pealing at 8:15 every weekday morning. At 8:25 the stroke quickened, and for the next five minutes the bell rang continually, while the boys gulped down their beefsteaks and hurried up College Hill. A number of them had it timed so that they could slip into their seats precisely on the last stroke, at 8:30. The alphabetical seating by classes made it easy for student monitors to check each class for latecomers or absentees. Though present, most of the students were not in what one called "a devotional frame of mind." Many remained slumped in their seats when the call was given to rise for the first hymn; quite a few were surreptitiously reading textbooks or popular magazines behind their neighbor's back. There was whispering, even occasional talking. A good speaker like Old Doc, with his homely New England stories, or (in the beginning) President Gates could conquer the students' attention; but as a rule, an almost palpable feeling, sharper than impatience but not quite hostility, pervaded the congregation. When the fifteen minutes were up they broke for the exit, disregarding the tradition that the faculty went first, then the seniors, and so on.[26]

Doubtless students had complained about chapel services as long as Amherst had existed, but in the eighties and previous decades their protests had been mainly about the dullness and inadequacy of the services. The students of the nineties were apparently the first to question the existence of the requirement itself. In Calvin's freshman year the student newspaper took a poll and found 76 percent of the whole student body, and even more among the upper classes, opposed to compulsory chapel. It seemed radically inconsistent, one protester wrote, with "the modern conception of Christianity as a religion of love." By the following year, the opponents had organized. The College Senate—a uniquely Amherst institution, which allowed students a small share in governing the college—passed a resolution against compulsory chapel, with support from at least one Amherst trustee. That was as far as the movement had progressed in the middle of Calvin's sophomore year. The following spring it was to run into a brick wall in the person of Merrill E. Gates.[27]

Sophomore work was not quite as much drudgery as the freshman year; the professors, for the most part, were better. But Coolidge found it dull. He was continuing math under Olds, and doing well. In German, Professor Richardson was popular with many students for his joviality and fondness for spicy anecdotes, but he made little impression on Coolidge. Latin and Greek remained uninspiring; in the latter Coolidge read Demosthenes's speech "On the Crown." described as the greatest speech of the greatest orator in history, under the venerable Professor William S. Tyler. His comment to John foreshadowed some of the withering remarks he would be famous for in later life: "Eloquence does not seem to grow very fast if after 2200 years we can produce nothing to rival this speech." He sat in the front row but was not always attentive; an anecdote of this class had Professor Tyler asking him to raise his head and commenting, "I can't talk through your skull." In the fall term his grade was a barely passing fifty. Probably the course he liked best was rhetoric, under the stout, bearded, deep-voiced John F. Genung, a scholarly, kindly man who had his students polish their writing style in a series of essays.[28]

With the excitement of politics and the enjoyment of friends, the fall and winter terms of sophomore year passed rapidly for Calvin. Classwork was basically routine. There were diversions: 1892 was an outstanding football season for Amherst, and Calvin was probably at the climactic game with Dartmouth in November, played on a Pratt Field which was "a little too thin to walk on and a little too thick to swim in." Amherst won, 30–2. He went home at Christmas; the train ride now was also routine, and he looked forward to talking with other collegians who would be riding home with him. As often happens to college students, his home towns, Ludlow and Plymouth, were slowly changing, becoming less familiar. Professor Sherman had left B.R.A. to take a post in Massachusetts. Rufus Hemenway had taken a job in Detroit. Henry Hicks was dying of Bright's disease. Loren Pinney, his long-suffering roommate of the eighties at B.R.A., was now studying law in Stickney's office. In Plymouth, Jennie Chamberlin, John's hired girl for some years, was leaving to work in Norwich, now that Carrie Coolidge had taken charge of the household, and John was getting set to fix up the house to please Carrie, with a bay window in the sitting room. It was now Amherst that was more real.[29]

The first thing Calvin did on returning from Christmas vacation was to change his lodgings. He did not move far, only up South Pleasant Street to Morse's boarding house, which was at the top of the hill next to President Gates's residence. He would continue to walk, sedately dressed in his derby and his overcoat, to the post office downtown or to the lecture hall every day at the same time by the same route. He explained to John that the new room was cheaper and warmer. Both features were important, but the main attraction was that he was moving in with friends: Percy Deering, Emmons Bryant, also of the class of 1895, and Carl Gates, the president's nephew, who belonged to the class of 1896. They shared a suite of rooms on the top floor. When he had changed his boarding house earlier in the fall, one reason had been that he wanted to sit with a table of his own class; probably the same reason accounted for this move. The new room, though more spartan in furnishings than the one at Trott's, seemed a welcome change. After a year or more as an outsider, he was becoming a full-fledged member of the class of 1895, claiming his share in what a member of his class called "the sunny dream"

> Of youth, which knows no doubt, no fear,
> And thinks of friends and friendships near....
> In Amherst town.[30]

14

Beyond the Provinces

Rain, rain, rain—sometimes a drizzle, sometimes a downpour. The Boston sidewalks were a jostle of umbrellas, mackintoshes, and rubbers. Carriages and wagons sloshed past. The red-brick buildings of Scollay Square were dimly visible from Coolidge's seat in the horse car. Water dripped from the jaunty striped awning on the car, from the telephone wires overhead. The bronze statue of John Winthrop, dripping in the center of the triangular square, was especially forlorn. It was chilly, too, for June—only in the mid-fifties—and men who had begun wearing their summer linen underwear were regretting it. (Most likely Coolidge still had on his winter flannels; he seems to have had only one or two pairs of underwear in all, which he wore throughout college.) Across the river in Cambridge, Harvard was having its worst Class Day in memory.[1]

Bad as the weather was, Coolidge kept peering through the rain from his seat beside Deering, anxious not to miss a thing. Boston was a metropolis of half a million, incomparably larger than any place he had ever been. There was much in it that was new and strange: for example, this canary-yellow vehicle like a miniature open railway carriage, one of many brightly painted cars that ran on rails down the middle of the cobblestoned street, carrying him, Deering, and other classmates to their destination, the Tremont House, for the class supper that would mark the end of their sophomore year. It was 24 June 1893.[2]

Ahead, the gleaming tracks continued up Tremont Street, through an urban panorama more complex and varied than anything Coolidge could have seen in his almost twenty-one years; there were, to quote a contemporary Boston guide, "the old pitch-roofed brick houses, the long triple-balconied front of the Boston Museum, the green trees of the burial ground, the dark low tower of King's Chapel, ... the lofty white marble pile of the Parker House," and amid all this, the glowering sandstone portico of the Tremont House.[3]

It was actually visible from Scollay Square, if one knew where to look—one long block away, over the horse's rump, at the corner of Beacon Street—a three-story building with an odd, massive granite portico, supported on five Doric columns, that reached almost to the curb. In its heyday, two generations ago, it had been the leading hotel in Boston; now it was an outdated business struggling to survive. It had closed a few years before for complete renovation, including complete electrical wiring, but the move came too late. The venerable building was too old-fashioned to save. Only a year and a half after the sophomores' class supper, in December 1894, it would shut down for good.[4]

Part of its problem was that the site it occupied was too valuable. Downtown Boston was undergoing a building boom in the 1890s, as the new style of commercial construction took hold, with tall buildings like those of New York and Chicago. Perhaps Calvin could see to his left the incredible outline of the Ames Building, at sixteen stories the tallest in the city; it was one of several massive new structures that dotted the area. At least one, the Carter Building, only a block from his hotel, was in the new "skyscraper" model, with a frame of steel girders and walls of ornate terra cotta that supported no part of the structure but were merely for decoration. Both it and the Ames Building were thoroughly electric, and served by the passenger elevators that had made tall buildings possible.[5]

There were no elevators, of course, in the Tremont House; it was too small. It was luxurious, though, in a dim, old-fashioned way. The high-ceilinged, carpeted lobby and reading room, the Greek columns and moldings inside, the tall curtained windows evoked the Boston of Daniel Webster and Charles Sumner. It did not have room telephones (no hotel, not even the best, did before 1894), but it most likely did have the electric bell system for summoning the bellboy, maid, or other employees. On the second floor was a row of private dining rooms, at least two of which must have been reserved for the class of 1895. The cuisine was French, as at most pretentious hotels, and there was a lot of it at the class supper.[6]

This was a grand occasion for the class of 1895. Most of the members were on hand, dressed in their best: long frock coats, kid gloves, canes, and quite possibly top hats, which were making a comeback. Formal dress, however (black tie, dinner jacket, and cummerbund), which was just becoming standardized during this decade and had yet to acquire the name "tuxedo," was not required. Not until his senior year would Coolidge attend an occasion at which he needed to wear a dress suit. The '95 colors, pink and olive, no doubt dominated the decorations. According to the newspaper report of the supper, the juniors-to-be feasted and held "high carnival" to a late hour; at least one of them, the normally staid Carleton Kelley, became so exuberant and profane that when report of his words got back to Amherst later, he was called before Old Doc to explain. They sang the songs proper to the occasion, like "Once again we've met together," all the traditional college and fraternity songs, and probably popular hits like "Ta-ra-ra-boom-de-ay," a London music hall import that had swept the nation's campuses, including Amherst, in 1892. Many voices were raised in song throughout the evening, but chances are that Coolidge's contribution to this part was small. Indeed, so was his contribution to the entire supper. He was not on the program; as in his freshman year, he was just a face in the crowd.[7]

For the class, it was a time to look back with satisfaction over the events of the sophomore year—and so it was for Coolidge. His most satisfying achievement had come in April, when the grades from the winter term arrived. His mark had risen from a two to a three. In other words, he was doing satisfactory work; he had found how to cope with the severity of Amherst learning. He had written several good essays for Genung, and Tyler had grudgingly passed him in Greek while making the rest of the class take another exam. Now he had time, he felt, to relax, to socialize with his roommates, sell them maple sugar from home, and regale them with stories of Plymouth life. During a visit home on spring vacation, for instance, he had learned that his sixty-nine-year-old grandmother was getting married again, to a widower, an elderly minister named George Putnam who had been married to a cousin of hers. This was news that needed no dry wit to make it amusing—"When I tell any one about it they always laugh," Calvin wrote his stepmother—but he probably added some anyway, for Reverend Putnam, though an upright man, did not seem to have a great deal of sense and was known for his rambling sermons. More and more, Calvin enjoyed bring the sophisticated college man, looking back on Plymouth with ironic affection.[8]

The same term, his roommates began introducing him to the less serious side of college life. Calvin had already acquired the reputation among his class as a nondrinker and nonsmoker who never swore and never socialized. But during the spring, Deering and company, including a couple of sporting freshmen who also roomed at Morse's, managed to talk him and Carl Gates into a jaunt to Northampton. The whole group returned later that evening, filled with "the spirit for singing rollicking songs." They posed for a gag photograph in the house, attired only in their shirts, bare-legged and sporting a variety of odd headgear. Coolidge, wearing a top hat and looking solemn, was in the middle.[9]

His roommates, meanwhile, were discovering that under Coolidge's reserved exterior lurked an unsuspected vein of humor. It appeared, for example, in the air gun incident that spring. Some student in the house, maybe one of his roommates, had one; Coolidge got it, aimed out the window, and used it to pepper the president's gardener next door in the behind. This incident took place in the spring, when the student controversy with Gates was at its height, and perhaps Calvin was taking out student resentment on the gardener as a proxy. But it equally well may have had no political content; it was the sort of prank a Vermont country boy would love for its own sake.[10]

More characteristically, there was the story of him and his roommate Carl Gates, a serious young man who was studying to be a minister like his uncle.

Coolidge and his roommates, back from partying at Northampton in spring 1893. Coolidge is at the center, in the top hat. (Amherst College Archives)

He was deep in his assignment one evening when Calvin came in and began systematically pushing every other book on his bookshelf back so far that the title could not be read. He had gotten to the end of the shelf when Gates looked up and asked him what he was doing. "Trying to teach you to swear," Coolidge said.

Probably the most exciting event of the year for Coolidge had been his participation, with the rest of his class, in an unsuccessful attempt to liberate a bronze statue of the nymph Sabrina from the class of 1894 (the class's Anabasis, one classically minded member called it, invoking the story from Xenophon). Coolidge had undoubtedly been there, although he had written his parents nothing about it; like the jackass affair at B.R.A., it was simply too thrilling an event to miss.[11]

The contest for possession of Sabrina was a relatively new part of interclass rivalry at Amherst. It had begun in 1887 when members of the class of 1890 stole her (the statue was always referred to as a person) from a barn near Amherst after the college administration had had her removed from the campus because of student vandalism. The class of 1890 had sought to keep her out of the clutches of their rival '91, and also to pass her on to their ally '92, which was also '93's rival. The struggle for possession thus turned into a mock war between the odd- and even-numbered classes, a war whose rules were still evolving.[12]

In Calvin's sophomore year, the class of 1894 had the statue, having stolen her from a Railway Express office in Springfield as she was being shipped to Boston for display at the class of 1893's sophomore banquet. No one knew where they were hiding her. (In fact, she was under the floor of a barn in New Hampshire belonging to friends of junior class president Harlan Stone.) But it seemed probable that they would try to pass her on to the class of 1896 during the year, and since the unwritten rules of the contest dictated that the transfer take place at some public class function, the freshman class banquet seemed a likely time. The sophomores' mission was to intercept the statue and/or prevent the freshmen from having their banquet. Accordingly, in February, when the freshmen chartered a special train on the New London Northern and arranged to board it at a special stop a mile south of the station, the sophomores got wind of the plan and resolved to stop it.[13]

Calvin was doubtless among the sophomores who gathered to surprise the freshmen's special train that February night. This was the sort of contest he enjoyed, a game whose rules he understood perfectly. But his experience was of no help to his class, who had a rather frustrating evening. They commandeered the train at Amherst and dogged the freshmen as far as Millers Falls. At this station the freshmen jumped out and challenged the sophomores to battle. The sophomores, thinking that this was a ruse to get them off the train, which was going to Brattleboro, where they expected the class supper would be held, stood their ground. It was indeed a ruse, but not the one they expected. The train carried them on to Brattleboro; meantime, the freshmen boarded a second waiting train to Greenfield, where they had arranged for their banquet. The encounter between the two groups of derby-hatted, overcoat-wearing collegians at a country depot on a February night must have been dramatic; unfortunately, the only vignette of it concerns seventeen-year-old Jimmy Lawson of '95, a Phi Delt from Brooklyn, who "plunged off a railroad train head first and turned his face into pulp" trying to stop the departing freshmen. (Casualties like this were a fairly normal part of college students' mock battles; as long as no one died, they occasioned little comment.)[14]

Ninety-five had been unsuccessful in trying to stop the freshman banquet; but they did succeed in their larger purpose. The juniors, alarmed by the close call, decided not to hand over Sabrina that year. The transfer would have to take place the following year; there would be another chance for '95 to intercept the statue.[15]

Now the sophomore year was over, and Coolidge was for the first time in Boston, a world away from Plymouth. His hotel room, carpeted and electrified, made the Echo Lake Inn or even the Amherst Hotel seem rustic. The bathrooms had running water, with gleaming porcelain tubs and toilets in every room; Plymouth was still in the age of the copper-lined washtub, the china washbasin, the chamber pot and privy. Saturday morning, when the weather cleared and the sun came out, he could see the city in all its glory. The crowds, the skyscrapers and elevators, the uniformed hotel employees, the enormous new library with its statues and murals, the policemen with their tall helmets and tight buttoned coats, the well-dressed women in their elaborate hats and veils—not to mention the electricity and the steam heat—had no counterparts at home.[16]

Of course there were some similarities. One feature common to both places, so common indeed that Calvin hardly noticed it, and radically different from late-twentieth-century America, was their dependence on the horse for local transportation. The smell of horses, the piles of dung in the streets, the early-morning ringing of hammers in blacksmith shops, were as integral to Boston as to Plymouth, and would remain that way for another ten or fifteen years.[17]

But the differences were what struck Coolidge most. When he came to Boston, his train had pulled into a massive, two-towered brick station that could have passed for a courthouse in Vermont, with a marble-and-hardwood lobby off of which opened barber shops, restaurants and the like; the contrast with the weatherbeaten little depot in Ludlow was overwhelming. In Boston the air was filled with telephone wires; in Plymouth the first line was being strung that very summer, from Ludlow to the Union and up the mountain to the Notch. The newspaper announcement of the first telephone at the Union, in Levi Green's store, suggested Plymouth's cautious attitude toward the new device: "All wishing to converse with outsiders, will have their wants promptly attended to."[18]

Late Saturday afternoon found Calvin passing Levi Green's store, rattling up Notch Mountain with his luggage in his father's buckboard. The railroad had whisked him home from Boston in a matter of hours, and he was ready to doff his coat and begin helping John in the field. It was the beginning of another college summer. It was momentous in one way, because this was the July in which he turned twenty-one and legally became a man, but in most ways it was uneventful, indeed rather dull. There was no celebration of any kind for Independence Day at the Notch, and probably only the most cursory observance of his birthday. He enjoyed his usual round of activities with Dell Ward, Levi Lynds, and the Gilson girls; doubtless he worked at farm chores and got a bit of reading done. He called on his grandmother and made mild fun of the way she fussed over her flock of chickens. The only thing out of the ordinary was the construction work on the cow barn. John's barn had been struck by lightning the preceding August (Eddie Wilson, the hired man, had been inside it milking at the time) and had burned to the ground. Rebuilding was going slowly. John had laid the foundation the previous fall; this summer framing was under way, and he would get it clapboarded just in time for winter. But in general the summer passed quietly, and in mid-September Calvin was on the train back to "old Amherst."[19]

Amherst, in terms of technology, was between Boston's urban modernity and Plymouth's early-American primitiveness, but more like Plymouth than Boston. It often struck people as a somewhat artificial survival of old New England on the edge of the metropolitan northeast. It did have a thoroughly modern water and sewer system, barely a decade old, so that some householders could have modern plumbing fixtures and Pratt Gymnasium could have showers when it was working; but not all houses were connected to it. On the other hand, there was no telephone service at all. The streets were of crushed gravel at their best, mud at their worst, with a street-sprinkling tank that drove around in summer to lay the dust. Although there were a few asphalt or concrete sidewalks uptown, on which elegant town ladies and professors' wives paraded with their sunshades, the paths across the Common were often ankle-deep in mud. As for lighting, most streets were lit with gas, though arc lights were being tried out that fall on selected streets. The college library stacks had electricity of an uncertain and wavering sort, but most college buildings too were still on gas, which, according to the student newspaper, usually failed to give "sufficient light for even ordinary purposes." (One class of 1895 witticism had Professor Richardson asking Coolidge to remove his hat in German class, and Coolidge refusing because he didn't "want to ignite the gas.") Northampton, by contrast, was much more electrified; indeed, from high spots in Amherst at night it was possible to see the faint glow over Northampton in the western sky.[20]

Coolidge arrived in Amherst 13 or 14 September to begin his junior year: "the time of plug hats and seats in front of Prexy at church," as the yearbook put it, since juniors had the dubious honor of sitting directly in front of President Gates at morning service, and the traditional privilege of wearing plug (i.e., top) hats and carrying canes for ceremonial occasions. He purchased his cane in Amherst, using money his stepmother had given him for his birthday, and also picked up a top hat somewhere. His rooming arrangements were already taken care of; he and Percy Deering had agreed to share quarters on the second floor at Mrs. Avery's, on South Prospect Street. The rooms were "well lighted and pleasant," and the location was good, directly behind the Alpha Delta Phi house, only a block or so from the business district.[21]

What was really exciting about junior year, however, was the freedom it offered in the course of studies. Coolidge now had almost all the required courses behind him—no more Latin or Greek, no more mathematics. There remained only two terms of physics, or as he sometimes called it in his letters home, using the old name for the subject, "natural philosophy." This was drudgery indeed for Coolidge, who had no taste whatever for science; but the rest of the course made up for it. He and Deering both enrolled in first-year French under the new professor Edwin Grosvenor, a relaxed, scholarly man who had spent years in the Near East and liked to fraternize with the students. They, like almost all the other juniors, also signed up for Logic and Public Speaking with their old friend Professor Frink, a course that featured a weekly series of public debates and orations in the chapel. And finally, Coolidge had the chance to study the subject that was most meaningful to him, history.[22]

History, at Amherst—all history, from the ancient world to the modern United States—was taught by one professor, Anson D. Morse, a tall, slight man in his late forties with a short, wispy beard, modest, soft-voiced, and rather feeble in health. Amherst underclassmen knew him as the owner of a splendid orchard on Northampton Road whose luscious fruit, overhanging the fence, they regularly pilfered in fall. Some, like Coolidge, had also heard and chuckled over the rumor that Morse's rich father-in-law gave him ten thousand dollars for each grandchild and that that was why his family was so large. But more serious Amherst men knew of him as a scholar who specialized in the rise, development, and importance of political parties. He was a Vermonter, which may have given him extra credibility for Coolidge. His course, which promised to be excellent, would cover the entire junior year and extend two terms into the senior year.[23]

Another feature that was going to make junior year different, it was clear from the beginning of the term, was the fact that he was rooming with Deering. For the first fall in his college career, he would be rooming with a classmate, and thus integrated into the communication network of the class of 1895. Moreover, Deering, although not a member of any society, had come to be an important man in the class. Two inches shorter than Coolidge but twenty-nine pounds heavier, he was the starting fullback on the football team, in a school where football was becoming more and more important. Shortly after the beginning of school, he was named to the class executive committee: so was Ernest Hardy. Inevitably, some of their prestige rubbed off on their friend Coolidge. In September, when Deering was running for a position on the board of the *Olio*, the student yearbook, Coolidge got out and secured votes on Deering's behalf, accosting his classmates just as he had seen John do before town meetings in Plymouth, speaking to men, like Ulysses Blair, who hardly knew him up to then.[24]

This prestige-by-association, however, did not impress everyone. Early in the term, both Deering and Hardy were approached by Beta Theta Pi, which had suffered some losses among its junior-class members through transfers and dropouts and was looking for a few new additions from the class. Hardy accepted the invitation to join; Deering refused unless the Betas would make Coolidge a brother as well. Some leading Betas—led, according to one account, by Dwight Morrow—balked at this; Coolidge, they felt, was still too countrified, not a good mixer, in short unsuitable material for a society. As a result, Deering remained an ouden through his junior year, and so did Coolidge.[25]

Social snubs like these must have rankled, but Coolidge said nothing about them to his parents, or indeed to anybody. He kept up his usual pattern of behavior: hard study, quiet regularity. As always, he was not going to change his ways to suit anyone else (except, of course, his father). Since Deering was prominent on the team that fall, he followed the fortunes of the Purple and White—not, indeed, going to out-of-town games, which might have entailed missing classes, but attending all home games and watching silently, or with an occasional word for acquaintances. It was a rather frustrating season for Amherst, which had been champion of its league the year before. The team loss several of its early games; it did beat Trinity on 25 October, in what Coolidge characterized to his parents as "not much of a foot-ball game but a good slugging match," but that game was marked by a lot of spectator rowdiness and booing of the "umpire," as the referee was called. Next it went to Boston for a contest against the local Athletics, and lost 26–0; by Deering's account, the Athletics "were as big as mountains, and came through the line like steam engines."[26]

On 2 November Calvin wrote his father, in a letter that managed to touch on academics, politics, and football,

> In view of the fact that yesterday I put up a debate said to be the best heard on the floor of the chapel this term, in view of the fact that my name was read as one of the first ten in french, and in view of the fact that I passed in Natural Philosophy with a fair mark whereas many failed, and lastly in view of the fact that the purchase clause of the Sherman Bill has been repealed thus relieving the cause of financial panic can you send me $25 the forepart of next week?

The twenty-five dollars that Calvin sought so earnestly was for what was considered the climactic game of the season, the contest with Dartmouth on 11 November. In the preceding year or two the New Hampshire college had become Amherst's chief athletic rival, and the year before Amherst had defeated them decisively in football. This year's match was to be in Hanover, and Calvin, like most of the student body, was convinced that "our team needs the support of the whole college to win the game," even to the point where he was willing to wheedle money out of his father by parading his academic prowess and political orthodoxy.[27]

In the event, even the support of the whole college was not enough to give Amherst victory. A much heavier Dartmouth team, which included some players of doubtful eligibility, humiliated the Purple and White 36–0 that Saturday, in front of Coolidge and over half the student body, about 225 men in all. Coolidge had come up, probably, by the morning train along with a hundred or so fellow students and spent the night in Hanover before returning. He thus missed the most spectacular part of the weekend, in which the main body of Amherst students, returning Saturday night in a restive mood, became disorderly at the Greenfield train station, first stealing food from the restaurant, then plates, silver, and signs, then attempting to loot railroad property like baggage carts. When he got back on Sunday, the college was abuzz with talk of the incident. Coolidge, however, wrote his stepmother the following day "There is nothing new here as I know of to write about," adding only that he had seen Dr. Putney of St. Johnsbury Academy on the train back from Dartmouth.[28]

He was selective in reporting about his own activities, as well. Back in October he had written John about that year's Field Day, in which his class again won the cider: "[W]e had a big time drinking it at the gym last night with songs and speeches and the tossing of freshmen up in the blanket." What he failed to mention was that at the end of the meet he had taken part in the traditional Plug Hat Race, in which all the junior class, wearing their top hats and carrying their canes, scrambled down Pratt Field, with the last seven contestants having to treat the rest of the class to a supper. Deering had undoubtedly been among the first finishers; Hardy, for all his bulk, had managed a respectable showing; but Coolidge was among the last seven. Not dead last; that place had been taken by Russell Prentiss, a nineteen-year-old Psi U from Brooklyn, who was so overwhelmed by the ridiculousness of it all that he collapsed with laughter in the middle of the field. But Coolidge was one of the "Immortal Seven," as his classmates ironically called the group. By mid-November he would have to find a way to pay for his share of the dinner; moreover, since custom also required that each of the losers respond to a toast, he would have to give his first nonclassroom speech before the class of 1895. Silent, unobtrusive Calvin Coolidge was finally going to have to take center stage in front of his classmates.[29]

15

A New and Gifted Man

For many men in the class of 1895, the Plug Hat Dinner of 23 November 1893, in Hitchcock Hall, marked the first time they realized that their thin, redheaded classmate from Vermont was not just an odd character whom they passed occasionally on the street, but a person of substantial talent. It was a relaxed, jocular occasion, held in the new dining hall the college had just installed in an old mansion across College Street from the campus. The menu, according to the recollection of some of the thirty-odd men who were there, was largely oyster stew and beer. The last item is hard to believe, particularly in a college building in what was officially a temperance town, but the oyster stew seems right. It was, in any case, an oysters-and-beer sort of gathering. Russell Prentiss was toastmaster; the other six losers followed him, each with a humorous, personal speech. Coolidge's, which drew astonished cheers and applause from the audience, was entitled "Why I Got Stuck."

No text of the speech seems to have survived. This may be no great loss; it was probably not deathless prose. Witnesses remembered Coolidge's turning his pants pockets out to dramatize how much the dinner had cost him—this touch was surely authentic. They remembered his making fun of his own rustic image ("You wouldn't expect a plow horse to make time on the race track or a follower of the plow to be a Mercury"), and his winding up with the reminder that "the Good Book says that the first shall be last and the last shall be first." What struck his hearers was not classic wit, but the discovery that this classmate who never said or did anything could stand up with poise, laugh at himself and at others, and package his thoughts in crisp, funny sentences.[1]

The same revelation came to others in Henry A. Frink's debating classes that fall. Every man had to take turns defending one side of the question. On the morning when Coolidge's first turn came, Jay Stocking, a very smooth, articulate fraternity man who was often toastmaster at class functions, recalled that "opinion was divided as to whether he would rise and say he was unprepared or whether he would content himself with saying that he stood for the affirmative." But when he rose to speak "the class had the surprise of its life. He spoke cogently, fluently, and with a good sense of humor, and won his case hands down." Stocking summed up, "It was as if a new and gifted man had joined the class."[2]

Coolidge turned out to be formidable in debate. Not only could he present his own side cogently and fluently, as Stocking said; he could also demolish an opponent's case in one or two telling sentences. For the rest of junior year, the class looked forward to his debates eagerly, and, according to one account, he won them all. He certainly won some challenging ones. In January, he defeated Bert Pratt, the captain of the football team, in a debate over presidential versus parliamentary government, with Coolidge upholding the foreign (i.e., parliamentary) side. In February, he managed a victory on the unpopular proposition that the influence of football on college life was more harmful than beneficial. In March, his turn came to compete in the weekly oratorical contest for a prize of fifty dollars in books, the winner to be decided by vote of the class. He took his assigned topic, "The Story of the Cid and Its Meaning," turned it into a ringing affirmation of the idea that righteousness will always prevail in the long run, and won the prize.[3]

This change in Coolidge's status, from obscurity to general respect as a skilled speaker, which was to become part of the class of 1895's shared mythology, took place in a very short time. Its suddenness can be seen in the recollection of William Boardman, the Latin scholar who had briefly been Coolidge's fellow student at St. Johnsbury. Boardman had had to drop out of college in the middle of sophomore year to work in New York City, and did not return until October of junior year. On his return, he remembered, "one of the changes which struck me was that the two most prominent members of the class were Calvin Coolidge and John P. Deering." He exaggerated, of course; at no time were Coolidge and Deering the two most prominent members of their class. But what he probably meant to say was that the prestige of Coolidge and Deering had increased more startlingly than that of any other two students: Deering in football, Coolidge in debate. The fact that they roomed together made them an even more conspicuous pair.[4]

Coolidge's status continued to rise for the rest of his junior year, indeed for the rest of his college career. His classmates valued his humor, once they had discovered it, and took to hanging around him in hopes of hearing some clever saying. By senior year, most of them thought of him as a funny man, whose wit, delivered in a hollow Yankee voice that tickled his urban classmates, was "sarcastic," or according to others, "subtle" or "subdued." Stories circulated about his remarks. One of them, extant in various forms, is perhaps best told in Deering's version. He and Coolidge were boarding together at the eating place of Jack Collins, who kept a large number of dogs at his house, of various breeds. One night, when frankfurters were served, Coolidge refused to dig in. Instead, he got all his tablemates to beat the table with the butts of their knives and forks until Collins produced or accounted for each of the dogs. Then he said "Thank you," and began to eat. He could even be witty in other languages. Another Amherst tale had him responding to some kidding about his fiery hair by punning on the college motto "Terras irradient" (They shall enlighten the earth); "Terras irradio" (I am enlightening the earth), he quipped.[5]

The typical Coolidge story, as it evolved on the Amherst campus in those years, had a dependable pattern, that of Coolidge sitting quiet and observant as a conversation went on or a situation developed, and then concluding it with some profound, deeply funny observation. His timing was superb, as not only his Amherst classmates but also his Plymouth neighbors recognized. The summer after his junior year, when the Gilson girls put on a minstrel show in Coolidge's Hall, with a friend from Brooklyn, a Mr. Sprawl, as interlocutor, it was Calvin who furnished the jokes and acted as end man, rattling off the laugh lines in blackface, wearing a piece of curly black astrakhan cloth for a wig. ("His own father couldn't have picked him out of the line," Dell Ward remembered.) Quite naturally for a young man who had been disguising his fears most of his life, his control, his capacity for deadpan humor, was enviable.[6]

By senior year, he had come to be a very well-known figure in his class. Men like Dwight Morrow, who had blackballed him from Beta Theta Pi only the year before, now respected him and were happy to associate with him. In September of his senior year, the class had to choose its speakers for graduation the following spring. Calvin decided to go after the post of the Grove Orator, who made the humorous speech reviewing the class's accomplishments. As he had done the previous fall on Deering's behalf, he called on all the members of his class soliciting support ("I put more work into it than Alfred [Moore] did into Freemen's Meeting," he wrote John), and won by fifty-three votes to eighteen. He would be one of only six men to speak at the Class Day ceremony.[7]

Even beyond his class he began to acquire a reputation. He was pointed out to underclassmen as one of the notable seniors, a deep scholar who rarely spoke but always had the correct answer, a serious student who never looked at magazines but continually read an ! reread Homer, Dante, Shakespeare and the Bible. (This image was not quite accurate; he read the newspapers religiously to keep up with political developments, and also enjoyed *Truth*, a popular humor magazine.) Younger college men would stop and stare awestruck at him, standing alone on the hill beside the College Church, gazing out over the Pelham Hills, and wonder what sort of thoughts were going through his mind. Despite the respect he had won from his contemporaries, his social style remained that of a loner. Men in the classes behind his—in other words, those who knew him during the later years of his Amherst career—described him in practically the same words as his classmates in earlier years: "retiring, silent," "solitary," "reticent," a man one might see crossing the campus alone with an armful of

books, a man who "ran with a small crowd largely of his own choosing."
The junior who saw him standing alone behind the College Church returned an hour later to find Coolidge still fixed in the same spot, staring
eastward, deep in thought.[8]

Coolidge, to the end of his years at Amherst, was the same person he had
always been, whose shyness, whose deep-rooted fear of other people's discovering his inadequacy, kept him from sharing this achievements except
with a few. "It needed a good deal of seeing Coolidge to begin to appreciate him," one classmate commented; another added, "Those who got into
personal contact with him had to go the whole way."[9]

He did have friends as a senior, principally the two who had been closest
to him since sophomore hear, Ernest Hardy and Percy Deering. He hung
around a good deal with Hardy; a satirical classmate called him Hardy's
"laconic shadow." But he and Deering were still closer. They were on first-
name terms now—"Percy" and "Cal." At the beginning of senior year they
moved into new digs on South Prospect Street, a few doors down from
where they had been living, in the house of a veterinarian, Dr. Paige. They
had comfortable rooms, with hot and cold water and even electric lighting if
the tenants wanted to pay for it. (There is no indication whether Coolidge
and Deering did.) Calvin had become enough of a college man to want to
furnish the place elegantly; he persuaded his stepmother to make five
ruffled pillows of various sizes for their sofa (two were to be dark red with
yellow ruffles). At Thanksgiving he brought Deering home with him to Plymouth, and the local folks were invited to a kitchen dance in honor of the
guest. The summer after graduation, he spent a week at the Deerings' place
in Maine. He tolerated, and even to a degree emulated, his roommate's
cigar smoking, beer drinking, and mild profanity.[10]

The crowning social achievement of his senior year came the January before graduation, when he and Deering were initiated together into a new
fraternity. Actually, it was not completely new; it was a chapter of Phi
Gamma Delta, the same society on behalf of which Coolidge had been
approached as a freshman. Six Amherst men had started a chapter in the
winter of 1893–94, had rented an old mansion on Northampton Road, with
tennis court, library, and billiard room, for a clubhouse, and were prospect-
ing about for new members. The contact with Coolidge and Deering may
have been made through one of the founding members, Benjamin Ray,
who was Hardy's best friend. In any case, they, along with two sophomores, took the "sacred vows" shortly after returning from Christmas
vacation.[11]

"Cooley," as they called him, was pleased to be in a society at last. More
important, Phi Gamma was pleased to have him. As he wrote John, "the
fraternity, which I joined, rec'd congratulations quite as much as did I." He
and Deering did not move into the fraternity house, preferring to stay at
Paige's; but in other respects the membership changed his habits, particu-

larly his spending habits, dramatically. First he found that he had to have a dress suit for social functions; he purchased one for fifty-five dollars, tailor-made in Northampton, within a week of joining. Then there were initiation fees, term fees, and the cost of the pin ("College men are always proud to wear a society, greek letter pin and are very seldom seen without it," he assured John), even though he planned to get an inexpensive pin, perhaps only twenty dollars. There were trips to society functions in Northampton and New Haven. There were modish recreations like fencing with the Fencing Club at the gym, for which he acquired a mask and a set of foils. (In one way, on the other hand, fraternity membership saved him money: when he had a major paper due in history, he turned it over to a junior Phi Gamma to type up.)[12]

Some scattered pieces of evidence suggest that he took an even more radical step during his last two terms at Amherst: he tried to learn to dance

Coolidge as an Amherst senior. (Forbes Library)

and invited some Smith girls over to social functions. Certainly by belonging to Phi Gamma Delta he was under some pressure to do so. The societies sponsored virtually all the male–female socializing there was at Amherst, and virtually all of these important activities revolved around dancing. It was almost the duty of a fraternity man to be able to dance and cut a good figure in society. It seems that Coolidge tried to be a loyal member and learn "the arts of the drawing room"; but the attempt (and he may have made it only once) was a failure, not surprisingly for someone so radically unsure of himself. Dance steps and the art of chatting with vivacious strangers proved too much of a challenge. When he invited a girl to Amherst for his graduation, it was not a Smith student, but Lena Clark of Keene, whom he had dated during his senior year at B.R.A.[13]

In terms of social prestige, Coolidge had gone from nearly complete isolation to general acceptance in the space of two years. In terms of his classmates' respect, he had gone still farther. He moved from anonymity to a place among the top ten or fifteen men in his class—despite his peculiarities, the long silences, the limp handshake, the gurgling chuckle that passed for a laugh, the queer habit of rubbing the underside of his chin in deep thought. One naturally searches for a reason behind this sudden celebrity, whether Coolidge's classmates had simply been slow to recognize his excellence, or whether he himself had developed since freshman year.[14]

Coolidge favored the second alternative, at least so far as his academic achievements were concerned. "In junior year," he recalled, "my powers began to increase and my work began to improve." College records bear him out. The last two years he spent at Amherst were scholastically much stronger than the first two. In fact, the best average he achieved in his twelve terms at college was the winter term of his junior year, in which he made an 86.25, very nearly a four on the five-point scale. It was not only his debating that did it, though that was very strong. His work in French was so good that it earned him a personal letter of commendation from Professor Grosvenor. In senior year his Italian became adequate to the task of reading the *Commedia* in the original. In the same year he placed among the Hyde Fifteen, the top orators in his class, and wrote an essay on the causes of the American Revolution that was judged by a national jury in an intercollegiate contest and won him a gold medal. "I think I must stand very well in college now," he wrote his father a few months before graduation.[15]

Several reasons account for his improved work. As a junior and senior he could take courses more congenial to him, history and philosophy rather than classics and mathematics. He could drop German, which he disliked, and take up French and Italian, which he enjoyed and did well at. It is also true that it had taken him several terms to slough off the disadvantages of his country background and limited education. Several of his classmates from rural and small-town backgrounds, like Fairbanks and Booth, never did, and stayed in academic hot water their entire Amherst careers.[16]

Probably the crucial factor was that he succeeded in developing a remarkably sensitive control over the way he expressed himself. He developed a masterly command of style, especially for a twenty-one-year-old. In his earlier years at Amherst he was still a devotee, as one classmate recalled, of the "Daniel Webster school of oratory," rich, ornamented rhetoric with lots of fustian, as his July Fourth oration at Plymouth showed. But at some point in his sophomore or junior year, probably encouraged by the appreciation of friends for his brief, epigrammatic way of talking in company, he decided to try using a similar approach in public. This was the style that brought down the house at the Plug Hat Dinner, that impressed his opponents in debate, and that ended up as the basis of his mature speeches: a spare style, based on simple sentence structures and frequent short sentences. It could be pointed and specific at times, but the general tenor of a Coolidge speech was oddly abstract, a speech from which the speaker himself was absent. He almost never used the word "I"; in some of his mature political speeches the word does not occur at all. Instead, there were broad statements, enunciated with the confidence of revealed truth and often phrased in striking, even challenging language. "The influence of right is imperishable," began his prize oration on the Cid. "The mantle of truth falls on the Grove Orator on condition that he wear it wrong side out," was the first sentence of his Grove Oration. When he had a point he wanted to argue, his introductory generalization could be startlingly abrupt. One professor assigned him a paper on the evils of inherited wealth, a popular topic in the depression of the nineties; Coolidge began, "Since wealth *per se* cannot be an evil neither can inherited wealth be an evil."[17]

This was his hallmark style, but he had others. What one might call the professorial mode, the offhand, ponderous sort of expression, studded with facts and a hint of condescension, in which late-nineteenth-century intellectuals communicated with the public, was well within his grasp. He did not use it as a rule, but it cropped up now and then, as in a letter to John in his senior year:

> I see Holmes is dead, the Autocrat of the Breakfast table on whom the years sat so lightly and who had only just declared that he was 85 years *young*. No one but Gladstone is left of those great men that were born in 1809. Darwin is gone, the great expounder of evolution, a scientist equal to Newton. Our own Lincoln finished his lifes work when he struck the shackles from four millions of slaves [note the fashionable Gallicism] and saw the surrender of General Lee. The nineteenth century is slipping away. We are to live in the 20th century and must prepare for it now.[18]

Then there was, surprisingly, a popular-literature style, which appeared in print only once. The college literary magazine for October of his senior year contained a short story by Coolidge entitled "Margaret's Mist," basically a conventional dime Western, set in the Adirondacks near Ausable Chasm, which he had visited that summer on an excursion from Plymouth. (Midge Gilson had been his companion, as she always was at Plymouth summer events.) It showed, if nothing else, that he had a near-infallible ear for magazine writers' cliches. The characters, the situations, and the prose were all derivative; the plot Coolidge himself dismissed to his stepmother as a "highly improbable yarn."[19]

The reason behind the story was that summer's excursion; the dramatic Adirondack scenery had so impressed Coolidge that he wanted to write about it, and devised the story as a vehicle. The "peaks of the Adirondacks" and the "ever varying glimmer" of the lake were what the story was really about. Calvin's deep, heartfelt response to natural beauty usually took the form of standard nineteenth-century romantic prose. "The sun is just going down; we have such beautiful sunsets here!" he wrote to John from his room at Paige's. "Far out over the Hadley meadows, over the city of Northampton, to the line of the Berkshire hills, the sky is purple and gold. Some one is playing the chimes of the college church. The harmony blends with the scene." He did not work at making his description of nature or of his response more detailed and precise. Feelings about nature were important to him; evocative writing about them was not.[20]

Oratory, as at B.R.A., remained the really important thing. "There is nothing in the world gives me so much pleasure as to feel that I have made a good speech and nothing gives me more pain than to think I have made a poor one," he wrote John in 1895. No wonder: public speaking had come to be his main channel of communication with his classmates. Carefully he worked on his speeches, both humorous and serious, trying to see how simply he could express his ideas and at the same time keep them free from any trace of his country origin. "I do not always want to remain a rustic in my ideas and in my appearance," he said in the same letter. By the end of his college years he was ready to move on to the clipped, idealistic speeches of his public career.[21]

Most of Coolidge's progress at Amherst, then, was the fruit of his own efforts, as he told John: "My growth has been slow but I think it is substantial and must have been made on my own merits as I have not been pushed forward by the influence of someone else." But he also received a good deal from his years there. Not the first two years: those were almost a total loss in terms of learning, except for picking up some general culture through lectures, concerts, and occasional conversations. But in the last two he came into contact with two of Amherst's best teachers, who crystallized his thinking in important ways: Anson D. Morse in history and Charles E. Garman in philosophy.[22]

History, as Morse presented it, was a subject full of meaning. It was essentially political, the story of the human rise from barbarism and servitude to self-government and democracy. It had heroes: men like Simon de Montfort and Luther, Cromwell and Jefferson, rebels all against some kind of oppres-

sion, helped on by progress, that wonderful warm engine that Morse, like so
many late-nineteenth-century Americans, sensed churning beneath the sur-
face of history. Where "conditions are healthful and progress is normal," he
wrote in a major paper the year Coolidge was studying under him, "the
humblest citizen becomes to the full measure of his capacity a sharer" in
the goods of society, including political power. To Morse, there was nothing
wrong with political parties; each was "the self-realization of a group of citizens within the state." This broad, basically optimistic vision of history
Morse presented with remarkable sweep and detail. According to Alfred
Stearns of the class of 1894, who had a chance to compare, his notes were
superior to those of students from either Harvard or Yale.[23]

Morse's vision held the full attention of Calvin Coolidge, who followed
the deeds of its heroes, many of whom he had already studied because of
their oratory, and accurately picked up the basic intent of the course. It
was, he wrote years later in his autobiography, "a thesis in good citizenship
and good government." For a young man who was so deeply committed to
the Republican party, it was doubtless reassuring to hear that political parties were the normal and right way to approach questions of power. And
Morse's faith in progress confirmed what Coolidge had already figured out
for himself to some degree: great powers and great truths guided human
affairs; a man had only to recognize them and align himself with them in
order to accomplish great things. A year before he began studying with
Morse, Coolidge had written his father of his conviction that

> genius is the ability to harmonise with circumstances and just as by a slight pres-
> sure of the finger we can turn on the most powerful current of electricity or open
> the valve of a mighty engine so genius taking advantage of natures laws with seem-
> ingly little effort rules the world, when it directs itself along the right channels.

But it must have been cheering to hear his thought restated, with abundant supporting detail, by this likable, understanding scholar who was
known for his insistence on factual accuracy.[24]

Coolidge had already studied two terms with Morse, and his class was approaching the English Civil War, when he began Charles E. Garman's
course in psychology the spring term of his junior year. The course extended from that point through the entire senior year, four terms in all. It
was called, indifferently, psychology or philosophy, because it began with a
rigorous study of the mind in the light of the latest scientific knowledge and
then went on to consider various philosophical and ethical systems. But
Coolidge had known about Garman long before entering. Garman's Psychology was the most remarkable course in the college and one of the most
remarkable in the country; Garman was a magnet to students, because of his
brilliant mind and the mystical aura that surrounded him. "We looked on
Garman," Coolidge said, "as a man who walked with God."[25]

He was a distinctive figure, a pale, slender, clean-shaven man with deep-set dark eyes, wrapped in an overcoat in all but the hottest weather, for fear of chills. His course, which was reputed the hardest in the college, involved an inordinate amount of reading. ("None of my work is very difficult," Coolidge wrote home in October of his senior year, "except Psycology [sic] that takes about thirty five hours each week and then one does not get all that is in it.") Nevertheless, it fascinated students, because Garman was entirely open to the latest scientific knowledge and unafraid to discuss evolution, the structure of the mind, mass psychology, arguments against God's existence and other controversies with a thoroughness and depth that left students gasping. Most students who took the whole course ended with a renewed faith in God and a belief in serving others, but even those who did not considered it a life-changing experience. "I don't believe, Professor," Dwight Morrow wrote Garman in the spring of 1894, "that you can fully appreciate what a strong hold you have on Amherst today. It isn't only with the senior class with whom you come in contact. Underclassmen go to the seniors for advice continually because they know that the seniors have something which they have not."[26]

Garman was not a combative person—quite the reverse, in fact—but his quiet power over the students inevitably attracted the attention, and occasional envy, of other dominant personalities. In the spring of 1894, as Coolidge prepared to begin his course, the philosophy professor was locked in polite, discreet, unpublicized combat with President Gates. The dapper president had been trying, with some success, to consolidate his own hold on Amherst. In the spring of Coolidge's sophomore year, he had managed to stymie the student effort to end compulsory chapel, after a series of noisy confrontations at his office in Walker Hall. The following year, he had taken on the College Senate, which had passed an anti–compulsory chapel resolution, over the issue of its power to discipline misbehaving students (for instance, the rioters who had sacked the Greenfield railroad restaurant). Matters had now reached the point that the student senators were waging a newspaper war, with angry public letters to justify their position, against the president and his allies among the faculty. Now Gates decided to deal with Garman, who was vulnerable to attack because of the way he taught his course. He did not use a text; instead, he made up pamphlets of his own writing and summaries of other works, printed them (with the aid of a black servant) on a press at his own home, and distributed them to the students with the condition that they were not to be shown to anyone outside the course and were to be returned when that part of the course was completed. The reason for this remarkable secrecy was that they contained statements of some very controversial positions—Darwinian, materialistic, atheistic—which Garman intended to discuss in class but did not wish presented as samples of his thinking. Gates, who was nothing if not orthodox, asked to see copies of the pamphlets and to sit in on Garman's discussions;

Garman responded that he was welcome to take part if he would sit in on the entire course, not just a portion. Jealous of Garman's popularity and suspicious of his doctrinal soundness, Gates began a series of bureaucratic maneuvers meant to make Garman's position at Amherst so uncomfortable that he would resign and go elsewhere.[27]

Coolidge was probably vaguely aware of this conflict as he began the course. Rumors were out among the students that spring that Garman had accepted a position at the University of Michigan and would be gone next year; in fact, they were the reason for Morrow's letter. Coolidge had lost his earlier admiration for Gates. "I understand that the Trustees are getting unsatisfied with him," he wrote his father. "I am not looking for his removal very soon but think it will come in time if he does not change his policy. He is narrowing down continually the breadth of principle that has character-ized Amherst in the years past." Not a rabid opponent of Gates, as many of his classmates were, he did not carve obscene comments about the presi-dent into the desks and beams of Walker Hall classrooms, as they did. A student in the class below his remarked, "One would as soon expect to see the Sphinx rise up and gallop madly down the Nile as to find Coolidge swept up and along by any college clamor or fad or excess." But he was doubtless relieved to learn in the fall of 1894 that Garman had been persuaded to stay by an intense letter-writing campaign by students and recent alumni, and by their pressure on Gates to increase his salary and leave him alone. It was Gates's first big setback, the first in a series that were to lead, as Coolidge had predicted, to his resignation within a few years.[28]

The fall term found Coolidge with sixty-six of his classmates, the great majority of the senior class, in the overheated Room 10 of Walker Hall, which Garman, because of ill health or hypochondria, always insisted be kept at nearly eighty degrees for his classes. Not all seniors elected the course; a few were frightened away by its reputation. But those who were there were enthralled. Despite the large number of students, Garman con-ducted the class almost as a seminar. He sometimes passed around brief questionnaires to see if everyone had read the material and how they had reacted to it, or asked for a brief summary of different passages, orally or in writing; but then he proposed a question, or questions, based on the read-ing (Does God exist objectively or is He just a creature of the human imagi-nation? For that matter, is there a human imagination, or merely a set of chemical responses in the brain?) and asked students to confront it on the basis of their reading. He rarely offered an answer of his own; what he did offer were precepts to help students tackle the question logically: "Process not product"; "Carry all questions back to fundamental principles"; "Weigh the evidence"; and, repeatedly, "Gentlemen, define your terms."[29]

The results, as the course went on, were spectacular. First tentatively, and then with increasing conviction, students responded. "Truly he drew men out," Coolidge was to write of Garman. The class turned into an animated discussion, with Garman refereeing, keenly commenting on the positions taken. It began at eleven forty-five; often the twelve forty-five bell would ring for lunch, and Garman, seated behind the desk, would say, "The bell has rung, gentlemen. I'm perfectly willing to continue the discussion if that is your wish, but no one is required to remain." But, as Alfred Stearns of the class of '94 recalled, "remain we did to a man and the arguments continued for fifteen, thirty, and occasionally forty-five additional minutes, while waiting dinners grew cold or irate boarding-house keepers in disgust swept the tables clean, leaving only Deuel's soda-fountain to minister to empty stomachs." Even after class, the discussion went on. At meals in the DKE house, William Boardman recalled, the seniors "disputed Garman's principles. They quarreled over the meaning of his words. They were enthusiastic over the man and enthused by the stimulus of his teaching."[30]

Few professors could have taught philosophy as Garman did, because few possessed his prodigious memory, his wide reading, and above all the keenness of mind that enabled him to respond to a student's comment with a penetrating query or illustration that forced the student to perceive the answer on his own, without having it thrust on him. Garman's brilliance made him wonderfully flexible; he was ready to follow wherever the students wished to go. As a result, his course was never quite the same from year to year. But beneath the flexibility there was a constant purpose. He felt that it was crucial for students to choose a basic system of beliefs, based on reasoning, as a guide to future action, at it was possible to know the truth, and, once one knew it, to act on it. His first objective was to supply them with the mental tools to make their choice. He had already made his own. He was a Christian, deeply committed to the idea of service to others; that commitment, indeed, was the reason why he taught at all. As the course went on through the winter and spring terms, the ideas of service and helping others moved more and more to the center of discussion.[31]

Many, perhaps most, of Garman's students valued the course especially for the analytical sharpness it gave them, the ability to discern basic intellectual and moral issues underlying practical questions. Certainly Coolidge did. "I am confident," he wrote Grandmother Coolidge in January of his senior year, "I have gained a power of grappling with problems that will stand by me all my life." Under Garman's influence, he experienced a surge of confidence in his abilities that he had probably never felt before. Over and over, that year, he referred to his "power" in letters to his family; "[C]areful work now will be a source of power to rely on in the future"; "[T]he time will surely come when to know [historical books] will be power to me"; knowing and observing the laws of human nature gave "power to rule." Certainly he handled philosophical concepts with an ease inconceivable in the shy, rustic Coolidge of four years before, as when he casually dropped the following aside into a letter on practical topics: "It is not true that all knowledge comes from experience, if it had to do so we not only would never know any thing about religion but would never know that two and two are four"; or when, in the manner of his mentor, he used scientific concepts to convey religious truths: "[God] works by processes and is limited by conditions so He can send a stronger current over larger wires."[32]

His confidence surged over into his plans for life after graduation. He had long hoped and assumed that when he was through with Amherst he would return to Plymouth, where he felt comfortable, and farm or keep the store, silently enjoying all the learning he had amassed at college but not doing anything in particular with it. But in senior year, impressed with his own performance under Morse and Garman, he began to waver. Early in the year when he had had to fill out a class questionnaire about his postgraduate plans, he put down his real sentiments in humorous language: "Nothing, I reckon. Must rest after these four hard years." But in January he wrote John a daring alternative idea: "I have not decided what I shall do next year, shall probably go into the store or go to a law school at Boston or New York." In terms of Morse and Garman, the choice made sense. Studying law in a swarming city far from Plymouth would afford limitless opportunities for study, analysis, debate, observation, all the things Calvin had learned to do well, if his father would only foot the bill. In terms of his own future, he was not yet committing himself to a high-powered metropolitan legal career, but he was at least suggesting it as an option he would be willing to consider in time.[33]

John was skeptical about law school. Father and son tossed the idea around in letters throughout the spring, and it is clear, though nowhere stated specifically, that John had reservations about the expense and did not see why Calvin could not study in the traditional manner, by entering some New England lawyer's office as an unpaid assistant and mastering the law as he learned the procedures of the office. Calvin would have none of that. It is probably fair to say that he wanted either of the two environments where he now felt secure: a college, learning under great professors, or, failing that, the easy insularity of the Notch. Toward the end of the semester, as it became apparent that John probably would not put up the money for law school, Calvin reminded his father in a postscript, "I have not decided to study law." For him, in other words, the alternative to law school was not a law office; it was returning to Plymouth and taking over the store from Les Walker.[34]

Returning home was not just a retreat to familiar surroundings; it also fit in with Garman's other teaching, his ideal of duty and service to others. As a early as junior year, when he had just begun studying psychology, Calvin had written his father a letter that in effect anticipated Garman's thinking. "Would you like to have me start in the store and live in Plymouth and live for Plymouth? Perhaps I could make it prosperous enough so that it would not be dependant upon the Home Missionary Society for the support of a Minister." In April of senior year he picked up the same thought: "I have not decided yet that I want to leave Plymouth, not because I like the place to live in, I do not, not because I could do more good there, there are larger fields, but because I may owe some debt to the place some duty that claims my first consideration." In the manner of many an idealistic young college man, but unusually for Calvin, who rarely challenged his father's values, he had already indicated to John that making a lot of money was not a priority with him: "I expect to sell out the present in terms of the future and am not in any hurry to get rich." There was, no doubt, an element of rationalization in all this. Calvin wanted to go back to the Notch because he felt comfortable with the people there, because he knew the rules of social interaction; but he also meant to go back imbued with Garman's ideals and logical power.[35]

The question was still very much undecided as warm weather settled over Amherst and June graduation approached. It would be a festive week, not unlike the county fair at Woodstock: farmers drove in with their wares from the surrounding countryside; there were booths of food and drink on the Common, and a special gymnastic drill exhibition in the Gym. The seniors had elected not to wear caps and gowns, but the ceremony in Johnson Chapel would still be colorful. The class was rehearsing its "alumni yell," which they would deliver en masse after getting their diplomas, and which contained the pointed lines "Hooray—hooroo—/ We're through Gates with you."[36]

Coolidge spent his last few weeks at Amherst working at his low oak desk with its double row of pigeonholes, cranking out his Grove Oration, polishing the sentences and sharpening the allusions. It was possible for a Grove Oration to be just a long catalogue of good-humored ribbing, poking fun at the faculty, the administration, and one's classmates, but Coolidge wanted something tighter and more interesting. Moreover, he had nothing else to work on. There were speaking contests and debates for the seniors, in which several of his acquaintances—Morrow, Ray, and Hardy, for instance—were involved, but he had not placed in the finals for these; his role was simply to be the class wit. He showed up at Walker Hall to have his picture taken with the class, standing in the rear again, holding a book, near a pillar. But this time, he was surrounded by friends: Hardy, Ray, Deering, all his Phi Gamma brothers. As in freshman year, however, he was staring into space over the heads of the class, and as in freshman year, he looked slightly different from the majority of his fellows. This time it was not his hat, but his hair. Almost all the men of the class of 1895 parted their hair in the center, as the fashion of the nineties dictated; Coolidge, however, had let his grow long, and wore it in a great romantic shock over his forehead.[37]

The commencement ceremony was to be on Wednesday, the twenty-sixth. His father and stepmother were coming down for the occasion. John had taken the momentous step (for him) of buying a new coat for the gradua-

The senior picture of the Class of 1895. (Amherst College Archives)

tion, after extensive consultations with Calvin about the proper style. (Calvin had become an authority on correct attire in his last years at Amherst, with the right sort of suits, gloves, shoes, hats, even tennis trousers. His wardrobe, though not large, was fashionable. He never dressed up, but he never looked informal.) They would come on the train and pick up Miss Clark at South Vernon station. To represent the rest of the town, Levi Lynds was coming separately. A disabled veteran and local eccentric, he could well afford to take a day off and go to a Plymouth boy's graduation. Calvin was delighted he was coming, but warned him to put up in Northampton, as Amherst was going to be impossibly crowded.[38]

It is not clear whether any of the Plymouth party were in Amherst around midafternoon the day before commencement, when the class of 1895 emerged from their formal Class Day ceremony in College Hall and headed for the College Grove—the tall, shady trees in the very center of the campus, behind Johnson Chapel—for the more relaxed part of the day, the Grove Oration and the Grove Poem. The seniors lighted their corncob pipes and lay back on the grass to hear Coolidge's effort, which he read in a solemn, poker-faced manner. Before long he had his classmates roaring with laughter and demanding repetition of the personal digs at faculty and students with which it abounded. When he repeated these, he did it in exactly the same dry tone, not cracking a smile.[39]

The speech was an enormous success. The Grove Oration contained many hallmarks of Coolidge's mature style. It was short and unembellished. The paragraphs were brief—indeed, one could almost call it a collection of unrelated one-liners. At the same time, it was not just a series of crackerbarrel witticisms. There were learned allusions—to De Quincey, Shakespeare, Milton, and Horace Greeley, among others—as one would expect in a college oration. The vocabulary was eclectic, but most of the humor was simple, quiet, and occasionally devastating. ("Only last Memorial Day, Lockwood delivered two addresses before people.") Coolidge did not share his generation's addiction to puns and word-play; the speech was funny because it was based on a close observation of people's foibles. But a great many of the references were sly, sometimes so indirect as to be totally opaque at the distance of a century. (Coolidge, with his distaste for confrontation, was fond of glancing, allusive comments.) "Compton has sometimes been unfortunate—when he could not read between the lines" probably referred to the use of a "horse" in class. The "tenebrific star" that "did ray out darkness" over the Amherst system was doubtless Gates. But what is one to make of this reference to Old Doc: "Was he the only member of the faculty that was eminently fitted to hear Egan's apology for talking French at the sophomore supper, or had Egan infringed upon the domain of the physical department?" Interspersed with these digs, however, were examples of the plain Coolidge style, dry, restrained, a little ironic:

Gentlemen of the Class of '95—O, you need not look so alarmed. I am not going to work off any song and dance about the cold, cruel world. It may not be such a misfortune to be out of college. It is not positive proof that a diploma is a wolf because it comes to you in sheep's clothing.[40]

The next morning, he and seventy-four other Amherst men climbed the stage in College Hall, wearing their best suits, and received their diplomas. They listened restively to Gates's address, delivered their alumni yell, said their goodbyes with all the reserve and repressed emotion called for by the occasion, and went back to their fraternity houses and boarding houses to pack for the trip home. Many of them, as they packed for the train, knew what lay ahead for them—not Coolidge. It was either his last summer on the farm before beginning a career in law, or the first summer of a life spent quietly in Plymouth among friends and family. It was up to John. Either would do. Calvin was used to living with uncertainty.

Afterword

This sketch of Coolidge to age twenty-three has been written with an effort to avoid focusing on his later rise to the presidency. The idea has been to present him as a young Vermonter of his time, fairly typical (with individual abilities and handicaps, to be sure), reluctantly discovering the world around him. But the question of his later career cannot be evaded entirely. This final section tries to sketch a connection between the solitary, hard-working college student of the preceding pages and the odd, laconic president of the Jazz Age.

Coolidge's hope of returning to Plymouth for good eluded him throughout his life. Between the *Autobiography* and his letters it is possible to reconstruct what happened in the summer after his graduation. John decided not to underwrite law school for Calvin, but at the same time refused to let him take over the Notch store. Calvin pleaded with him in vain to change his mind; two years later, as he faced the expense of opening a law office in Northampton, Massachusetts, he was to remind his father with dry irony, "I suppose that is what you contemplated ... when you sent me down here two years ago—rather than let me try to live in Plymouth."

Actually, John did not "send" his son to Northampton; he merely insisted that Calvin take a position in a lawyer's office. Calvin had written a lawyer, an old acquaintance of his father in Montpelier, about this possibility, and was awaiting an answer when he heard, unexpectedly, from Ernest Hardy, who had gone back home to Northampton. Hardy was clerking in a law office there, and thought there might be room for another clerk if Calvin might be interested. Northampton was fairly familiar ground to him, and he enjoyed Hardy's company, so he applied and was accepted. When he won admission to the bar, John helped him open an office of his own in Northampton. Meanwhile, he and Hardy had begun dabbling in local Republican politics with a good deal of success. In 1905, he married Vermont-born Grace Goodhue, who taught at the Clarke School for the Deaf and, perhaps for that reason, was one of the few young women not frightened by his long, impenetrable silences. The following year Hardy married and left town to live in the West, while Coolidge continued his local political activity. The improbable sequence of events that led him from there to national prominence is set forth clearly in the *Autobiography*, and in the biographies of Fuess and McCoy.

In a sense, then, Coolidge failed to achieve the dream of his youth. But the failure was only apparent, because the dream itself was only instrumental, a way of dealing with the fears that beset him throughout his life, the fear of hostile strangers detecting and criticizing his inadequacy, belittling and eventually destroying him. By retreating to the Notch, where he knew the rules of all the verbal and social interactions that took place, he could have avoided that threat, but in the end he found a different strategy for dealing with it: political activity. By seeking and winning public office he could prove to John, and thus to himself, that he was a worthy person. Nothing in his words or actions indicates that he had any of the other goals that start men out on a political career: desire for money, thirst for power, an ideological agenda to promote. He was simply doing what he had done for years: trying to win his father's approval. For the same reason, he was committed to doing the job well, with all the intelligence, integrity, and rhetorical skill he had. He had these abilities in such abundance, it turned out, that they outweighed the crippling shyness of his early years, which normally would have scuttled any hopes for political advancement.

From this viewpoint, Coolidge's early years constitute an impressive success story—the story of a sensitive, idealistic boy of more than average intelligence learning to cope with a terrible psychological burden. Reading, study, and daydreaming formed a large part of his defenses, as they do with most reticent people. But more useful to him were the other devices of disciplined routine effort, mastery of rhetoric, keen observation, and emotional control, all of which he picked up little by little. The cultural norms of the area where he grew up helped him. He was not expected to be outgoing, gallant, or aggressive; Yankee culture rewarded him for being silent, observant, and diligent. But the task of concealing his fear was heavy, unremitting work, and perhaps explains the paucity of close friendships he formed during adolescence and, indeed, throughout life. He was simply too occupied in shoring up his own psychological defenses to have much time to give to other people.

Another challenge of his early years was that of low vitality. He was subject to a variety of respiratory ailments, and doubtless one reason, apart from shyness, that he held aloof from activities with other boys was that they were physically exhausting. He liked the outdoors, but most of his pastimes there were sedentary, like fishing and riding. In his only recorded athletic competition, the Plug Hat Race in his junior year, he finished last, or nearly last. "Cal always hated exercise," Percy Deering recalled, "and never took an inch of it if he could help it. Walk? O, he'd walk to classes, but that would be enough to last him for a week." Hitchcock's anthropometric measurements for him, which still survive at Amherst, make the point statistically: in weight, in lung capacity, in number of pushups and pullups, and in total strength, Coolidge was at or near the bottom of his class.

At bottom, Calvin and his father probably both regarded this lack of vigor as a sign of impending death. Yet for all Calvin's low vitality, he outlived several of his schoolmates: his roommate Alfred Turner, the athlete, died only a few years out of college; his Amherst acquaintance Royal Booth contracted tuberculosis and died at an Army hospital in New Mexico in the early 1900s; Henry Hicks, his friend at B.R.A., died of Bright's disease while Calvin was still in college. But Coolidge, though he survived, was psychologically prepared to join them. As far as we know, he entertained no dreams, no long-range plans for the future. "Do the day's work," was a favorite maxim of his in maturity, and it was equally true of his growing up, in both the positive and negative senses. Do the day's work, yes, with all possible care, intelligence, and honesty; but also, do only the day's work, make no long-range agenda, set no future goals for achievement. Time and again, important decisions in Coolidge's early life were taken at the last minute, with no suggestion of advance planning. This is not to say that the Coolidges were not prudent and saving; Yankee culture had taught them to be. But Calvin did not go in for great dreams of future accomplishment. As far as he knew, he had no future. He preferred to let the future come to him.

Most of Coolidge's early friends (Dell Ward, Warren Spaulding, Allen Wilder, Henry Brown, Herbert Moore) did what he had hoped to do, lived and died in Windsor County, farming or operating small businesses. Thomas Moore did move as far as New Hampshire. Albert Sargent became an attorney in Montpelier. Rufus Hemenway, on the other hand, returned from the Midwest to spend most of his life as a businessman in Ludlow. Midge Gilson taught music and commuted between Brooklyn and Plymouth most of her life, and Coolidge's B.R.A. sweetheart Lena Clark married his B.R.A. classmate George Levey and spent her life in Ludlow. John Coolidge lived to see his son become president, as did many others of that generation (John Wilder, for example). All were still in or near Plymouth.

Coolidge's two closest friends in college had careers similar to his own, minus the political luck: Deering returned to his home town in Maine and became a successful lawyer and judge; Hardy became a leading attorney in Portland, Oregon.

As for the environments in which he grew up, Amherst College has changed a good deal. Most of the college buildings of Coolidge's time are gone; only a few of the oldest survive. The town, on the other hand, is fairly intact. All four buildings where Coolidge roomed are still standing, though not marked in any way. In fact, there is no memorial of Coolidge's presence anywhere in Amherst.

Plymouth Notch remains remarkably unchanged. The hills are rather more forested; there are fewer flower gardens and almost no working farms. But thanks to the Coolidge family, Plymouth neighbors, and the State of Vermont, buildings have been preserved or restored so that the hamlet looks almost as it did a century ago. Most of the houses are now museums, not residences, and the Coolidge Home attracts thousands of tourists every year, but the place retains its serene beauty. The remoteness, the self-contained quality of the spot continue to inspire wonder that any inhabitant should have gone on to greatness in the outside world—least of all a young man so quiet, so diffident, and so profoundly unambitious.

Notes

Abbreviations used in the Notes and Bibliography are as follows:

AGQ *Amherst Graduates' Quarterly*
ALM *Amherst Literary Magazine*
AS *Amherst Student*
CC Calvin Coolidge
FL Forbes Library, Northampton, Mass.
JC John Coolidge
VH *Vermont History*
VHS Vermont Historical Society
VS [Woodstock] *Vermont Standard*
VT [Ludlow] *Vermont Tribune*

Chapter 1. The Fourth of July

1. I got the time of moonrise from an 1885 pocket diary in the Arden Taylor Collection at the Vermont Historical Society (hereafter VHS). The weather is from [Ludlow] *Vermont Tribune* (hereafter VT), 10 July 1985, and the monthly summary for July in the [Woodstock] *Vermont Standard* (hereafter VS), 27 August 1885. Fireflies are mentioned in Fisher, *Hillsboro People*, 1, Taber, 60, and Duffus, 129.

2. A train schedule as of any given date in these years is on the front page of VT. Descriptive sources on train travel in these years are numerous. See, for instance, Frederic, 311–16. On the grimy windows and the smell of the coach, see Ripley, 98, 100. For street lamps, see Harris, 77, and Cooley, 138.

3. Three good general sources for Fourth of July noisemaking in Vermont and New England are C. Johnson, *Farmer's Boy*, 96, 98; Leach, 137–38; and Wood, 123–25. Entries in schoolboy diaries like those of D. B. E. Kent and Arthur E. Sherman, both in VHS, suggest how much the celebration meant to the boys themselves. Kent, aged eleven, wrote on 1 July 1886, "The boys are all talking about the 4th," and on 3 July, "The great day has come and gone." (The Fourth was a Sunday in 1886, and the firecrackers were set off the day before.) Sherman, sixteen, went to Underhill on the Fourth in 1892 and "bought fire crackers 38c Caps 5c Pistol 10c torpedoes 5c matches 5c ring 10c candy 3c." (4 July 1892).

4. VT, 5 July 1889; 10 July 1891; Watson, 77. On vandalism, see, for instance, VT, 7 July 1893. The diary of Sidney Johnson, a Newbury farmer and town leader (VHS), suggestively notes for 4 July 1893, "24 panes of glass in semenery [*sic*]." In Charles H. Hoyt's play *A Temperance Town*, about small-town Vermont in the 1880s, a young man threatens: "You just wait till the Fourth of July, and if I don't have his sign down and my name over the door for a saloon, my name ain't Jones" (Hoyt, 156). But there were also pranks on Halloween; cf. VT, 8 November 1889. The quotation is from VT, 8 July 1892.

5. "Horribles" in Windsor County are mentioned in VT, 9 July 1886; VT, 27 June, 11 July 1890; VT, 3 July 1891; and VS, 9 July 1891. For "horribles" elsewhere, see, for instance, Fellows and Freeman, 31. A broadside for a parade of horribles in Woodstock in 1874 is in VHS. "Various and indescribable": VS, 9 July 1885.

Regarding accidents, see Jennison, 11; "Diary of a Vermont Boy," 165; VT, 10 July 1891 and 12 July 1889. For other disasters and near-disasters, see Watson, 77, and Twombly, *Heritage*, 45. General background on the use of explosives in Fourth of July celebrations is in Appelbaum, 125–29.

6. For one example of a formal celebration, see the report from Mechanicsville in VS, 9 July 1885. Another example, from Felchville, is in VS, 9 July 1893. "Gaims": Leslie, 122.

7. VS, 9 July 1885; VT, 10 July 1885.

8. VT, 10 July 1885; *New York Times*, 9 September 1923, 4, 3. See note 10 to this chapter on the rivalry for possession of the cannon. George Moore: VS, 25 February 1886. Plymouth Notch is more elaborately described in chapter 2. For the elm tree, see, e.g., the photographs in Ward, Mahon, and Chiolino 90, 110.

9. Stage passengers' fright: see Archer. An accident on Notch Mountain in 1868 is mentioned in G. S. Adams, 130. Plymouth Union is described in Ward et al., 71–76, 88; Kavanagh, 13, and Child, 172, 623. For an example of lumbering there, see VT, 19 February 1886. Child's list of farms (424–33) shows the largest ones in Plymouth near the Notch. Details of one farm operation in 1887 are in Leslie, passim. Other mentions of farming are VS, 4 February 1886, and 1 December 1887.

10. The rivalry between the young men of Plymouth Notch and those of Plymouth Union for possession of the town cannon is a central motif of this chapter. There are several independent local sources for it. They all agree that it was a familiar feature of late–nineteenth-century life in Plymouth, and that the raids on the cannon took place generally around the time that possession of it was most important: the Fourth of July. But they differ on several other points: how and when the rivalry began, how long it lasted, and what unwritten rules governed its conduct. This note lists the sources of information, compares their versions, and explains how I arrived at the conclusions given in the text.

First, the sources.

We have the recollections of four Plymouth men who were alive when the rivalry was in its heyday. John J. Wilder, who recounted his version to Forrest Crissey in 1923 (Crissey, 166), was a participant in the struggles, by his own account. So was Dell Ward, who also talked to Crissey (Crissey, 159, 161). Ernest Carpenter, of Five Corners, taught school at the Notch in the 1880s and doubtless knew many of the men involved (Carpenter, 96). Ernest Kavanagh, who wrote his account in the 1930s (Kavanagh, 13–14), was several years younger than the others; though he grew up in the area, much of his account is probably hearsay.

The accounts given by town historians and Coolidge biographers mostly derive from these recollections. Where they vary, they may embody another strand of local tradition—maybe accurate, maybe fabricated or imperfectly recalled.

Finally, there is a uniquely valuable contemporary source: a letter from a correspondent in the Union, reprinted in VT, 10 July 1885.

Wilder's account deals with a single clash shortly after the Civil War, in which the Notch boys captured the cannon from the Union and there was nearly a pitched battle on the road between the two places. Wilder said that the fight for the cannon had been going on for some years at this time; he also implied that this raid was the last and that thereafter the Notch had possession of the cannon. If the incident took place in, say, 1870, Wilder would have been twenty-three and Norman Taylor, the ex-athlete who led the Union forces, forty. The disparity in age seems a little strange.

Dell Ward's story is shorter and more general. To his generation, he said, the clashes over the cannon were a game, nothing more, in contrast to the seriousness with which Wilder's generation fought over it. (Ward, born in 1871, was a full twenty-four years younger than Wilder.) The last raid, in which the Notch boys stole and kept the cannon, was in 1892. He and CC took part, with Allen Wilder, Herb Moore, Hen Willis, Hen Brown, Edwin [Elwin] Bailey, and Thomas Moore. They stole the cannon on the early morning of the Fourth, hauled it up the mountain, and hid it in John Wilder's barn and then in his house. This story is told in chapter 12.

Carpenter recounts the 1892 raid in terms so similar to Ward's as to suggest that he was using Ward's account. Probably he was. Ward, whom he had taught, was a participant. Carpenter was not, so he just accepted Ward's version. He adds that the cannon had been cast at Tyson Furnace and had been a joint purchase by the Union and the Notch, but that the right of possession was never clear. Sometimes the Union would steal it from the Notch and sometimes vice versa.

According to Kavanagh, the cannon was cast at Tyson just after the Civil War. Both sides had possession of it at different times. Once, the Union boys recaptured it by ambushing the Notch boys at the top of the mountain when they brought it there to fire it. They held it for some years; then the Notch people recaptured it and have held it ever since, hidden in Wilder's house.

Later biographers and local historians have added a few variations. Blanche Bryant, who mostly repeated Ward's account, added that it was known as the Tippecanoe Cannon because it had been cast at Tyson Furnace just before 1840 (Bryant, 13). The recent volume by Ward et al. stated that it was cast by D. Taft & Sons of Taftsville for the town by popular subscription after the Civil War (111). Ward's source was a *Rutland Herald* article from 1963, reproduced in Watson, 24, which lists the subscribers, Civil War veterans like A. T. Moore and C. C. Hall. Cameron Rogers's early Coolidge biography contains an obviously distorted version in which Coolidge found out where the cannon was located and swiped it singlehanded (Rogers, 36–37).

Finally, there is the 1885 article, a unique source in that it is the only one that is not self-consciously relating a tradition. It describes a single theft of the cannon, a few days before 4 July 1885, by the "Notch boys," backed by two unnamed selectmen (evidently John Wilder and M. G. Moore, Herbert's father, since there were only three selectmen and the third, C. C. Hall, was from the Union). "We were used to that caper," says the article, expressing the Union viewpoint, "because they had done it before." The article refers to "our old rusty cannon that we had used nearly forty years," and says that an old man stood guard at the head of Notch Mountain to warn of any Union attempt to retake the cannon. (This could have been Seth Wilder, John's father, who lived near that point.) The author seems to assume that the cannon rightly belonged at the Union.

Together with these, I should mention one other small source, an isolated reminiscence from a boyhood friend of Coolidge reported in the *New York Times* of 9 September 1923 (4: 3). He recalled one 3 July when Coolidge was fifteen or sixteen (i.e., 1887 or 1888) and was mightily excited because he was part of the squad that had charge of the cannon and fired it all night.

On the basis of these sources, I conclude, first, that the cannon was indeed as old as Wilder and Mrs. Bryant stated: it was cast in the 1840s, probably at Tyson Furnace. The cannon referred to in the Ward and Watson books must have been another, purchased after the Civil War, about whose ownership there was never any controversy. (Possibly this latter cannon was the one that was borrowed from Plymouth and exploded at the 1896 Bridgewater Fourth of July celebration, as related in Jennison, 11.)

Secondly, in the raids on the cannon, the Notch boys were typically the aggressors, the Union boys the defenders. All the detailed accounts (for 1870 or so, 1885, and 1892) describe the Notch boys' stealing the cannon from the Union, never the reverse. In fact, no source except Kavanagh reports the Union's stealing it from the Notch, and in Kavanagh the theft is a well-deserved setback to the Notch boys' overconfidence. This pattern suggests that the 1885 correspondent was right in stating that the cannon was "at home" at the Union.

But this conclusion seems paradoxical, in that the Union was a relatively new settlement, in fact newer than the cannon. Moore, *Plymouth*, [21], states that it grew up in the 1860s when the stage road was rerouted. (The pages in Moore's book are not numbered; in this and subsequent notes I have supplied the numbering.) This statement cannot be quite correct as it stands, for an 1859 map, reproduced in Ward et al., 52, shows "Unionville" with quite a few houses. Moore's account, however, is the only statement of any town historian as to the founding of the Union, and probably correct in essentials. Beyond question, the cannon did not originally belong to the residents of Plymouth Union; so the next question to address is how and when it came to be in their keeping. The answer given in the text is the most logical to me: when the Union overtook the Notch in size and importance, the town authorities decided to relocate the town cannon there. Probably this transfer took place no earlier than the Civil War, perhaps later; it was not until 1867 that the locale of the March town meeting was changed from the old town hall behind the Notch church to Levi Green's hall at the Union (Town records, Book C). Clearly, the change took place only because the voters of the Union were more numerous and were able to impose their will at town meeting. The raids, then, were the Notch boys' (and men's) way of expressing their resentment. (For a precisely parallel struggle over a town cannon, in the town of Amherst, Massachusetts, at an earlier date, reference See, 9.)

I should note that a careful study of newspaper and town records during the 1880s has turned up no mention of how the cannon was returned to the Union after the raid of 1885, to be ready for the raid of 1892.

In this narrative, I have taken the friend's account in the *New York Times* and applied it to the 1885 raid, when CC was thirteen. I think it is accurate to do so. The friend himself was evidently not quite sure of CC's age at the time, and I have found no other evidence to suggest that another raid on the cannon took place in 1887 or 1888.

"The Notch boys came": VT, 10 July 1885.

11. On work clothes, see Coolidge, *Autobiography*, 19, and the pictures in Ward et al., 15, 19, 20, 72, 82. John Wilder: Crissey, 166.

12. *New York Times*, 9 September 1923, 4: 3.

Chapter 2. Pastorale

1. A good map of the Notch in 1869 is in Ward et al., 6; an excellent photograph, taken in the winter of 1885, is on the cover of Bryant. For other descriptions, see Woods, 73, and *New York Times*, 12 September 1926.

2. Carpenter, 41, in 1925 described the Notch as having "five or six farm houses, a store, a church, a cheese factory, and a school house." Herbert L. Moore's count in 1935 (*Calvin Coolidge*, 5) was "four farm houses, two tenements, a cheese factory [built after 1885], a store, a schoolhouse, a church, and exactly twenty-nine people ... when they are all at home." The varying counts illustrate the difficulty of defining the Notch exactly. Moore and Carpenter may have been thinking of the Brown farm or the Coolidge homestead, or the Moore house on Schoolhouse Hill. All the build-

ings in the text, at any rate, are shown on the 1869 map in Ward et al. (The Coolidge home at that time still belonged to S. N. Butler.) See also the photographs in ibid., 89–110, especially the photo of the Coolidge home on 110. Occupants of the homes in 1880 are listed in the manuscript U.S. Census of that year. On the Moor–Wilder House, see C. Coolidge, *Autobiography*, 7. The best source on the Coolidge House is the *Guide Book* of the Vermont Division for Historic Preservation.

3. The general store is discussed more extensively later in this chapter, the schoolhouse in chapter 5. On the church, see the photos in Ward et al., 98–100; C. Coolidge, *Autobiography*, 17; Carpenter, 133; Vermont Division for Historic Preservation, 14; Hyde Leslie diary, entry of 6 November 1887. Woods, 77, documents the Coolidge family's close relationship with the church. A Sunday school is mentioned in C. Coolidge, *Autobiography*, 17–18; Leslie 13, 20 November 1889, and 11 December 1887; VS, 4 August 1887 and 8, 15 September 1887; VT, 24 March 1889. The school organized in 1887 had A. F. Snow as superintendent. Almeda Coolidge to CC, 2 June 1891, Coolidge Family Papers, VHS, however, verifies Mrs. Coolidge's strong interest in it.

4. A map showing the boundaries of the Notch school district is in Ward et al., 6. The Coolidge farm is pictured in ibid., 95, and described in an essay by CC, "Grandmother's Kitchen," in the Coolidge Family Papers, VHS. On Almeda Coolidge, see Fuess, *Calvin Coolidge*, 14; Kavanagh, 11; and M. S. Brown, 9. James Brown's farm: Ward et. al., 92, and Bryant, 5.

5. The individual post office addresses and farm locations given in Child, 424–33, make it possible to determine the extent of territory served from the Notch post office. Messer Hill, Pinney Hollow, Lynds Hill, and about half of the Five Corners neighborhood were included; the rest of the Five Corners inhabitants received their mail at Bridgewater Corners. For the location of these neighborhoods, see Ward et al., 89, 121, 123, 126. Stagecoach: Black River Academy, *Catalogue*, 1885–86, 22.

6. Carpenter, 145–46; Hard, 93. A reprint from the *Boston Gazette* in VS, 17 September 1885, describes the five-hour journey by stage from Ludlow to Woodstock via the Union and the Notch. A coach of the kind used on the route can be seen in the Farm Museum; its changeover to wheels in the spring was usually noted in the newspaper (e.g., VT, 2 April 1886, 29 April 1887, 4 May 1888, 29 March 1889, 3 April 1891). I infer that the job of stage driver changed hands frequently from the fact that I have not found the same individual mentioned twice in connection with it during the eight years covered by this study. Men mentioned once include John P. Farmer (VT, 29 July 1892), Mr. Carpenter (VT, 11 September 1885), Clayton Allard (G. S. Adams, 130), Mr. Billings (VT, 26 February 1886), Mr. Earle (VT, 29 January 1892), and Merritt Sawyer (VS, 3 September 1885).

7. Levi Lynds to CC, 20 January 1900, Coolidge Family Papers, VHS; Leonard, 91; J. C. Carter, "Trip," 239.

8. Hopkins, 10–11; Flanders, 17; Beck, 1–2, 4, 5, 19; VS, 25 February 1886 and 24 June 1886; Freeman, *Nun*, 113.

9. VS, 11, 17 November 1886, 13 November 1890, 26 February 1891; Curtis, Curtis and Lieberman, *Return*, 20, 28; C. Coolidge, *Autobiography*, 9–10; McCoy, 6. The ownership of the Notch store can be followed through the local newspapers and the records of R. G. Dun & Co. at the Baker Library, Harvard University. As late as 1883 CC's uncle Frank Moor was operating it (Child, 430). After him it was briefly in the hands of Edwin E. Earle, who failed in January, 1884 (R. G. Dun & Co. Papers, Vermont, 25: 314). George Moore succeeded him in the spring and ran the store until Leslie J. Walker bought him out at the end of 1888 (VT, 7 December 1888, 4 January 1889; R. G. Dun & Co., Papers, 25: 379). Walker operated it through the end of the period covered in this study; see Levi Lynds to CC, 20 January 1900, Coolidge Family Papers, VHS. On George Moore's interrupted college

career, see VT, 19 October 1888, 10 May 1889. Storekeepers' problems: Carson, 77–80; Beck, 11, 14; *Rutland Herald*, 29 July 1889; Hopkins, 10–11; Duffus, 29; interview, Jerry tapes.

10. In Perkinsville, for instance, on the Fourth of July, 1888, a majority "did not celebrate except in the hay field" (VS, 12 July 1888). Haying in Vermont, according to an old saw, started the week after the Fourth of July (*New York Times*, 19 September 1931); but in Plymouth it regularly started late in June (Carpenter, 73) and ran into August (VT, 14 August 1885, South Reading; 20 August 1886, Five Corners; 26 August 1887, Plymouth). On James Brown's farm in 1887, haying began 18 June and finished 8 August (Leslie, 117, 132—the number of wagonloads is from the latter page). Brown's acreage is from Child, 425. A photograph of haying in Plymouth is in Ward et al., 20.

11. Duffus, 169; Freeman, *Nun*, 17; Carpenter, 75; Trudo, 124; Cooley, 199; Leslie, 120, 121, 127; Fuller, 227; Hard, 143; Pettingill, 66. On smocks, see C. Coolidge, *Autobiography*, 19–20. Glover, 143, maintains that smocks were not worn during haying, as they were too hot. The point seems reasonable; but the photos reproduced in Curtis et al., *Return*, 33, 76, show CC pitching hay in a smock, and we have his own word that such pictures were not posed. Consequently I conclude that in Plymouth smocks were indeed worn during haying.

12. Photographs like those in Curtis et al., *Return*, 58, and Ward et al., 90–91, show that Vermonters in these years commonly drove to fairs and local celebrations. Riding horseback, on the other hand, was a means of transportation not often mentioned except as an exercise for schoolchildren (VT, 28 April 1893). Perhaps some Vermonters perceived it as arrogant or snobbish; at any rate, during the depression of the 1870s one well-to-do Rutland family had their children give up horseback riding to avoid offending their poorer neighbors (Ripley, 193). Walking, on the other hand, was common, but always in a practical setting; CC, a few years later, regularly walked four miles to visit his aunt (diary, 7, 17 April 1887), and poorer people walked long distances in search of work (Freeman, *Nun*, 126–27).

I have had surprising difficulty in finding good general sources on horse-drawn vehicles of the nineteenth century. Several styles are illustrated in Meyer, 76. The democrat wagon is mentioned in such contemporary sources as Hunt, Hunt, and Malton, 72, Davis, 184, and Ware, 29.

13. Sumner, 4; Ware, 23; Tarr, 272; Meyer, 5–7; C. M. Snyder, 9–10, 62–75.

14. C. Coolidge, *Autobiography*, 27–28, does not state in so many words that JC was in the habit of taking his family to Independence Day festivities, but it makes clear that he was a regular attender of public events. CC recalled that "usually" there was a picnic celebration on the Fourth of July, and this recollection may very well mean that he, John, and the others usually attended a nearby celebration on that day, for it does not seem that the Notch held a picnic regularly—nor, indeed, did the Union, despite Carpenter, 96. The portrayal here of the family en route to a celebration, then, is an inference, not backed by direct evidence.

Actually, in this paragraph, I have taken the more serious liberty of endowing JC with a vehicle he may not have possessed, a surrey. There is good evidence for only two horse-drawn vehicles (on wheels) in the Coolidge household, a buggy and a buckboard. The buggy, mentioned in C. Coolidge, *Autobiography*, 10, is on exhibit in the Coolidge homestead. The buckboard, mentioned in CC to JC, 14 November 1913 (Lathem, 122) and the ms. notes on the Taylor–Coolidge suit, Coolidge Family Papers, VHS, seems to have been used a lot and may well be the "wagon" CC mentions in *Autobiography*, 29 ("Whenever the hired man or the hired girl wanted to go anywhere they were always understood to be entitled to my place in the wagon, in which case I remained at home.") The problem with these vehicles, however, is that each seated only two. If JC wished to go anywhere with more than one passenger, he would have had a problem. It is possible, of course, that the elder Coolidge never drove anywhere with more than one person; there is certainly no evidence for large family outings. (The only reference I can find to his taking more than one passenger is Calvin Coolidge's diary entry of 31 January 1886: "John Mat [the hired girl] and Ab went up to McW[ain's]"; but this trip would have been made in a sleigh.) Moreover, as the next chapter shows, the relationship between him and his son was very close, so close that perhaps he took Calvin to festivities and left Abbie behind; but that conclusion, so repugnant to current ideas of family togetherness, seems to me to demand harder evidence than what is presented here. (This problem is also alluded to in the notes to chapter 4.) Accordingly, I have assumed that John took the whole family and that he owned or borrowed a carriage large enough to hold everyone.

His public career and that of his father are conveniently summarized in E. D. Coolidge, 169. On his father, Calvin Galusha Coolidge, see also C. Coolidge, *Autobiography*, 13–14, Carpenter, 61, and Kavanagh, 10. Plain John Coolidge: Sargent, part 2; Bryant, 9. Dislike for courtesy titles: Hartt, 567–68; Damon, 249; C. Johnson, *New England*, 170.

15. Kavanagh, 10; *Autobiography*, 24. Mentions of JC's work in law enforcement are in VT, 9 December 1887, 9 March, 8 June 1888, 14 June, 22 November 1889. The quoted material is from VT, 8 January 1886. The Plymouth town records contain assessments for real property and for watches. JC and John Wilder were among the few men in town assessed for a watch in 1886—Wilder for ten dollars, Coolidge for five. There are several good photographs of John Coolidge in Curtis et al., *Return*, 20, and C. Coolidge, *Autobiography*, opposite 48. In likening his features to an Indian's, I do not mean to be taken as implying ethnic heritage—although, in fact, there was a tradition of Indian blood in the family of his grandmother, Sally Thompson Coolidge (C. Coolidge, *Autobiography*, 14).

16. Toye, 4; Child, 426, 624. Copies of his fire insurance policies, covering apparently almost everyone in the town of Plymouth, are in Coolidge Family Papers, VHS.

17. Kavanagh, 10–11; Orton, 19; McCoy, 6; Vermont Division for Historic Preservation, 3, 5. The R. G. Dun & Co. Papers at Harvard are lacking the volume that would verify that JC worked for the company, but the tradition that he did is early and seems plausible. Ample evidence exists to show that JC was an active farmer: "The corn ground is nearly plowed shall plant next week if nothing happens," (JC to CC, 15 May 1891, Coolidge Family Papers, VHS); "Father must have made enough sugar now so that be can get the bounty," (CC to Carrie B. Coolidge, 22 April 1892, Coolidge Family Papers, VHS); "It is most time for the threshers to come around, is it not?" (CC to JC, 20 September 1894, Blair Collection). Child, 425–26, lists him with 200 acres, ten dairy cows, and one hired man in 1883. CC's interview in *New York Times*, 19 September 1931, mentions haying on his farm. He certainly sold some farm produce, moreover: Woods, 71, mentions maple sugar and milk; there is a mention of selling butter in C. Coolidge diary, 21 February 1887; and when CC first went to the academy in Ludlow, his father was carrying a calf to be sold in Boston (C. Coolidge, *Autobiography*, 32).

It is evident from the figures in Child's gazetteer, however, that Coolidge farmed on a much smaller scale than most of his neighbors. John Wilder farmed 600 acres; James S. Brown had 300 acres and thirty cows; James Ayer had 440 acres and twenty registered Holsteins. Since Coolidge was away from home so frequently, moreover, he lacked the time to give consistent attention to his farm. No account that I have seen suggests that farm profits were more than a small part of his total income. An article in VT, 17 August 1923, mentioned his owning the family farm but added that he had "hired farmers to work it for him either by the month or 'on shares' since he was a very young man." The quotation on his skills is from C. Coolidge, *Autobiography*, 12.

The blacksmith is mentioned in ibid., 10–11, but not named. I have conjecturally identified him with Henry Willis, who worked for Coolidge around 1880 (Archer; Crissey, 169; Town Records) and again around 1890 (VT, 3 May 1889; VS, 14 December 1889).

18. C. Coolidge, *Autobiography*, 10: "He was a good business man, a very hard worker, and did not like to see things wasted." M. S. Brown, 7: "[A] prosperous man. He wasted nothing." Fuess, *Calvin Coolidge*, 23n: "he was regarded by some [neighbors] as unreasonably 'near.'" On the necrotic vein of Yankee humor, see Damon, 251. The Mencken quote is from his essay "Coolidge," first printed in the *Baltimore Sun*, 30 January 1933, reprinted in Mencken, 222.

19. Victoria Moor Coolidge died 14 March 1885; this and the other family information are from Bryant and Baker, 116. Actually, Almeda Coolidge had been a second mother to CC long before his mother's death, and he had spent much of his boyhood in her house (Sargent; Crissey, 8).

20. Flowers: personal observation. Fourth of July noises: Freeman, *Nun*, 45.

Chapter 3. The Invalid's Son

1. Gossip is so universal a trait that it hardly requires footnoting, but simply to show its existence in late-nineteenth-century rural Vermont I offer the following citations. Williamstown, Vermont: "everybody knew everybody else's business. A man couldn't even have an illicit sexual relationship in our town without everybody, including ten-year-old boys, knowing about it" (Duffus, 65). Brattleboro: "With the strangers ... the town has little to do, but it knows everything, and much more also, that goes on among them. Their dresses, their cattle, their views, the manners of their children, their manner toward their servants and every other conceivable thing, is reported, digested, discussed, and rediscussed" (Kipling, 8). Western Vermont, 1920s: "Though no one ever does much talking, Vermonters just sit and visit, trying to pry loose some gossip without giving up anything" (Gordon, 148). Six 1886 letters from Alva Peck to CC in the Coolidge Papers, VHS, provide a good example of the kinds of things Vermonters talked about. See Twombly, *Heritage*, 65, for another sample. The Blanche Bryant quote is from Bryant, 9; and see also the marvelous example in Kipling, 122–23.

2. The "jackknives" story is from Steele, 219. On Moore, see Scott, 6–7, and Carpenter, 135–38.

3. Carpenter, 114–15; Vermont Division for Historic Preservation, 13. A photograph of a Sunday School picnic from this period, including CC, is reproduced in Curtis et al., 56–57.

4. C. Coolidge, *Autobiography*, 13, 30; Fuess, *Calvin Coolidge*, 30; Vermont Division for Historic Preservation, 12; Bryant, 7.

5. Washburn, *Coolidge*, 14; Hennessy, 18; H. T. Brown, 311; Carpenter, 100; Toye, 3, 5; Curtis et al., 56–57; C. Coolidge, *Autobiography*, 24, 26. "I don't think Calvin really knew what play was," his father is quoted as saying, in Washington *Post*, 6 August 1923. On his reading, Coolidge, "Books," 144–45, contains a long list of books he had read by age twelve. Dan Macuin, five years younger than Calvin, once recalled playing with Newman Wilder, about the same age, and Calvin by the mill near Plymouth Union (VT, 20 June 1924); the recollection hints that Coolidge, like many timid youngsters, may have preferred to play with younger children when he played at all.

6. C. Coolidge, *Autobiography*, 27; Woods, 80; Kavanagh, 7, 9; Carpenter, 115; Toye, 5; Crissey, 9; *Boston Herald*, 2 August 1923.

7. Ben Sawyer is mentioned in Archer, and in Leslie, 147, note. The Wheeler descendant was Warren R. Taylor, who had a double dose of Wheeler blood; see his letter to Minnie B. Walker, 11 March 1907, in Coolidge Papers, VHS.

8. Green, 10, commented on CC's resemblance to his mother. Pictures of all four grandparents are in Curtis et al., 16, 18. The characterization of the Coolidges as tall, stolid, and domineering probably applies best to Calvin's father and to his paternal grandmother, who was a Brewer before her marriage, but Calvin Galusha Coolidge was also a forceful personality. There is much less data on previous generations of Coolidges. See C. Coolidge, *Autobiography*, 4–5, 14–16. "[M]y great grandsire ... used to be a giant in strength," wrote CC in a college essay on his family, and since he was writing from the perspective of the Coolidge homestead, he probably meant his Coolidge great-grandfather ("Grandmother's Kitchen," Coolidge Family Papers, VHS).

One wishes for more data on the Moors, with whom Calvin had many more traits in common. On Hiram D. Moor, see C. Coolidge, *Autobiography*, 30; VS, 26 January 1888; C. Coolidge diary, 12 January 1886 ("Grandpa Moor came home tonight and he has a long story to tell, you bet"); and especially John G. Sargent's sketch in "Our President-Elect," *The Republican Woman*, January 1925, copy in FL. Almost all the material there is on Abigail Moor is summarized in Lathem, 8n. She died in Calvin's sophomore year at college. His comment was: "She has died as she lived, very quietly and without any trouble to any one." In a letter from college to his stepmother (to Carrie Brown Coolidge, 18 February 1894) he recalled her stoic sayings designed to buffer the impact of a New England winter, like "February is a short month and March is soon gone."

A photograph of Victoria Moor Coolidge is in C. Coolidge, *Autobiography*, 30; she is eloquently described on pages 12–13.

9. A good general introduction to the terror of tuberculosis is Mooney; see especially 9–10, 24, and 183–84. See also VT, 23 September 1892; Biggs, 763; E. Hitchcock, *Personal Health Lectures*, 26–27; "Facts about Consumption," *Public Opinion*, xiv (24 December 1892), 283 84; and Vermont, *Registry ... of Births, Marriages and Deaths ... for ... 1879*, 121, 123. The last source also shows that the counties to the east of the Green Mountains, including Windsor, had an even higher rate than Vermont as a whole. Consumption, in fact, was known as the "New England disease" (Pattee, 60).

10. On Koch, see Lowell, 6. One can get a feel for the various views on consumption from J. H. Young, 38; articles in *Science* 10: 32 (15 July 1887), 38–41 (22 July 1887), 99–100 (26 August 1887); and Vermont *Registry for 1880*, 127–29. On the belief in the inheritability of tuberculosis, see Biggs, 759–60, and, for a vivid individual example, "Memoirs of Daniel Ransom," 20. The deaths of the Coolidges are in the Vital Records of the Town of Plymouth, at the town clerk's office, and their interrelationships can be pieced together in Bryant and Baker, passim. Curiously, Victoria Coolidge's death was not recorded at all in the Plymouth book. Frank Moor's was, however; for more details on his health, see VT, 26 February, 7 May 1886, 10, 24 May, 28 June 1889; VS, 25 February 1886, 17 February 1887, 21 March 1889; and C. Coolidge, diary, 10 February 1886, 25 February 1887. In his freshman physical examination, a record of which is in the Amherst College Archives, CC listed "consumption" as the cause of his mother's death, and "pleurisy" and "bronchitis" among the diseases he himself had had. CC to JC, 25 September 1894, Blair Collection, FL, makes it plain that CC and his father both thought of tuberculosis as a real possibility in his case; John had insured his son's life but was concerned that the policy might not cover tuberculosis.

11. On Dr. Boyden, see VT, 9 October 1885, 19 February 1886, 13 September 1889; M. E. Dimick diary, 6 February, 19 December 1884; and C. Coolidge diary, 1,

5 March 1890. The "Dr. Rodman" referred to in Carpenter, 46, sounds just like Dr. Boyden and is in fact probably a mistake for him; county records do not mention a doctor named Rodman. Dr. Lane was a personal friend—Fuess, *Calvin Coolidge*, 47, refers to him as the family doctor—but he did not practice much in Plymouth otherwise. Carpenter, 46, points out that Charles Scott, although the only physician in town in 1890 (Bryant and Baker, 344), was not popular in the Notch and had no practice there. On treatments for tuberculosis, see Fuller, 285, and "Consumption," *Science*, 15 July 1887, 5: 32. On death customs in Plymouth, see Carpenter, 140, Curtis et al., 36, and C. Coolidge diary, 9 January and 3 April 1887. On Levi Green, see Moore, *Plymouth*, 21, and Child, 427.

12. JC's recollection is from Toye, 2 1/2. CC, however, worried about his health as a young man; he wrote in his diary for 13 April 1887, "I am feeling very well now days and hope I shall continue the same until school is done." His colds documented in the diary include the following entries: 2 January 1886; 14–17 March 1886, in which he went to bed for over twenty-four hours, ate oranges as a remedy, and which left him feeling "not very strong"; ibid., 20–27 March 1887, in which he was in bed at least a day and was "troubled to breathe"; letter of 29 January 1888 ("some cold"), in Lathem, 7; 14–17 January 1890, when he was bedridden at least a day with a "hard headache"; 2–3 February 1890. The following letters also document his illnesses: Almeda Coolidge to CC, 22 April 1891 (oranges again); CC to Carrie Brown Coolidge, 15 May 1892, VHS; CC to John Coolidge, 25 September 1892, in Lathem, 37n (difficulty in breathing); CC to Carrie Brown Coolidge, 18 January 1894, VHS (difficulty in breathing). Small wonder that he recalled always feeling cold in springtime as a schoolboy (CC to JC, 4 May 1924, in Lathem, 187). His fondness for oranges appears again in the Vrest Orton's interview of Dallas Pollard (Orton, Pollard interview, 10). Other sweet things he liked are mentioned in chapters 5 and 6. Oranges are hardly mentioned in accounts of New England food habits in the 1880s except in a holiday context (e.g. Damon, 159).

13. C. Coolidge diary, 3–4 January 1887; CC to JC, 21 February 1892, Blair Collection; CC to Carrie B. Coolidge, 25 February 1892, VHS.

14. On JC's discipline, see Whiting, 34, and Toye, 5. For another Vermont father, see Earle, 11. Almeda Coolidge was anxious about her grandson's health; see her letters to CC, 24 and 28 February 1886, VHS. From college he wrote her: "I wish you would not think I am sick all the time, every time I hear from home they say you are worrying about me and going over to the Notch late at night to hear from me" (to Almeda B. Coolidge, 6 June 1892, Special Collections, Amherst College). CC's occasional distaste for his chores appears in such recollections as Jennie Chamberlin's (Crissey, 8) of a time when he, as a boy, annoyed by having to bring in firewood, deliberately left all the doors open to let the cold air in as he filled the woodbox. Most of the time he was more compliant. As to farm work, Kavanagh, 6, states that he had little to do, as CC's own quote, in Crissey, 9, confirms. On his reading, see Orton, Pollard interview, 6.

15. CC's shyness and its underlying fears are so central to this account that it is important to consider the sources for them carefully.

At the outset one should note that there are really two different, though closely related, subjects involved. CC's behavior as a boy around other people is recounted in the statements of neighbors, friends, and acquaintances, and there is fairly abundant evidence for it. His feelings about other people, on the other hand, are traceable only in his own utterances, and there are very few of those.

As to his behavior, there is a consensus. "My boy was always shy and quietlike," JC was quoted as saying (Dennis, 24). On another occasion he said, "I don't think Calvin really knew what play was" (*Washington Post*, 6 August 1923). Henry Brown, his schoolmate, recalled that he was "quieter than most lads" and "did not enter the more boisterous games" (H. T. Brown, 311). Oric Ward, another school-mate, described him as "a quiet sort of fellow" who kind "of kept to himself" (Toye, 3). The aloofness was reciprocated; according to his cousin Park Pollard, who spent summers in the Notch, he was simply ignored by the other boys: "I think the boys had the least interest in Calvin of any person that ever lived in Plymouth" (Orton, Pollard interview, 4). His teacher Ellen Dunbar confirmed, "He didn't play much with the other boys," and added suggestively "he always seemed to be thinking of something.... One could never become familiar with him" (Toye, 5; Hennessy, 18). The only divergent account, that of Ernest Kavanagh, who insisted that he was "just one of the gang," was written by a neighbor at least eight years younger who did not know him well.

CC as a boy, then, was quiet, aloof, and reluctant to engage in contact sports, but none of the neighbors' accounts gives any hint why. The only evidence on that score comes from a confession that CC made as an adult to his political friend and bene-factor Frank W. Stearns. So revealing that it has been quoted by almost every Cool-idge biographer, it exists in several slightly different secondhand variants; I quote in full the version from Stearns himself, published in 1935 (G. Coolidge, May, 247):

"They say that I have a poker face. I suppose I know what they mean. When I was a boy, there were perhaps fifty inhabitants of Plymouth. I knew them all, of course. But if I was aware that one of them happened to be in my mother's kitchen, it was a little short of torture for me to go in "

"At the age of ten or twelve," he went on, "I made up my mind that I must overcome that feeling. Gradually I did, but some of it still stays with me."

Several points emerge from this recollection. First, that CC's silence and impas-sivity were a mask assumed to conceal his discomfort in the presence of others. Sec-ond, that he had felt this discomfort originally with neighbors as well as with strangers. Third, that around age ten he began trying to cope with it—and, one can add, was generally successful. As one biographer pointed out, his childhood shyness was not regarded as peculiar or pathological (Fuess, Calvin Coolidge, 25). Finally, that despite his success in coping, the feeling in some form stayed with him all his life.

What this feeling of terror consisted of, or why it was "torture" for him to encoun-ter another person, is examined in a subsequent note.

16. The most useful book I have found for understanding theoretical and clinical concepts of shyness is John A. Daly and James C. McCroskey, eds., *Avoiding Com-munication*, especially the essays by Arnold H. Buss ("A Conception of Shyness") and Gerald M. Phillips ("Reticence: A Perspective on Social Withdrawal"). The quote on avoiding communication is from G. M. Phillips, 52.

17. The correlation between shyness and low self-esteem in one sample was .51 (Buss, 44). G. M. Phillips (55–57) makes the point that shy people fear looking fool-ish: "There is more than just a touch of paranoia associated with reticent behavior. Reticents believe that other people pay a great deal of attention to them." In addi-tion, "Reticent humans see themselves failing at most social enterprises. They will not argue because they know they will lose; they do not ask questions because they despair of getting the syntax right; they avoid social contact because they fear rejec-tion; they choose their work to avoid talk." The "horrifying experience" quote is from ibid., 58. Buss (52–53) observes that shy people particularly fear give and take, the unexpected. Tyskowa's article, summarized in *Psychological Abstracts*, points out the central importance of high performance standards in producing shy behavior. One could, in fact, almost characterize Phillips's "reticence" as chronic audience anxiety, the feeling of having a critical audience constantly evaluating one's performance.

Almost all these behavior patterns seem to apply to CC, but they only prompt a further question: Why was his self-esteem so low? Many conditions in his life—his being one of the better students in school, for example, or his being the son of one of the leading men in the community—would seem to promote high self-regard. Some writers (H. T. Brown, 311; W. A. White, 16) have suggested that his small size and slight build bred caution and diffidence, but this seems an inadequate explanation of fears that were very strong.

These fears, moreover, carried on into his adult life—as CC himself conceded—even into his presidency. Some of his behavior patterns were those of a man repeatedly tormented by feelings of inadequacy. "Ike" Hoover, the chief usher at the White House, felt that CC had the most "[e]gotism, self-consciousness, or whatever you call it" of any of the nine presidents he had worked for, noted his distaste for social events and strangers, and noted, too, his capacity to lose his temper and fly into a rage over something that seemed of trifling importance (Hoover, 232–33, 256, 273). Robert Washburn, a Boston journalist who knew CC before, during, and after his presidency, observed the same trait: "One who has always been very close to him told me that Calvin has often used him as a punching bag. Calvin was fitted up without a safety valve, so that his boiler does often blow up." Washburn went on to suggest an amateur's diagnosis: "Our hero has never known what it is to be happy. He is sensitive, with a full appreciation of his limitations.... He has an inferiority complex" (Washburn, *My Pen*, 65, 66).

Letters home during his early adult years reveal one area in which CC was clearly sensitive: criticism from his father. Minor criticisms stuck with him over a long period; for example, three years after graduation from Amherst he reminded John in a letter, "You made a good deal of fun of me when I was in college for putting two *o*'s in lose" (23 September 1898, in Lathem, 95). When JC dismissed his winning a silver medal in a college essay contest with the remark that it would "buy no bread and butter," CC reacted by neglecting to inform his father when he went on to win the national gold medal (10 January 1896, in ibid. 78 and note). When he was aware that he had done something wrong, his letters home could take on an abject tone, as when he lost a pocket book containing a few dollars: "I am very sorry and know I deserve much blame" (16 June 1891, in ibid., 20); but when he was simply defending himself against implied criticism, his phrasing was sinuously diplomatic. "You called my attention very carefully," he wrote during his senior year, "to how much the Dartmouth book agent was doing on his vacation ..., so I have taken pains to explain what I was doing for perhaps you did not see that so plainly and I was sure you would like to know" (21 May 1895, in ibid., 70). Repeatedly he referred to JC's dismissal of him and his ideas: "I do not suppose this is of so much interest to you" (13 November 1892, in ibid., 40), or "I do not now recall any idea which was taught me at college with which you agreed" (12 July 1897, in ibid., 81). In this vein, the longest statement of his feeling toward his father is in the letter just cited. With its feelings of inadequacy barely camouflaged by irony and its undercurrent of resentment toward John's direction, it is more than the utterance of a dutiful son: "I have tried to do the best I could by my feeble efforts to carry out other plans which did not appeal to me very strongly and if I have sometimes faltered, if I have failed to meet with the success you desired, forgive me—I think I tried my best."

My working assumption throughout this account is that the feelings manifest in these letters can be extended both backward and forward in time to account for most of CC's low self-esteem: his intense worry, for instance, about the quality of his schoolwork, discussed in chapters 6, 7 and 11, and doubtless related to JC's stress on performance, which is discussed further in a later footnote to this chapter; or his acceptance of a career in politics, as mentioned in the Afterword. One cannot trace CC's feelings toward his father back to any specific incident, but perhaps the general situation explains enough: an intelligent, sensitive boy growing up in the household of a blunt, stern, demanding father, with only an invalid mother to mediate between them. Perhaps it is not too much to say that JC became for his son a stern, godlike, accusing figure, who could be placated but never confronted, and before whom, even after his death, his son was still genuflecting: "My father had qualities that were greater than any I possess.... I cannot recall that I ever knew of his doing a wrong thing" (quoted in Fuess, *Calvin Coolidge*, 23).

18. Buss, 43, found a .50 correlation between shyness and physical fear. On sledding, see for example C. Coolidge diary, 30 January 1886, 1, 2, 5, 9, and 10 February 1886, 9 April 1887. On riding, see C. Coolidge, *Autobiography*, 42 and *Boston Post*, 7 January 1933. The incident of his breaking his arm is in chapter 7.

19. G. M. Phillips, 60. Carpenter, 115–16, mentions his wit as a boy. Crissey, 156, gives the judgment of a schoolmate, Dell Ward: "He was shy and bashful with strangers, but he was fond of goin' with the young folks he'd grown up with." Kipling, 7, has an outsider's impression of the Vermont drawl in this era. The two friends were Thomas Moore and Warren Spaulding, respectively; see chapter 5. For recitations by CC, VS, 31 December 1885, 6 January 1887.

20. On cats: C. Johnson, *Farmer's Boy*, 77; Hard, 22; Leonard, 45; Pettingill, 61, 67; Kavanagh, 5; C. Coolidge diary, 11 January 1886; Curtis et al., 52; CC to JC, 18 September, 21 September 1892 (Lathem, 36); CC to JC, 24 January, 26 April 1892, 7 January 1894, Blair Collection; CC to Carrie B. Coolidge, 27 November 1892 (Lathem, 37n) and 1 May 1892 (Coolidge Family Papers, VHS). On horses, C. Coolidge, *Autobiography*, 14–15, 42.

21. G. M. Phillips, 62, and Kaplan, 440, mention programmatic activity as a device for avoiding interaction. On CC's pleasure in obedience, see C. Coolidge, "Books," 18. His cousin Dallas Pollard likewise stressed his intense concentration, as a boy, on performing well: "I think that he had his mind made up that every job that he took that he would do as well as he possibly knew how no matter how small it was or how big ... " (Orton, Pollard interview, 7–8). Washburn, *Calvin Coolidge*, 15, has the woodbox anecdote, which according to Coolidge's former teacher Ernest Carpenter (115) may be apocryphal, but was characteristic of his attitude toward work. The quote from JC is from Dennis, 24; very similar quotes are in Toye, 4, and Whiting, 20–21. The other quotes are from Carpenter, 115, and Toye, 3.

22. W. A. White, 30, describes JC as "a Republican war horse" of Plymouth—a somewhat misleading phrase, since it suggests that there was a Republican organization in the town and that JC played a key part in it. In fact, Plymouth was too small to have more than a rudimentary organization, and to the extent that it had one in the 1880s, JC held no major role. His name does not appear at all in the lists of state and county convention delegates for the period, and he rarely ran for more than local office. (He did serve in the state legislature in the 1870s and again in the 1900s.) It is true, however, that he was a dedicated Republican, read newspapers regularly (Carpenter, 62–63; C. Coolidge, "Books," 144), and followed state and national politics keenly. Several letters that CC wrote him from college attest to their common interest in politics: e.g., 19 June, 30 October, 13 November 1892 (Lathem, 35, 42n, 40–41). A better account of JC's local political activity is in Carpenter, 127.

Regarding town meetings in Plymouth, C. Coolidge, *Autobiography*, 21–23, is succinct and accurate. Mrs. Eliza Ward of Plymouth Union described Levi Green's hall to me. Town meetings in this era were often full of hot, violently personal debate (Kavanagh, 11; VT, 28 May 1886), and occasionally influenced by liquor, if the clipping dated 14 October 1884 in the Coolidge Family Papers, VHS, is to be believed. On CC's activities, see Crissey, 162; C. Coolidge, *Autobiography*, 23; and Alva Peck to CC, 21 May 1886, Coolidge Family Papers, VHS.

23. On JC as a legal adviser, see C. Coolidge, *Autobiography*, 24–25, and Carpen-

ter, 62–63. On the Stickney family, see Kent's article, "William Wallace Stickney." Moore, *Plymouth*, 20, refers to J. W. Stickney as a "petafoger" [*sic*]. But JC and the Stickneys were unquestionably close (interview with Erminie Pollard, June 1987, Proctorsville, Vt.). When there was a robbery in the Five Corners area, "Stickney and Coolidge" were reported appearing "in company" to investigate it (VT, 23 October 1885). In 1893, JC became a director of a new savings bank in Ludlow headed by W. W. Stickney (ibid., 5 May 1893). Later on, when W. W. Stickney became governor of Vermont, he appointed JC to a colonelcy in the state militia. (For this reason some biographers of CC have adopted the habit of referring to JC as "Colonel Coolidge." For the 1880s and 1890s, however, the title is anachronistic, and I have avoided it.)

24. "Caring is the significant report in the life histories of reticent people," states G. M. Phillips, 54. His observation on shy people as listeners is on 55. On CC's participation in games, see Carpenter, 100–101. The quote from CC is taken from Frank Stearns's account in G. Coolidge, May, 247.

25. C. Coolidge, "Books," 144; Webb, vii, 4; VT, 25 September and 23 October 1885, 19 and 26 February, 5 March, 1 October 1886; Moore, *Calvin Coolidge*, [20]; Carpenter, 58–60; Bryant and Baker, 34; VS, 10 December 1885; Hartt, passim.

26. Crissey's *Saturday Evening Post* article on CC's Plymouth background was entitled "They Call Him Cal." The title was more than journalistic hype; Alva Peck's 1886 letters to CC, in the Coolidge Family Papers, VHS, begin "Dear Cal." CC himself, however, always signed his full name to letters, even those to friends and family (Ross, 13).

Examples of Yankee reserve and silence are innumerable. Those cited here, from Weld, 242; Russell, 19; E. L. Bigelow, 255; and Damon, 59–60, are only a sampling. But the central point here is not that such behavior was widespread, but that it was admired. Fred Pattee's father, on a New Hampshire farm in the 1880s, put it plainly: "Talk never gets work done. Don't ever talk unless you have something on your mind, and when you're on a job, there'll be nothing on your mind but the job. Work, don't talk" (Pattee, 73). The comment of Hyde Leslie, a Plymouth farm worker, about James Kavanagh in his diary makes the point by contrast: "Charles Blanchard did more shoveling than 2 like James Cavenough He called it working here today more talk than work" (Leslie, 128). Basic data on Kavanagh's birthplace, family, and war service are from Plymouth Town Records, the 1880 manuscript U.S. Census, and Aldrich and Holmes.

On fear of strangers, see Gordon, 2; Martin, 236; Kent diary, 3 August 1891.

27. Washburn, *Calvin Coolidge*, 14; Sawyer, 34; Toye, 3; Orton, Pollard interview, 7.

28. Earle, 23, 41; Leslie, 167; Alva C. Peck to CC, 21 May 1886, Coolidge Family Papers, VHS; Beck, 23–24; C. Coolidge, *Autobiography*, 14.

29. CC's unusual fondness for practical jokes in the White House appears in several memoirs (e.g., Parks, 150–51). Ross, 37–38, narrates a trick that CC played on his young son Calvin. Jr. A trick on his grandmother Coolidge is in chapter 12, and a letter to his stepmother Carrie Coolidge (17 January 1892, Coolidge Family Papers, VHS) seems to suggest a trick played on her ("How mean it was to put a mouse in the woodbox, it should have been put in the desk drawer where it might do some good"). Rogers, 44–48, a secondary and not altogether reliable source, tells of a prank played on George Putnam, CC's grandmother's second husband. The only family member CC seems never to have tried to fool was—not surprisingly—his father.

The incident cited in the text, that of cutting the teacher's switch, is given in both Crissey, 161–62, and Kavanagh, 8–9. It is only one of several. CC loved to tease animals and smaller children (Crissey, 9; Kavanagh, 9). He had a trick of sucking all the juice from an orange and then fluffing it up to make it look full (Orton, Pollard interview, 10). In district school, he shot wads of paper at the stove (Whiting, 30); at the academy, he played tricks on his roommates (C. Coolidge diary, 13, 20 January 1887). Jennie Chamberlin, a neighbor who worked in the Coolidge household when CC was small and again during his early college years, summed it up: "Fact is, Cal would rather hector somebody or something than eat raisin pie" (Crissey, 8–9).

30. *New York Times*, 9 September 1923, 4: 3.

Chapter 4. Six Miles from Anywhere

1. In Crissey, 9, CC recounted his boyhood trips to see the circus, beginning when he was seven and lasting at least until he went away to school in 1886. He described one such trip in some detail: "One of the most exciting experiences of my boyhood was that of starting for the first time for Rutland, with my father, to see the great Barnum and Bailey circus unload from the cars and put up the big tent. To accomplish this we had to start at three o'clock in the morning, after a candlelight breakfast that I was too excited to eat." That trip was probably not the one in this chapter, for the passage implies that he and his father went to Rutland more than once, and the trip described here, in 1885, was probably his last to see Barnum and Bailey's circus, whose presence in Rutland is attested by the *Rutland Herald*, 22–23 July 1885. But I have felt free to borrow details from his account of the first trip—the early departure, the excitement, the candlelight breakfast. One liberty I have taken is that of including Abbie in the party, although CC nowhere mentions her in these recollections.

"Chamber" for bedroom: Hughes, "Word-List," 7: 129; Hoyt, 81 (in his play "Temperance"). Getting up in winter: Duffus, 17–18.

2. Vermont Division for Historic Preservation, 9, 11–14; Woods, 77. Martha (Mattie) McWain was working for JC at the beginning of 1886 (C. Coolidge diary, 5 January 1886 and passim), and had worked for him during Mrs. Coolidge's last illness (Curtis et al., *Return*, 35). Orton, *Calvin Coolidge*, 76.

3. Vermont Division for Historic Preservation, 3–4, 7. On the privy, cf. the quote from a Hartland diary given in the Folklore Department of *Vermont History* (hereafter VH), 24 (January 1956): 87: "I took some physic tonight—it called on me at one o'clock—it was damed [*sic*] cold out there."

4. Hired men in Plymouth generally worked from April to April; so Warren Spaulding, who was working for Almeda Coolidge in January 1886 (C. Coolidge diary, 2 January 1886), was probably working for her the preceding July. On milking, see C. Johnson, *Farmer's Boy*, 9; Gordon, 20; and Fisher, *Arlington*, 212–13.

5. Shrewsbury road: Earle Brown interview.

6. Crissey, 9; *Rutland Herald*, 22 July 1885; Durant and Durant, 86–88.

7. *Rutland Herald*, 23 July 1885; Durant and Durant, 80, 86–88; Murray, 253–56; Leach, 73–75; Sherwood, 26–27.

8. Durant and Durant, 67, 79; *Rutland Herald*, 23 July 1885.

9. *Rutland Herald*, 23 July 1885; Sherwood, 68–75; Curtis et al., *Return*, 12; cf. Crissey, 169.

10. *Rutland Herald*, 23 July 1885; Sherwood, 139–40; Taber, 216–17; Duffus, 23.

11. Twombly, *Vermont*, 70–72, 74–75; Bassett, passim; *Rutland Herald*, 5 October 1885. Indoor plumbing was occasionally pictured in advertisements in the *Vermont Tribune*, none of whose readers had it in their homes; see, e.g., VT 24 February 1888. On JC's travel to Boston, see C. Coolidge, *Autobiography*, 9–10, and *New York Times*, 19 September 1931.

12. C. Johnson, *New England Country*, 35; Twombly, *Genealogy*, 37; VT, 28 January 1887.

13. The decline of rural New England in the last quarter of the nineteenth century has been the subject of a lot of writing, most of it of very high quality. Harold Fisher Wilson's *The Hill Country of Northern New England* impressively summarized the evidence of economic, social, and demographic decline from the Civil War on. More recently, Hal S. Barron and Holman D. Jordan (see Sources Cited) have modified Wilson's picture a little, pointing out that not all towns suffered depopulation, that some farmers were able to adapt to changing conditions and become more prosperous, that many late–nineteenth-century writers on the topic were city dwellers who projected their fears about social decay, crime, vice, and racial decline onto the hill country (Hartt's article is a good example), and that it was (and is) very easy to exaggerate the decline and portray it as a catastrophe.

I have tried to profit from all these writings in this account. Plymouth's problem, it seems to me, was primarily one of depopulation, and the annual *Reports* of the secretary of state, summarizing births and deaths for each year, make clear that the cause of the problem was emigration, since there was a slight excess of births over deaths, at least during the 1880s. Population figures for Vermont in general are from Newton, 189, and Wilson, 103–7. Where these emigrants went is discussed in Newton, 182, Wilson, 132–39, and Barron, *Those*, 187–89. Contemporary comments on the emigration are in Kipling, 10, and Dana, 5. Abandoned farms are described in Hard, 25, 42, 126.

14. Ward et al., 11, 15–17, 22. Carpenter's account of the Kingdom church (138) puts its closing during the pastorate of Mason Moore, that is, during the 1880s. For Ninevah, see Fletcher, especially 8, and VT, 5 October, 7 December 1888, 1, 14 June, 12 July, 6 December 1889, and 29 August 1890. A gang of counterfeiters had flourished in nearly the same part of town during the Civil War; Richard Moore interview, Jerry tapes. The quotation is from Cady, "Plymouth," 217.

15. Wilson, 154, and Currier, 385–89, give the institutional picture (a dimension not addressed by Barron or Jordan) for New England in general. Figures for Plymouth schools are from Child, 172, and *Vermont School Reports*: 28 : 110–11, 166–67; 30: 130–31, 186–87; and 32: 153–54, 272–73. Newspaper items occasionally add details; for instance, District 2, between the Kingdom and Five Corners, had had no school for several years when Florence Cilley taught a term there in the winter of 1888 (VT, 9 February 1888); when Geneva Wilder taught there three years later, she had only one pupil (JC to CC, 27 May 1891, Coolidge Family Papers, VHS). The Pinney Hollow school in the winter of 1886 had only seven students, and some children from the area went instead to the Notch district school (VT, 16 December 1886). The Frog City school, District 10, was dilapidated and abandoned even in the 1880s (Ward et al., 68). On churches: Child, 172, 609; Vermont Historical Records Survey, 9. There was occasional public comment about the absence of clergy, e.g., VS, 1 December 1887: "We need a missionary here," or VT, 26 April 1889, "I don't know where there is more need of a missionary than here in Plymouth." Roads: Kavanagh, 11; C. Coolidge, *Autobiography*, 22.

16. VT, 3 May 1889, 9 September 1887.

17. VS, 10 December 1885.

18. VS, 17 November 1887; Child, 431. Fenn, 126, describes a comparable development in West Windsor. On the shift to dairying, see: Barron, "Impact," 324–30; Wilson, 192–93; VT, 19 October 1888; Abbott, "'Gramp' Abbott's," 33; Spear, 17–21; Chase, 449–52; and Newton, 193. According to a land classification map (c. 1945) in ibid., 183, almost all land in Plymouth is Class 4 land, "in which returns from farming have been so low that the land has been or is being abandoned insofar as any agricultural use is concerned, or which, because of rough topography, stoniness, un-

productive soils, or all three, are definitely unsuited to agriculture." On the other hand, in Chelsea, the town most intensively studied by Barron, over half the land was Class 2, suitable for agriculture.

19. Child, 173, 652; VT, 19 November 1886, 30 January 1891; VS, 17 January 1889. For an example of a young man's farming in the summer and driving a team in the winter, see the notice of Matt C. Hall in VT, 27 May 1887. The quotation is from Taber, 249.

20. Leonard, 202; Crane, 174–75; figures for lumbermill workers and sawmill workers in 1880 U.S. Census of Plymouth; VT, 31 July 1885, 28 January, 11 March, 15 April 1887, 8 February 1889, 16 January 1891; VS, 27 January 1887, 12 March 1891; Kavanagh, 13. A photo of Hubbard's mill is in Ward et al., 53; for a general description of a New England sawmill, see C. Johnson, *New England*, 173–74.

21. The general mineral wealth of Plymouth, including the iron deposits and the caves, is described in Child, 169–70; Carpenter, 89–91; and Cummings, 119. Several of those interviewed on the Jerry tapes (e.g., Richard Moore) describe the production of lime, and a clipping on the Plymouth Caves, in a scrapbook at the B.R.A. Museum, describes them in detail. The occurrence of placer gold is documented in such sources as Moore, *Plymouth*, [3]–[4], and VT, 19 August 1887. Abbott, "Gold," 15–16, mentions early explorations.

The story of the mining boom in the early 1880s is well told in Abbott, "Gold." Some accounts (e.g., Curtis et al., *Return,* 13) portray the entrepreneurs of this period simply as city swindlers, but in fact there are variant stories of why the mines failed: see Trudo, 124; Carpenter, 90; VS, 27 October 1887; and VT, 4 November 1892.

22. Basic statistics on Tyson in the 1880s are in Child, 173, 623. For background on the Tyson House, see *New York Times*, 20 April 1924. VT, 20 August 1886 and 29 July 1892, indicate that its popularity went back at least to 1869; and ibid., 11 June, 10 September 1886, give a glimpse of the vacationers' activities. On "Lake Adsulule," see ibid., 13, 20 August 1886, and VS, 11 August 1887. The first use of "Lake Amherst" I have found is in VT, 19 August 1887. On the Beers map of 1869, reproduced in Ward et al., the two lakes are collectively designated "Plymouth Pond," and that name was still used in some quarters in the 1880s (Twombly, *Heritage*, 55), while other local people called it "Tyson Lake" (VT, 25 December 1885). Clearly, then, the name "Echo Lake" was not universally accepted at that time and must have been relatively recent. Another attempted rechristening—"Ticehurst" for Notch Mountain—is reported in ibid., 28 August 1885. Ludlow Pond was renamed "Rescue Lake" in 1881 (Child, 151). The quotation is from VS, 6 August 1885. I found reports on Hubbard's construction of the Echo Lake Inn in VT, 11 November, 9, 30 December 1887, 10 February, 27 April, 8 June 1888, and R. G. Dun & Co. Papers, Vermont, 25: 280.

23. Visitors to the Tyson House and the Echo Lake Inn came from Boston (VT, 21 August 1885, 20 August 1886), Chicago (VT, 10 September 1886), Indianapolis (VT, 19 August 1887), New York (VT, 6 June 1888), Kansas City, Albany, Washington, Toronto (VT, 20 July 1888), Providence, and Savannah (VT, 3 August 1888). On tramps and gypsies in Plymouth, VS, 31 March 1887, VT, 18 October 1889, 7 August 1891, and Evelyn Whittemore interview, Jerry tapes. (It is not clear whether these wandering horse-traders were true Romany gypsies; what is certain is that they passed through Vermont in bands, were considered sharp traders and dangerous customers, and were always called "gypsies.") An entry in the Kent diary, VHS (3 August 1891), illustrates how frightening tramps seemed to local residents; and cf. Martin, 236. A boy who grew up later in Vermont recalled that foreigners, to him, were "strange and terrifying people" (Gordon, 2).

24. Kipling, 122, put it vividly: "The air [of rural Vermont] which kills germs dries

out the very newspapers. They might be of to-morrow or a hundred years ago. They have nothing to do with to-day—the long, full, sunlit to-day. Our interests are not on the same scale as theirs.''

Some of Almeda Coolidge's Sunday School material is in the Coolidge Family Papers, VHS. On conversation in the store, see C. Coolidge, *Autobiography*, 28–29, and cf. Wood, 78.

25. Freeman, *Pembroke*, 35.
26. Coolidge, "Books," 19.

Chapter 5. Winter in the Notch

1. The Vermont School Register for District 9 is in the Plymouth town records; the Register for 1885–86 was the one used here. See also VT, 24 July, 11 September 1885.

2. Stone, 180, recalls the importance most pupils, boys especially, attached to being early for the first day of school. CC's friendship with Thomas Moore is clear from his diary for 1886. Thomas was the son of Ephraim A. Moore (Bryant and Baker, 280), whose house (labeled "T. Moore") can be located on the F. W. Beers 1869 map in Ward et al., 6. A photo of it is in ibid., 94. Ages of all the students are in the Register. On attendance laws, see VT, 11 December 1885, and Newton, 204; on academies, Zinar, 217, and *Report of the Observance . . .* , 28.

3. Photos of the dresses women teachers wore in this era in Plymouth are in Ward et al., 68, 112, 113. Ina Davis, who never married, is described in Davis, *Reading*, II: 211, as a "school teacher now [1903] deceased." Her birth date is from Vermont Vital Records. On boarding around, see "Boarding 'Round," 166, and the Vermont teacher's comment in Hoyt's play "A Midnight Bell" (Hoyt, 59): "Oh dear, with this boarding around every week, a country schoolteacher's life is not a happy one." Boarding around seems to have been discontinued in rural Massachusetts by this time (C. Johnson, *Country School*, 57), but the Coolidge diaries and the other sources cited here show that it was still common practice in Vermont. "Unclaimed blessing" is from Carpenter, 109. On the age of teachers, see, for example, Downing, 243; Guernsey, 4; and *28th Vermont School Report*, 21–33.

4. An exterior photo of the school is in Ward et al., 113. The only extant descriptions of the interior are Kavanagh, 7, and C. Coolidge, *Autobiography*, 31. I have supplemented them with recollections of the equipment that was standard in rural schoolrooms, from Downing, 243; Guernsey, 4; "Boarding 'Round," 165; M. L. Johnson, 47; Roundy, 132; and C. Johnson, *Country School*, 59–65. The carvings on the desks in one Plymouth district "were hard to execute and lasted for years" (Fletcher, 2). Apropos of their content, the superintendent in one eastern Vermont district observed in 1878, "A society for the suppression of obscene pictures and literature would find a fruitful field of operation. Nothing short of fire would purify some of them" (Zinar, 204). Ripley, 87, remarked on the "unspeakable" filth of the school privies in West Rutland. On the condition of the school building, see the Register. Construction of the new building can be followed in VT, 28 May, 16 September 1886, and VS, 27 May 1886. Frost: VS, 17 September 1885. Handbell: cf. Guernsey, 4, and C. Johnson, *Country School*, 66. Since watches were subject to taxation in Vermont in the 1880s, it is possible to learn from the town records who possessed them.

5. Memorizing: Zinar, 210–11. Seating: Roundy, 132, suggests this arrangement. Textbooks: Fuess, *Calvin Coolidge*, 27; "Boarding 'Round," 165. Toeing the crack: Fletcher, 2; C. Johnson, *Country School*, 67; M. L. Johnson, 47. Reading: C. John-

son, *Country School*, 73. *A, b, abs*: Downing, 243. Memorizing pieces: Stone, 179, Kent diary, VHS, 24 February 1886. Diagramming: Twombly, *Heritage*, 55. Noisy slates: Guernsey, 4; Wood, 78. Multiplication tables: Fletcher, 2; Downing, 243. Mental arithmetic: M. L. Johnson, 47.

6. Lunch hour: Fletcher, 3; Hard, 66; "Boarding 'Round," 165. Afternoon subjects: C. Johnson, *Country School*, 74; Crissey, 162. Fletcher, 2, has a sample of didactic verse. Examinations were in use in Newbury, as the Leonard Johnson diary, VHS, 7, 12 January 1886, shows; but in nearby Thetford oral question-and-answer still prevailed (Zinar, 210–11). In Zoa Townsend Fletcher's Plymouth school district, school lasted until 4:00 P.M. (Fletcher, 3). "Diary of a Vermont Boy," 166, suggests that this was the usual time.

7. Discipline is mentioned in nearly every account of Vermont district schools. See, for example: Carpenter, 109; Crane, 97; Duffus, 37; Twombly, *Heritage*, 67; Guernsey, 4; Nash, 44; Fletcher, 7; Stone, 180; "Diary of a Vermont Boy," 164; entry of 8 July 1886, Kent diary, VHS.

8. Fletcher, 3; Carpenter, 110; Earle, 24; Fuess, *Calvin Coolidge*, 29.

9. There were three possible marks for conduct in the school register: plus, minus, and zero. Coolidge received a plus all three terms. Minuses were very rare; in fact, Miss Davis gave none. Johnnie Wilder and Harry Rowe received zeroes all three terms (School Register, 1885–86, Town Records). The author of "Boarding 'Round" used the term "between age," (165). For a concrete example of a student whose conduct deteriorated at this age, see Twombly, *Heritage*, 46.

As for the fall weather, many remarked, according to VT, 9 October 1885, "that they never saw the trees don their gay colors so early in the season, the maple orchards being at the height of their glory." CC's love of natural beauty appears throughout this narrative; see especially chapter 13.

10. Weather: VT, 25 September, 6 November 1885. County fair: Curtis et al., *Return*, 59; VS, 1 October 1885. The fair was a regular event in CC's life, as in that of most Plymouth residents; he thought of late September and early October as "fair time" (CC to Carrie Brown Coolidge, 28 September 1892, Coolidge Family Papers, VHS; cf. C. Coolidge, *Autobiography*, 27). Fall tasks: Cooley, 192, 200; Leslie, 140–56; VT, 20 November 1885; C. Coolidge, *Autobiography*, 27. Mending walls: CC to JC, 2 October 1892, 23 October 1894, Blair Collection; Crissey, 9. Cattle: CC to Almeda B. Coolidge, 23 November 1891, 25 November 1892, Special Collections, Amherst College.

11. Report cards: Twombly, *Heritage*, 46. According to Fussell, 30, teacher examinations were given only in May and November. In Plymouth, the only dates for teacher examinations I have found were 27 November 1886, in Green's Hall at the Union, and 26 November 1887, at the Notch schoolhouse (VS, 25 November 1886, 17 November 1887)- -the last Saturday in November in both cases. I conjecture that the date of the 1885 examination followed the same pattern. JC as school superintendent: VT, 18 September 1885. CC and teacher examination: C. Coolidge, *Autobiography*, 31.

12. Sizer, 2, 29, 36–40; Huse, 26–27. Noble, passim, describes a fairly typical academy.

13. VT, 18 September, 23 October, 4 December 1885.

14. M. L. Johnson, 47; Farnsworth, 19; Ripley, 92.

15. "Boarding 'Round," 166; Kavanagh, 7–8; Carpenter, 45; Duffus, 37.

16. C. Coolidge diary, 6, 7, 15, 19 January 1886; District 9 School Register for 1885–56, Plymouth Town Records. Herbert Moore: Bryant and Baker, 271, 274; VT, 5 November 1886; Harriet Moore to Sarah Coolidge Putnam, c. 1900, Coolidge Family Papers, VHS. Matt Hall: VT, 27 May 1887, 9 April 1889; Richard Moore interview, Jerry tapes.

17. Cleghorn, 35; M. G. Marshall, 163; Earle, 9; Crane, 46–47; J. C. Carter, "Christmas," 308–10; Ripley, 195; Wood, 105; C. Johnson, *Farmer's Boy*, 157–63. Local newspapers carried advertisements for Christmas goods (e.g., VT, 18 December 1885, 7 December 1888). Christmas greens: VT, 6 November 1885, VS, 18 November 1886.

18. C. Coolidge, *Autobiography*, 28; Carpenter, 97. A document in Ward et al., 99, shows the existence of the tradition as early as 1869. For the 1885 celebration, see VS, 31 December 1885; VT, 25 December 1885, gives the weather. For local celebrations in other years that give more information on community practices, see VS, 29 December 1887, and VT, 28 December 1888. Applause: Twombly, *Genealogy*, 35.

19. Cooley, 201; Kipling, 5, 9, 117; Taber, 246; Steele, 210; Hard, 58; Carpenter, 97–98.

20. VT, 8 January 1886; C. Coolidge diary, 2, 3, 15, 28, 30 January 1886.

21. Kavanagh, 12; Ward et al., 77, 103; and Bryant and Baker, xi: these refer mainly to the public dances held at the hotels. Many of them were announced in the local newspapers: see, for example, VS, 18 February 1886, or VT, 11 February 1887. Twombly, *Heritage*, 73 (entry of 12 November 1887), gives a view of a winter dance from the vantage point of a stablehand. Kitchen dances: Carpenter, 99–100 (cf. Fleming, 31, 60, for a similar picture in neighboring Sherburne); Orton, Pollard interview, 3; VT, 4 February 1887; VS, 16 October 1890; Curtis et al., 54–55.

All sources agree that Coolidge did not enjoy dancing and rarely went to dances (Carpenter, 100–1; Orton, Pollard interview, 3), and Curtis et al., *Return*, 19, quotes a local saying that "The Coolidges never dance." Toye, 2, however, states that Abbie did dance on at least one occasion, to her grandmother's displeasure. It was not uncommon for some members of a family to dance and others not to. The young Pollards of Proctorsville, for instance, were split on the issue: Dallas and Park danced, but Fred did not (Erminie Pollard interview). On CC's reasons for not going to a dance or not staying at one once there see, e.g., C. Coolidge diary, 5 February 1886 ("A party at Thomas. I could not go on account of toothache") or 11 February 1887 ("went to a party at J. J. Wilder's. I had a very good time but did not stay only till 11:00").

22. Skating: C. Coolidge diary, 6, 7, 8 January 1886. Sliding: ibid., 30 January, 1, 2, 5, 9, 10 February 1886, 9 April 1887; Curtis et al., *Return*, 53: J. A. Carter, "Christmas," 309; "Diary of a Vermont Boy," 167, entry of 26 December; Hoyt's play, "A Midnight Bell," (Hoyt, 79); VS, 29 January 1891. Hunting: C. Coolidge diary, 15, 16, 30 January, 6, 13, 20 February 1886; Thomas Moore to CC, 23 March 1886, Coolidge Family Papers, VHS. Winter costume: Taber, 225, 227. Game: Moore, *Plymouth*, [22]; Crane, 104; *New York Times*, 19 September 1931; C. Coolidge, "Grandmother's Kitchen," Coolidge Family Papers, VHS. On deer, see C. W. Johnson, 91. Deer sightings near Plymouth were reported in VT, 22 July, 19 August, 14 September 1887.

23. Kipling, 120; Taber, 14, 19, 75, 80: C. Coolidge diary, 1 February 1886.

24. C. Coolidge diary, 6, 10, 22 January 1886; Crissey, 8, 166; C. Coolidge, "Grandmother's Kitchen," Coolidge Family Papers, VHS; C. Coolidge, "Books," 144–45; Curtis et al., 19; Sargent.

25. Entries in C. Coolidge diary, for 5, 6, 17, 20, 21, 24, 26 and 31 January 1886 suggest that John, Mat, and Abbie were all gone on most of these dates, and that Calvin was alone in the house. Warren Spaulding: C. Coolidge diary, 3 ("The teacher went over to see Warren. At least he thought she did"), 15, 16, 21 January, 2, 14 February, 7 March 1886. As late as 1892 CC still had a warm regard for Warren and was praising him to his father (letter of 8 March 1892, in Lathem, 32). Others in the community seem to have thought highly of him too; see VT, 4 January 1889, 7 November 1890.

26. CC's being sent to school at Black River Academy (B.R.A.)—or to some academy, at any rate—was in some ways a normal, foreseeable step in his upbringing. As Coolidge's *Autobiography* points out (38), both his parents and his grandmother Coolidge had attended B.R.A.; moreover, it was almost routine for the children of financially secure farmers in Plymouth to attend a term or two there. A glance over B.R.A. catalogs for the eighties shows two children (and a grandchild) of James S. Brown, two children of James "Strawberry" Brown, a daughter of John Wilder, a son of J. W. Stickney, five Moore children from various Notch families, and three children of Nathaniel King, who lived near Tyson, in addition to CC and his sister Abbie. Still, there is one striking feature about CC's entrance in 1886. He was very much younger than most Plymouth students who attended. The average age of the seventeen students from Plymouth whose age could be determined on their entrance to B.R.A., exclusive of CC and Abbie, was seventeen, and none was younger than fifteen. Calvin and Abbie, on the other hand, were both thirteen when they entered. The fact suggests either haste on their father's part or eagerness on their own to get off to boarding school.

It is clear from the sources that CC, though a bit nervous, was also enthusiastic about going away to school. He recall it in his *Autobiography* as his "first great adventure.... Going to the Academy meant a complete break with the past and entering a new and untried field, larger and more alluring than the past, among unknown scenes and unknown people" (38). Closer in time to the reality was his diary entry of 4 March 1886, in his second week at B.R.A.: "Had a good time down here but not so good as I expected." This entry suggests that he had built up a vivid image of academy life and had high expectations of it. For this reason, it seems likely to me that he had mentioned to John his interest in attending, and that John, for the reasons cited in the text, had seconded his idea.

The first mention of a decision to attend B.R.A. is in C. Coolidge diary, 13 February 1886: "John went to Ludlow to see about my going to school at that place." But it seems plausible that the idea had come up before. The teacher examination, which CC had passed in November, was a sort of primitive Scholastic Aptitude Test; that is, students sometimes took it "for pastime," just to get an idea of how well they were doing in their schoolwork (cf. VT, 4 May 1888). It could well be that he had taken it not from a desire to teach but to show his father that he was indeed qualified for an academy.

27. CC (diary, 8 February 1886) records the trip to Woodstock to look at a school but does not explicitly say that he was considering attending it; that is my inference. The village is well described in Curtis et al., *Times Gone By*, passim. VS, 12 January 1888, notes that the Maloy boys of Five Corners were at the high school there.

The schedule of B.R.A is obvious from C. Coolidge diary, 22 February 1886. The schedule in the B.R.A. Catalog, 1885–86, 25, mistakenly shows the term as beginning on 21 February. For the offerings and fees, see ibid.

28. C. Coolidge diary, 13, 14 February 1886; Almeda Coolidge to CC, 24 February 1886, Coolidge Family Papers, VHS.

29. C. Coolidge diary, 17, 18, 19 February 1886; C. Coolidge, *Autobiography*, 32; Carpenter, 100. Sweet tooth: CC was not at all reticent about his food preferences. His diary and correspondence throughout his youth contain repeated references to his fondness for molasses candy (diary, 17, 27 February 1886, 16 April 1887), maple sugar (diary, 13 March 1886, 27 March, 19 April 1887; CC to JC, 12 March 1893, FL), and pie (CC to Carrie B. Coolidge, 11, 26 October 1891, Coolidge Family Papers, VHS). Honey was an exception. He had overeaten some in early childhood and become violently ill; he disliked it the rest of his life (Quint and Ferrell, 47–48).

30. C. Coolidge, *Autobiography*, 32–33; C. Coolidge diary, 21 February 1886. M. L. Johnson, 7, and Damon, 59–60, articulate the standard Yankee viewpoint about

emotional reserve; but it is hard to be sure whether it applied to the Coolidges. In later life CC regularly kissed his father when greeting him; see chapter 12 and notes for further discussion.

Chapter 6. A Railroad Town

1. A good brief description of Ludlow at the end of the century, reprinted from *Stone* magazine, is in VT, 4 November 1892. The second edition of Harris's *History of Ludlow* contains numerous photographs from the 1880s and 1890s, which I use repeatedly in these chapters. On the depot, see VT, 27 May, 28 October 1892, 13 January 1893. A photograph showing part of it is in Shaughnessy, 52.

2. There are several slightly different versions of JC's parting words to CC; this one is from Carpenter, 25. Cf. W. A. White, 24, and Fuess, *Calvin Coolidge*, 32. JC to CC, 1 March 1886, Coolidge Family Papers, VHS, documents the fact that CC was rooming at Miss Boynton's.

3. The 1869 Beers map, available at the B.R.A. Museum, and the 1880 U.S. Census manuscript, help to locate Miss Boynton's house. Iron bridge: VT, 26 October 1888. Academy hill: VT, 3 January 1890; VT, 14 June 1956 ("March Storms Bring Memories of School Days to Mrs. William Butler"). Shoes with rubbers: C. Coolidge, *Autobiography*, 32.

4. For the building's history, see Harris, 63–64. VT, 23 June 1938, ("Frank Sherman Writes on B.R.A. in Retrospect"), mentions the town's use of the upper floors, and C. Coolidge diary, 1 March 1887, shows that it continued in the 1880s. The percentage of students from the village and town of Ludlow, calculated from the addresses given in the school catalogs, was 63 percent in 1885; 48 percent in 1885–86; 52 percent in 1886–87; 68 percent in 1888–89; 64 percent in 1889–90; and 53 percent in 1890–91. Almost all the rest were from the surrounding towns: Plymouth, Reading, Cavendish, Weston, Mount Holly, and Shrewsbury. The school district's connection with B.R.A. is clear from *History of Black River Academy*, 125, 129; for parallel instances and the basic state law, see Fussell, 17; E. R. Snyder, 86; and Sizer, 44.

5. Sizer, passim, supplies excellent background on American academies in general; see also the good brief summary in Krug, 3–7. The list of outstanding academies in Vermont at the end of the century is based on Spear, 13. Their relation as "feeder schools" to the colleges is summarized in Collar's article: "The preparatory schools and many academies, make the fitting of boys and girls for college their chief aim. With high schools this is a subordinate end" (Collar, 425). The proportion of B.R.A. students in each of the three courses is taken from the catalogs; for the English course the figures are 1885 winter–spring 82.5 percent; 1885 fall 85.9 percent; 1886–87 80.5 percent; 1888–89 72.5 percent; 1889–90 69.1 percent; 1890–91 68.4 percent. The decline in the late eighties and early nineties probably had to do with Principal George Sherman's effort, discussed in the next chapter, to steer more students into the Classical, college-bound course. The curriculum is described in the catalogs; e.g., 11–15 in the 1887 catalog. Krug, 6, suggests that it was absolutely typical for its time.

6. The irregular attendance at B.R.A. was typical; compare Sizer, 29, and Vinovskis, 555. The figures for 1888–89 are from that year's catalog. Out of 123 students, fifty-nine attended all three terms; forty of them were from Ludlow. Thirty students attended two of the three terms, thirty-four only one.

7. The quotation is from Vinovskis, 555, a parallel to B.R.A.'s situation. A B.R.A. advertisement in 1888 put it this way: "Students are strongly urged to remain in school to complete the studies commenced." B.R.A. commencement cere-

monies can be followed in *History of Black River Academy*, 147. By the time CC graduated in 1890 they had become quite elaborate; see chapter 8. Diplomas and their rationale are mentioned in Grizzell, 334. The percentage of students graduating is, again, from the B.R.A. catalogs; only 35 percent of the students in the 1888–89 catalog, for instance, are in the complete list of graduates, *History of Black River Academy*, 147ff. Other years are similar. In all these respects, cf. Barre Academy, in Noble, 142.

8. The interior layout of the old building and some of the faculty are described in Mary Pollard's article (VT, 16 June 1955: "Mary Pollard Recalls Old Times at B.R.A.; First Class met in Old Bakery Room"). The process of setting up the term's schedule is outlined in *The Tribune Junior*, 7 March 1890, B.R.A. Museum. The 1885–86 catalog has the faculty roster, as well as the names of Henry Brown and Florence Blanchard; on the latter see also Bryant and Baker, 7–8, and C. Coolidge diary, 19 January 1886. More on Henry Kendall is in VT, 16 January 1891. Male principal: Sizer, 198.

9. CC's diary for 1885 gives the course schedule, and Mary Pollard's article (VT, 16 June 1965) supplies the context.

10. CC's marks at B.R.A. are given in a footnote in Lathem, 19. They fluctuated from a low of 81.3 (spring term, 1888) to a high of 91.6 (winter, 1886–87). His class standing for the 1886 spring term was quite low: sixty-second (report cards, Coolidge Family Papers, VHS). On his civil government course, see C. Coolidge, *Autobiography*, 40.

11. CC's general ability with figures is evident from the calculations of interest and return on investment that pervade his letters from college on. But he said of algebra, with regard to his term at St. Johnsbury in 1891, "I had no use for the subject" (Fuess, *Calvin Coolidge*, 42); and at Amherst he was sure that he did not want to take any more mathematics than the college required (CC to JC, 12 January 1892, Blair Collection). His difficulties at B.R.A. are covered in this and the next chapter. As for Clara Prior, see her photo in the B.R.A. Museum collection, and C. Coolidge diary, 8, 9 March 1886. It may be worth noting that some current studies suggest a connection between difficulty in mathematics and low self-esteem among adolescents (Bower, 184–86).

12. The report card (Coolidge Family Papers, VHS) shows five absences during this term; for the cold, see C. Coolidge diary, 15, 16, 17 March 1886. Compare "I have good lessons always" (ibid., 4 March 1886) with "Have a quite [*sic*] a lot of lessons behind" (ibid., 17 March 1886). Henry Brown: H. T. Brown, 312. Deadpan humor: Thomas Moore to CC, 23 March 1886, Coolidge Family Papers, VHS. Honor roll: VT, 2 April 1886.

13. CC to JC, 29 January 1888 (Lathem, 7); "Memories of Black River Academy"; Twombly, *Heritage*, 56, 58.

14. CC's concentration: cf. C. Coolidge diary, 20 April 1887, "I cannot study much for I am so out of doors that if I try to study I am thinking of something else." Literary society: B.R.A. catalog, 1889–90, 21. Athletics: C. Coolidge, *Autobiography*, 44. There were casual athletics, particularly baseball; see VT, 19 April, 3 May 1889. Social events: VT, 2 April 1886. Morning assembly: VT, 17 June 1954 ("Memories of Black River Academy by an 'Old Grad'"). Spruce gum: see Wilder.

15. VT, 27 August 1886, 23 September 1887; Child, 152.

16. Harris, 21, 77–78; VT, 10 July 1885, 23 April, 28 May, 27 August 1886, 11 April 1890, 30 October 1891; Kipling, 111; Alva C. Peck to CC, 29 May 1886, Coolidge Family Papers, VHS.

17. The first mention of a long-distance telephone in Ludlow is the line to Weston in 1889 (VT, 12 July 1889). Child, 152, lists the stores; many of them, including Raymond's and Sherman's, are profiled in the credit reports of R. G. Dun & Co. Bakery:

VT, 17 June 1954 ("Memories of Black River Academy by an 'Old Grad'"); VT, 16 December 1887, 27 September 1888. See also the photographs and sketches of local businessmen in *Ludlow and Her Neighbors*, 3–17. On drugstores: Duffus, 171; VT, 5 August 1892, M. L. Johnson, 23, and Curtis et al., *Times Gone By*, 57.

18. John Keating: VT, 17 July 1885. Hammond Hall: Ibid., 25 September, 30 October 1885, 5, 19 February, 16 April 1886, 4 March, 1, 29 April, 13 May, 30 September 1887. Clerks: Martin, 233. Lampposts: VT, 21 May 1886. Ludlow House: VT, 16 April 1886, 21 December 1888; photograph in Harris, 3rd ed., appendix. On prohibition and its enforcement generally, see Graffagnino, 102, 105, and M. L. Johnson, 23–24. Delivery carts: VT, 26 March 1886, 29 August 1890; photograph in Harris, 3rd ed., appendix. Clothing: Nash, 45; Cleghorn, 77; Macomber, 176; M. L. Johnson, 21–22; Fisher, *Memories*, 181–85.

19. VT, 5 March 1886, 11 February, 15 April, 23 September 1887; C. Coolidge diary, 1, 19 March 1886, 15 January, 25, 27, 28 February, 1, 12 March, 10, 17 April 1887. A handcar of this period is exhibited at the Shelburne Museum. For the Canadian Northwest car, see ibid., 12 January 1887; VT, 14 January 1887. Another recollection of Proctorsville–Ludlow rail travel, a little later, is in Crane, 143.

20. CC's weekend activities in Ludlow deserve a little comment here. He left the impression at B.R.A. of a boy closely tied to his home and family. His schoolmate Ada Barney remembered years later that he regularly went home twice a week (VT, 28 October 1920); in fact, he did not and could not have, but the recollection shows the kind of image he presented. His neighbor and classmate Henry Brown, James Brown's youngest brother, recounted how his family came for him every Friday and brought him back to Ludlow every Sunday, perhaps implying that JC did likewise (H. T. Brown, 312). CC himself stated (*Autobiography*, 43), "Sometimes I walked home Friday afternoon, but usually my father came for me and brought me back Sunday evening or Monday morning." This version, of CC's going home nearly every weekend, has passed into several biographies (Hennessy, 19; W. A. White, 24). The problem is that it seems not be true on the basis of contemporary evidence. CC's surviving diaries for 1886, 1887, and 1890 cover a total of twenty-five weekends during the school term: on ten of them he went to Proctorsville; on eight he stayed in Ludlow; on five JC came and took him home; on one he hitched a ride with a Plymouth neighbor; and on one he walked home by himself. Granted, the diaries cover mainly January, February, and March, winter months when weather could be severe; but November and December, also school months, cannot have been much easier in that respect and probably had the same travel pattern. Probably in fall he went home more often; consequently, I have hedged a little in the text and suggested that he went to Proctorsville on weekends "perhaps more often" than to Plymouth. What is certainly true is that CC wanted to go home much more often than he actually did, and never knew until the last minute whether it would suit his father to come for him; one of the most poignant pictures in the diaries is that of CC sitting up in Stickney's law office all afternoon, watching Main Street traffic in vain to see if he could spot John's buggy: "so I was left but I did not care much" (diary, 6 January 1887). JC seems often to have changed his mind at the last minute, coming unexpectedly or failing to come when he had said he might (see, e.g., ibid., 1 April 1887).

21. Don C. Pollard: Lathem, 95n; Orton, Pollard interview, 9. The Pollard store can be followed through the reports in R. G. Dun & Co. Papers, Vermont, 25: 292, 332, 377. CC's enjoyment of his work in the store is evident from diary entries like 27, 28 February, 27, 28 March 1886, and 29, 30 January, 26 February 1887. Cavendish Gorge: Fuess, *Calvin Coolidge*, 35. Aunt Sarah: C. Coolidge, *Autobiography*, 44; C. Coolidge diary, 16 April 1887.

22. CC's 1886 and 1887 diaries record only two Sundays when he went to church in Ludlow: 6 February and 24 April 1887. But considerable evidence suggests that

most of Plymouth shared his casualness in this respect. M. E. Dimick of Five Corners, whose diary is in VHS, often worked on Sundays in 1884 and attended meeting only occasionally. Likewise, the diary of Arden Taylor of Plymouth, also in VHS, contains this entry for 12 August 1877: "All went to church but me and I staid and read Dickens." The diary of the farm hand Hyde Leslie for nine months of 1887 shows that he attended church on seven Sundays in that period and stayed away on twenty-nine. Both the *Vermont Tribune* and the *Vermont Standard* at different times took Plymouth people to task for excessive fishing on Sundays (VT, 24 May 1889; VS, 24 May 1888). A rather defensive comment by a correspondent in the *Standard* suggests that Plymouth mores were talked about by outsiders: "One might think from an article in some of our newspapers that nothing of the kind of religious feelings entertained by civilized communities, generally, were ever heard of with us" (VS, 10 December 1885). It is probably a mistake, however, to try to infer anything about religious beliefs from this behavior. As Fred Pattee remarked of his upbringing in New Hampshire, "Never did we talk religion in the home. Like sex it was never mentioned, yet it was always present.... We knew our world and had no doubts. God, as He had been revealed to man through the Bible, was to us as much an actuality in our thinking as were our parents" (Pattee, 66).

23. Sunday dinners are described in Twombly, *Heritage*, 81; Duffus, 156; and Gordon, 12, from which the quote is taken. For Thanksgiving dinner, see Twombly, *Heritage*, 27; "Diary of a Vermont Boy," 167; VT, 23 November 1888; Humphrey, 23; M. G. Marshall, 163; Nash, 45; VH 26: 53; and Earle, 9. A Thanksgiving dinner bill of fare from the Notch, from the household of James and Ella Ayer, is described by their niece Eliza Hoskison in an interview on the Jerry tapes: mashed potatoes and gravy, pork, roast beef, turkey, chicken pie, onions, squash, turnips, beets, pickles, relish, macaroni and cheese, and desserts that included raisin, pumpkin, mince, apple, and berry pies. My sources for beverages include *New York Times*, 24 August 1924, clipping in Forbes Library, Northampton, Mass. (hereafter FL); Hunt et al., 72 (in which small children were given "coffee milk" as a first step toward drinking coffee); Leach, 123; J. C. Carter, "Christmas," 308, 310; J. C. Carter, "Trip," 243; Hoyt's play, "A Midnight Ball" (Hoyt, 56); "Expressions," 357; W. P. Bigelow, 261 (white sugar was called "coffee sugar"). CC was fond of coffee with cream and associated it with his grandmother's house; see his letter to her, "33 [*sic*] November 1891," Special Collections, Frost Library, Amherst College.

24. Boiled victuals, in several different combinations, are mentioned in Twombly, *Heritage*, 27 (beet greens, dandelion greens, boiled mush with cowslip greens), and Nash, 44 (peas, beet greens, and new potatoes on one occasion, pole beans, cabbage, and beets on another). Other meatless meals are in ibid. (succotash and tomatoes) and in the Kent diary, 24 January 1886 (turnips), 11 March 1889 (oatmeal), 11 February (hasty pudding), 21 February (beans), 3 April ("maccheroni"), 30 August 1891 (sweet corn and cucumbers). Boiled dinners are discussed in Gould, 126; Crane, 172; VH 19 (July 1951): 188; and C. Johnson, *New England Country*, 63. E . Young's account (257) emphasizes the basic ideal of thrift: "A shrewd lady always saw to it that there were four meals in the pot. She served the contents hot for dinner, cold for supper, and the next morning a hash was made. Finally, the next day, a soup was compounded of the fragments with a pint of beans added."

25. Codfish: Flanders, 17; "Boarding 'Round," 167. Woodchuck: Pettingill, 61. Flanders, 14, mentions "that festival dish, chicken pie." Salt pork: Crane, 167–68; *New York Times*, 24 August 1924, clipping in FL; and Andrews, 23 (in which salt pork was the backup meal when the dog ran off with the Christmas dinner).

26. Wilson 120; Kipling, 116; Gordon, 14 (farm cooking from a later era); Crane, 169; "Boarding 'Round," 166–67; Duffus, 42. CC's praise of his Aunt Sarah's bread is documented in Donald and Waterhouse, 9, and his fondness for hot cereal is from

ibid., 3. Other favorite foods: salt pork, doughnuts (Crane, 167–70, and Flanders, 15–16); tripe, buckwheat cakes (Mason, 25); Indian pudding (E. Young, 257, and Charles Hoskison interview, Jerry tapes); pickles, doughnuts (Hunt et al., 71).

27. Oysters: Twombly, *Heritage*, 68; "Diary of a Vermont Boy," 167; Leach, 16; J. C. Carter, "Christmas," 310; Winslow, 46; Hunt et al., 71. Tropical fruits: Twombly, *Heritage*, 75; M. G. Marshall, 158; Duffus, 19; VS, 2 August 1888. The quotation on bananas is from Ripley, 166. Commercial chewing gum is mentioned in ibid., 113; but Wrigley's, the brand that epitomized the product to most Americans of this generation, was introduced only in 1898. Other brands, however, had been manufactured since the 1870s (Flexner, 141).

28. Duffus, 56–57, "Boarding 'Round," 165; Crane, 169–70; "Memoranda," Sidney Johnson diary, VHS; Twombly, *Heritage*, 56; C. Coolidge diary, 2 February 1887, and "cash accounts" in back of 1887 Diary; CC to Carrie B. Coolidge, 4 October 1891, and Thomas H. Moore to CC, 23 March 1886, Coolidge Family Papers, VHS.

29. The reference to chunks is actually from a letter later in 1886 (CC to Abbie Coolidge, 29 November, quoted in Fuess, 33), when he was boarding at another place; but practices were similar at most boarding houses, and there is no doubt that CC got his wood from Plymouth. The use of chunks is explained in C. Johnson, *Farmer's Boy*, 12. On laundry, see JC to CC, 1 March 1886, Coolidge Family Papers, VHS.

30. Alva Peck to CC, 29 May 1886, Coolidge Family Papers, refers to "the crowd at Miss B's," but it is not clear who made up that crowd. CC mentioned another boarder simply as "Fred" (diary, 23 March 1886), and this may very well have been Fred Colburn, who had just returned to Ludlow from three years in the West; see the sketch of him in *Ludlow and her Neighbors*, 19–20. Possibly another boarder was nicknamed "Hile" (Alva Peck to CC, 21 May 1886, Coolidge Family Papers); this could have been Hiland Stickney, Lawyer Stickney's nineteen-year-old brother, who was clerking in his office for a year or so before going to college (Bryant and Baker, 388; VT, 24 February 1888). John's instructions are in his letter to CC, 1 March 1886, Coolidge Family Papers.

31. C. Coolidge diary, 17 February, 11, 16 March 1886; letters from Alva Peck to CC in Coolidge Family Papers, VHS. The quote, which probably alludes to masturbation, is from Peck's letter of 22 June 1886; another cryptic passage probably on the same subject is in his letter of 21 May 1886.

32. George Raymond and Dick Lane are mentioned in CC to JC, 22 November 1891, in Lathem, 26, and C. Coolidge diary, 28 March 1887, and Win Bixby in CC to W. M. Bixby, 24 April 1926, Personal Letters (microfilm), FL. Frank Day is mentioned in Alva Peck to CC, 21 May 1886, Coolidge Family Papers, VHS. Vice in Ludlow was chronicled in VT, 26 August 1887, 20 June, 29 August 1890, and alluded to in VS, 29 November 1888. The "Beehive" is also noticed in Harris, 162. Park Pollard: Alva Peck to CC, 22 June 1886.

33. 1887 diary; *American Catalogue*, 178. A select list of Murray Hill publications is found in the back of Foote. On Foote, see Reed, 16.

34. Sugaring in general: Taber, 29, 192–93, 231; Ward et al., 20; Curtis et al., *Return*, 48–49; Ripley, 185–86; Kipling, 10; *Rochester*, 88; Trudo, 124–25; Bryant and Baker, x; Carpenter, 83, 85; Hance, 130–31; Ludlum, 40. According to Carpenter, 130, sugaring at the Notch could begin as early as February and run as late as May 1, but I narrowed the time frame in the text by using the Leslie diary (100–3) and CC's comment in a letter from college, "I shall be home in five weeks, boiling sap, I hope" (CC to JC, 21 February 1894, in Lathem, 54). CC's knowledge of sugar and sugaring is clear from the following: C. Coolidge diary, 19, 21 April 1887; Hennessy,

7; CC to JC, 14 April 1892, 12 March 1893, FL; and CC to Carrie B. Coolidge,
1 March 1893, FL.

35. VT, 30 April, 14 May 1886; Alva Peck to CC, 14 May 1886, Coolidge Family
Papers, VHS. Spring: VT, 13 May 1887, 25 May 1888, 10 May 1889; Taber, 234, 235;
C. Johnson, *Farmer's Boy*, 65; Curtis et al., 50; Kent diary, 6 September 1891.

Chapter 7. The Academy Dude

1. Newspaper clipping, dated 8 March 1925, in scrapbook at B.R.A. Museum;
Bryant, 9; VT, 17 June 1954 ("Memories of Black River Academy"); Hemenway, 5;
New York Times, 14 August 1927. CC's autograph book is in the B.R.A. Museum.
On Clara Pollard, see the class photographs also in the B.R.A. Museum, and C. Co-
lidge diary, 10, 19 January, 3, 9 February 1887.

2. "Papa": C. Coolidge diary, 16, 17, 18, 21 February 1887 and passim; "John":
ibid., 2, 4, 5, 11, 17 January 1886 and passim. Profanity: ibid., 6, 21 January 1886.
Expressions of a similar sort are in Hard, 51, 91; "Diary of a Vermont Boy," 166;
and "Expressions," 63. CC disliked hearing profanity as an adult (*New York Times*,
30 August 1928), and, according to a friend of his early manhood, "swore not at all"
(Dennis, 20); but cf. chapter 15. The accounts for his jewelry trade are in the back of
his 1887 diary; they cover January and part of February. Typical entries are: "chased
ring L. .20," "1/2 doz. collar but. L. .10," "1 band ring .75." Ring: Fuess: *Calvin Coolidge*, 33.

3. Toye, 6; Orton, Pollard interview, 3; VT, 28 October 1920 ("A Coolidge
Story"). VT, 21 April 1921 ("Sparking a Girl in Vermont," by Daniel L. Cady), is a
conventional but detailed example of how a boy's dress might improve under a girl's
influence. On Ada Barney, see Barney, 18–19.

4. C. Coolidge, *Autobiography*, 44; Bryant, 9; Toye, 6. "Oh, hell": cf. Ripley, 218.
Oaths: VT, 29 January 1886. In the same vein, the entry of 3 February 1891 in the
Kent diary, VHS, is probably to be read "had a mud fight, and beat Olney's ass."
Spaulding's program, in the 1888–89 B.R.A. Catalog, is in the Widener Library, Har-
vard University. In "Susie F. Wilder's Graduation, 1889," B.R.A. Museum, the word
"pass" is used in quotation marks in this sense, implying that it was still novel.

5. Crissey, 9; Sawyer, 35; Lathem, 38.

6. C. Coolidge diary, 9 January, 6 February, 24 April 1887; C. Coolidge, *Autobiography*, 29–30. For CC's hair, see photographs.

7. CC boarded at Pinney's all three terms of the 1886–87 school year, as is evident from his diary and from the autograph book in which one of his roommates
identified himself as "one of Pinney's tribe." See also VT, 8 October 1886. Men's
clothing: Waugh, 117, 156, and passim; Cunnington and Cunnington, 285–309; Kidwell and Christman, 115–21. The quotation is from Oscar Wilde (Waugh, 156).

8. CC to JC, 28 August 1887, Coolidge Family Papers, VHS; Lathem, 7, 9; Fuess,
Calvin Coolidge, 33.

9. The evidence on CC's roommates at B.R.A. is good for his first two years but
spotty thereafter. His autograph book in the B.R.A. Museum is dated on the first
page "B.R.A. J. Calvin Coolidge Plymouth Vermont November 1886" and signed
in November by S. R. Kendall of Pittsford, Henry E. Lawton of North Springfield,
and Fred E. Colburn of Ludlow, all of whom identify themselves either with B.R.A.
or Pinney's boarding house. From the diary for the winter and spring of 1887 it is
clear that Colburn and Newton E. Turgeon (who also signed the autograph book

later) were his roommates in the winter and George Harris and Loren Pinney (also a signer of the autograph book) either then or in the spring.

CC to JC, 28 August 1887, Coolidge Family Papers, VHS, establishes that he roomed with Henry Hicks (and perhaps others) in the fall term of that year. I have found no other contemporary evidence about his roommates from then until his graduation in 1890. Ada Barney recollected that he boarded on Pleasant Street in early 1888 (VT, 28 October 1920), which perhaps means that he was still at Pinney's. Albert Sargent, however, recalled having "slept with" (i.e., roomed with) him as a student (Toye, 6); possibly, then, he also roomed at the Sargents' house on Pleasant Street. He is also said to have roomed at Mrs. Sherwin's on Pleasant Street (Fuess, *Calvin Coolidge*, 32), and Alice Lockwood's recollection of his "skirmishing with Lena across the lawn from our house" (Ross, 98) may refer to this period, as Mrs. Sherwin lived next door to the Lockwoods. Herbert Moore remembered rooming with him at Parker's (Fuess, *Calvin Coolidge*, 32); this recollection is easy to date, since Moore attended only one term, in the fall of 1888 (B.R.A. Catalog, 1888–89).

Finally, during his postgraduate study at B.R.A., narrated in chapter 10, he roomed at Rufus Hemenway's house on Pleasant Street.

On CC and his roommates, see his diary entries of 13, 20, 24, 25 January, 6 February 1887, and Fuess, *Calvin Coolidge*, 35.

10. This story is told in the following: VT, 8 October 1886; VS, 7 October 1886; C. Coolidge, *Autobiography*, 41; and Toye, 6. It is clear that he was attempting a circus trick. The only circus I can find a record of in the vicinity that summer is the Doris circus (*Rutland Herald*, 3, 5, 10 August 1886). A contemporary poster for it, advertising "The Great Egyptian Boalupus," is at the Shelburne Museum.

11. C. Coolidge diary, 2, 3 February, 2, 13, 20 March, 20 April 1887.

12. C. Coolidge diary, 6, 14 January 1887; C. Coolidge, *Autobiography*, 40.

13. Background on the Ludlow Toy Manufacturing Company and its owners is in Child, 398–99. A report dated 1885 in the R. G. Dun & Co. Papers, Vermont, 25: 306, describes its directors as among the best men in the community. A catalog of the company for 1876 is in the B.R.A. Museum, along with one of its doll carriages. For descriptions of very similar factories in Mechanicsville and Lyndon, see O. S. Marshall, 11, and Twombly, *Heritage*, 44. On swimming in its pond, see VT, 14 August 1891.

14. CC's account of this work, and the only source for it, is C. Coolidge, *Autobiography*, 40–41. He does not date the experience and states only that he worked "some" at the factory, which he calls simply a "cab shop." This was the way the factory was referred to in Ludlow; see, for instance, the newspaper item cited above. JC is authority for the statement that his son's earnings were placed in a savings account (Toye, 6). For the work day, see Twombly, *Heritage*, 44, and Watson, 41. A sampling of his fellow workers is listed in the Ludlow town directory (Child, 394–401).

Since CC gave no date for his work at the toy factory, my dating is necessarily conjectural; but a look at CC's personal history and the history of the plant narrows the options considerably. The diary for his first term, spring 1886, shows no work on Saturdays; on the other hand, production ceased entirely at the factory in the fall of 1889 and was at a "low ebb" all that year (VT, 15 February, 11 October 1889). Presumably, then, CC was employed some time between the fall of 1886 and the end of 1888. It seems, however, that from the time it was auctioned in November 1887 it was running simply to use up the remaining stock (R. G. Dun & Co. Papers, Vermont, 25: 306), a situation in which the owners would be unlikely to hire extra help. CC's diary for the first four months of 1887 shows no employment at the plant; indeed, he usually left Ludlow on weekends. Thus, it appears that he could have worked there only in the fall of 1886 or the fall of 1887. The first period seems most likely, since it was a time of good business and heavy volume (R. G. Dun & Co. Papers, ibid.; VT,

17 September, 15 October 1886). In that case, though, the job was brief: from the opening of school in late August to his accident in early October, a matter of a few weeks.

15. Lathem, 4n; C. Coolidge diary, 8, 11, 17, 26 January, 1, 3, 7 February, 14 March 1887; Fuess, *Calvin Coolidge*, opposite 34. "I stood 93.4 this last half," CC wrote in his diary on 10 February, " ... so I am going better as 93.4 is the highest I ever stood."

16. My warrant for asserting that enrolling in the classical course was CC's idea is a passage in the *Autobiography*, 38, about his years at B.R.A.: "What I studied was the result of my own choice. Instead of seeking to direct me, my father left me to decide." This seems like a straightforward general statement. Actually, like much in the *Autobiography*, it implies more than it really says. The decision to go on from B.R.A. to college, I argue in the next chapter, was not CC's but his father's; but the kernel of truth in the statement is probably that studying the classics was CC's idea. The quotations come from Orton, Pollard interview, 7, and Toye, 5.

17. *History of Black River Academy*, 124–27; CC to JC, 8 October 1887, in Lathem, 5; VT, 17 June, 7 October 1887.

18. VT, 14 October 1887, 29 January, 17 February, 7 December 1888; VT, 14 June 1956, ("March Storms"); VT, 16 June 1955 ("Mary Pollard Recalls"); Bryant, *Calvin Coolidge*, 13.

19. VT, 3, 10 December 1886, 17 June, 22 July 1887; VS, 2 December 1886. The changes in administration can also be followed through the school catalogs for the years 1886–89. Photographs of Sherman and Chellis are in the B.R.A. Museum. CC paid tribute to both in his *Autobiography*, 45–46, in a passage that shows his fascination with ancient history. For later eras, see C. Coolidge diary, 19, 28 March 1887.

20. VT, 23 September 1887. (CC's cap is on exhibit in the B.R.A. Museum.) The debating society and the revamped curriculum are from the 1889–90 *Catalogue*; see also George Sherman to Ernest W. Gibson, December 1888, in B.R.A. Museum. Class exercises: VT, 17 May 1889; "Susie F. Wilder's Graduation." Advertisement: VT, 17 May 1889. The percentage of students enrolled in the Classical and Latin Scientific courses during these years, by year, follows: 1885–86, 15 percent, 1886–87, 20 percent; 1888–89, 28 percent; 1889–90, 31 percent; 1890–91, 32 percent. Sherman's seriousness and high ideals are apparent from some papers relating to his career, preserved by his daughter and given to the Sherman Memorial Room, Brimfield Public Library, Brimfield, Mass. Unfortunately, they contain almost no material relating to his years at B.R.A.

21. Grades: Lathem, 19n. Greek: C. Coolidge, *Autobiography*, 41. Homesickness: C. Coolidge diary, 3 February, 3 March, 8 April 1887. Abbie's attending: Fuess, *Calvin Coolidge*, opposite page 34; CC to JC, 29 January 1888, in Lathem, 7.

22. Blizzard: VT, 16, 23 March 1888; VT, 16 June 1955 ("Mary Pollard Recalls"); VT, 14 June 1956 ("March Storms"). Abbie At B.R.A.: Abbie Coolidge to JC, 4 March, 2 April 1888; A. S. Sawyer to JC, 15 April 1888, Coolidge Family Papers, VHS.

23. Fuess, *Calvin Coolidge*, 33; C. Coolidge diary, 12 March 1887; CC to JC, 8 October 1887, in Lathem, 5. For background on the medicine show, see VT, 4, 11, 18 March 1887; VS, 10, 24 March 1887; Strickland, 259–60; J. H. Young, 169–70. CC and Hood's sarsaparilla: C. Coolidge diary, 21 March, 4 April 1887; VT, 24 February 1888; J. H. Young, 61, 74–75.

24. Fuess, *Calvin Coolidge*, 32; Curtis et al., *Return*, 64; VT, 16 September 1892. The frequency of his visits home is discussed in the notes to chapter 6. On neighbors' seeing him and JC en route to Ludlow, see Bryant, 9, and CC to JC, 14 November 1913, in Lathem, 122.

25. VS, 23, 30 August 1888; VT, 9 November 1888; VT, 14 June 1956, ("March

Storms"). The second edition of Harris's *History of Ludlow* contains photographs of Ludlow during this campaign.

26. VT, 9, 16 November 1888.

27. 1887 C. Coolidge diary, entry of October 28. CC had stopped keeping the diary regularly in April of 1887, so this entry, which certainly refers to a national election year, should probably be assigned to 1888 rather than 1887.

28. *History of Black River Academy*, 127; VS, 20 September 1888. The building, substantially unchanged, is now the B.R.A. Museum, and my description of it is taken from personal observation.

29. *History of Black River Academy*, 127–28; VT, 7 December 1888. There were definitely rest rooms in the building; in the planning stage, the building committee had contacted manufacturers of "sanitary appliances" (ibid., 12 June 1887).

30. "It was not until I came to read the Orations of Cicero in my Latin course," CC wrote later, "that I began to have any realization of the value of literature for its own sake. What he said ... gave me a new interest in the spoken and written word" (C. Coolidge, "Books," 145). The useful summary of the Classical course in Lathem, 19n, shows that Cicero was a junior-year subject. For the nomenclature of classes, see ibid., 6n. The class schedule for 1888–89 appears on a card inserted into the catalogue of that year; I consulted the copy at FL, which also gives the number of students enrolled in each course.

31. C. Coolidge, "Books," 145–46; C. Coolidge, *Autobiography*, 41; card in 1888–89 B.R.A. catalog, FL. Some of the student compositions in the Susie F. Wilder scrapbook, B.R.A. Museum, have clearly been reviewed and corrected by a teacher. CC's farewell speech: VT, 17 May 1889.

32. C. Coolidge diary, 14, 15 February, 2, 9 March 1887. Public speaking played a similar role for CC's contemporary Woodrow Wilson; see Weinstein, 133.

33. Toye, 6.

34. The basic story is in VT, 15 November 1889. Some supplementary details are from Orton, Pollard interview, 10. Miss Butler's room number and class assignments are from the schedule card in the 1888–89 catalog. For similar pranks elsewhere, see G. S. Adams, 52; Patton and Field, 250.

35. VT, 15, 22 November 1889. JC's presence is attested in the latter issue, in connection with a law enforcement matter.

36. A *Rutland Herald* report, two weeks after the incident, stated that the board had "succeeded in finding out several of the culprits" and was "now considering the best plan to bring them to justice" (19 November 1889); but nothing appears to have been done by the school authorities, except perhaps for the one expulsion recalled by Mary Pollard (VT, 16 June 1955). This fact, together with the phrasing of the *Herald* article ("considering the best plan" seems to imply that the culprits were not within the board's jurisdiction, and that hence it was not obvious how to deal with the incident), suggests that the pranksters were not students at all; see below.

Allis's sellout, a sudden, unexpected move (VS, 12 December 1889), was probably connected in some way with the local feud that he had been carrying on for some time with the "Sargent gang," as he called them. At this distance in time, it is hard to determine exactly who his adversaries were. But at one point during the jackass affair, he suggested in print that it had been staged to divert public attention from their mishandling of village affairs. It is hard to believe that Allis's departure was not somehow provoked by the controversy, but no evidence exists to elucidate the connection.

37. Two early sources to assert CC's connection with the incident were Adin Demary (see the bibliography) and Ernest W. Gibson (*New York Times*, 14 August 1927), both of them contemporaries who had lived or attended school in Ludlow. An early biographer, Hennessy, 20, stated that there was a "lingering suspicion" that CC

knew more than he admitted about the incident, and Blanche Bryant, his Plymouth neighbor, said cryptically that he had a "smiling" knowledge of it (Bryant, 9). Charles E. Crane assumed in his remarks at Plymouth in 1948 that CC was a participant. The passage in his *Autobiography* is on 42–43. Those who denied CC's connection included JC (Toye, 5), Dallas Pollard (Orton, Pollard interview, 10), and Erminie Pollard (personal interview, June 1987). The engagingly written account in Webb is pure fiction.

38. Orton, Pollard interview, 10–11. Agan made a comment in 1923 (Green, 18) that suggested his involvement, and it may be worth noting that after the affair he left town and did not return for three years; see his biography in VT, 24 June 1920.

Chapter 8. Graduation and a Change in Plans

1. A full account of the Trades Carnival is in VT, 31 January 1890.

2. The closing of the cab shop is from VT, 15 February, 11 October 1889. The quote from the Springfield newspaper is from ibid., 26 October 1888; and see also 25 November 1887. But the *Tribune* itself exasperatedly called Ludlow a "backwoods town" in its issue of 8 May 1891. According to the U.S. Census returns of 1880 and 1890, the town's population decreased by 237 during the decade, from 2,005 to 1,768. The Vermont vital statistics show a natural decrease of about twenty-two; hence, about 215 people, eleven percent of the population, must have emigrated.

3. VT, 31 January 1890.

4. C. Coolidge pocket diary, entries for 1, 3, 4, 14, 24 January 1890, C. Coolidge Papers, VHS. C. Coolidge, *Autobiography*, 42, mentions studying French and getting up at 3:00 A.M. to prepare; the hours in the diary entries suggest, however, that 4:00 or 5:00 A.M. was more typical. The members of CC's graduating class at B.R.A. were photographed together in a picture that has been widely reproduced (e.g., in Curtis et al., *Return*, 66). CC is the second from left in the back row. The names of the other members have been given variously and sometimes inaccurately. The correct identifications were given in a clipping from the *Boston Post* (no date) in the Sherman Papers, Brimfield Public Library, and verified by checking them against an 1887 photo in the Black River Academy Museum, which includes many of the same students; their names follow. Back row: Abbie King, CC, Henry Hicks, Clara Pollard, Amos Pollard, Front row: Rufus Hemenway, Jessie Armington, Albert Sargent, Ellen Adams. Abbie to JC, 7 October 1889 (CC Papers, VHS), mentions rooming at the Hemenways'. The vignette of her walking home with CC is from Addie Wheeler's recollections in VT, August 1, 1924.

5. A photo of Roy Bryant is in the B.R.A. Museum. Sociables are mentioned in VT, 1, 8 November 1889, and 4, 25 April 1890. Compare a similar party in Rutland described in Fuller, 1. Jane Spafford's experience is in VT, 17 June 1954 ("Memories of Black River Academy"). The tone of student socializing is captured in an item in *The Tribune Junior*, 7 March 1890, in a scrapbook at B.R.A. Museum: "It is rumored that Gorham Parker is rejoicing because several of the new students are young ladies. Gorham's head is level."

6. "Susie F. Wilder's Graduation, 1889," scrapbook in B.R.A. Museum; VT, 10 April 1891; Alice M. Lockwood to CC, 28 October 1923, C. Coolidge Papers, LC; C. Coolidge diary, 31 March 1890.

7. "Susie F. Wilder's Graduation" describes Lena Sargent. For Lena Levey's family, see Harris, 219. Both she and Lena Clark are mentioned in Bryant, 14–15, although Bryant seems to think that Calvin was interested in her sister Nell. CC's

album contained photographs, on the same page, of Lena Levey and either Lena or Nell Clark. He described "Miss Clark" as having black hair and "medium stature" in a letter to JC, 22 June 1895, Coolidge Family Papers, VHS. The Spaulding catalog is in the Widener Library at Harvard.

8. Rothman (especially 207–208 and 231–34) supplies the general background for boy–girl relationships in this era. For rural New England in particular, see Hartt, 565–66, and C. Johnson, *Farmer's Boy*, 146–50.

9. Class officers are listed in the 1890–91 catalog (24). For the Adelphic Literary Society, see VT, 10, 24 January 1890. Bryant, 13, maintains that Sargent was one of CC's three best friends at B.R.A. Clearly, they were involved in many activities together; but Sargent's own recollections (Toye, 6) were distant and critical, and seemed to imply that the two men had not kept in touch since high school. The minstrel troupe is mentioned in VT, 7, 21 March 1890. (The "disgraceful whistling, yelling, hand clapping and stamping ... in the rear of the hall" when they performed gives some idea of Ludlow audience manners.) On CC's acting in minstrel shows, see Carpenter, 101. This acting cannot be dated precisely; the account in Rogers, 36–37, places one show in the summer of 1890. Rogers's book, however, is a blend of fact and fabrication and cannot be trusted in detail. CC's best-authenticated acting in Plymouth came during his college days and included a part in a minstrel show (Crissey, 161); but his diary entry of 4 January 1887 shows an earlier interest in drama. ("Went down to Pville [*sic*] to a drama it was good too.... Shall not tell the faculty I went down." Curtis et al., *Return*, 65, incidentally, quote this passage but mistranscribe "drama" as "dance.")

10. VT, 10 January, 28 February 1890; C. Coolidge diary, 10–11, 14–17, 19 January, 2–3 February 1890.

11. C. Coolidge diary, 28 February, 1, 2, 5, 6 March 1890; *Autobiography*, 47; VS, 6 March 1890; VT, 7 March 1890; B.R.A. Catalog, 1889–90, 11; Fuess, *Calvin Coolidge*, 36. The doctor mentioned in the *Autobiography* must have been Bryant, with whom CC remained in contact for years. The third physician treating Abbie was Dr. O. W. Sherwin of Woodstock.

12. The death rate among American children and adolescents in the twentieth century is extremely low: 0.3 per thousand in 1980 for persons five to fourteen years old, 1.2 for persons fifteen through twenty-four (Bogue, 208). In Vermont in 1880 it was considerably higher: about 4.9 in the first group and 6.5 in the second (1880 U.S. Census; Vermont *Registration* for 1879 and 1880).

Child's 1883 Windsor County directory classified physicians by the kind of theory they espoused (i.e., allopath, homeopath, etc). On the varieties in Plymouth, see Carpenter, 46–49. These divisions, however, ware not purely a rural phenomenon; a New York City student at Amherst expressed sympathy for the illness of a classmate who "was a Homeopath and had to take awful Allopathic drugs" (Frederick A. Blossom to Sarah Blossom, 14 October 1894, Blossom Papers). On prescriptions and folk remedies, Fuller, 225–27, and Steele, 214–16, are excellent; see also Fleming, 36; Twombly, *Heritage*, 71; and Lathem, 38n. Laudanum: "Use of Opium"; VT, 20 June 1890; Damon, 264; Leslie, 161.

13. Meda Kavanagh: C. Coolidge diary, 9 January 1887. Orson Butler: VT, 26 March, 1 October 1886. Willey Winn: C. Coolidge diary, 24 February 1887; VT, 25 February 1887. Martha Lynds: VT, 4 January, 15 February 1889. Lula Hall: VT, 14 February 1890. Abbie's funeral: VT, 14 March 1890. A copy of the memorial program is in the Sherman Papers, Brimfield Public Library.

14. "Oh, she was one of the sweetest girls I ever knew. Laughed as easily as anyone I ever saw, fat and jolly ... she was wonderful company" (Orton, Pollard interview, 3). "Happy day": CC to JC, 8 March 1892, in Lathem, 32. CC's mention of her in the *Autobiography*, 47 likewise stresses his "memory of the charm of her presence." Mother's portrait: Ross, 15.

15. Achsah Sprague, the spiritualist preacher and healer of the Notch, active in the 1850s, is noted in Ward et al., 114; see also the sketch of her in the *Dictionary of American Biography*. For spiritualist meetings in the eighties, see Carpenter, 135; VT, 2 October 1885, 29 January, 11, 25 June, 2 July 1886; VS, 19 September 1889; and Bryant and Baker, 443. On religious sentiment in Plymouth, see Carpenter, 140.

16. Abbie's membership: Herman P. Fisher to JC, 30 April 1890, Coolidge Family Papers, VHS. "Am ashamed": C. Coolidge diary, 5 January 1890. The most complete statement of CC's religious beliefs is in his *Autobiography*, 66–70, but it reflects the impact of his later study with Charles E. Garman (see chapter 15) and may not state the thoughts of his adolescence. Indeed, one could argue on the basis of ibid, 54–55, that he later felt he was lacking in faith when he came to Amherst. Beyond doubt, however, he knew the Bible, as most literate people did in that era; see ibid., 17, and Fleser, "Rhetoric," 45. After the funeral: CC to JC, 12 March 1890, Blair Collection.

17. Understanding of CC's decision to attend college is hampered by a lack of direct contemporary evidence. One has to rely on either inference or later recollections by the parties involved, CC and his father.

There is, literally, no surviving mention of CC's plans to attend college until 7 September 1890, four months after his graduation from B.R.A., when he wrote a letter to Amherst College asking about their conditions for admission that fall. Later letters contain statements that help to illuminate CC's attitude toward college in general and Amherst in particular, but there is no direct discussion of the decision to attend. In this account, then, I have turned to recorded actions before 1890 that suggest such an intent, and to statements made about the decision after the fact.

Two actions suggest interest in college. First, CC's enrolling in the Classical course in 1887, discussed in chapter 7. This was more than a token gesture, for practically all Classical graduates of B.R.A. in the late 1880s and early 1890s did in fact go on to college, like Albert Sargent and Abbie King of CC's own class; they generally went to Middlebury College, which was only an hour away, beyond Rutland, on the Central Vermont. But CC's other action suggests a last-minute change of plans: he suddenly enrolled in the French course at B.R.A., in the middle of a term. He states the fact but gives no explanation of it (C. Coolidge, *Autobiography*, 42). Clearly, however, it was a sudden decision that entailed a lot of work for him. "Studied French considerable," he noted in his brief diary 4 January 1890. In the autobiography he states that he had to rise early in the morning to catch up on his French. He was not studying for credit, at least not at first; he received no official grade for French in the winter term (see his grades in Lathem, 19n). He went on with it, however, in the spring term and received an 80. This flurry of activity suggests a decision by CC or his father that French was a desirable course for a graduate to have, a decision that makes sense only if he proposed going on to college.

18. Who made these decisions? CC's account (*Autobiography*, 48) seems to imply that he did: "It had been my thought, as I was but seventeen, to spend a year in some of the larger preparatory schools and then enter a university." JC later also sought to propagate the impression that CC was making the decisions; he told George Olds (and Olds told an Amherst alumni dinner) that he had originally intended to apprentice CC to a pharmacist and dropped the plan only when CC, who wanted to attend college, reminded him that pharmacists in Vermont were required to sell rum (*New York Times*, 14 March 25). He also told a reporter that the choice of Amherst had also been CC's (M. E. Hennessy, "The Story of Calvin Coolidge," newspaper clipping, scrapbook in B.R.A. Museum).

But there are reasons for believing that JC systematically exaggerated the role his son played in his early career decisions and sought to minimize his own influence. The pharmacist story seems rather too pat, and the assertion that CC chose Amherst is definitely not true: "But it was suddenly decided that a smaller college would be preferable, so I went to Amherst" (*Autobiography*, 48). The phrasing is clearly intended to underline the fact that going to Amherst was not CC's decision. It must have been JC's. As chapters 9 and 11 detail, CC was initially unhappy at Amherst and made several vain attempts to go home for good. He later wryly told his father, "I have tried to do the best I could by my feeble efforts to carry out [your] plans which did not appeal very strongly to me" (12 July 1897; Lathem, 81); this does not sound like the statement of a young man who felt himself essentially in control of his career. Bearing all this evidence in mind, one has difficulty in concluding that CC was enthusiastic about college or that he influenced his father in a direction the elder Coolidge would not have taken otherwise.

For CC's desire to be a storekeeper, see *Boston Post*, 7 January 1933, and C. Coolidge, *Autobiography*, 16.

19. CC to JC, 3 May 1895, in Lathem, 68. College costs are taken from *Catalogue ... of the University of Vermont ... 1890–91*, 66–67, national income figures from Cochran and Miller, 261. On JC's desire for CC's success, see C. Coolidge, *Autobiography*, 174: "the tenderness and care he had lavished upon me ... in the hope that I might sometime rise to a position of importance."

20. Absentmindedness: C. Coolidge diary, 28 March 1886, 31 January, 1 February, 20 April 1887. The quote is from Carpenter, 78–79.

21. Orton, Pollard interview, 6; C. Coolidge, "Books," 144–45; C. Coolidge diary; 27 February, 19, 20, 28 March 1887. CC recalled the attitude toward reading in the Notch, that "evening and rainy days were about all the time it was thought well to devote to books" (C. Coolidge "Books," 145). The same hostility toward reading as a waste of time appears in Hard, 10. But some Vermonters were avid readers, even some in Plymouth; Arden Taylor, for instance, read Dickens (Taylor diary, entry of 12 August 1877, VHS), and a small-town intellectual was portrayed in a contemporary play, "A Temperance Town," as saying "Dickens is my Bible" (Hoyt, 175). Dr. D. F. Rugg of Hartland read not only Dickens but Hugo, Swift, Cooper, and Wilkie Collins (Rugg diaries for 1885 and 1887, passim, VHS). In addition, quite a few young Vermonters enjoyed a kind of reading CC was apparently not exposed to: the popular *Youth's Companion* magazine (Twombly, *Heritage*, 44; "Diary of a Vermont Boy," 166).

22. Strictly speaking, the statements in this paragraph are based on inference; no direct statement of Sherman's support exists. But a couple of pieces of supporting evidence—a detailed, cordial letter from Sherman to CC the following year (5 June 1891, Coolidge Family Papers, VHS), and his praise for CC's commencement speech, noted below—make it abundantly clear that Sherman liked and admired his pupil. It is also evident that he played a crucial role in sending CC to Amherst; I discuss the point further below. JC's service on the B.R.A. board can be followed in the annual catalogs of the academy.

23. This paragraph is based on a close reading of the statement in the *Autobiography*, 48: "It had been my thought, as I was but seventeen, to spend a year in some of the larger preparatory schools and then enter a university." I am guessing here that CC felt justified in calling it his thought to attend a prep school for a year because it was a concession he had wrung from his father; the underlying supposition is that he was reluctant to go away to school, as I think the evidence given in chapters 9 and 11 plainly shows. For Park Pollard's attendance at Vermont Academy, see VT, 7 January, 4 March 1887, and C. Coolidge diary, 29 January 1887. CC's apparent failure to even consider attending Middlebury, the destination of most B.R.A. graduates, is striking but not easy to explain. Nor is it obvious why his plans called for attending a university rather than a smaller institution. Costs at Middlebury were similar to those at the University of Vermont; see *Catalogue of Middlebury College ... 1889–90*, 33.

24. VT, 9 May 1890, and cf. the elaborate ceremonies in ibid., VT, 17 May 1889; CC to JC, 19 April 1890, in Lathem, 9, 11n.

25. The commencement program and list of graduates are in the *Annual Catalogue ... of Black River Academy for 1890–91*, 24, and can be compared with the previous class in the previous year's catalog. Fleser, "Jam Tempus Agi Res," is an analysis of CC's speech, which was entitled "Oratory and History." (The title of Fleser's article comes from the motto of the class of 1890.) Sherman's praise of the speech: CC to JC, 19 April 1890, in Lathem, 9.

26. There are thorough descriptions of the ceremony in VT, 30 May 1890, and VS, 29 May 1890. George Sherman to CC, 5 June 1891, shows that B.R.A. graduation ceremonies could be reviewed even in the Montpelier press; Carrie Brown to CC, 27 May 1891, discusses the 1891 ceremony in detail, with careful notes on what the graduates wore. Both letters are in the Coolidge Family Papers, VHS. CC's speaking voice can be sampled in recordings preserved at the Forbes Library. It was not a tenor voice, and it was not a "quack," despite the exaggerations of later biographers. The text of the speech is from Fleser, "Jam Tempus," 46.

27. *Annual Catalogue ... for 1890–91*, 24. For Henry Hicks, compare the class photograph with earlier photographs, all in the B.R.A. Museum.

28. Fourth of July: VT, 4, 11 July 1890. Coolidge Hall: VS, 11, 17 November 1886, 10 April, 1 May 1890.

29. Newton, 184, 193; Chase, 449–52; VT, 19 October 1888; Wilson, 192–93, 202, 208; and Barron, "Impact," 327, supply the background. On early interest in cheese factories, Heinritz, 132; Humphrey, 227. Interest in 1890s: Fenn, 126, 151; VT, 10 May 1889, 10 January 1890. In Plymouth Notch: VT, 28 February 1890. A capsule account of founding and building the factory is in Lathem, 10–11n.

30. VS, 17 April, 22 May, 16 July, 5 November 1890; VT, 6 June 1890.

31. The long, complex Taylor case is difficult to piece together, since there seems to be no one authoritative account. I have used several partial sources and attempted to fill in the gaps with inferences; I may well have some details wrong. My main sources for the beginnings of the case are the account in VT, 29 May 1891; a brief version from Sherburne, in Fleming, 37; and Taylor's own rambling, disjointed defense (Warren R. Taylor to Minnie S. Walker, 11 March 1907, Coolidge Family Papers, VHS).

32. VT, 27 May, 3 June 1887, 29 May 1891; VS, 26 May 1887.

33. This account follows JC's deposition in the Coolidge Family Papers; cf. VT, 18 January 1889. The quotations are from Taylor's letter cited above. Taylor's countersuit is referred to in VT, 6 December 1889; the Coolidge Family Papers contain several pages of notes presumably gathered by JC to help in his defense.

34. What is known about the decision to send CC to Amherst is easily summarized. The decision was taken "suddenly," CC stated in his autobiography (48), and it was not his decision; i.e., it was his father's. It was made late in the summer, for CC's letter of inquiry to Amherst was written only at the beginning of September, a couple of weeks before the term started (Lathem, 13n).

That Sherman's influence was crucial in the decision is nowhere stated but seems certain. He was the only Amherst graduate whom the Coolidges knew at all well, and he had a friendly interest in seeing Calvin attend college. It is difficult to imagine who else could have convinced JC that CC ought to attend.

The real question that this paragraph tries to address is why the decision was made so very late. In other words, what new factor entered the picture that made JC decide to enroll CC in 1890 rather than 1891, and why did Amherst suddenly become a possibility? The answer I suggest here is wholly conjectural; no direct evidence supports it. One has to turn, instead, to a few small pieces of evidence that seem to provide information about CC's brief attempt to enter Amherst in 1890.

In the fall of 1891, as he was becoming settled at Amherst, CC wrote his new step-mother, Carrie Brown Coolidge, that his new lodgings were "about opposite where Weaver had a house last year, of course you don't know about that but my father does" (20 September 1891, in Coolidge Family Papers, VHS). The reference to Weaver is tantalizing. It turns out that there were no Weavers resident in Amherst at that time; at least none appear in the town directories for the years closest to 1890. There was, however, a Harry B. Weaver enrolled as a student at Amherst in both 1889 and 1890, although he did not graduate (Amherst College, *Biographical Record*), and a listing of freshman addresses in the *Student*, 6 October 1890, shows him as staying at "Mr. Weaver's." He was the only freshman so listed. The *Springfield Republican*, 1 September 1890, announced that A. H. Weaver had "opened a boarding-house in the house owned by the college on South Pleasant street, at the foot of College Hill." This A. H. Weaver appears to have been Harry's father, Albert H. Weaver of Wales, Massachusetts. Absalom Gardner's extraordinary "Compendium of the History, Genealogy, and Biography of Wales" (1873), in the town records (consulted on microfilm at the New York Public Library), throws some light on Albert Weaver. He had, after many sacrifices, registered at Amherst in the 1860s, but then had had to drop out because of financial problems. Naturally, he would have been very anxious for his son to succeed there, and had probably taken the step of moving to Amherst to give him support. An interview with a local informant in Wales, who knew Harry Weaver later in his life, indicates that he shared his father's veneration for Amherst College and was very proud of having attended. (The informant, who wished to remain anonymous, also suggested that Harry had had a drinking problem as a young man, which may be associated in some way with his failure to graduate.)

How did CC come to know the Weavers, who were not well-known figures in Amherst—on the contrary, little more than transients there? The obvious explanation is that he boarded or intended to board at Weaver's house. Here a connection with George Sherman becomes possible, for Sherman was from Brimfield, the town next to Wales. Given the network of acquaintance that existed among Amherst graduates and supporters, it seems highly likely that Sherman and Weaver had known each other for some time. If Weaver planned to open a boarding house on 1 September doubtless he was casting about for possible tenants during August, and Sherman, as principal of an academy, would have been a logical person to ask. One could even conjecture that Weaver offered a cut rate on the price of room and board which made the deal attractive enough to persuade JC to enroll his son, given all the other advantages of Amherst. For the costs of an Amherst education, see F. W. Hitchcock, 98, 103.

"Down below" was a Vermont way of referring to Massachusetts; see Hughes, "Word-List," 133.

35. My reading of CC's reaction is connected with my belief that the illness that prevented his entering Amherst was largely psychosomatic (see the next chapter). For CC's feeling about the distance, see his letter to JC, 11 September 1894 (Lathem, 60): "It does not seem so very far from home to be down here now, not near so far as it used to seem."

Chapter 9. Nerves

1. At the outset, I think I should set forth the factual evidence that supplies the skeleton for this narrative. C. Coolidge, *Autobiography*, 48, states that CC went to Amherst in 1890 to take the entrance examination but returned home sick. VS, 25

September 1890, states that he left for Amherst on 15 September, a Monday, and returned on the following Thursday, 18 September. The railroad was the standard means of intercity travel in 1890, and the *Travelers' Official Railway Guide* for September (57, 58, 143) gives the schedules and connections between Amherst and Ludlow. There was only one route (via the Central Vermont and the New London & Northern) and only two trains a day from Ludlow to Amherst, one leaving at 7:46 A.M. and arriving at 11:12 A.M., with connections as described in the text, the other leaving at 12:30 P.M. and arriving at 4:40 P.M., with the same connections. As far as I know, there is no reason to believe that he took one of these trains rather than the other; my selection of the 7:46 is based on a guess that he might have wanted to arrive in Amherst earlier in the day. I think it likely that he traveled to Amherst alone; later in these notes I explain my reason for believing that his father accompanied him on the return trip.

On conditions in the Ludlow station yard, see VT, 27 May 1892; for weather in this period, *Bulletin of the New England Meteorological Society for 1890*, 5, 13, and the *Springfield Republican*, 11–15 September 1890.

2. Shaughnessy, 52; VT, 25 October 1888, 31 January 1890.

3. VT, 23 September 1887; Flanders, 14–15; Harris, 123; Skinner, 47; cf. CC to JC, 24 August 1897: "I know coal stoves are not good for me" (Lathem, 82n). J. M. White, 438, 443. For the scheduling, see above.

4. The announcement of the Amherst examinations is in the catalogue for 1890.

5. Hunt et al., 70; Porter, 306; J. H. White, 440–41.

6. *Traveler's Official Railway Guide*, 58; J. H. White, 403; Ripley, 100; Duffus, 81.

7. Samuel B. Marsh to CC, 9 September 1890, in Lathem, 13n.

8. Rockingham Bicentennial Committee, 75, 79. Sounds of a railroad yard: Hibbard, 721–22. Later in his Amherst years Calvin, returning to college, often rode the train from Ludlow with an acquaintance named George Sheldon, who attended Harvard and had to leave the train at the Falls to take the Boston train. CC to JC, 3 December 1893, 7 January 1894, Blair Collection.

9. *Traveler's Official Railway Guide*, 143; J. H. White, 429.

10. Barry et al., 54–58, 62, 64, 120.

11. On having to change trains at Brattleboro, see CC to JC, 6 January 1892, in Lathem, 28. This letter, incidentally, suggests that CC was unfamiliar with the connections of the afternoon train to Amherst, perhaps an indication that his earlier trips had been made on the morning train.

12. *Traveler's Official Railway Guide*, 57; personal observation; F. W. Hitchcock, 72.

13. The depot was on Main Street, where the homes of Emily Dickinson's family and other established Amherst people were located; see F. W. Hitchcock, 68–72. Common: Fuess, *Calvin Coolidge*, 44. A cultivated outsider's impression of the village is in Longsworth, "Growth," 151. For contemporary pictures of the business block, see Bierstadt, 26; for the Episcopal church and town hall, F. W. Hitchcock, 61, 65.

14. It seems generally conceded that the Amherst College buildings "of the early nineties were not impressive" (C. Coolidge, *Autobiography*, 63). One alumnus, indeed, referred to the college's "meagre buildings and hideous architecture" (Fuess, *Amherst*, 287). But the site was striking, and the whole perhaps exceeded the sum of its parts. F. W. Hitchcock, 113–41, contains a building-by-building description of the campus in 1891, with photographs of the structures referred to in this paragraph. The steep hill south of the campus is mentioned in Stearns, 101.

15. As noted in the preceding chapter, in a letter to his stepmother in 1891 (20 September, in Coolidge Family Papers, VHS), CC mentioned the location of Weaver's boarding house and added, "of course you don't know about that but my father

does." The clear implication is that JC had been in Amherst and was familiar with Weaver's house. If that is the case, one needs to choose between two possibilities: either JC accompanied CC to Amherst on Monday, or he brought him back on Thursday (or, of course, both). In the absence of any evidence, it seems more logical to suppose that he brought CC back on Thursday, when he was seriously ill, than that he rode down with him on Monday. For what it is worth, when CC entered St. Johnsbury Academy the following year he took the train there alone (Lathem, 15n). A letter to his father describing St. Johnsbury remarks, "The town is situated a great deal like Amherst the depot is down low and you come up the street to the hotel just the same" (19 April 1891, in Lathem, 16). CC's mention of the hotel in this connection may indicate that his father spent a night there when he came after his sick son; it need not, however, for the Amherst House was something of a village landmark. In any case, for this narrative I have assumed that CC went to Amherst alone and returned in his father's care.

If that happened, then CC must have telegraphed his father from Amherst on Wednesday morning, since the telegram would have required at least a couple of hours to get from Ludlow to Plymouth, and it would take JC at least a couple of hours to get to Ludlow for the 12:30 train. Given the miserable weather in central Massachusetts on Wednesday (*Springfield Republican*, 18 September 1890), one could construct a scenario in which CC, already feeling ill, and depressed over his performance on the previous day's examination, got up on Wednesday morning, saw the pouring rain, and decided to take to his bed and wire his father. There is no evidence as to whether he took one day of the examinations or both, but if the illness was as serious as he said it was, his missing a part of the examination (especially the part he dreaded most) seems entirely likely.

Chapter 10. Performances

1. VT, 10 October 1890. Two weeks earlier (26 September), the Plymouth column had reported, "Calvin Coolidge, who returned home from Amherst College sick, is improving." The quote is from Kipling, 8. Other items: VT, 3, 24 October 1890.

2. Warren Taylor had made snide comments about John's wasting money sending Cal to B.R.A., as is evident from CC to JC, 14 November 1913, in Lathem, 122. Other enemies are alluded to in Carpenter, 127–28.

3. VT, 28 June 1889.

4. C. Coolidge, *Autobiography*, 48. CC said that he had recovered by "early winter"; a letter of his to Carrie Brown Coolidge (8 November 1891, Coolidge Family Papers, VHS), in which he mentioned how lonesome it felt in 1890 after the cheesemakers left in mid-November (VT, 28 November 1890), suggests that he was probably up and around for some time before they left. Repairs on store: VS, 13 November, 11 December 1890, 26 February 1891; VT, 23 January 1891.

5. CC to Carrie Brown Coolidge, 8 November 1891, 15 May 1892, Coolidge Family Papers, VHS; VT, 28 November 1890; *Autobiography*, 48; C. Coolidge, "Books," 146.

6. VT, 5, 12 December 1890, 2, 23 January 1891.

7. The basic and almost the only source for the following account of performing "Under the Laurels" is Dell Ward's recollection in Crissey, 161; but it is detailed and consistent, both internally and with other available evidence (e.g. Carpenter, 101). Ward suggests as the date the winter of 1891, before CC left for Amherst, and indeed this would seem to be the only possible date for it, as CC was not home for

any length of time during the winter thereafter, or for five years before. The list of performers given in Crissey supports this date as well; all of them were living in the Notch that winter. Unfortunately, neither of the local newspapers mentions the performance. On the whole, though, I find Ward's account convincing and have followed it closely in the next few paragraphs; if not otherwise noted, all details are from this source.

On amateur theatricals during the winter, Fisher, *Hillsboro*, 188–89, is good. There are many notices of them in Plymouth and elsewhere in VT, e.g., 10 February, 2 March 1888, 8 March 1889, 13, 20 February 1891. Clara Moore: Curtis et al., *Return*, 54; VS, 21, 28 April 1887.

8. Denison, passim; Carrie Brown to CC, 27 March 1891, Coolidge Family Papers, VHS; VT, 10 April 1890, 5 February, 6 August, 10 December 1891. For Dell Ward's family connections, Bryant and Baker, 420–22.

9. CC and theater: Carpenter's recollection that CC "sometimes took part in amateur theatricals and minstrel shows" has no indication of a date and may refer to this production or earlier activities (Carpenter, 101). The generally unreliable Rogers mentions his participating in a minstrel show in 1890, and while the date is to be taken with skepticism, there may be some basis for the story (Rogers, 35–36). Certainly, CC was interested in theater; while at B.R.A. he slipped down to a drama at Proctorsville one evening when he should have been studying, and the following week attended a comic operetta, "Sir Marmaduke," produced by a traveling Boston company (C. Coolidge diary, 4, 13 January 1887). CC's reference to this play, in which he also mentions Clarence Blanchard and Len Willis, is in his letter to Carrie B. Coolidge, 19 November 1895 (Coolidge Family Papers, VHS).

In this connection, it is worth recalling Mack Sennett's remark that, during CC's presidency, theater people regarded him as a fellow performer and admired his acting skill (Sennett, 23).

On CC's role in "Under the Laurels," see Denison, 13, 16, and passim.

10. On the Vermont Liberal Institute, see Ward et al., 72–73, Bryant and Baker, 443, and *Vermont Historical Records Survey*, 10. In 1889, a group from the Notch had presented a play at the Wilder House (VT, 8 March 1889). Special effects: Denison, 6.

11. At a Plymouth dance in these years, one witness recalled, CC "sat on the corner of the kitchen table, swung his feet and watched the others dance"; but when the Portland Fancy country dance was played, "he caught each girl in turn and balanced with her. He seemed to enjoy cuttin' in that way better than dancing the whole figure" (Jennie Chamberlin, in Crissey, 9).

12. C. Coolidge, *Autobiography*, 48; VS, 19 March 1891; CC to JC, 28 March, 3 April 1891, Blair Collection; Lathem, 8–9n. The spring term at B.R.A., in which CC is listed as a postgraduate student, began 3 March (B.R.A. Catalog, 1890–91, 5, 11). Other postgraduate students are listed in the 1888–89 and 1889–90 catalogs. Rufus Hemenway: VT, 2 May 1890, 3 April 1891.

13. JC's remarriage: C. Coolidge, *Autobiography*, 51–52. Carrie Brown: Child, 425; Sargent; Carpenter, 58; Fuess, *Calvin Coolidge*, 42; H. T. Brown, 311; VT, 15 September 1887. Her long letter to CC, 27 May 1891 (Coolidge Family Papers, VHS) suggests that by that date there was an understanding between her and JC. This understanding doubtless went back earlier in time, but I have found no earlier reference to it.

14. VT, 6 March 1891. By 28 March CC had written to Amherst about admission; see his letter of that date to his father, Blair Collection, which also contains the quotation in this paragraph and a mention of Dick Lane's concern about fraternities. The other information on Lane is from VT, 4 July 1890, 30 January 1891, and Fuess, *Calvin Coolidge*, 47. Rufus Hemenway grew a mustache sometime between

graduation and the summer of 1892, when the picture of him and several friends on an excursion to Killington, now in the B.R.A. Museum, was taken.

The earliest reference to CC's shaving I have found is a year and a half later (CC to Carrie B. Coolidge, 18 November 1892, Coolidge Family Papers, VHS).

15. B.R.A. Fifty-sixth Annual Catalogue, 4; VT, 27 February 1891; A. E. Wilder to CC, 3 May 1891, Coolidge Family Papers, VHS; Vermont Vital Records.

16. VT, 3, 24 April, 8 May 1891. The popularity in New England of the new safety bicycles, beginning around 1890, can be followed in collections of photographs like Curtis et al., *Times Gone By*, 61, or Sandler. For the craze in another Vermont community, see Humphrey, 253. In intercollegiate competition the changeover from the high-wheeled bicycle to the newer model came in 1892 ("'Twas Fifty Years Ago," 307). For the Crane family, see the remarks by Charles E. Crane at Plymouth Church, 29 August 1948, copy in FL.

17. Sherman's plan is outlined in CC to JC, 3 April 1891, in Lathem, 14n. Collar discusses admission by certificate in New England colleges (433–34). Sherman's classmate was Audubon L. Hardy; see Fuess, *Calvin Coolidge*, 40. CC's switch to St. Johnsbury was so sudden that it caught the Plymouth correspondent for the *Vermont Standard* off guard. The 16 April issue of the *Standard* announced merely that CC had finished his review studies at B.R.A. and was coming home; only in the 23 April issue did the correspondent add that he had gone to St. Johnsbury.

18. Mead, passim.

19. Russell, 8; Start, 712; Fairbanks, 362–63; CC to JC, 19 April 1891, in Lathem, 16–17 and note; 10 May 1891, Blair Collection.

20. CC to JC, 14 April 1891, in Lathem, 15. On the flush toilet, see Wright, 205, and M. G. Marshall, 164.

21. Charles E. Putney to CC, 7 April 1891, in Lathem, 14n; Calvin to John Coolidge, 27 April, 14 May 1891, Blair Collection; Fuess, *Calvin Coolidge*, 40–42.

22. 1891 Catalog, 5–7; on the excellence of the course work, Russell, 10.

23. CC to JC, 24, 27 May 1891, Blair Collection; 31 May 1891, in Lathem, 18. A photograph of the main building is the frontispiece of the 1891 catalog.

24. Rain: VT, 19 June 1991. Drought: 1891 *Bulletin*, 166–67. Theft: CC to JC, [16 June] 1891, in Lathem, 20. Taylor suit: VT, 29 May 1891.

25. VS, 2 July, 10 September 1891; Freeman, *Nun*, 417; Crissey, 156; Bryant and Baker, 188–89; VT, 10 July 1891. On mosquitoes, cf. Twombly, *Heritage*, 81, on fishing in Reading in 1888. ("The mosquitos bit all the way. Brushed them with one hand and fished with the other.")

26. VT, 3, 10, 17, 31 July, 14 August 1891; VS, 9, 16 July, 6, 13 August 1891; C. Coolidge, *Autobiography*, 52.

27. A paragraph in his autobiography (49) describes CC's visit to the Bennington celebration with his father. Background on the celebration is in Graffagnino, 116, and *Dedication*, passim. VS, 20, 27 August, names people from the Notch who attended.

28. Heinritz, 133–34, the diary of a Grafton farmer who traveled to the celebration by wagon, is a good comparison. For details, see *Dedication*, 69, 70, 74–76, and Graffagnino, 116.

29. *Dedication*, 105; W. A. White, 31; C. Coolidge, *Autobiography*, 49; Marx, 270.

30. *Dedication*, 151–53.

31. On drinking in Vermont during prohibition years, sources are abundant; see Graffagnino, 102–105; Ripley, 157; Steele, 217; M. L. Johnson, 23–24; VT, 5 May 1921 ("Signs of Spring in Vermont"); and Hoyt's play, "A Temperance Town" (Hoyt, passim). VT, 22 August 1889, contains a report of an excursion to Ausable Chasm in which the return trip was marred by "[b]lasphemy, obscenity, and filthy ejections from nauseated stomachs."

Chapter 11. Into the Vortex

1. A copy of the 1895 freshman class picture is in the Amherst College Library. No book is visible in the picture, but CC's classmate Carleton Kelley recalled that he was holding one (Boston *Globe*, 12 August 1923). W. J. Rand recalled his chin as a prominent feature (Oklahoma City *Oklahoman*, 12 August 1923). These and other newspaper clippings for August 1923 are in the Amherst College Archives, Frost Library.

2. Basic background for the class picture is "The Annual Picture Rush," an article from the *'88 Olio*, reprinted in Ball, 69–73. This, and Hamilton, 86ff., which dates from the next decade, are the only sources I have been able to find on the picture rush, as distinct from the cane rush, which is mentioned in nearly every account of student life at Amherst (see below). Yet it seems evident that the two were functionally connected; that is, the sophomores' main objection to the freshman class picture was that freshmen used it as an occasion for showing that they were carrying canes, which they were forbidden to do. (CC's oblique and not very helpful recollection in the *Autobiography*, 53, was that it "would not have been judicious for [a freshman] to appear on campus with a silk hat and cane, but as none of the other students resorted to that practice this restriction was not a severe hardship.") Indeed, in the 1888 account (Ball, 72), the picture rush turns into a struggle over "a twenty-five cent cane," in which blows are exchanged and clothes torn, as they were in the cane rush itself. Nothing of that sort, however, seems to have happened to the class of 1895.

The evidence as to hazing in the early 1890s is ambiguous. (For hazing in New England colleges in the 1880s, cf. Patton and Field, 237–38.) Some forms were evidently frowned upon and some tolerated. Harlan Stone's biographer could write (Mason, 45) that there was a "strong tradition" at Amherst against hazing, and a notice in the Amherst *Student* (hereafter AS), 5 November 1892, warning solemnly that "Amherst College has given up all forms of individual hazing" and that violators' names would be published in the paper "with the necessary adjectives" seems to corroborate his statement. Alfred Roelker, Jr., of CC's class, published a story in the college literary magazine in which a student accused of hazing a freshman was tried by the college senate, a student body, and faced expulsion if convicted (Ball, 119, 120). Group hazing, on the other hand, was apparently permissible. The following year, Calvin was to recount that he and some other sophomores, after their class won an intramural meet, "caught three freshmen and made them dance and sing and make a speech congratulating us" (CC to JC, 23 October 1892, in Lathem, 48n); and after the same event the next year, freshmen were tossed in a blanket in the gym (CC to JC, [12] October 1893, in Lathem, 47). Hazing in fraternities was standard ("We'll paddle him.... We'll take the freshness out of his hide," in *Amherst Literary Monthly* [hereafter ALM], 6 [March 1892]: 369). Hazing of freshmen off campus was not unusual; Aubrey Barnes of CC's class recalled being shut up in an upper Pullman berth by a sophomore en route to Amherst (Law, 13). There was also some hazing on campus; two items in the *'94 Olio*, 194, seem to imply that paddling freshmen or making them paint their faces took place in the dormitories, and a writer in the ALM (6 March 1892]: 410) recalled being grabbed and ducked under the ice-cold shower in the gym as a freshman. "Three freshmen have been hazed so far," Frederick Blossom reported to his mother in early October of 1894 (n.d., Blossom Papers): one had been visited by a group of sophomores who tried to "smoke him out" of his room by filling it with cigarette and cigar smoke; the other two had been forced to sing and dance by upperclassmen in their own fraternity.

Perhaps the reason there was relatively little hazing on campus in the early 1890s was that few freshmen roomed in the dormitories (see below). Later in the decade and early in the 1900s, when the dormitories were occupied again, there is a good deal of hazing mentioned, much of it taking place there (B. Johnson, 92–93, and Hamilton, 27–28, 56, 60–63).

3. Fuess, *Amherst*, 205; cf. Patton and Field, 241. Several good sources exist for the cane rush; the best is Frederick A. Blossom's letter to his mother, 15 September 1895 (Blossom Papers). See also CC to JC, 18 September 1892, in Lathem, 36; Law, 81; and B. Johnson, 90. Patton and Field, 240, though more general in scope, corrobates the Amherst sources.

4. C. Coolidge, Grove Oration, AS, 25 June 1895.

5. W. A. White, 34, says that CC attended every meeting of his class for his entire four years. Chapel is discussed at greater length in chapter 13; the points in this paragraph are only that freshmen sat in the gallery (F. W. Hitchcock, 136); that seating was alphabetical (*Amherst Graduates' Quarterly* [hereafter AGQ], 19: 214), doubtless for the purpose of checking attendance, which was taken (Ball, 43; Frederick A. Blossom to Sarah Blossom, 16 December 1894); and that chapel was at 8.30 A.M. It had been at eight o'clock in the 1880s (Rounds, 737); the change was apparently made in September of CC's freshman year (AS, 26 September 1891), perhaps by newly appointed president Merrill E. Gates, who is also discussed in chapter 13. In the final alphabetical roster of the class of 1895, CC's name occurs between those of Isaac M. Compton and George Critchlow (Amherst College, *Biographical Record*); but both Critchlow and the man who came after him in the roster of graduates, Richard F. Dana, transferred to Amherst after freshman year. In 1891, CC would have sat next to Davis. Compton: '95 *Olio*, 64, '96 *Olio*, 170. On Davis: AS, 5 March 1892, 18 February 1893, '94 *Olio*, 190, '95 *Olio*, 62, 162, '96 *Olio*, 158. The anecdote about varnishing the seats is related in Fuess, *Amherst*, 219. It is a little hard to assess, for it speaks of the freshmen's sitting downstairs for the first time, whereas F. W. Hitchcock and *Hampshire Gazette*, 15 September 1893, maintain that freshmen sat in the gallery.

6. F. W. Hitchcock, 103–4, 128; Fuess, *Amherst*, 159; Le Duc, 128–30; CC to Carrie B. Coolidge, 11 October 1891, Coolidge Family Papers, VHS; E. Hitchcock, *Personal Health Lectures*, 3 (and cf. J. Tyler, 265); AS, 7 November 1891. A photograph of the interior of Pratt Gymnasium is in *Bierstadt*, 14. On cold showers, see ALM (6 [March 1892]: 410). The availability of hot water in the gym is a little mysterious. On the one hand, a proposal for a "swimming tank" was turned down because there was no way to heat the water (AS, 11 March 1893); on the other hand, in the fall of 1892 hot water was available in the gym on Wednesdays and Saturdays (AS, 24 September 1892).

7. Patton and Field, 150; J. Tyler, 266; Law, 85; E. Hitchcock, *Anthropometric Manuals*, 14–15; Stearns, 126–27; C. Coolidge, *Autobiography*, 53–54; P. C. Phillips, 220; CC to Carrie B. Coolidge, 20 September 1891, Coolidge Family Papers, VHS; AS, 12 December 1891. CC's measurements are in his anthropometric record, in the Amherst College Archives. Notations in these records suggest that there may have been other measurements besides those officially recorded; one page, for instance, contains a five-unit code for describing the foreskin: "1. completely retracted, 2. partially covered," etc.

8. E. Hitchcock, *Gymnastic Exercises*, 7–11. A sample exercise, from ibid., 20, runs:

> Movement 2. Direction A.—Forcibly thrust the right bell forward horizontally on count one, and return to breast on count two, continuing thus through eight counts.
> Same with left bell, through eight counts.
> On count one, forcibly thrust the right bell forward horizontally, and return on count two;

on count three thrust left bell forward in same manner, and return to breast on count four; continuing thus alternately through eight counts.
Forcibly thrust *both* bells forward simultaneously through eight counts.
Direction B.—Repeat all the movements of A horizontally outwards.
Direction C.—Repeat all the movements of A perpendicularly upwards.

More details on the drill are from C. Coolidge, *Autobiography*, 56–57; Stearns, 126; Patton and Field, 59; F. W. Hitchcock, 104; and Leach, 17–18. The last description is of interest because it dates from the 1870s and shows how little the drill changed in two decades. An item in the AS, 24 September 1892, conceded that many students found the drill monotonous. CC mentioned the uniforms in letters to his father, 15, 25 October 1891, in Lathem, 25, 26n. On Bishop, see Law, 16–17, and '95 Olio, 138, 162. "Chimes from the Dumb-bells," in Ball, 32–33, purports to reproduce one of "Old Doc's" passionate rebukes to misbehaving students, and in fact contains enough expressions confirmed in other sources so that it may be a fairly faithful rendering. See also Fuess, *Amherst*, 230, and Amherst College, Class of 1895, *Decennial Class Book*, 16. CC to Carrie B. Coolidge, 8 November 1891, Coolidge Family Papers, VHS, is the source of the quotation.

9. Class meetings are mentioned in AS, 3 October, 12 December 1891, and Law, 65. See also note 10.

The average age of the men in the class at graduation was twenty-two years, ten months ('95 Olio, 64); CC was almost exactly twenty-three. Fred Gray, thirty-one at graduation, was the oldest member; Robert Mainzer, Alfred Roelker, and Ernest Hardy were the youngest at twenty.

E. Hitchcock, *Anthropometric Manual*, 11–15, gives figures on the physical characteristics of Amherst men: the average height was 5'7"; CC's height was 5'9".

In E. Hitchcock's tabulations of eighty-one freshmen, five were described as auburn-haired, as against fifty-six brown, twenty fair, and three black (AS, 19 December 1891); Ransom P. Nichols, a classmate of CC, however, remembered only three redheads: CC, Hardy, and himself (*Boston Globe*, 12 August 1923). Hitchcock actually described CC's hair as "golden," not auburn (Anthropometric records, Amherst College Archives); but the consensus of his classmates was that it was red.

As to residence, the *Biographical Record* lists 99 members of the class, seventy-five graduates and twenty-four nongraduates. Based on the biographical data it gives, along with the addresses given in AS, 3 October 1891, the residences of the class can be grouped as follows.

Massachusetts	31
other New England	12
New York	31
Pennsylvania–N.J.	7
Midwest and West	18

Another, possibly more pertinent way of grouping the students is under the headings of metropolitan versus rural. Forty-eight of the ninety-nine members of the class came from large cities or established preparatory schools; forty-three were from smaller communities in New England and New York; eight came from small towns in other parts of the country. The metropolitan majority, therefore, was numerically very tenuous, and Charles Andrews's recollection, in his letter to Claude M. Fuess (25 January 1938, Fuess Papers), that urban and rural students were about evenly represented certainly applied to the class of 1895. I set forth in the next few paragraphs the reasons why the urban students had an influence disproportionate to their number.

10. Stearns, 82–83; ALM, 9 (January 1895): 297–98; Roelker, "A Political Deal," in Ball, 121–23; Frederick A. Blossom to Sarah Blossom, 22 September 1895, Blossom Papers. A student in the late 1880s summed up bluntly, "As the most able and influential men are chosen for societies, the remaining fourth are practically without influence in college affairs, and the societies meet with no opposition" (Rounds, 741). Statistics on fraternity affiliation are from AS. The freshmen not pledged, in addition to CC, were the following: Fred Gray, of Ogdensburg, N.Y.; Robert Mainzer, of New York City; George Fairbanks, of Ayer, Mass.; Ernest Hardy, of Northampton, Mass.; John Percy Deering, of Saco, Maine; Isaac M. Compton, of Morristown, N.J.; Royal Booth, of Holliston, Mass.; Tracy Griswold, of Elmira, N.Y.; Benjamin Ray, of Leeds, Mass.; Ransom Nichols, of Greenfield, Mass.; Thomas Hennessy, of Milford, Mass.; and Robert Dunbar, of Portland, Maine.

11. Le Duc, 125–26; Fuess, *Amherst*, 243.

12. Veysey, 265–66, 280; Hays, 72; Le Duc, 60; W. P. Bigelow, 310–13.

13. AS, 7 May 1892.

14. Le Duc, 124–26; Fuess, *Amherst*, 288–89; F. W. Hitchcock, 147; Mason, 817; B. Johnson, 98; [Northampton] *Hampshire Gazette*, 23 September 1890. Frederick A. Blossom to Sarah Blossom, 24 October 1894, Blossom Papers, mentions rivalry and bad feeling between two fraternities without giving the reason.

15. The houses are described in Fuess, *Amherst*, 193, 287–89, and F. W. Hitchcock, 147–58. On the Alpha Delta Phi house in particular, see Stearns, 81; King, 150; and Frederick A. Blossom to Sarah Blossom, 12 September 1894, 20 January, 6, 9 October 1895, Blossom Papers.

16. Stearns, 81; Frederick A. Blossom to Sarah Blossom, 12 September 1894; F. W. Hitchcock, 154; AS, 13, 20 February 1892; Nicolson, 31; Fuess, *Amherst*, 193.

17. Fuess, *Calvin Coolidge*, 47, uses the term *rushing*, as does Hamilton, 15ff., referring to the early 1900s. I have found no contemporary use of the word at Amherst before 1895, when representatives of all the societies agreed to a set of "'rushing' Resolutions" (AS, 15 June 1895). On the other hand, there are at least two contemporary references to the "campaign": Rounds, 741, from the late eighties; and Frederick A. Blossom to Sarah Blossom, 19 June 1895, Blossom Papers. The process is minutely described in those two sources, in Hamilton, 15–21, 32, and in [Northampton] *Hampshire Gazette*, 23 September 1890, from which the quote is taken.

18. Fuess, *Calvin Coolidge*, 48; Mason, 55; Frederick A. Blossom to Sarah Blossom, 14 October 1894, Blossom Papers.

19. Fuess, *Calvin Coolidge*, 47–48; Frederick A. Blossom to Sarah Blossom, 21 November 1894, Blossom Papers; B. Johnson, 83; Nicolson, 34; *Boston Globe*, 12 August 1923. Although CC stated in the *Autobiography* that the fraternities did not leave him "without an invitation to join them," C. G. Brainerd of the class of 1896, a fraternity brother of CC in the newly formed Phi Gamma Delta society during his senior year, wrote CC's biographer Claude Fuess (3 February 1933, Fuess Papers) that he was certain no fraternity had offered him a bid as a freshman. The slightly tortuous construction of CC's sentence suggests some sort of technicality or evasion, and I have chosen to use Brainerd's version.

20. Gibes at Booth, Compton, and Fairbanks are abundant in the student publications of the class of 1895; for an example in which the three were linked, see *'96 Olio*, 170. Booth and Fairbanks, as seniors, received some votes from their classmates as the man most likely to succeed, but as their classmate Charles Andrews commented to Claude Fuess (26 January 1933, Fuess Papers), the votes were "highly and entirely ironical as everybody in the class would recognize."

21. Fuess, *Amherst*, 289; Frederick A. Blossom to Sarah Blossom, 2, 6, 12 October 1894, Blossom Papers. For examples of society activities, see AS, 22 October 1892, 18 February 1893.

22. J. L. Harrison Notes; Fuess, *Calvin Coolidge*, 46; CC to JC, 16 September 1891, in Lathem, 21; 23 September 1891, Blair Collection. F. W. Hitchcock, 103, classified a room rent of thirty dollars per semester as "economical"; seventy-five dollars was "liberal." Room rent in the dormitories could be as low as twelve dollars per semester.

23. C. Coolidge, *Autobiography*, 54; F. W. Hitchcock, 135–36; AS, 26 September 1891, 23 January 1892; Rounds, 739; ALM, (November 1891): 216; Ball, 105–106. A photo of a student's room from the nineties is in the Herbert O. White Scrapbook, Frost Library, Amherst College. See also Frederick A. Blossom to Sarah Blossom, 2 October, 18 November 1894, 6, 20 January 1895, Blossom Papers. The letter of 20 January gives an idea of the student aesthetic: "I received from Sister Sue, a small box of home-made pralines, a letter, and a picture frame embroidered with violets, with a kodak of Miss Porter sitting on one of those rocky promontories at the lake. That is on my knick knack shelf with the cardholder I won at Allie's, three Japanese boxes, the azalea and my silver drinking cup, while five girls' cards are pinned against the wall. My room really looks very comfortable now."

24. Lathem, 21; CC to JC, 23 September 1891, Blair Collection; CC to JC, 15 October 1891, in Lathem, 25; CC to Carrie B. Coolidge, 18 October 1891, 10 January 1892, Coolidge Family Papers, VHS; AS, 14 May, 22 October 1892; '94 *Olio*, 99; '95 *Olio*, 76, 86.

25. Woods, 99. CC's continuing interest in college athletics can be followed in his letters home (e.g., in Lathem, 26, 33, 38, 41, 43); it seems to have waned, however, in his junior and senior years. On Pratt Field, see Fuess, *Amherst*, 285. The facility was only a few months old in the fall of 1891; a sketch of the grandstand is in F. W. Hitchcock, 129. On intercollegiate and intramural sports, AS, 17 October 1891, 17 December 1892; Stearns, 16–17, 96–97; and Le Duc, 133.

26. A report of the meet is in AS, 17 October 1891; a ticket and eight-page program are preserved in the Herbert O. White Scrapbook, Amherst College Library. Photographs of track and field athletes are in the *Olio*. CC's report is in his letter to JC, 15 October 1891, in Lathem, 24.

27. Danzig, 17, 20–25, 28–29, 31; AS, 10 October 1891; CC to JC, 7 October 1891, in Lathem, 26n; *New York Times*, 4 August 1923; Barnes, 151.

28. *Springfield Republican*, 22 November 1891. For general background, see Bergin, passim.

29. CC to JC, 22 November 1891, in Lathem, 26; *Springfield Republican*, 22 November 1891; Tower, 115, 170ff.; Atlas of Springfield, 1899, in Connecticut Valley Historical Museum.

30. 1899 Atlas; Tower, 9; *Springfield Republican*, 22 November 1891. There are photographs of the field in the Connecticut Valley Historical Museum in Springfield.

31. CC to JC, 22 November 1891, in Lathem, 26; Betty Cutter to Mrs. Cutter, 20 November 1892, E. C. Morrow Papers, Smith College; Bergin, 44–47. Bergin estimates the crowd at twenty-five thousand.

32. CC to JC, 23 October, 11, 27 November 1891, Blair Collection; CC to Carrie B. Coolidge, 18 October, 26 November, 6 December 1891, Coolidge Family Papers, VHS; AS, 14 November 1891, 12 November 1892.

33. CC to JC, 23 September 1891, Blair Collection; CC to Carrie B. Coolidge, 11 October, 29 November 1891, Coolidge Family Papers, VHS.

34. Woods, 93–94; recollections of U. J. Blair, *Boston Globe*, 12 August 1923; Ball, 73. CC apparently did not study before breakfast; in the winter term, when his first class was at 11:45 A.M., he calculated that he had "three solid hours in the forenoon for study" (CC to JC, 8 January 1892, in Lathem, 29). As a senior, he rose around 7:40 every day, and went to bed at 12:00 or 1:00 A.M. (CC to JC, 10 October 1894, Blair Collection); I am assuming that he did the same as a freshman, when he

was intensely worried about his grades. Alarm clocks were in common use among Amherst students; one is mentioned in ALM 9 (November 1894): 180. The midnight chapel bell is mentioned in ibid., 6 (June 1891): 119. On CC as a student see Jay Stocking to C. M. Fuess, 3 March 1933, Fuess Papers, and recollections of George Olds, *New York Herald*, 4 August 1923.

35. "Ex-Vermonter," 205; recollections of W. J. Rand, *Oklahoma City Oklahoman*, 12 August 1923.

36. Jay Stocking to C. M. Fuess, 3 March 1933, Fuess Papers; recollections of Thomas F. Hennessey and Walter C. Seelye, *Boston Globe*, 12 August 1923. The statement about the student newspaper is based on a tabulation of all members of the class of 1895 mentioned in AS, September 1891–June 1893. It does not include addresses, which were given for all students.

37. This paragraph is based on a recollection of A. B. Tyler printed in the *Springfield Republican*, 8 January 1933. Tyler, who was in the class of 1894, was not a wholly reliable witness; some parts of his memories, such as CC's applying for financial aid, are wrong. But it is quite plausible that a friendship developed between CC and Booth, oudens both, during freshman year. Booth is not identified by name in the article, but the circumstances of his life are unmistakable. For more on him, see his photo in the *'95 Olio*; AS, 5 November 1892; "A Royal Youth," *'94 Olio*, 195; and Law, 20. CC may also have been friends this year with Fred Gray, an ouden, and his roommate George Jones, who roomed nearby on South Pleasant Street; see Jones's recollection in the *Boston Globe*, 12 August 1923, which he assigned to "the first of our college course." It could have been either freshman or sophomore year, as he and Gray roomed together both years.

The quote is from CC's letter of 7 January 1892 to his father, in Lathem, 28.

38. CC to JC, 22 November 1891, in Lathem, 26–27; CC to JC, 17 December 1891, Blair Collection; CC to Carrie B. Coolidge, 20, 29 November 1891, 10 January, 11 February, 6 March 1892, Coolidge Family Papers, VHS. From the letter of 22 November it is clear that CC had no knowledge of his grades and was worried about them.

Frederick A. Blossom to Sarah Blossom, 16 December 1894, Blossom Papers, describes midwinter exams. New London trains: Stearns, 9.

Kissing his father on the lips when he greeted him was CC's custom in maturity; it can be seen, for instance, in some of the footage in John Karol's documentary; but I do not know when he began it or why. Its occurrence here is a conjecture.

39. In a letter to his father 9 July 1897 (in Lathem, 79), anticipating the latter's criticism of his immediate career plans, CC referred to a time "when you sent me back to college five years ago ... rather than let me try to live in Plymouth." He was, in other words, charging his father with having sent him back to Amherst against his will at some point in 1892. (The same event, viewed from a complacent adult standpoint, probably underlies his account thirty years later in the *Autobiography* [60]: "During my first two years at Amherst I studied hard but my marks were only fair. It needed some encouragement from my father for me to continue.") The only question is at what point in 1892 this happened. As chapter 13 shows, CC returned to school that fall in a generally upbeat mood, whereas it is clear that he was miserable, to the point of physical illness, on his return from Christmas vacation of 1891. I assume, therefore, that this event took place in January, and that Calvin informed John of his unhappiness at Amherst; the letter clearly implies that his overriding Calvin's wishes was a conscious decision.

For samples of CC's advising his father on money and farm matters, see CC to JC, 2 March 1891 ("Do you intend to take any insurance? I think it is a good investment, as it is not likely that it is going to be easy to find a safe investment for money at 4 1/2 percent, above taxes, for the next twenty years; and if it should be higher you get the benefit; but I am not [an] authority in financial matters"), 11 December 1891 ("Have you seen Morgan about his note? it outlaws in about a month and if you don't get it soon you may loose [*sic*] it"), and 20 November 1892 ("You got a good price for your pork I think"), all in the Blair Collection. Clearly, father and son talked a lot about business, even in CC's adolescence; it is regrettable that so few samples of their discourse remain.

40. CC to JC, 6 January 1892, in Lathem, 27–28.

Chapter 12. The Sophisticate

1. CC to JC, 7 January 1892; CC to Carrie Brown Coolidge, 10 January 1892 (Lathem, 28, 30n).

2. Marsh's nickname of "Swampy" is mentioned in F. A. Blossom to Mrs. Blossom, 24 October 1894, Blossom Papers; and see also AS, 27 June 1893, where the student slang to "pull a three" is also used.

CC's report of his grades is in his letter to JC, 14 January 1892 (Lathem, 27n). The actual grades are in the Registrar's office at Amherst. CC had earned a 2.75 average, which, as a penciled note on the side of the record shows, was equivalent to 68.75 percent. Although I have not found a conversion table in the Registrar's records for turning the five-point grades into percentages, marginal notes in the grade records of Calvin and other students make it possible to compute the relationship. A grade of 2 equaled 50 percent; a 3, as stated in the text, was 75 percent; and a 4 seems to have been 88 percent. This system was more stringent than the one at Harvard, where 40 percent, at least on the entrance examination, was a passing mark (Collar, 433); but there are indications that 40 percent was sometimes considered a passing grade at Amherst too (Calvin to Carrie B. Coolidge, 25 October 1891, Coolidge Family Papers, VHS).

The one-to-five system and its failure to take fractional marks into account are described in an article from the '85 Olio, the college yearbook, reproduced in Ball, 31, with an example of how it worked. F. A. Blossom described it in a letter to his mother, 13 January 1895 (Blossom Papers), and Stearns, 87, explained what each grade on the scale meant. CC described it in his letter to his father cited above, and a complete series of report cards is in the Coolidge Family Papers, VHS. Two, according to CC in his letter to his father, was "the average" grade; fours, by all accounts, were rarely awarded and highly prized (CC to JC, 8 November 1893, 27 January 1895, Lathem, 49, 64; AS, 7 May 1892; Blossom to Mrs. Blossom, cited above). The system, thus, resembled the twentieth-century American A-B-C-D-F scale, except that there were only three passing marks.

So far as students' report cards were concerned, the grading system remained unchanged during CC's years at Amherst; internally, however, there was a change. In 1892–93, the registrar began recording individual course grades and yearly averages as percentages. Increasingly, students began thinking of their work in terms of percentages; CC, for instance, referred to a ninety in philosophy in a letter to his father in his junior year (11 March 1894, Blair Collection.)

(I am grateful to Gerald Mager and Daria D'Arienzo, Registrar and Archivist respectively of Amherst College, for their help with the topics discussed in this note.)

3. Fuess, *Amherst*, 259; C. Coolidge, *Autobiography*, 58–59; CC to JC, 7, 12 January 1892, in Lathem, 28, 29n; Fuess, *Calvin Coolidge*, 50; Nicolson, 36. Bierstadt, 21, has a photograph of a Walker Hall recitation room; for the gas jets, see AS, 3 December 1892.

CC's freshman grades in mathematics were 3.5, 3.25, and 3.25 for the three terms.

In ancient languages all but one of his marks were below three. (Registrar, Amherst College).

4. Fuess, *Amherst*, 235–36; Fuess; *Calvin Coolidge*, 55; Stearns, 87–88; *'96 Olio*, 169; Amherst *Student*, 26 September, 3 October 1891.

5. AS, 16 January, 21 May 1892, 21 January 1893; Stearns, 120–21; "They Never Came Back," *'94 Olio*, 156; *'95 Olio*, 26; Law, 19.

6. Fuess, *Amherst*, 263–64; Stearns, 87; "Eph's Dream," *'94 Olio*, 178; *'95 Olio*, 26; *'96 Olio*, 183; C. Coolidge, Grove Oration, AS, 25 June 1895; CC to JC, 22 November 1891, in Lathem, 27. Wood was probably the "heartily disliked" Latin instructor referred to in B. Johnson, 87.

7. Le Duc, chapter 5, especially 76–77, is excellent on this topic. The expression *drudgery* is from CC to Carrie B. Coolidge, 11 February 1892, Coolidge Family Papers, VHS, but was probably not original with him. A student poem in the AS, 13 February 1892, could dismiss "Oedipus the King" as the "[u]ncouth production of some old Greek."

8. *'96 Olio*, 182; Fuess, *Calvin Coolidge*, 56; ALM 7 (October 1892): 187–88; AS, 15 November 1890 ("cramped up over a small piece of cardboard"), 13 February 1892 ("horsing all the Greek I could afford"), 27 June 1893 ("O some men crib for passing, / And some to pull a three"); Frederick A. Blossom to Sarah Blossom, 14 October 1894, 24 March, 3 November 1895, Blossom Papers; F. W. Hitchcock, 94.

The minimum requirement in ancient languages at Amherst was three terms of Latin and three terms of Greek in freshman year, plus three terms of either Latin or Greek in sophomore year (Amherst *Catalogue* for 1891–92, 46).

9. Lathem, 30n; Stearns, 89–92; B. Johnson, 98; Frederick A. Blossom to "K," 24 October 1894, Blossom Papers; CC to JC, 9 October 1892, in Lathem, 38; Fuess, *Amherst*, 242; Luther E. Smith to C. E. Garman, March 1898, Garman Papers; C. Coolidge, *Autobiography*, 62. A photograph of the reading room is in Bierstadt, 5; Longsworth, *Austin*, 339n, mentions Dickinson.

10. Mason, 61; Frederick A. Blossom to "K," 24 October 1894, Blossom Papers; B. Johnson, 99.

11. B. Johnson, 106; Fuess, *Amherst*, 230; F. W. Hitchcock, 104; P. C. Phillips, 219; J. Tyler, 266; Allen, 82; Mason, 53. A quotation, perhaps apocryphal, passed on by an Amherst graduate and preserved in a scrapbook in the Hitchcock Papers, epitomizes this blend of religious fervor and physical frankness: "Trust in God and keep your bowels open." The quotations in the text are from E. Hitchcock, *Personal Health Lectures*, 3, 4.

On shaving, see Frederick A. Blossom to Sarah Blossom, 24 February 1895, and *'95 Olio*, 147. CC was shaving by his sophomore year (to Carrie B. Coolidge, 6 November 1892), but it is not clear when he started.

12. E. Hitchcock, *Personal Health Lectures*, 12–13, 18–19, 22–23.

According to a survey in the *Student*, 19 December 1891, 26 percent of the freshman class smoked. Cigarettes were certainly popular; see Jump, 185, and *Amherst Literary Monthly* 7 (April, 1892): 30. But on the vogue for pipes, which seems to have begun at Yale, see ibid., 7 (April 1892): 26; (June 1892): 138; Ball, 106; and AS, 7 November 1891, 23 January 1892.

13. E. Hitchcock, *Personal Health Lectures*, 34; Kinsey, Pomeroy, and Martin, 410, 513. Cf. Rothman, 239–40.

14. C. Coolidge, *Autobiography*, 51, gives CC's account of the sports and shows his obvious distaste for them: "they were not looked on with favor, and they have not survived. While the class has lost many excellent men besides, yet it seems to be true that unless men live right they die." The term, with its overtones of drink, gambling, and sex with prostitutes (Wentworth and Flexner, 511; Flexner, 450), was widely used at Amherst in the 1890s; a student could allude to the attitude of "the

sporting element" in a particular course (John H. Chase to C. E. Garman, 31 September 1896, Garman Papers), or identify a fraternity brother as "one of the three outstanding 'sports' of the undergraduate body" (B. Johnson, 100). There was even a term, *cubeb sports*, for men who pretended to lead a sporting life, as one might smoke a cubeb, or medicinal cigarette, instead of the real thing (AS, 25 February 1893; *'95 Olio*, 195). The unofficial Sigma Phi Delta society featured in the *'94 Olio* (116–17), which admitted no member who "retires earlier than 2:05 A.M. . . . who spends more than 15 minutes on any lesson . . . who goes to 'Hamp' less than twice a week, who looks with disfavor on the fair sex, and who does not cut over in church and chapel more than 8 times, not counting Monitor bribes," probably included a good many of the sports, including eleven from the class of 1895. In that connection, it is worth noting that four of the eleven (Beer, Booth, Kingsland, and Twichell) had died by 1929, when CC wrote the passage in his *Autobiography* about the sports' dying young as a result of their misspent lives (Amherst College, *Biographical Record*).

Northampton: Law, 19; Patton and Field, 264–67; Rounds, 740; Stearns, 198, 202; ALM 6 (May 1891): 61; 9 (May 1894): 44. The last evening train from Northampton to Amherst was known as the "drunk." (AS, 12 November, 1892; Jump, 183) Rounds (737) was legally accurate but factually in error when he stated that "Amherst is a temperance town so far as students are concerned." Evidence to the contrary includes Jump, 187; Stearns, 69, 176; Allis, 280–81; AS, 23 January 1892; *'95 Olio*, 146; and ALM 9 (May 1894): 43. "Forty-nine bottles" is alluded to in ibid., 9 (May 1891): 83. Beer had been available in bottles since the 1850s, but more widespread refrigeration in urban areas and better bottling technology caused a surge in sales in the late 1880s (Anderson, 94; Arnold and Penman, 76, 80). Two instances of janitors' dispensing alcoholic beverages are in Stearns, 55–60, and F. M. Allan to F. A. Blossom, 8 July 1895, Blossom Papers.

15. AS, 5 December 1891; CC to Carrie B. Coolidge, 4 February 1892, Coolidge Family Papers, VHS; Morgan, 65–66; Betty Cutter to Mr. Cutter, 20 January 1893, Elizabeth C. Morrow Papers. The program for the 1894 Senior Prom in the Edward W. Capen Papers, Hartford Seminary, lists twenty dances: ten waltzes, eight two-steps, and two polkas. "Eddie Writes to Pa" is in the *'95 Olio*, 169.

16. "Eddie Writes to Pa"; CC to Carrie B. Coolidge, 4 February 1892, Coolidge Family Papers, VHS; CC to JC, 18 June 1892, in Lathem, 35.

17. CC to JC, 8 January 1892, in Lathem, 29; 11 November, 20 November, 27 November 1891, Blair Collection.

Urban slang: ALM 7 (May 1892): 83, 84; (November 1892): 321–22.

18. *'96 Olio*, 204 (for another example, see ibid., 158); F. M. Allan to F. A. Blossom, 5 July 1895, Blossom Papers.

19. This point is treated more fully in chapter 14.

20. An account of the supper, listing the speakers, is in AS, 27 February 1892. CC's letter to his stepmother, dated 18 February 1892 (which must be an error for 19 February), is in the Coolidge Family Papers, VHS. A program for the supper is in the Herbert O. White Scrapbook, Amherst College Library. See also *'94 Olio*, 34; Law, 65; CC to Carrie B. Coolidge, 25 February 1892, Coolidge Family Papers, VHS.

21. The unsettled bill is mentioned in AS, 26 March, 28 May 1892. Patton and Field, 246–47, shows how general this casual vandalism was.

22. CC to JC, 14 April, 31 January 1892, 23 September 1891, Blair Collection; CC to Carrie B. Coolidge, 27 January 1892, Coolidge Family Papers, VHS. Report cards are in ibid.

23. Charles M. Stebbins to Claude M. Fuess, 31 December 1934; James B. Cauthers, speech to Phi Gamma Delta dinner, 20 February 1929, Fuess Papers.

24. CC to JC, 12 January, 7 February 1892, Blair Collection. I assume that these

letters refer to the same sort of insurance discussed in CC to JC, 25 September 1894, ibid., in which JC did in fact take out a policy on CC's life. On CC's dress, see Charles A. Andrews to C. M. Fuess, 25 January 1938, Fuess Papers.

25. CC to Carrie B. Coolidge, 17 April, 1, 15, 29 May 1892, Coolidge Family Papers, VHS; AS, 12 December 1891; 30 April, 7, 28 May 1892; Stearns, 123: '95 *Olio*, 187; ALM 7 (April 1892): 28. Fuess, *Amherst*, 301; Rand, 175. An Amherst commencement from the 1870s is described in Leach, 57ff.; compare the "old-time commencement" portrayed in Patton and Field, 272. CC to JC, 8 March, 19 June 1892, in Lathem, 32, 35.

26. On Ned the cat, see CC to JC, 18 September 1892, in Lathem, 36 and 37n; also CC to JC, 26 April 1892, Blair Collection, which probably refers to the same cat. On the woodchuck, H. T. Brown, 312, and Lathem, 104n. The horse is discussed below.

27. CC wrote an essay about Lynds, probably his sophomore year at Amherst, under the title "An Inconsistent Man"; it is in the Coolidge Family Papers, VHS. In the same collection, see Lynds to JC, 13 August 1872, and Lynds to CC, 20 January 1900. See also VS, 21 May 1891; Crissey, 165; and CC to John Coolidge, 20 March, 8 November 1894, Blair Collection. For Lynds's military service, see his gravestone in the Notch cemetery, Peck, 69.

28. Bryant and Baker, 188–89; Bryant, 14; Crissey, 156; Ward et al., 6, 83. VT, 11 July 1890, 10 July 1891, 8 July 1892; VS, 17 September 1891.

29. Crissey, 156. CC referred often to his horse in his letters home. See his letters to JC, 15 October 1891, 9 October 1892, in Lathem, 25, 38–39; 11 November 1891, 12, 19, 31 January, and 21 February 1892 in the Blair Collection; and to Carrie B. Coolidge, 12 June 1892, Coolidge Family Papers, VHS.

30. Crissey, 161.

31. Ripley, 231; Freeman, *Pembroke*, 116.

32. VS, 30 June, 7 July 1891; VT, 1 July 1892; Crissey, 166.

33. VT, 8 July 1892. Typical food at a midsummer picnic is described in Gordon, 149, and Freeman, *Nun*, 45; see also the Charles and Eliza Hoskison interview on the Jerry tapes. The opening of the speech is from Toye, part 4.

34. I copy the rest of the speech from Hennessy, 32–34.

35. Crissey, 166.

36. As stated in the Notes to chapter 1, the only independent source for the 1892 raid on the cannon, with which I close this chapter, is Dell Ward's account in Crissey, 156, 161. Bryant, 13–14, adopts this account but then confuses it with the 1870 raid also in Crissey. Carpenter, 96, is not an independent source, but simply an endorsement of Ward's version. There is no newspaper mention of the incident, to my knowledge. Still, the fact that three Plymouth Notch neighbors of approximately the same generation endorsed this account gives it credibility.

On the Wilder House, see the report on Norris Wilder in the R. G. Dun & Co. Papers, Vermont, 25: 335. Herbert Moore: VT, 1 April 1892. Hen Brown: VT, 23 May 1890, 15 May 1891, 15 April 1892.

37. The phonograph is mentioned in VS, 23 June 1892.

Chapter 13. The Sunny Dream

1. CC to JC, 2 October 1892, Blair Collection; F. W. Hitchcock, 127; cf. *Northampton Daily Herald*, 15 October 1892: "The beautiful October weather is thoroughly appreciated and the beauty of the eastern and southern views embracing the Pelham hills and the Holyoke range will repay a considerable journey to see."

2. *Northampton Daily Herald*, 3 October 1892, identified this as the Walter Emerson concert, which featured "[b]rilliant renderings of difficult selections" and a solo on a gold cornet. I have been unable to learn anything more about Walter Emerson.

3. The essay, titled simply "The days of chivalry are passed," is among the Coolidge Family Papers, VHS. CC to JC, 18 September 1892, in Lathem, 36; F. W. Hitchcock, 57, 61; *'95 Olio*, 179.

4. CC to JC, 18, 25 September 1892, in Lathem, 36, 37n; CC to Carrie B. Coolidge, 21 September 1892, Coolidge Family Papers, VHS; Stearns, 69.

5. "Choice indecencies": Coolidge's Grove Oration, AS, 25 June 1895. Morrow: Nicolson, 25, 30, and passim. Kingsland: *'94 Olio*, 116; Law, 53, 70; AS, 25 June 1895. Twichell: *'94 Olio*, 116; *'95 Olio*, 138; Law, 104. Penney: AS, 5 December 1891; *'95 Olio*, 195. Andrews: numerous photographs in the *'95 Olio*. Blair: CC to JC, 25 September 1892, in Lathem, 37n. In sophomore year, Booth's name began to be mentioned in connection with wagering on football games (*'95 Olio*, xl, 166).

6. The best source on the boarding houses at this time is Rounds, 738–39, 742. See also King, 103–104; Edward Hitchcock Scrapbook, 1891–92, 15, Amherst College Library; Ball, 50; and Frederick A. Blossom to Sarah Blossom, 28 September 1894, Blossom Papers.

7. Rounds, 738–39; Charles A. Andrews to Claude M. Fuess, 26, 31 January 1933, Fuess Papers; recollections of A. B. Tyler, *Springfield Republican*, 8 January 1933; Frederick H. Allan to Frederick A. Blossom, 5 July 1895, Blossom Papers.

8. Ball, 43, 167; Frederick A. Blossom to Sarah Blossom, 28 September 1894, Blossom Papers; CC to Carrie B. Coolidge, 4, 11 October, 26 November 1891; 21 January, 24 November 1892, Coolidge Family Papers, VHS; CC to Almeda B. Coolidge, 33 November [*sic*] 1891, Special Collections, Amherst College.

9. Rounds, 737, assumes that a student walks to breakfast. CC's boarding arrangements are discussed in a letter to his father, 18 September 1892, in Lathem, 36 and 37n. His judgment of the fare at Trott's is discussed in a letter to Carrie B. Coolidge, 4 October 1891, Coolidge Family Papers, VHS. He was to eat at many different houses before leaving Amherst; his roommate Percy Deering recalled several in his response to Claude M. Fuess's queries, Fuess Papers. Fred Blossom, likewise, changed boarding houses in the middle of his freshman year (to Sarah Blossom, Easter Sunday, 1895, Blossom Papers). Most of CC's board receipts are in the Coolidge Family Papers. "Coons": ALM, IX (December 1894, 1895), 255; *'95 Olio*, 168.

10. Rounds, 737–38; CC to Carrie B. Coolidge, 25 February 1892, Coolidge Family Papers, VHS; Frederick A. Blossom to Sarah Blossom, 6 May 1895, Blossom Papers; G. Coolidge, May: 252 (Frederick H. Law).

11. The interviews with CC's college classmates in the *Boston Globe* (12 August 1923) identify Hardy and Deering as his closest friends and mention that the relationship existed by sophomore year. Deering's own account is among them. For Hardy, who remained a close friend for some years after college, see Feiker, 20, 49. His background is from the biographical sketch in Carey, 3: 376, and the Northampton city directories for the period. Deering's explanation for the friendship between him and CC is in an undated letter to Claude M. Fuess in the Fuess Papers.

12. Hardy: Law, 45; Feiker, 20; AS, 12 December 1891, 27 February, 21 May 1892, 29 April, 6, 13 May 1893; *Hampshire Gazette*, 22 March 1907. Deering: Law, 34; "To Deering," *'94 Olio*, 195; *New York Times*, 4 August 1923; Dartmouth–Amherst football program, November 1894, Herbert O. White Scrapbook, Amherst College; AS, 18 February, 6 May 1893; Biddeford (Me.) *Daily Journal*, 6 January 1947.

13. Hardy and CC were partners in local Northampton politics after college, and both seem to have enjoyed it (Feiker, 20). Hardy was a Republican in later life

(Carey, 3: 376), though in the statistics of the class yearbook he called himself a Democrat (*'96 Olio*, 199), presumably in jest. Deering's political background was mentioned above. For CC's politicking at college, see chapter 15.

Republican activities are noted in CC to JC, 28 February 1892, in Lathem, 31 and note; Fuess, *Calvin Coolidge*, 48; and AS, 5, 19 March, 7 May 1892.

14. Mason, 55; AS, 15 October, 5 November 1892. On torchlight parades, see Collins, passim.

15. AS, 29 October, 5 November 1892; C. Coolidge, *Autobiography*, 22.

16. CC to JC, 30 October, 13 November 1892; to Almeda B. Coolidge, 17 November 1892, Special Collections, Frost Library, Amherst College; AS, 12 November 1892; Mason, 56.

17. *Hampshire Gazette*, 30 September 1890; AS, 7, 14 May 1892. The Austin Dickinson–Mabel Todd affair is the subject of Polly Longsworth's fascinating *Austin and Mabel*; it was common knowledge in the community long before CC came to Amherst (see Longsworth, *Austin and Mabel*, 121n).

18. CC to Carrie B. Coolidge, 20 September 1891, quoted in Lathem, 21; Fuess, *Calvin Coolidge*, 45; Stearns, 98–99, 104; Jump, 187.

19. Jump, 186; Mason, 50; Stearns, 100; Fuess, *Calvin Coolidge*, 45.

20. Weisenburger, 168–79, 236–42; P. A. Carter, 10–12, 14, 18–20, 34–35, 81–83.

21. Jump, 188; Le Duc, 140; Stearns, 20. Numerous letters to Charles E. Garman in the Garman Papers at Amherst College afford glimpses of student doubts: e.g., Elizabeth McCurdy, 24 March 1893; Luther E. Smith, 17 March 1895; Mabel E. Stearns, 27 April 1893 ("He [Charles D. Norton] professes a cold belief in a Nature God"); Horace Bigelow, 4 February 1894 ("Prayer means very little to me"), Roberts Walker, 21 February 1897 ("I am running on a 'provisional government,' hoping to find the Truth in time"); and Emma L. Kingsland, 24 September 1894, quoting her son Nelson: "I don't know Mamma, I believe in God & that we should live aright but there are so many things I don't know, things that cannot be proven. I don't know whether to believe Christ is divine or not." Fred Blossom probably spoke for many other students after attending one Bible class conducted by the college: "I can enjoy the service, but I can't stay and have Dr. Tuttle or President Gates tell me things I don't believe" (to Sarah Blossom, 30 September 1894, Blossom Papers). Like any college students, Amherst men spent hours discussing religious beliefs and problems; see, for instance, Fred Blossom to Sarah Blossom, 21 October 1894. On students and revivalist preaching, AS, 23 January 1892, and CC to Carrie B. Coolidge, 10 January 1892, in Lathem, 30n. Average attendance at prayer meetings is given in AS, 29 October 1891.

22. Le Duc, 34; Dyer, 151; W. P. Bigelow, 310–13; B. Johnson, 101; Stearns, 96.

23. Stearns, 101, 106ff.; Jump, 186; Gates to Garman, 10 June 1893, Garman Papers; Fuess, *Amherst*, 252. Burges Johnson (100–1) relates an account of Gates's being outprayed himself, by a sporting fraternity brother of Johnson's whom he was trying to convert, which suggests some limitations of verbally aggressive Christianity. In the student's words, "I used to belong to the Christian Endeavor Society when I was a kid back home and knew how to pray, so I started in and I prayed all around Prexy. We both stood up. He looked at me queerly and shook hands in the way he does, taking my hand in both of his, and said good-bye. That was all there was to it."

24. C. Coolidge, *Autobiography*, 54: *'94 Olio*, 164; CC to JC, 7 February 1892, Blair Collection. Actually, compulsory chapel attendance was an issue as early as CC's freshman year (see AS, 7 November 1891, 7 May 1892), but the debate became much more public and heated the following year, as described in the text.

CC's views in the *Autobiography* (54–55), where he tries to explain the hostility he and other students felt toward the requirement on grounds of general student fractiousness, are much more sympathetic to compulsory worship than those in his letter of 7 February 1892.

25. ALM 6 (March 1892): 411; Calvin to Carrie B. Coolidge, 17 April 1892, Coolidge Family Papers, VHS. The college church is described in F. W. Hitchcock, 127; a photograph of the interior is in Bierstadt, 16. Dr. Burroughs: CC to JC, 25 September 1892, in Lathem, 39n. Snell's comment: '94 Olio, 162.

26. Chapel: AS, 26 September, 14 November, 12 December 1891, 20 February 1892; Stearns, 102–103, 119; Ball, 43, 68; ALM 6 (January 1892): 502 [302]; AGQ 19: 214. "Devotional frame of mind": Rounds, 737.

27. Patton and Field, 200; AS, 7 November 1891; '94 Olio, 166; AS, 29 April, 6 May 1893; Mason 50ff.; Le Duc, 140; Jump, 188; Fuess, Amherst 253.

28. CC to JC, 18, 25 September 1892 (in Lathem, 36, 37n); Ball, 30–31, 33; Ross, 275; CC to JC, 15 January 1893, quoted in Fuess, Calvin Coolidge, 56; Fuess, Amherst, 231–33; Stearns, 130–31; '95 Olio, 27, 146. There are essays apparently written for Genung's course in the Coolidge Family Papers, VHS, and the Edward W. Capen Papers, Hartford Seminary.

29. Fuess, Amherst, 300; Amherst Record, 16 November 1892; VT, 14 April 1893; CC to JC, 3 December 1893, Blair Collection VT, 20 May, 16 September, 18 November, 16 December 1892, 6 January, 3 February, 10 March 1893; Curtis et al., Return, 25.

30. CC to JC, 6 January 1893, in Lathem, 45; John P. Deering to J. L. Harrison, 29 May 1940, FL, states that CC roomed with Carl Gates, and Deering with Bryant; but Bryant also claimed to have roomed with CC for a time (AGQ 31 [August, 1942]: 245), and it seems most likely that the four had some sort of suite. From an anecdote related by Deering in the Boston Globe (12 August 1923) it is apparent that their rooms were on the top floor. CC to Carrie B. Coolidge, 21 September 1892, in Lathem, 37n; W. J. Blair recollections, Boston Globe, 12 August 1923; Frederick Houk Law, "In Amherst Town," '95 Olio, 175.

Chapter 14. Beyond the Provinces

1. On the weather and the clothing appropriate for it, see the Boston Globe, June 24, 1893; on the sights, King's Handbook, 11, 83. On undergarments, CC to JC, 10 October 1894, Blair Collection.

2. The horse-drawn trolleys are described in Morison, 27, and one is pictured in the Boston Public Garden sketchbook of Maurice B. Prendergast, which dates from 1892 (16). A ticket to the supper is preserved in the White Scrapbook, Frost Library, Amherst, 23. General statistics on Boston are in Herndon, passim.

3. King, 11.

4. There are good exterior photographs of the Tremont House in the collections of the Bostonian Society. For its history, see the excellent account in Williamson, 16–18, 28.

5. Herndon, 32–38; Damrell, 67–84.

6. Williamson, 16–17, 69, 214; see the interior photographs in Stevens, 330, 333, 340.

7. Boston Herald, 24 June 1892. On dress, see Cunnington and Cunnington, 285–90, 298, 309 and CC to JC, 27 January 1895, in Lathem, 63. Pink and olive are the class of 1895 colors in the White Scrapbook (1), although a report in AS, 12 December 1891, names Yale blue as the class's choice. The Grove Oration (in AS, 25 June 1895) mentions Kelley's words. On music at Amherst, see, e.g., Fuess, JCC, 44; Le

Duc, 139n; AGQ 18 (November 1928): 15; AS, 12 December 1891. "Ta-Ra-Ra-Boom-De-Ay" is mentioned several times in 1892 student publications (e.g., ALM 7 [December 1892]: 322).

8. Report cards, Coolidge Family Papers, VHS. CC to JC, 6 January 1893, in Lathem, 45. On Almeda Coolidge's remarriage, see the notes in ibid., 10, and Rogers, 44. CC's classmates' reaction: CC to Carrie B. Coolidge, 19 April 1893, Blair Collection.

9. For CC's reputation, see a mock advertisement in the '95 Olio, xxvi, for a school called "Temperance Hall" in which Compton, Coolidge, and W. S. Tyler were listed as leading instructors. For the jaunt to Northampton, see Deering's reminiscences, Boston Globe, 12 August 1923. The photograph is in the Amherst College Archives.

10. The anecdotes in this and the next paragraph are both from Deering's recollections in the Boston Globe, 12 August 1923. Neither is dated, but both can be assigned to the last half of sophomore year, the only period when CC roomed at Morse's, next door to the president's house; also the only period when he roomed with Carl Gates.

11. The story of the struggle for Sabrina, related in this and succeeding paragraphs, comes from Fuess's Amherst and Shoop's work on the rivalry. The "anabasis" comparison is from Law, 60.

12. Fuess, Amherst, 352; Shoop, 42–46, 54; B. Johnson, 92–93.

13. Fuess, Amherst, 352; Shoop, 64ff., 76ff.; Mason, 46–48.

14. Shoop, 88–89; Law, 60; cf. an incident recorded in Frederick A. Blossom to Sarah Blossom, 23 January 1895, Blossom Papers, in which a freshman trying to board the train to his class supper struck a sophomore who attempted to detain him on the head with a steel umbrella: "The blow must have nearly killed the fellow."

15. Jump, 189.

16. More modern conveniences are mentioned in Williamson, passim, and Damrell, passim. A photograph in the Bostonian Society collections shows a policeman on duty in front of the Tremont House. For women's dress, see the Prendergast sketchbook. On state-of-the-art plumbing in the 1890s, see Wright, 201, 205, Williamson, 61, 64, and the enthusiastic account of the 1895 addition to the Massachusetts State House in Damrell, 96: "The plumbing is open to view in every detail"; there are "washbowls and closets" in each suite; and "The main toilet room on the third floor ... is a thoughtfully planned and admirably executed piece of work."

17. A good evocation of Boston in the horse-drawn age is Morison, 21–31.

18. King's Handbook, 42–43. The progress of the telephone in Plymouth can be followed in VT, 12 August, 18 November, 23 December, 1892, 17 February, 10 March, 1893. The quotation is from the 10 March issue.

19. VT, 30 June 1893. Barn: ibid., 18 August, 23 September 1892; CC to JC, 25 October 1893, Blair Collection, FL. Chickens: CC to Carrie B. Coolidge, 19 November 1893, Blair Collection.

20. "We lived so far from industry that we didn't know the industrial revolution had happened," wrote Mary Heaton Vorse of growing up in Amherst at this time. "Yet within a few miles of us were the manufacturing towns of Holyoke, Chicopee, and Springfield" (Quoted in Abramson and Townsend, 217–18). Rand, 77–78, 84, 89–90; F. W. Hitchcock, 52; Annual Report, 1893, 22; King, 112–13; Longsworth, "Growth," 154; AS, 22 November, 6 December 1890, 21 October, 4, 11 November 1893; '95 Olio, 151; CC to Carrie B. Coolidge, 8 October 1893, Blair Collection.

21. '95 Olio, 27; CC to JC, 27 September 1892; CC to Carrie B. Coolidge, 29 October 1892, Blair Collection; Harrison; city directories, Jones Library, Amherst. The house was 13 South Prospect; the modern numbering is 37.

22. Amherst Catalogue for 1891–92, 46; CC to JC, 2 November 1893, 11 March

1894, Blair Collection. CC's grade of 67 for his first term of physics was the lowest he was to make in his last two years at Amherst (Registrar, Amherst College). AS, 14 October 1893. Stearns, 133–35; Fuess, *Amherst*, 260. Deering's study of French is obvious from the fact that CC gave him his old French dictionary to use (CC to Carrie B. Coolidge, 25 September 1893, Blair Collection.)

23. Stearns, 129–30; Fuess, *Calvin Coolidge*, 57; Morse, xli–xlii and passim; CC to JC, 30 January 1895, Coolidge Family Papers, VHS.

24. Men of the same class tended to room in the same places; according to AS, 3 October 1891, only thirteen freshmen were in lodgings where there were no other freshmen. CC was one. Of the thirteen, moreover, only three were oudens and thus cut off from the other great channel of extracurricular communication, the fraternity meeting: George Fairbanks, Robert Mainzer, and CC. In the fall term of sophomore year, seventeen sophomores roomed where there were no other men of 1895 (*'94 Olio*, 36–38). Again, only three were oudens: Fairbanks, CC, and Royal Booth.

Deering was 5'7" and weighed 150 pounds, according to AS, 18 November 1893. CC's measurements for April of his junior year, from the Anthropometric Measurements in the Amherst College Archives, were 5'9" and 121. Executive committee: AS, 30 September 1893. Politicking: Whiting, 44.

25. This account is from Lucius R. Eastman to Claude M. Fuess, 27 January 1933, Fuess Papers. Eastman mentions only one vacancy to be filled, so it may be that Hardy was offered the chance to join after Deering declined. The phrases applied to CC are from Scandrett, 190, where a 1907 letter from Morrow about his college days is cited.

26. CC to Carrie B. Coolidge, 8, 29 October 1893; CC to JC, 25 October, 2 November 1893, Blair Collection; AS, 28 October 1893.

27. CC to JC, 2 November 1893, in Lathem, 50; and see the other letters cited on that page and on 43. It is just possible that CC had an additional motive for requesting money at this time; see note 29 to this chapter.

28. AS, 18 November, 9 [2] December 1893; Fuess, *Amherst*, 253; Stearns, 110; CC to Carrie B. Coolidge, 13 November 1893, Coolidge Family Papers, VHS.

29. CC to JC, [12] October 1893, in Lathem, 47–48; AS, 14 October 1893; Fuess, *Calvin Coolidge*, 52; *'96 Olio*, 198. The requirement that the seven losers provide a dinner for the entire class must have placed an extraordinary burden on a student who, like CC, was getting by on small remittances from home. It was not the sort of expense that he would have enjoyed asking his father to cover; perhaps, therefore, part of the 25 dollars he requested for the Hanover trip went to pay for his dinner obligation.

Chapter 15. A New and Gifted Man

1. Fuess, *Calvin Coolidge*, 52; *'96 Olio*, 178; King, 102–5.

2. Stocking to Claude M. Fuess, 3 March 1933, Fuess Papers; Fuess, *Calvin Coolidge*, 61.

3. Fuess, *Calvin Coolidge*, 60; CC to JC, 2 November 1893, 14 January 1894, Blair Collection; CC to Carrie B. Coolidge, 18 February 1894, Coolidge Family Papers, VHS; recollections of Saxe Hanford, Rochester *Democrat*, 6 August 1923. CC's previous biographers, like Fuess, *Calvin Coolidge*, 61, and the generally accurate Lathem, 50n, have described the March competition as an annual event to determine the best speaker in the junior class. It was, in fact, one in a series of weekly competitions which began in November and for which the prizes in the first semester were bound copies of George W. Curtis's orations (AS, 4 November 1893, 27 Janu-

ary 1894). CC's accomplishment was thus not so grand as previous accounts have implied; moreover, he was not the sole winner of the contest in his week, since the class's vote was a tie between himself and H. L. Williston. Still, it was a victory of some significance; as CC pointed out in a letter to his father, Williston was one of the best orators in the class (CC to JC, 11 March 1894, in Lathem, 50n). The manuscript, untitled, is in the Coolidge Family Papers.

4. Boardman's recollections are in the *Boston Globe*, 12 August 1923, along with those of many other Amherst classmates, which together document CC's sudden rise to esteem. Boardman recalled that he returned to Amherst in his sophomore year, but AS, 14, 21 January, 21 October 1893, indicates that it was his junior year.

5. Recollections of U. J. Blair and Lucius R. Eastman, *Boston Globe*, 12 August 1923; recollections of Merton Griswold, *Worcester Telegram*, 5 August 1923; recollections of George Olds, *New York Herald*, 4 August 1923; Feiker, 4, 38; Dennis, 20.

Deering's version of the boarding-house story is in the *Boston Globe*, 12 August 1923; for a variant, see Fuess, *Calvin Coolidge*, 46. The other story is from Rogers, 50–51, not a very reliable source; but it dovetails with CC's bent for languages and could possibly be true. For another example of a typical story, see the recollections of George Jones or James S. Lawson, *Boston Globe*, 12 August 1923, and on such stories in general, Woods, 102, and Washburn, *Calvin Coolidge*, 24.

6. Crissey, 161; VT, 24 August 1894. Sennett, 23, praised CC's sense of timing.

7. Morrow had changed his opinion about CC by senior year; Charles A. Andrews to Claude M. Fuess, 26 January 1933; Jay Stocking to Fuess, 3 March 1933, Fuess Papers. Indeed, he seems almost to have adopted CC; cf. "Ex-Vermonter," 205; Scandrett, 190 ("Dwight said ... that he admired him"); and Nicolson, 34–35. C. Coolidge, *Autobiography*, 70; CC to JC, 21 September 1894, in Lathem, 71–72n.

8. C. J. Adams, 280, 285; "Ex-Vermonter," 205; recollections of Frederick S. Fales, in Fuess, *Calvin Coolidge*, 64; recollections of W. J. Rand, *Oklahoma City Oklahoman*, 12 August 1823. On CC's newspaper reading, see the excellent notes in Lathem (e.g., 53, 55, 60, 62). He sent his stepmother a copy of *Truth* he found enjoyable in his junior year: CC to JC, 18 April 1894, Blair Collection; there are also notes in the Coolidge Family Papers of money spent on the magazine.

9. Recollections of A. B. Tyler, *Springfield Republican*, 8 January 1933; Jay Stocking to Claude M. Fuess, 3 March 1933, Fuess Papers.

10. Handwritten copy of an alumni bulletin, written by Walter Fiske and dated 14 October 1895, in the CC biographical file, Amherst College Archives; CC to JC, 10 September 1894, in Lathem, 58 (and see 59n); AS, 20 October 1895; CC to Carrie B. Coolidge, 16, 19, 20 September, 15 October, 21 November 1894, Coolidge Family Papers, VHS. (I am assuming that the dance referred to in Crissey, 9, when CC brought a friend home from college, took place at Thanksgiving of 1894. I find no reference to any visits by other friends.) CC to JC, 30 August 1895, ibid.

Deering, in his *Boston Globe* interview, 12 August 1923, related a story that concluded with CC' saying "Well, I'm damned." That CC smoked cigars and drank beer shortly after leaving Amherst is evident from G. Coolidge, February 188; Feiker, 5; and JC interview, *Trenton Times*, 9 August 1923, clipping in B.R.A. Museum. It seems reasonable to suggest that he began under his roommate's tutelage.

11. AS, 13 [9], 13 [16] December 1893, 27 January 1894, 19 January 1895; Weaver, 125, 127.

12. JC to CC, 27 January 1895, in Lathem, 63, 65n; 3 February 1895, ibid., 66; 20 January 1895, Blair Collection. The last letter cited makes it clear that the money for the dress suit was CC's own, from his savings account at the Rutland Trust Bank; John, however, paid for the pin. Fencing: Leon Ensworth recollections, undated newspaper clipping attached to CC's desk in Amherst College Library; cf. AS, 28 January, 4 February 1893 for more on the fencing instruction available at Amherst. Ensworth was also the student who did CC's typing.

13. Hennessy, 24–26; Woods, 103; and Ross, 11, suggest that CC made a few efforts of a social kind; but this kind of activity cannot have played a significant part in his life. Classmates like "Jeff" Davis could not recall that he ever called at either Smith or Mount Holyoke (*Boston Globe*, 12 August 1923). For the general context of male–female socializing at Amherst, see the Elizabeth Cutter Morrow Papers, Smith College. Lena Clark: CC to JC, 22 June 1895, Coolidge Family Papers.

14. Feiker, 4, 38; Dennis, 20; interview with John P. Deering, *Boston Globe*, 12 August 1923.

15. C. Coolidge, *Autobiography*, 60; CC grade records, Registrar's Office, Amherst College; CC to JC, 10 September 1894, 27 January, 21 May 1895, in Lathem, 58, 63, 70; Ross, 275; C. Coolidge, *Autobiography*, 73–74.

16. Charles A. Andrews to Claude M. Fuess, 26 January 1933, Fuess Papers. Both Fairbanks and Booth almost failed to graduate; see M. E. Gates to Charles E. Garman, 6 May 1895, E. Hayward Fairbanks to Garman, 11 May 1895, Garman Papers; and *Springfield Republican*, 8 January 1933.

17. George Critchlow's reminiscences, *Boston Globe*, 12 August 1923; Woods, 105. Fleser's dissertation on CC's rhetoric is less helpful on this topic than one might expect, because it focuses on the continuities rather than the changes in his style. He does, however, spell out the qualities that made CC's mature style unique among his contemporaries: "simple," "direct," "clean," "pungent," and "gnomic" were some of the adjectives applied to it (65, 90). First, he used simple sentence structure (as opposed to complex, compound, or compound-complex) in almost half (47 percent) of his sentences, much more than other orators of his time. Second, he was fond of short sentences for emphasis (75). Third, as noted in the text, he was very sparing in references to himself (79). For the quantitatively minded, a comparison of his July Fourth oration of 1892 with the Grove Oration he gave three years later shows movement in the direction of his mature style. (I use the text of the July Fourth speech given in Toye, and a typescript of the Grove Oration from the C. Coolidge Papers in the Forbes Library.) In the 1892 oration, 45 percent of the sentences were grammatically simple; in 1895, 51 percent were. The average length of a sentence in the 1892 oration was twenty-four words; in the 1895 oration, it was eighteen. In the 1892 speech, which was just over a thousand words in length, he used "I" thirteen times; in the Grove Oration, 1,500 words long, "I" occurred only nine times. Probably the differing genres of the two speeches account for some of these changes; but taken all together, the figures suggest that he was, as his classmates felt, developing a new style of speaking.

Manuscripts of the other compositions cited, on the Cid and the evils of inherited wealth, are in the Coolidge Family Papers.

Curiously, in his maturity, CC told an inquirer that his style, if he had one, was "undoubtedly" a product of his legal training (in other words, that it emerged after college); but he prefaced that comment by saying, "I am not conscious of having any particular style about my writings" (Fleser, "Rhetoric," 91). This remark, coming from a man whose speeches and writings had long been the subjects of favorable comment largely because of their style, is hard to evaluate. Probably what he meant was that he was not conscious of following any existing stylistic model. But it also implies that he saw his Amherst years a little differently from the rest of his class, that rather than adopt a new way of speaking and writing, he had simply gotten more proficient at what he was doing already.

18. JC to CC, 22 November 1894, in Lathem, 61.

19. ALM, (October 1894), 140–46; Bryant, 14; CC to Carrie B. Coolidge, 28 October 1894, Coolidge Family Papers.

20. CC to JC, 16 February 1895, Coolidge Family Papers.

21. CC to JC, 27 January 1895, in Lathem, 63–64.

22. Ibid.; C. Coolidge, *Autobiography*, 60–70, stresses CC's debt to Morse and

Garman for his intellectual development. One should be clear, however, about what CC meant by intellectual development: a "general comprehension" of a subject (61), a "clearer comprehension" of one's rights and duties (62), a "power to weigh evidence ... and to know the truth" (65). CC was not an innovative thinker, as Fleser comments ("A New England Education," 159), at Amherst or later. Indeed, he placed little value on originality. Learning, to him, was simply the ability to apprehend preexisting truths, to express them in the clearest possible way, and to apply them in the broadest possible context.

23. C. Coolidge, *Autobiography*, 60–62; Morse, 24, 159; Stearns, 129–30.

24. C. Coolidge, *Autobiography*, 62; JC to CC, 13 November 1892, in Lathem, 42.

25. Occasional notices of the content of course work in AS (e.g., 3 March 1894) make it possible to follow the outline of Morse's course. On Garman and his course generally, see Le Duc's excellent account (102–18) and Waterhouse, 9–13. The quotation is from C. Coolidge, *Autobiography*, 65.

26. Recollections of Garman, by C. S. Sargent, and Morrow to Garman, 21 July 1894, both in Garman Papers, Amherst College Archives; CC to JC, 10 October 1894, in Lathem, 60n; Harlan F. Stone to William Allen White, 13 April 1933, Stone Papers, LC; Woods, 92–93; Patton and Field, 164–65, 232; Boardman, 14; Stearns, 142–47; Waterhouse, 10; Law, 16; Fuess, *Amherst*, 239–40.

27. Gates's struggles for domination are chronicled in Stearns, 106–16, and Fuess, *Amherst*, 250–54. His disputes with faculty and students were widely covered in the newspapers; see CC's reference in his letter of 4 February 1894 to Carrie B. Coolidge, Coolidge Family Papers. On Garman's personality see Sargent, "Recollections," 6–7, in the Garman Papers; on his pamphlets, Caldwell, 242–45, Waterhouse, 11, and many letters in the Garman Papers (e.g., Alexander W. McCurdy to Garman, 14 September 1893).

28. Fuess, *Amherst*, 251, 255–56; CC to JC, [21] February 1894, in Lathem, 54; Stearns, 118; AGQ, 14 (February 1924): 84.

29. AS, 27 October 1894; Gates to Garman, 18 April 1893, Garman Papers; Fuess, *Calvin Coolidge*, 58–59; Fuess, *Amherst*, 240; Stearns, 144–46, 153; Le Duc, 112. Waterhouse, 10, gives a synopsis of the topics covered. Various quizzes and compositions in the Coolidge biographical file in the Amherst College Archives throw light on Garman's teaching methods. (To be sure, they contain only CC's answers; one must infer the questions.) There were short quizzes, of three, four, or five questions; one or more questions might ask for the student's opinion on teaching methods or issues that had come up in the course. There were also essay assignments with five or six alternatives, from which Garman selected the one he wanted the student to complete; it is not clear whether this selection was personalized or random.

30. Stearns, 146–47, 152–53; Le Duc, 111–12; C. Coolidge, *Autobiography*, 64; Boardman, 14.

31. Stearns, 144–53; Le Duc, 105–106, 113–18.

32. Charles A. Andrews to Claude M. Fuess, 25 January 1938, Fuess Papers; Harlan F. Stone to William Allen White, 13 April 1933, Stone Papers, LC; CC to Almeda B. Coolidge, 20 January 1895, Special Collections Amherst College Library; CC to JC, 30 January, 13, 21 May 1895, in Lathem, 65n, 69n, 71; untitled manuscript in CC biographical file, Amherst College Archives. This emphasis on power corresponds to Garman's own, as expressed, for example, in the "Private Manuscript" he distributed to his class in the fall of 1895 (Garman Papers): "Psychology is only a test of what your real power is. Power reveals itself only by work done, character never shows itself except in overcoming resistance.... Psychology discovers the laws of mental action, and [it is] worth the attention of a Senior in College to consider carefully for a few short weeks that which is essential in mental action, at least to acquire the power of discriminating between the essential and the accidental"(7). I am indebted to Dr. Michael Platt for calling my attention to this pamphlet.

33. None of CC's surviving letters before January 1895 mention law as a possible career; two letters to his father mention the possibility of his returning to Plymouth to live. Speaking of his grandmother's farm on 12 March 1893, he suggested, "Perhaps I shall want it to live on when I am done going to school" (Lathem, 69). On 26 April 1894 he asked directly, in a letter to be cited below, "[W]ould you like to have me start in the store and live in Plymouth?.... Or would you prefer to have me enter some profession and go away and leave my community ... " (Ibid., 56). This second letter unavoidably suggests that John had been pressing him to follow a professional career, but one cannot know for sure, since the father's side of the correspondence is missing. CC's letter suggesting law school as a possibility, dated 7 January 1895, was, as usual, tentative and cautious: "shall probably go into the store or go to a law school at Boston or New York, that is about as far as I can get and think you will have to decide which I shall do" (ibid., 68n). Questionnaire: Fuess, *Calvin Coolidge*, 67.

34. The debate over law school can be followed in CC to JC, 21 April, 3, 13 May, 19 June 1895, in Lathem, 68, 69n, 73; CC's letters, particularly that of 19 June, often contained rejoinders to points raised by his father.

35. CC to JC, 26 April 1894, 7 January, 21 April 1895, in Lathem, 56, 68n, 69n.

36. Leach, 57ff. The classes of 1893 and 1894 had elected not to wear cap and gown (AS, 27 January 1894). The position of the class of 1895 is not a matter of record; but at the beginning of senior year Royal Booth, Isaac Compton, and George Fairbanks were named by the class as part of a seven-man Cap and Gown Committee, from which the other four members promptly resigned (AS, 29 September 1894), a sequence of events that suggests strongly that caps and gowns were not worn. The class yell is from the Mark Kimball scrapbook in the Special Collections, Amherst College Library.

37. CC's desk is in the Amherst College Library. The Grove Oration for 1894, by Percival Schmuck (reprinted in AS, 26 June 1894), had the same structure as Coolidge's with jibes at the faculty, the administration, the other classes, and members of the senior class; but it was much longer and a good deal less pointed. On the other oratorical events at commencement, see JC to CC, 21 May 1895, in Lathem, 70. CC claimed (*Autobiography*, 73) that he was simply following "college fashion" in wearing his hair long, but at least one Amherst contemporary remembered it as unusually long and distinctive (W. J. Rand, *Oklahoma City Oklahoman*, 12 August 1923).

38. The elder Coolidge's choice of a coat can be followed in CC to JC, 14 April 1895, Coolidge Family Papers; and 3 May 1895, in Lathem, 68. CC's dress: Dennis, 16; recollections of John P. Deering, *Boston Globe*, 12 August 1923; Charles A. Andrews to Claude M. Fuess, 25 January 1938, Fuess Papers; various bills for clothing in the Coolidge Family Papers, and the letter of 3 May 1895 cited above. Arrangements for graduation: CC to JC, 22 June 1895, Coolidge Family Papers.

39. The College Grove is shown on the map in W. S. Tyler, 92. Fuess, *Calvin Coolidge*, 65–66; recollections of George Critchlow, *Boston Globe*, 12 August 1923.

40. A full text of the Grove Oration is in AS, 25 June 1895.

Sources Cited

Manuscript Sources

Barney, Ada J. Statistics and Prophecy of the Class of '89. B.R.A. Museum.

Blair, John, Collection, Forbes Library.

Blossom, Frederick A. Papers, State Historical Society of Wisconsin.

Broadside. Woodstock, Vt., Vermont Historical Society.

Calvin Coolidge Biographical File, Amherst College Archives.

Capen, Edward W. Papers, Hartford Theological Seminary.

Coolidge Family Papers. Vermont Historical Society.

Coolidge, Calvin. Autograph book, B.R.A. Museum.

Coolidge, Calvin. Papers, Library of Congress.

Crane, Charles E. Typescript of remarks at Plymouth Church, 28 August 1948, Forbes Library.

Dimick, M. E. Diary, in Coolidge Family Papers, VHS.

Dun, R. G., & Co. Collection. Baker Library, Harvard University Graduate School of Business Administration.

Feiker, William H. "The True Story of a Great American," ms., Forbes Library.

Fuess, Claude M. Papers, Forbes Library.

Fuess, Claude M. Papers, Phillips Academy.

Gardner, Absalom. "A Compendium of the History, Genealogy, and Biography of Wales...." In Vital Records of Wales, Mass., 1762–1895 (microfilm).

Garman, Charles E. Papers, Special Collections, Amherst College Library.

Harrison, John L. Notes on Coolidge's residences in Amherst, Forbes Library.

Hemenway, Marion P. "Handwritten Account of the Hemenways' Visit to the Coolidges at the White House," Black River Academy Museum, Ludlow, Vermont.

Hitchcock, Edward. Papers, Special Collections, Amherst College Library.

Johnson, Leonard. Diary, Vermont Historical Society.

Johnson, Sidney. Diary, Vermont Historical Society.

Kent, Dorman B. E. Diary, Vermont Historical Society.

Kimball, Mark. Scrapbook. Special Collections, Amherst College Library.

"Memoirs of Daniel Ransom," Williams Public Library, Woodstock, Vt.

Morrow, Elizabeth Cutter. Papers, Smith College.

Orton, Vrest. Interview with Dallas Pollard. Typescript in B.R.A. file, Vermont Historical Society.

Plymouth town records. Plymouth, Vt.

Rugg, D. F. Diary, Vermont Historical Society.

Scott, Charles. "History of Plymouth," typescript, Calvin Coolidge Memorial Foundation, Plymouth, Vt.

Scrapbook, B.R.A. Museum.

Sherman Family Papers. Brimfield Public Library, Brimfield, Mass.

Sherman, Arthur E. Diary, Vermont Historical Society.

Stone, Harlan F. Papers, Library of Congress.

Taylor, Arden. Diaries, Vermont Historical Society.

Vermont School Register for 1884–85, Plymouth, District 9, Forbes Library.

White, Herbert O. Scrapbook and memorabilia, Class of 1895, Amherst College Archives.

[Wilder, Susie F.] " Susie F. Wilder's Graduation from B.R.A., 1889." Scrapbook, B.R.A. Museum.

Printed Primary Sources

Abbott, Collamer M. "'Gramp' Abbott's Life: Farming in Central Vermont, 1865–1913." VH, 39 (Winter, 1971): 31–42.

Adams, Charles J. "An Early Memory of Calvin Coolidge." VH, n.s., 22 (October 1954): 280–86.

Aldrich, L.C., and Frank R. Holmes, eds. History of Windsor County, Vermont. Syracuse, N.Y.: D. Mason & Co., Publishers, 1891.

The American Catalogue, 1884–1890. New York: Office of the Publishers' Weekly, 1891.

Amherst College. Biographical Record of the Graduates and Non-Graduates. Revised edition. Amherst, Mass.: The Trustees of Amherst College, 1939.

Amherst College. Catalogue 1891–1892. Amherst, Mass.: Amherst College, 1892.

Amherst College, Class of 1895. Decennial Class Book. Boston: Southgate Press, 1906.

"An Ex-Vermonter Recalls Calvin Coolidge: An Unpublished Letter Written in 1924." VH, 38 (Summer 1970): 204–6.

Andrews, Dawn K., ed. "'Family Traits': Vermont Farm Life at the Turn of the Century: The Sketches of Stanley Horace Lyndes." VH, 48 (Winter 1980), 5–23.

Archer, W. L. "The Old Stage-Driver," clipping from Rutland Herald in scrapbook at B.R.A. Museum.

Atlas of Springfield, Mass., 1899.

Ball, Walter S. Amherst Life. Amherst, Mass.: William Carpenter Howland, 1896.

Barnes, James. A Princetonian. New York: G. P. Putnam's Sons, 1896.

Bigelow, William P. "Shifting Emphasis." AGQ 1 (1912): 308–16.

Biggs, Hermann M. "To Rob Consumption of Its Terrors," Forum 14 (February 1894): 758–67.

Black River Academy. Fifty-first Annual Catalogue, 1885–86. Ludlow, Vt.: Warner & Hyde, 1886.

———. Fifty-second Annual Catalogue, 1887. Ludlow, Vt.: R. S. Warner, 1887.

———. Fifty-third Annual Catalogue, 1887–88. Ludlow, Vt.: R.S. Warner, 1888.

———. Fifty-fourth Annual Catalogue, 1888–89. Ludlow, Vt.: R.S. Warner, 1889.

————. *Fifty-fifth Annual Catalogue*, 1889–90. Ludlow, Vt.: R.S. Warner, 1890.

————. *Fifty-sixth Annual Catalogue*, 1890–91. Ludlow, Vt.: R.S. Warner, 1891.

"Boarding 'Round Fifty Years Ago." *Vermonter* 34 (November 1929): 165–68.

Boardman, Richard. "A Dartmouth Man on Garman." AGQ 17 (November 1927): 14–17.

Brown, Henry T. "Memories of Calvin Coolidge." VH, n.s., 21 (October 1953): 311–13.

Bryant, Blanche Brown. *Calvin Coolidge As I Knew Him*. DeLeon Springs, Fla.: The E. O. Painter Printing Company, 1971.

Bulletin of the New England Meteorological Society ... for 1889–91. Cambridge, Mass.: W. H. Wheeler, Printer, 1890–93.

Cady, Daniel. "Plymouth, Vermont." VH, 40 (Summer, 1972), 216–17.

Carpenter, Ernest C. *The Boyhood Days of Calvin Coolidge*. Rutland, Vt.: The Tuttle Company, Publishers, 1926.

Carter, Joseph C., ed. "A Quiet Christmas on the Farm (25 December 1883)," VH, 43 (Fall 1975): 307–10.

————, ed. "Trip to Clarendon Spa: July 4th, 1882." VH, 48 (Fall 1980): 239–43.

Chase, Frederick Hathaway. "Is Agriculture Declining in New England?" *New England Magazine*, n.s., 2 (1890): 449–52.

Child, Hamilton, comp. *Gazetteer and Business Directory of Windsor County, Vt., for 1883–84*. Syracuse, N.Y.: Printed at the Journal Office, 1884.

Cleghorn, Sarah N. *Threescore*. New York: Harrison Smith & Robert Haas, 1936.

Collar, William C. "The Action of the Colleges upon the Schools." *Educational Review* 2 (December 1891): 422–34.

Coolidge Calvin. *The Autobiography of Calvin Coolidge*. New York: Cosmopolitan Book Corporation, 1929.

————. "Books of My Boyhood." *Cosmopolitan* (October 1932): 18–19, 144–16.

————. "Margaret's Mist." ALM 9 (October 1894): 140–46.

Coolidge, Grace. "The Real Calvin Coolidge: A First-hand Story of His Life Told by 50 People Who Knew Him Best and Edited with Comment by Grace Coolidge." *Good Housekeeping* (February–June 1935).

Crissey, Forrest. "They Call Him Cal." *Saturday Evening Post* (25 October 1924): 8–9, 156–69.

Currier, Amos N. "The Decline of Rural New England." *Popular Science Monthly* 38 (1891): 384–90.

Damon, Bertha. *Grandma Called It Carnal*. New York: Simon and Schuster, 1938.

Damrell, Charles F. *A Half Century of Boston's Building*. Boston: Louis P. Hager, 1895.

Davis, Robert. "Middlebury Sketches V: The Middlebury-Bristol Ball Game of 1892." VH, 12 (October 1944): 183–85.

The Dediction of the Bennington Battle Monument, and Celebration of the Hundredth Anniversary of the Admission of Vermont as a State. Bennington, Vt.: Banner Book and Job Printing House, 1892.

Demary, Adin C. "Vivid Recollections." *Vermonter* 32, no. 12 (1927): 31.

Denison, T. S. *Under the Laurels*. Chicago: T. S. Dennison, [1881].

Dennis, Alfred Pearce. "The Man Who Became President." in Edward C. Lathem, ed. *Meet Calvin Coolidge*. Brattleboro, Vt.: The Stephen Greene Press, 1960.

"Diary of a Vermont Boy," VH, 25, no. 2 (April 1957): 164–67.

Downing, Lucia B. "Teaching in the Keeler 'Deestrict' School." VH, 19 (October 1951): 233–40.

Duffus, Robert L. *Williamstown Branch: Impersonal Memories of a Vermont Boyhood.* New York: W. W. Norton & Company, Inc., 1958.

Dyer, Walter A. "Dearly Beloved Grandparent." AGQ 18 (1929): 151.

Earle, Horatio Sawyer. *The Autobiography of "By Gum" Earle.* Lansing, Mich.: The State-Review Publishing Company, 1929.

"Expressions from a Hartland Diary," VH, 23 (April 1955): 63–64; (July 1955): 258; (October 1955); 356–57; 24 (January 1956): 87–88.

"Facts About Consumption." *Public Opinion* 14 (24 December 1892): 283–84.

Fellows, Dexter W., and Andrew A. Freeman. *This Way to the Big Show.* New York: The Viking Press, 1936.

[Fisher], Dorothy Canfield. *Hillsboro People.* New York: Henry Holt and Company, 1915.

Fisher, Dorothy Canfield. *Memories of Arlington, Vermont.* New York: Duell, Sloan and Pearce, 1957.

Flanders, Ralph E. *Senator from Vermont.* Boston: Little, Brown and Company, 1961.

Fletcher, Zoa Townsend. *Tales of Vermont One Room Schools.* Windsor, Vt.: The Chronicle Press, n.d.

Foote, E. B. *Science in Story: Sammy Tubbs, The Boy Doctor, and "Sponsie," The Troublesome Monkey.* New York: Murray Hill Publishing Co., 1885.

Frederic Harold. *The Damnation of Theron Ware.* Cambridge, Mass.: The Belknap Press of Harvard University Press, 1960; first published 1896.

Freeman, Mary E. Wilkins. *A New England Nun and Other Stories.* Ridgewood, N.J.: The Gregg Press, 1967; first published 1891.

———. *Pembroke.* New Haven: College & University Press, 1971; first published 1894.

Fuller, John H. "Medicine in the 'Good Old Time,'" VH, 23 (July 1955): 220–28.

Gordon, James, *Escape from Vermont.* New York: Henry Holt and Comapny, 1948.

Gould, Ralph E. *Yankee Drummer.* New York: McGraw-Hill Book Company, Inc., 1947.

Guernsey, Sarah E. "A Vermont Country School of the 1870's." *Mount Holyoke Alumnae Quarterly,* 32 (May 1948): 4–5.

Hamilton, James Shelley. *Butt Chanler, Freshman.* New York: D. Appleton and Company, 1908.

[Hard, Walter]. *Walter Hard's Vermont.* Brattleboro, Vt.: Stephen Daye Press, 1941.

Hartt, Rollin Lynde. "A New England Hill Town." *Atlantic Monthly* 88 (1899): 561–74.

Heinritz, Stuart F., ed. "The Life of a Vermont Farmer and Lumberman: The Diaries of Henry A. Thompson of Grafton and Saxtons River" VH, 42 (Spring 1971): 89–139.

Herndon, Richard, comp. *Boston of To-day.* Boston: Post Publishing Company, 1892.

Hibbard, George A. "As the Sparks Fly Upward." *Scribner's Magazine* 8 (1890): 721–34.

History of Black River Academy As Seen Through Various Publications. Springfield, Vt.: William L. Bryant Foundation, 1972.

[Hitchcock, Edward]. *The Subjects, Statements and Facts Upon Personal Health Used for the Lectures Given to the Freshman Class of Amherst College.* 4th ed. Amherst: n.p., 1893.

————. *A Manual of the Gymnastic Exercises As Practiced by the Junior Class in Amherst College.* Boston: Ginn, Heath & Company, 1884.

————. *Amherst College: An Anthopometric Manual.* Amherst: J. E. Williams, 1887.

Hitchock, Frederick W. *The Handbook of Amherst, Massachusetts.* Amherst: privately printed, 1891.

Hoover, Irwin H. *Forty-two Years in the White House.* Boston: Houghton Mifflin, 1934.

Hopkins, Anson Smith. *Reminiscences of an Octogenarian.* New Haven: The Tuttle, Morehouse & Taylor Company, 1937.

Hoyt, Charles H. *Five Plays.* Ed. Douglas L. Hunt. "America's Lost Plays," vol. 9. Princeton: Princeton University Press, 1941.

Huse, Raymond H. *The Autobiography of a Plain Preacher.* Boston: Meador Publishing Company, 1949.

Johnson, Burges. *Campus versus Classroom.* New York: Ives Washburn, 1946.

Johnson, Clifton. *The Country School in New England.* New York: D. Appleton and Company, 1893.

————. *The Farmer's Boy.* New York: Thomas Y. Crowell, 1907.

————. *New England and Her Neighbors.* New York: The Macmillian Company, 1902.

————. *The New England Country.* Boston: Lee and Shepard, 1893.

Johnson, Margaret L. *Tales of Old Woodstock.* Woodstock, Vt.: Woodstock Historical Society, 1957.

Jump, Herbert A. "Vignettees of the 'Nineties." AGQ 21, no. 3 (May 1932): 183–89.

Kavanagh, Ernest S. "Coolidge's Boyhood." In *The Real Calvin Coolidge,* vol. 4, 5–17. Plymouth, Vt.: The Calvin Coolidge Memorial Foundation, 1986.

[King, Moses]. *King's How-to-See Boston.* Boston: Moses King Corporation, 1895.

Kipling, Rudyard. *Letters of Travel, 1892–1913.* Garden City, N.Y.: Doubleday, Page & Company, 1920.

Lathem, Edward Connery, ed. *Your Son, Calvin Coolidge.* Montpelier, Vt.: Vermont Historical Society, 1968.

Leach, Valette Washburn. *Jedediah Bascom.* New York: The Abbey Press, 1902.

Leonard, Jonathan. *Back to Stay.* New York: The Viking Press, 1929.

[Leslie, Hyde]. *The Diaries of Sally and Pamela Brown, 1832–38; Hyde Leslie, 1887; Plymouth Notch, Vermont.* Edited by Blanche Brown Bryant and Gertrude Elaine Baker. 2nd ed. Springfield, Vt.: The William L. Bryant Foundation, 1979.

Ludlow and Her Neighbors. Ludlow, Vt.: Vermont Tribune Office, 1899.

Ludlow Toy Manufacturing Co. *Annual Catalogue and Price-List for 1876.* Ludlow, Vt.: R. S. Warner, 1876. At B.R.A. Museum.

Macomber, Loula I. "Fifty Years Ago On Our Farm." *Vermonter* 42 (December 1937): 175–76.

Marshall, Margery G. "A Mother's Memories." VH, 24 (April 1956): 155–65.

Marshall, Oscar S. *Journeyman Machinist En Route to the Stars*. Taunton, Mass.: Wm. S. Sullwold Publishing, Inc., 1979.

Martin, E. C. "A Monster of My Acquaintance." *Scribner's Magazine* 6 (1889): 233–41.

Meyer, Henry W. *Memories of the Buggy Days*. Cincinnati: n.p., 1965.

Middlebury College. *Catalogue of ... 1889–90*. Middlebury, Vt.: Register Company, Printers, 1889.

Moore, Herbert L. *Calvin Coolidge: From the Farm to the White House*. Privately printed, 1935.

Moore, Herbert L. *The Little Town of Plymouth, Vermont*. Plymouth: Herbert L. Moore, 1946.

Morison, Samuel Eliot. *One Boy's Boston, 1887–1901*. Boston: Houghton Mifflin Company, 1962.

Morse, Anson D. *Parties and Party Leaders*. Boston: Marshall Jones Company, 1923.

The '94 Olio. Amherst, Mass.: Published by the Junior Class of Amherst College, 1892.

The '95 Olio. Amherst, Mass.: Published by the Junior Class of Amherst College, 1893.

The '96 Olio. Amherst, Mass.: Published by the Junior Class of Amherst College, 1894.

Parks, Lillian Rogers. *My Thirty Years Backstairs at the White House*. New York: Fleet Publishing Co., 1961.

Pattee, Fred L. *Penn State Yankee*. State College: The Pennsylvania State College, 1953.

Peck, Theodore S., comp. *Revised Roster of Vermont Volunteers ... 1861–66*. Montpelier, Vt.: Press of the Watchman Publishing Co., 1892.

Pettingill, Samuel B. *My Story*. Lebanon, N.H.: Helen M Pettingill, 1979.

Phillips, Paul C. "Dr. Edward Hitchcock " *American Physical Education Review* 16, no. 3 (March 1911); 217 20.

Porter, Horace. "Railway Passenger Travel." *Scribner's Magazine* 4 (September 1888): 296–319.

Quint, Howard H., and Robert H. Ferrell, eds. *The Talkative President*. Amherst: The University of Massachusetts Press, 1964.

Report of the Observance of the Semi-Centennial of St. Johnsbury Academy, June 24 1892. St. Johnsbury, Vt.: Printed for the Trustees, 1893.

Ripley, Thomas Emerson. *A Vermont Boyhood*. New York: D. Appleton–Century Company, 1937.

Rounds, R. S. "Social Life at Amherst College." *Lippincott's Monthly Magazine* 40 (November 1887): 737–43.

Russell, Charles Edward. *Bare Hands and Stone Walls*. New York: Charles Scribner's Sons, 1933.

St. Johnsbury Academy. *Catalogue ... for the ... year ending June, 1891*. St. Johnsbury, Vt.: Caledonian Press, 1891.

Sargent, John Garibaldi. "Our President-Elect." *The Republican Woman*. Philadelphia (January 1925).

Scandrett, Richard. "Remembering Calvin Coolidge: An Oral History Memoir." VH, 40 (Summer 1972): 190–215.

Sennett, Mack. *King of Comedy*. Garden City, N.Y.: Doubleday & Company, Inc., 1954.

Sherwood, Robert E. *Here We Are Again*. Indianapolis: The Bobbs-Merrill Company, 1926.

Skinner, W. L. *Ramblings of the Woodstock Observer*. Woodstock, Vt.: The Elm Tree Press, 1938.

Spear, Victor I. *Vermont: A Glimpse of Its Scenery and Industries*. Montpelier: State Board of Agriculture, 1893.

Start, Edwin A. "A Model New England Village." *New England Magazine*, n.s., 3 (February 1891), 701–18.

Stearns, Alfred E. *An Amherst Boyhood*. Amherst, Mass.: Amherst College, 1946.

Steele, Fred E. "A Medical Practice in the Upper Reaches of the White River Valley, 1882–1903." VHS 37 (Summer 1969): 207–22.

Stevens, Benjamin F. "The Tremont House: The Exit of an Old Landmark." *The Bostonian* 1, no. 4 (January 1895): 329–44.

Strickland, Franklin N. "Dr. William S. Hopkins of Vergennes." *Vermonter* 44 (December 1939), 259–60.

Taber, Edward Martin. *Stowe Notes*. Boston: Houghton Mifflin Company, 1913.

[Toye, Joe]. "My Son, Calvin Coolidge," as told by John C. Coolidge to Joe Toye. *Boston Traveler* (14 August 1923), clipping in scrapbook, Forbes Library.

Travelers' Official Railway Guide for the United States and Canada. New York: The National Railway Publication Company, September, 1890.

Trudo, Sevilla. "Vanished Life among the Hills." *Vermonter* 36 (April 1931): 123–25.

"Twas Fifty Years Ago," AGQ 31 (August 1942): 307–9.

Twombly, John Felch. *Twombly Genealogy*. Aiken, S.C.: Privately printed, 1990.

———. *Vermont Heritage*. Aiken, S.C.: Privately printed, 1987.

Tyler, John M. "Edward Hitchcock: The Man." *American Physical Education Review* 6, no. 3 (September 1901): 264–66.

University of Vermont. *Catalogue of the Officers and Students ... 1890–91*. Burlington, Vt.: Free Press Association, 1891.

"Use of Opium." *Science* 10 (26 August 1887): 100.

Washburn, Robert M. *My Pen and Its Varied Styles*. Cambridge, Mass.: University Press, 1939.

Weld, Mildred A. "A Vermont Grandfather and Grandmother." VHS 19 (October 1951): 241–43.

Winslow, Henry W. "Forty Years Ago Around Willoughby." *Vermonter* 26, no. 2 (February 1921): 45–46.

Secondary Sources

Abbott, Collamer M. "Gold in Them Thar Hills." *New England Galaxy* 10 (Fall 1968): 14–21.

Abramson, Doris E., and Robert C. Townsend. "Versions of Community." In *Essays on Amherst's History*, 191–241. Amherst, Mass.: The Vista Trust, 1978.

Adams, Gladys S., comp. *Bridgewater, Vermont, 1779–1976*. N.p., 1976.

Allen, Mary Adele. *Around A Village Green*. Northampton, Mass.: The Kraushar Press, 1939.

Allis, Frederick S. "Thomas Cushing Esty." AGQ 30 (1941): 279–81.

Anderson, Will. *From Beer To Eternity*. Lexington, Mass.: The Stephen Greene Press, n.d.

Appelbaum, Diana Karter. *The Glorious Fourth*. New York: Facts on File, 1989.

Arnold, John P., and Frank Penman. *History of the Brewing Industry and Brewing Science in America*. Chicago: Privately printed, 1933.

Barron, Hal S. *Those Who Stayed Behind*. New York: Cambridge University Press, 1984.

— ——. "The Impact of Rural Depopulation on the Local Economy: Chelsea, Vermont, 1840–1900." *Agricultural History* 54 (April 1980): 313–35.

Bassett, T. D. Seymour. "A Case Study of Urban Impact on Rural Society: Vermont, 1840–80." *Agricultural History* 30 (January 1956): 28–34.

Beck, Jane. *The General Store in Vermont: An Oral History*. Montpelier: The Vermont Historical Society, 1980.

Bergin, Thomas G. *The Game: The Harvard–Yale Football Rivalry, 1875–1983*. New Haven: Yale University Press, 1984.

Bigelow, Edwin L. "Eliakim Bigelow: A Stowe Farmer." VHS 31 (October 1963): 253–71.

Bogue, Donald J. *The Population of the United States*. New York: The Free Press, 1985.

Bower, Bruce. "Teenage Turning Point." *Science News* (23 March 1991): 146–48.

Brown, Mary S. *Footprints of Calvin Coolidge*. Rutland, Vt.: Novak Publishing Co., 1938.

Bryant, Blanche Brown, and Gertrude Elaine Baker. *Early Settlers: Plymouth, Vermont*. Springfield, Vt.: William L. Bryant Foundation, 1975.

Buss, Arnold H. "A Conception of Shyness." In John A. Daly and James C. McCroskey, eds. *Avoiding Communication: Shyness, Reticence, and Communication Apprehension*, 39–49. Beverly Hills, Calif.: Sage Publications, 1984.

Caldwell, Eleanor E. "Garman Through Colored Glasses." AGQ 18 (August 1929): 242–45.

Carey, Charles H. *History of Oregon*. Chicago: Pioneer Historical Publishing Co., 1922.

Carson, Gerald. *The Old Country Store*. New York: Oxford University Press, 1954.

Carter, Paul A. *The Spiritual Crisis of the Gilded Age*. Dekalb: Northern Illinois University Press, 1971.

Cochran, Thomas C., and William Miller. *The Age of Enterprise*. Rev. ed.; New York: Harper & Row, 1961.

Collins, Herbert R. *Political Campaign Torches*. "Contributions from the Museum of History and Technology," no. 45. Washington: Smithsonian Institution, 1964.

Cooley, Harry H. *Randolph, Vermont, Historical Sketches*. Randolph, Vt.: Randolph Town History Committee, 1978.

Coolidge, Emma Downing. *Descendants of John and Mary Coolidge of Watertown, Massachusetts*. Boston: Wright & Potter, 1930.

Crane, Charles Edward. *Winter in Vermont*. New York: Alfred A. Knopf, 1941.

Cummings, Charles R. "In Adoration of Plymouth." *Vermonter* 23, no. 5 (1918): 116–23.

Cunnington, C. Willett, and Phillis Cunnington. *Handbook of English Costume in the Nineteenth Century*. London: Faber and Faber, 1959.

Curtis, Jane, Will Curtis, and Frank Lieberman. *Return to These Hills*. Woodstock, Vt.: Curtis–Lieberman Books, 1985.

Daly, John A., and James C. McCroskey, eds. *Avoiding Communication: Shyness, Reticence, and Communication Apprehension*. Beverly Hills, Calif.: Sage Publications, 1984.

Dana, John Cotton. *Vermont Explained by a Typical Vermont Village, Which Is to Say Plymouth*. Woodstock. Vt.: The Elm Tree Press, 1925.

Danzig, Allison. *The History of American Football*. Englewood Cliffs, N.J.: Prentice-Hall, Inc., 1956.

Davis, Gilbert A. *History of Reading, Vermont*. Vol. 2 (Windsor, Vt.: Privately printed, 1903).

Donald, Kathleen E., and John A. Waterhouse. *"Coolidge-Country" Cookbook*. Plymouth, Vt.: Friends of the Calvin Coolidge Memorial Foundation, 1988.

Durant, John, and Alice Durant. *Pictorial History of the American Circus*. New York: A. S. Barnes and Company, 1957.

Fairbanks, Edward T. *The Town of St. Johnsbury, Vt*. St. Johnsbury, Vt.: The Cowles Press, 1914.

Farnsworth, Russell H. *Over Cram Hill*. Burlington, Vt.: Queen City Printers, 1967.

Fenn, Mary Beardsley. *Parish and Town: The History of West Windsor, Vermont*. Taftsville, Vt.: The Countryman Press, 1977.

Fleming, Madeline C. *An Informal History of the Town of Sherburne, Vermont*. Rev. ed., n.p.: Privately printed, 1972.

Fleser, Arthur F., "Jam Tempus Agi Res: Oratory in History," *Quarterly Journal of Speech* 49 (February 1963): 46–49.

Flexner, Stuart B. *Listening to America*. New York: Simon and Schuster, 1982.

Fuess, Claude M. *Amherst: The Story of a New England College*. Boston: Little, Brown, and Company, 1935.

———. *Calvin Coolidge: The Man from Vermont*. Boston: Little, Brown, and Company, 1939.

Fussell, Clyde G. "The Emergence of Public Education as a Function of the State in Vermont: Chapter IV." VHS 29 (January 1961): 13–47.

Glover, Waldo F. "On Smocks for Vermont Farmers." *Vermonter* 29 (1924): 142–43.

Graffagnino, J. Kevin. *Vermont in the Victorian Age*. Bennington, Vt.: Vermont Heritage Press, 1985.

Green, Horace. *The Life of Calvin Coolidge*. New York: Duffield & Company, 1924.

Grizzell, Emit Duncan. *Origin and Development of the High School in New England before 1865*. New York: The Macmillan Company, 1923

Hance, Dawn D. *Shrewsbury, Vermont: Our Town As It Was*. Rutland, Vt.: Academy Books, 1980.

Harris, Joseph N. *History of Ludlow, Vermont*. 3rd ed. Ludlow, Vt.: Black River Historical Society, 1988; first published 1929.

Hays, Samuel P. *The Response to Industrialism: 1885–1914*. Chicago: The University of Chicago Press, 1957.

Hennessy, M. E. *Calvin Coolidge: From A Green Mountain Farm to the White House*. New York: G. P. Putnam's Sons, 1924.

Hughes, Muriel J. "Vermont Dialectical Expressions." VHS 19 (April 1951): 81–84.

———. "A Word-List from Vermont." VH, 27 (April 1959): 123–67.

Humphrey, Zephine. *The Story of Dorset*. Rutland, Vt.: The Tuttle Company, 1924.

Hunt, Emma A., Erling M. Hunt, and Virginia H. Moulton. *Roots and Branches of the Hunt-Fifield-Bailey Family and the Times in Which They Lived*. Claremont, N.H.: Privately printed, 1980.

Jennison, Peter S. *The History of Woodstock, Vermont, 1890–1983*. Woodstock, Vt.: The Countryman Press, 1985.

Johnson, Charles W. *The Nature of Vermont*. Hanover, N.H.: The University Press of New England, 1980.

Jordan, Holman D , Jr. "The Value of Census Data in the Writing of Vermont Town Histories." VH, 36 (Winter 1968): 19–25.

Kaplan, Donald M. "On Shyness." *International Journal of Psychoanalysis* 53 (1972): 439–53.

Kent, Dorman B. E. "William Wallace Stickney." *Proceedings of the Vermont Historical Society* 4 (March 1936): 17–20.

Kidwell, Claudia B., and Margaret C. Christman. *Suiting Everyone: The Democratization of Clothing in America*. Washington, D.C.: Smithsonian Institution Press, 1974.

Kilmartin, Thomas W. "The Last Shall Be First: The Amherst College Days of Calvin Coolidge." *Historical Journal of Western Massachusetts* 5 (Spring 1977): 1–12.

King, Stanley. *"The Consecrated Eminence."* Amherst, Mass.: Amherst College, 1951.

Kinsey, Alfred C., Wardell B. Pomeroy, and Clyde E. Martin. *Sexual Behavior in the Human Male*. Philadelphia: W. B. Saunders Company, 1948.

Krug, Edward A. *The Shaping of the American High School*. New York: Harper & Row, 1964.

Law, Frederick Houk. *Famous Men of a Famous Class*. N.p., n.d. Amherst, Frost Library.

Le Duc, Thomas. *Piety and Intellect at Amherst College, 1865–1912*. "Columbia Studies in American Culture," no. 16. New York: Columbia University Press, 1946.

Longsworth, Polly. "The Growth of Civic Consciousness." In *Essays on Amherst's History*, 139–61. Amherst, Mass.: The Vista Trust, 1978.

———. *Austin and Mabel*. New York: Farrar, Straus, Giroux, 1984.

Lowell, Anthony M. "Tuberculosis Morbidity and Mortality and Its Control." Part I of *Tuberculosis*, "American Public Health Association Vital and Health Statistics Monographs." Cambridge: Harvard University Press, 1969.

Ludlum, David M. *The Vermont Weather Book*. Montpelier, Vt.: Vermont Historical Society, 1985.

Marx, Rudolph. *The Health of the Presidents*. New York: G. P. Putnam's Sons, 1960.

Mason, Alpheus T. *Harlan Fiske Stone: Pillar of the Law*. New York: The Viking Press, 1956.

McCoy, Donald R. *Calvin Coolidge: The Quiet President*. New York: The Macmillan Company, 1967.

Mead, Edgar T., Jr. *Over the Hills to Woodstock*. Brattleboro, Vt.: The Stephen Greene Press, 1967.

Mencken, H. L. "Coolidge." In Alistair Cooke, ed. *The Vintage Mencken*. New York: Vintage Books, 1956.

Mooney, Elizabeth. *In the Shadow of the White Plague*. New York: Thomas Y. Crowell, 1979.

Morgan, Constance Morrow. *A Distant Moment: The Youth, Education, & Courtship of Elizabeth Cutter Morrow*. Northampton, Mass.: Smith College, 1978.

Munyon, Paul Glenn. *A Reassessment of New England Agriculture in the Last Thirty Years of the Nineteenth Century: New Hampshire, A Case Study*. "Dissertations in American Economic History." New York: Arno Press, 1978.

Murray, Marian. *Circus!* New York: Appleton-Century-Crofts, Inc., 1956.

Nash, Hope. *Royalton, Vermont*. N.p.: The Town of Royalton, 1975.

Newton, Earle. *The Vermont Story*. Montpelier, Vt.: The Vermont Historical Society, 1949.

Nicolson, Harold. *Dwight Morrow*. New York: Harcourt, Brace and Company, 1935.

Noble, John W. "Jacob S. Spaulding and the Barre Academy." VH, 29 (July 1961): 121–47.

Orton, Vrest. *Calvin Coolidge's Unique Vermont Inauguration*. 3rd ed. Rutland, Vt.: Academy Books, 1981.

Patton, Cornelius Howard, and Walter Taylor Field. *Eight O'Clock Chapel: A Study of New England College Life in the Eighties*. Boston: Houghton Mifflin Company, 1927.

Phillips, Gerald M. "Reticence: A Perspective on Social Withdrawal." Daly and McCroskey, 51–67.

Rand, Frank P. *The Village of Amherst*. Amherst, Mass.: The Amherst Historical Society, 1958.

Reed, James. *From Private Vice to Public Virtue*. New York: Basic Books, Inc., 1978.

Rochester, Vermont: Its History, 1780–1975. Burlington, Vt.: Queen City Printers, 1975.

Rockingham Bicentennial Committee. *A Pictorial History of the Town of Rockingham*. Bellows Falls, Vt.: n.p., 1975.

Rogers, Cameron. *The Legend of Calvin Coolidge*. Garden City, N.Y.: Doubleday, Doran & Company, Inc., 1928.

Ross, Ishbel. *Grace Coolidge and Her Era*. New York: Dodd, Mead, & Company, 1962.

Rothman, Ellen K. *Hands and Hearts: A History of Courtship in America*. Cambridge: Harvard University Press, 1987.

Roundy, Rodney W. "The District School: Town of Rockingham." VH, 16 (October 1948): 127–34.

Sawyer, Roland D. *Cal Coolidge, President*. Boston: The Four Seas Company, 1924.

See, Anna Phillips. *Amherst, Past and Present*. Amherst, Mass.: Tercentenary Committee, 1930.

Sennett, Mack. *King of Comedy*. Garden City, N.Y.: Doubleday & Company, Inc., 1954.

Shaughnessy, Jim. *The Rutland Road*. 2nd ed. San Diego: Howell North Books, 1981.

Shoop, Max, comp. *Sabrina, The Class Goddess of Amherst College*. Amherst, Mass.: Privately printed, 1910.

Sizer, Theodore R., ed. *The Age of the Academies*. "Classics in Education," no. 22. New York: Teachers College, Columbia University, 1964.

Snyder, Charles M. *Buggy Town: An Era in American Transportation*. Lewisburg, Pa.: Oral Traditions Project, 1984.

Snyder, Edwin R. *The Legal Status of Rural High Schools in the United States.* "Teachers College, Columbia University, Contributions to Education No. 24." New York: Teachers College, Columbia University, 1909.

Sumner, Philip. *Carriages to the End of the Nineteenth Century.* "A Science Museum Illustrated Booklet." London: Her Majesty's Stationery Office, 1970.

Tarr, Laszlo. *The History of the Carriage.* London: Vision Press, 1969.

Tower, James E., ed. *Springfield, Present and Prospective.* Springfield, Mass.: Pond & Campbell, 1905.

Tyler, W. S. *A History of Amherst College during the Adminstration of Its First Five Presidents from 1821 to 1891.* New York: Frederick H. Hitchcock, 1895.

Tyskowa, Maria. "The Personality Foundations of the Shyness Syndrome," *Polish Psychological Bulletin,* XVI (1985), 113–21. Summarized in *Psychological Abstracts,* 74: 1346.

Vermont Division for Historic Preservation. *Guide Book to the Coolidge Homestead at Plymouth Notch, Vermont.* N.d., n.p.

Veysey, Lawrence R. *The Emergence of the American University.* Chicago: The University of Chicago Press, 1965.

Vinovskis, Maris A. "Have We Underestimated the Extent of Antebellum High School Attendance?" *History of Education Quarterly* 28 (Winter 1988): 551–68.

Ware, Francis M. *Driving.* New York: Doubleday, Page & Company, 1903.

Washburn, Robert M. *Calvin Coolidge: His First Biography.* Boston: Small, Maynard, & Company, 1923.

Waterhouse, John Almon. *Calvin Coolidge Meets Charles Edward Garman.* Rutland, Vt.: Academy Books, 1984.

Watson, Pearl G., ed. *Taftsville Tales.* Taftsville, Vt.: Happy Valley Homemakers, 1967.

Waugh, Nora. *The Cut of Men's Clothes, 1600–1900.* London: Faber and Faber Limited, 1964.

Weaver, Warren, Jr. "Amherst Rounds Out Fifty Years." *The Phi Gamma Delta* 46 (November 1943): 123–33.

Webb, Kenneth. *From Plymouth Notch to President.* Taftsville, Vt.: The Countryman Press, 1978.

Weinstein, Edwin A. *Woodrow Wilson: A Medical and Psychological Biography.* Princeton: Princeton University Press, 1981.

Weisenburger, Francis P. *Ordeal of Faith.* New York: Philosophical Library, 1959.

Wentworth, Harold, and Stuart Berg Flexner. *Dictionary of American Slang.* New York: Thomas Y. Crowell Company, 1960.

White, John H., Jr. *The American Railroad Passenger Car.* "Johns Hopkins Studies in the History of Technology," n.s., no. 1. Baltimore: The Johns Hopkins University Press, 1978.

White, William Allen. *A Puritan in Babylon.* New York: The Macmillan Company, 1939.

Whiting, Edward Elwell. *President Coolidge: A Contemporary Estimate.* Boston: The Atlantic Monthly Press, 1923.

Williamson, Jefferson. *The American Hotel: An Anecdotal History.* New York: Alfred A. Knopf, 1930.

Wilson, Harold Fisher. *The Hill Country of Northern New England.* New York: AMS Press, Inc., 1967; first published 1936.

Wood, Leyland E. *Two Vermont Hollows*. Randolph, Vt.: L. E. Wood, 1976.

Woods, Robert A. *The Preparation of Calvin Coolidge*. Boston: Houghton Mifflin Company, 1924.

Wright, Laurence. *Clean and Decent*. London: Routledge & Kegan Paul, 1960.

Young, Elizabeth, "Boiled Dinner." VH, 23 (July 1955): 257.

Young, James Harvey. *The Toadstool Millionaires*. Princeton: Princeton University Press, 1961.

Zinar, Ruth. "Educational Problems in Rural Vermont, 1875–1900: A Not So Distant Mirror." VH, 51 (Fall 1983): 197–218.

Government Documents

Annual Report of the Town of Amherst. Amherst, Mass.: Carpenter & Moorhouse, 1893.

United States. Bureau of the Census. Manuscript 1880 census of Windsor County, Vt. Microfilm.

Vermont Historical Records Survey. *Inventory of the Town, Village and City Archives of Vermont*, no. 14. Windsor County, vol. 12, Town of Plymouth. Montpelier, Vt.: The Vermont Historical Records Survey, 1940.

Vermont, Secretary of State. *Report to the Legislature of Vermont, Relating to the Registry and Returns of Births, Marriages, and Deaths in the State* ... (1884; 1886; 1888; 1890–94).

Vermont, State Superintendent of Education. *Vermont School Report* (1884–92).

Periodicals

Amherst Graduates' Quarterly. 1912–42.

Amherst Student. 1890–95.

Biddeford (Me.) Daily Journal. 6 January 1947.

Boston Globe. 12 August 1923, Editorial and News Feature Section.

Boston Post. 7 January 1933.

New York Herald. 4 August 1923.

New York Times. 1923–33.

Newark News. 4 August 1923.

Northampton (Mass.) Herald. 1892–93.

[Northampton, Mass.] *Hampshire Gazette*, 1890, 1907.

Oklahoma City Oklahoman, 12 August 1933.

The Real Calvin Coolidge, 1983–92.

Rochester Democrat. 6 August 1923.

Rutland Herald. 1885–86, 1889.

Science News. 23 March 1991.

Springfield (Mass.) Republican. 1890–91, 1933.

Trenton Times. 9 August 1923.

[Woodstock] *Vermont Standard*. 1885–95.
[Ludlow] *Vermont Tribune*. 1885–95, 1920–56.
Washington Post. 6 August 1923.
Worcester Telegram. 5 August 1923.

Dissertations

Fleser, Arthur F. "The Rhetoric of Calvin Coolidge." Ph.D. diss. Indiana University, 1962.

Interviews

Brown, Earle. Interview, August 1986.
Jerry, Donna. Taped interviews with Plymouth residents Art Dix, Eliza Hoskison, Richard Moore, Norma Vivier, Victor Ward, Clitt Wheeler, and Evelyn Whittemore.
Pollard, Erminie. Interview, July 1987.
Ward, Eliza. Interview, July 1987.

Pictorial Materials

Barry, Harold A., Richard E. Michelman, Richard M. Mitchell, and Richard H. Wellman. *Before Our Time*. Brattleboro, Vt.: The Stephen Greene Press, 1974.
Bierstadt, E. *Sunlight Pictures: Amherst*. New York: The Artotype Publishing Co., 1891.
Curtis, Will, Jane Curtis, and Frank Lieberman. *Times Gone By*. Woodstock, Vt.: Privately printed, 1976.
Photograph collection. Bostonian Society.
Photograph collection. Connecticut Valley Historical Museum.
Prendergast, Maurice. *Large Boston Public Garden Sketchbook*. New York: George Braziller, Inc., 1987.
Sandler, Martin W. *As New Englanders Played*. Chester, Ct.: The Globe Pequot Press, 1979.
Ward, Eliza, Barbara Mahon, and Barbara Chiolino. *A Plymouth Album*. Randolph Center, Vt.: Greenhills Books, 1983.

Miscellaneous

Karol, John. "Calvin Coolidge: A Life for Our Time." Documentary film to be released spring 1995.
Recordings of Coolidge's speeches. Forbes Library.

Index

house, 38, 62; grooming, 80, 183; Grove Orator, 172, 176, 183, 185–86, 247 n.17; growth of self-confidence, 181–82; on gymnasium drill, 123, 124; health, 38, 86, 95, 105, 109–11, 149–50, 188, 199 n.10, 200 n.12; height and weight, 124, 245 n.24; helps recover Plymouth cannon, 148; history, interest in, 84, 149, 167, 178; homesickness, 85, 134–35, 144; humor, 69, 146; hunting, 61–62; image at Amherst, 133, 171–73; increased prestige at home, 146; intellectual development, 175, 248 n.22; isolation from fellow students, 81, 133; on isolation of Plymouth, 53; lack of long-range plans, 83, 189; law school, interest in, 182, 249 n.33; legal career, 187; loses Plug Hat Race, 169, 188; loses pocketbook, 118; on Merrill E. Gates, 155, 180, 185; in minstrel show, 172; moves to new lodgings, 159; natural beauty, love of, 149, 172, 177; Northampton, excursion to, 162; oratory, interest in, 89–90, 100–101, 139, 175–77; personality, 35, 173, 175; and Phi Gamma Delta fraternity, 144, 173–75; philosophy, interest in, 181–82; plans to attend college, 98–100, 103–4, 115, 223 n.17 and 18, 225–26 n.34; Plymouth, affection for, 145, 162, 182–83; political career, 188; political interest, 41, 87–88, 152–54, 178; postgraduate work at Black River Academy, 114–15; practical jokes, 44, 147, 162, 204 n.29; profanity, 78, 173, 217 n.2; reading, 99, 112, 144, 172; recitation, 60; reconciled to being at Amherst, 144; rejected by fraternities, 125, 128, 144, 234 n.19; religion, 72, 97, 157, 223 n.16; requests $25 from father, 168, 245 n.29; resents father's direction, 187, 202 n.17; residence in Amherst, 129, 159, 166–67, 173; riding, 39, 40, 146; rooms with John P. Deering, 166–67; at St. Johnsbury Academy, 117–18, 230 n.17; sells jewelry to classmates, 78; sells maple sugar, 162; sexual interests, 76; shaving, 115; short story, "Margaret's Mist," 176–77; shyness, 39–43, 81–82, 173, 188, 200–201 n.15, 202–3 n.17; singing school,

61; skating, 144; sledding, 61; smoking, 162, 173; speaking style, 143, 176–77, 247 n.17; speaking voice, 225 n.26; speeches, 100–101, 147, 170, 176, 247 n.17; studies at Amherst, 132–33, 150, 158, 166–67, 168, 175, 178, 180–82, 235 n.34; studies at Black River Academy, 68, 82–83, 85, 93, 219 nn.15 and 16; summer activities, 118; sweets, fondness for, 38, 64, 76, 211 n.29; takes teachers' examination, 57; theater, fondness for, 113, 222 n.9, 229 n.9; thirteenth birthday, 21; vacations from Amherst, 134, 145–48, 158, 177, 227 n.8; visits aunt, 72, 214 n.20; visits home from academy, 214 n.20; wants to drop out of college, 134, 236 n.39; wins essay contest, 175; wins oratorical contest, 171; wit, 40, 95, 158, 162–63, 171–72; work, attitude toward, 40–41; works at cab shop, 82, 218–19 n.14

Coolidge, Calvin Galusha, 40, 44, 47, 199 n.8

Coolidge, Carrie (Brown), 114, 119, 129, 158–59, 204 n.29, 229 n.13

Coolidge, John, 22, 35, 62, 65, 76, 91, 94, 96, 97, 145, 146, 189; attends graduation at Amherst, 183, 185; barn struck by lightning, 165; on CC, 200 n.15; character, 32–33; and cheese factory, 102; circus, fondness for, 46; clothes, 32; colonel in state militia, 204 n.23; considers apprenticing CC to pharmacist, 223 n.18; as farmer, 197 n.17; as father to CC, 38, 62–63, 104, 112, 182, 186–87, 214 n.20, 224 n.19; and general store, 25, 101, 112; gives party, 64; home, 22, 45–46, 158–59; income, 32, 38; Indian blood in family, 197 n.15; as law officer, 32, 46, 58; legal experience, 41; locates hidden cannon, 148; mending walls, 57; political experience, 27, 32, 41, 50, 203 n.22; refuses to let CC leave college, 134; remarriage, 114; sends CC to Black River Academy, 63–65; sends CC to college, 98–100, 104, 114, 223–24 n.18, 225–26 n.34; sends CC to St. Johnsbury Academy, 116; suggests CC enter law office, 182, 187, 249 n.33; superintendent of schools, 57–58; takes CC home from Amherst, 109–10, 228 n.15; takes